Puffballs, earthballs, and earthstars, page 267

Jelly-like fungi, page 272

Morels, false morels, and elfin saddles, page 276

Cup-fungi, page 285

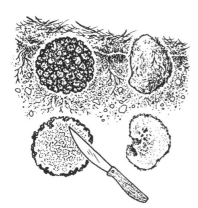

Truffles and false truffles, page 297

Odds and ends, page 302

MUSHROOMS
of the PACIFIC NORTHWEST

Steve Trudell & Joe Ammirati

Illustrations by MARSHA MELLO

TIMBER PRESS FIELD GUIDE

To the memories of
Ben Woo, Kit Scates Barnhart,
and Dan Stuntz, for their many
contributions to mushrooming
in the Pacific Northwest

CONTENTS

PREFACE

Generally speaking, the Pacific Northwest (PNW) encompasses all of Oregon, Idaho, and Washington, plus portions of northern California, western Montana, southern Alaska, and southern British Columbia (B.C.), Canada. The most characteristic part of the PNW biological region, however, lies north of a line that roughly coincides with the 44th parallel of latitude, extending eastward from Florence to Springfield/ Eugene to Bend to Ontario, Oregon, and then through Boise to Idaho Falls, Idaho. The northern limit is in southern B.C. and Alaska at the transition to the boreal forest region. For most people, the PNW evokes images of towering trees festooned with lichens and clubmosses, dripping from the seemingly incessant rain. However, this picture is not complete without an assortment of mushrooms decorating the forest floor for anyone who takes time to look down.

Mushrooms, as we broadly define them, represent numerous small to large, conspicuous fungi that have evolved an array of different forms and colors. They occur as decomposers, living on dead organic materials, and as symbionts with plants, animals, and other fungi. Because of these lifestyles, mushrooms play major roles in the functioning of ecosystems where they provide nutrients to trees and other plants, recycle those nutrients by breaking down wood and other plant materials, and cause damage as plant pathogens. Many species have intercontinental distributions across the Northern Hemisphere, others occur at the continental or regional scale, a smaller number

are more localized, and some have global distributions. Where fungus species occur today reflects a complex of interactions with other organisms and the physical environment over time. Temperature, moisture, soil, topography, vegetation, and other factors influence where fungi grow, when they produce their fruitbodies, and how their spores are dispersed from one location to another.

People from many cultures have long histories of gathering mushrooms for food, medicine, and mind-altering effects and, in the process, have accumulated considerable knowledge about poisonous and deadly species. In addition, mushrooms have been used for a variety of other purposes, including tinder, dyes, clothing, and decoration in the form of illustrations, carvings, and icons. The use of mushrooms by peoples in diverse cultures invariably has involved some system of names to facilitate acquiring and exchanging information about them. While almost all cultures have developed a system of common names for their most notable edible and poisonous mushrooms, none have assigned names to all mushrooms, so the overwhelming majority have no common names. Beginning around the late 1700s, mushrooms began to be studied, given scientific names, and arranged in classification schemes. That activity continues today, and gradually many fungi for which there were no previous names have been given scientific names. For identification purposes, it is better to use these names so that communication within and across cultures and societies is as precise and effective as possible.

Mushroom-hunting has always had a certain number of devotees, but it has become increasingly popular over the past 50 or so years, partly in response to the wide variety of high-quality books and other resources now available for mushroom identification. However, surprisingly, few of these resources were developed specifically for the PNW. Mushroom books and field guides for North America first appeared around 1900. Some of the better known early works include *Our Edible Toadstools and Mushrooms* (W. H. Gibson 1895), *One Thousand American Fungi* (Charles McIlvaine 1900), and *Mushrooms: Edible, Poisonous, etc.* (George F. Atkinson 1903). From these early contributions through the 1960s, mushroom books were based mostly on eastern U.S. species and were illustrated with black and white drawings or photographs of varied quality. During this period, two books covering fungi in the PNW appeared—Margaret McKenny's short *Mushrooms of Field and Wood* (1929) and G. A. Hardy's *Some Mushrooms and Other Fungi of British Columbia* (1947).

In 1949, Alexander Smith produced *Mushrooms in Their Natural Habitats*, which provided descriptions and photographs of a large number of mushrooms, including many from western North America. The fungi were illustrated with color stereo-photos by Portland, Oregon, photographer William B. Gruber, presented on View-Master reels. Although this made use of the photos somewhat cumbersome, it ushered in the era of all-color mushroom guides. The second half of the 20th century saw a steady increase in the publication of mushroom books and a gradual transition from black and white to color photos. Three books that appeared in the 1970s and early 1980s have had a particularly wide impact—*Mushrooms of North America* (Orson K. Miller, Jr. 1972), *The Audubon Society Field Guide to North American Mushrooms* (Gary H. Lincoff 1981), and *Mushrooms Demystified* (David Arora 1979 and 1986)—and the latter, although focused on coastal central California, has received wide use in the PNW. Additional books on fungi of B.C. and southwestern Canada, Idaho, and California have come out over the years, but only one dealt with the whole PNW and included all color photographs— *The New Savory Wild Mushroom* (Margaret McKenny and Daniel E. Stuntz, revised by Joseph F. Ammirati in 1987). Although it has served Northwest mushroomers well over the years, it covers only 200 of the larger, more common mushrooms with a major emphasis on edible species.

Thus, *Mushrooms of the Pacific Northwest* is a much-needed, color-illustrated guide to the mushrooms of our region, providing general information on their ecology and identification. It covers over 450 edible, poisonous, ecologically important, and just-plain-interesting species using accurate color photographs and concise discussions of their salient features. We hope it will serve you well—whether you are a hardcore mushroomer, part-time chanterelle- or morel-chaser, curious hiker, or around-town naturalist—and that it perhaps motivates you to learn more about these fascinating, but usually unseen, organisms that help make our lives possible.

ACKNOWLEDGMENTS

Obviously, over the years, many people have contributed in some way to making this guide possible, but thanking them individually would take precious page-space away from the mushrooms. However, a few particularly instrumental people deserve special mention.

Alan Bessette, Arleen Bessette, and Bill Roody set the standard for high-quality color mushroom books with guides such as *Mushrooms of Northeastern North America*, *North American Boletes*, and *Mushrooms of West Virginia and the Central Appalachians*. Marsha Mello's charming and accurate illustrations effectively convey key concepts and were made possible by the generous support of the Daniel E. Stuntz Memorial Foundation (http://www.stuntzfoundation.org/). Dr. Denis Benjamin provided a wealth of information on mushroom poisoning and reviewed those portions of the manuscript that discuss it. Drew Parker went above and beyond to provide a fine last-minute photograph of *Cleistocybe vernalis*. Thank you all.

In addition, SAT would like to thank Dr. Kenneth Wells for introducing him to mushrooms in class and on a field trip to Mendocino County, California, many years ago, and Drs. Harry Thiers and Orson Miller for their knowledge, advice, and enthusiastic encouragement during those first years of learning a new field, and their continuing friendship thereafter. The mushroom world is just not the same without Harry and Orson. I also thank my wife, Sally Graupman, for just about everything. She found many of the mushrooms for the photographs, kept the dogs from stepping on them, tolerated boxes of fungi in the refrigerator and stacks of papers on the dining-room table, was the number-one supporter of this project, reviewed large portions of the manuscript, and, most of all, worked hard to keep the mortgage paid and food on the table so that I could indulge in mushroom-hunting and book-writing. Everyone should be so lucky.

PRELIMINARIES

What Are Mushrooms?

The word "mushroom" means different things to different people. If asked to form a mental image of a mushroom, most people probably would picture something plant-like, with a stem and top together forming an umbrella-shaped object. Under the top there would be a series of plate-like structures somewhat like pages in a book. This concept is exemplified by the familiar grocery-store button-mushroom, *Agaricus bisporus*. For some people, that is the only mushroom, all similar things being called "toadstools." Others use mushroom to refer to all edible large fungi, and toadstool to refer to the poisonous ones. Use of the latter term, however, requires that you know about the edibility of the fungus, so we will not use it. For still other people, including us, mushrooms encompass a much broader concept. We consider a mushroom to be anything that a mushroom-hunter might pick, thus including a wide variety of objects of different sizes, shapes, and colors, as illustrated in this book. But what are these mushrooms? Although presenting many different appearances, all are linked by their common function.

Mushrooms are the sexual reproductive structures produced by certain fungi. ("Fungus" is singular, "fungi" is plural and usually pronounced "fun′ jī," but also "fun′ jē" or, especially in Great Britain, "fun′ ghē" with a hard "g." Thus, jokes about the mushroom being invited to parties because he is a real "fun guy" are grammatically incorrect.) Mushroom-forming fungi often are referred to as macrofungi or macromycetes (from the Greek, *macro* = large, *myc* = a fungus). But what are fungi? For the past half-century, the organisms comprising the fungi have been placed in their own biological kingdom (traditionally the highest level in the categorization of life) and formally known as fungi. Besides the fungi, there are plants, animals, protists (for mostly microscopic fungus-, plant-, and animal-like organisms larger and more complex than bacteria), and monera (bacteria and other small simple microscopic organisms). In recent years, information from molecular and biochemical studies has resulted in creation of a higher category, the domain, and a proliferation of new kingdoms. This has resulted in many organisms traditionally studied by mycologists (mycology is the study of fungi), such as slime molds, being moved to new kingdoms. However, the mushroom-forming fungi and their close relatives do seem to form a natural evolutionary group and the kingdom Fungi is likely to remain a kingdom into the future. The fungi with which people usually are most familiar are the molds that appear on neglected food items in kitchens. These are similar in many respects to the mushroom-fungi, but do not produce large fruitbodies.

To put the mushroom in the context of the whole fungus, the life cycle of *Amanita phalloides*, the death cap, is shown inside the back cover. The purpose of the mushroom is to produce and release tiny reproductive propagules, or dispersal units, called spores, which function much like the seeds of plants. Most mushroom spores are somewhat larger than bacteria but, with rare exception, still much too small to be seen individually without a microscope. If a windblown spore is fortunate enough to land in a spot with suitable moisture, temperature, and nutrient conditions, it can germinate to form a new fungus body. This body, called a mycelium (plural = mycelia), is made up of many thin, complexly interconnected, tubes called hyphae (pronounced "hī′ fē," singular = hypha) that grow into and through the soil, wood, cheese, or other substrate in which the fungus lives. This hyphal or mycelial body type sets fungi apart from plants, animals, and even most other microorganisms. Hyphae grow at their tips and thereby extend the mycelium and allow it to explore widely and intensively within the substrate.

Most fungi have multiple mating types, or "sexes," and reproduction cannot occur until the mycelium of one mating type merges with the mycelium of a compatible type. Once this has happened, sexual reproduction, including the formation of mushrooms, can occur, thus completing the life cycle. It is worth noting, however, that many fungi rarely, or perhaps never, undergo sexual reproduction. They either spread vegetatively by extension of their mycelia, or produce spores without having to merge with another compatible individual. Most of those molds in the kitchen, for instance, fall into this category.

As you might expect, the different parts of mushrooms have been given names. Inside the back cover, this time on the right, is a figure that shows the main parts of a gilled mushroom, *Amanita phalloides*, and for comparison, a spine-fungus and a bolete. Many more features are defined and illustrated in the Glossary, and we suggest you spend some time going over them. Learning the terminology will make it much easier for you to communicate with others about mushrooms and will facilitate identifying them.

Why Do People Hunt Mushrooms?

For most mushroom-hunters, the quest is fueled by a desire to find a wild foodstuff, perhaps in the process satisfying some ancestral hunter-gatherer urge. Some, particularly in the Pacific Northwest (PNW), hunt to provide income, selling their mushrooms to buyers who resell them to markets and restaurants, or ship them overseas. Growing numbers of people collect certain species for medicinal or health-promoting purposes. For others, mushrooms are a source of beauty, to be "immortalized" (as New England mushroom guru Sam Ristich was fond of saying) on film or with watercolors or other medium. A rather specialized group uses them as a source of dyes for

The brilliant yellow mycelium of *Piloderma bicolor* is a common sight in Pacific Northwest forest soils. The visible strands are made up of many microscopic hyphae.

Commercial mushroom-harvesting is big business in the Pacific Northwest.

The pigments in many mushroom-fungi can produce beautiful colors in wool.

coloring wool and other fibers. For still others, mushrooms are objects of study—what are the different types? how many kinds are there? what functions are they performing in the ecosystems in which they live? Whatever your principal interest in mushrooms, learning something about their fascinating biology will increase your understanding of the world in which we live. Learning the names of the fungi you encounter is an important first step in this process, as it will allow you to discuss particular fungi with others and look up information about them in books or using the internet.

Where and When Do You Find Mushrooms?

The PNW justifiably is known as a mushroom paradise. Mushrooms can be found everywhere in the Northwest and in every month of the year. However, they are more abundant in some places than in others and at certain times of the year. Generally speaking, the combination of mild to warm temperatures, ample moisture, and the presence of trees makes for the most abundant and diverse fruitings. Such conditions most often are found in the forests west of the Cascade Mountain crest at low to moderate elevation. However, forests are not the only places where mushrooms grow, and a surprising number of species can be found even in urban and suburban areas, some occurring only there.

Our region experiences a moderately mediterranean climate, with cool wet winters alternating with warm mostly dry summers. Precipitation is mostly in the form of rain at low elevation. The proportion falling as snow increases with increasing elevation so higher areas usually are covered with snow throughout the late fall, winter, and early spring months. Thus, the main occurrence of moist mild weather is in late spring–early summer and fall. Spring and summer fruiting is most abundant at moderate to high elevations where moisture is provided by melting snow or thundershowers. This produces an interesting set of species, referred to as "snowbank mushrooms," characteristic of the montane areas of western North America. However, far more mushrooms fruit in fall, and the September–November period is what most PNW mushroom-hunters normally mean by "mushroom season."

Speaking of "fruiting," use of this term for the production of mushrooms requires comment. Strictly speaking, fruiting refers to the production of fruits, which are found only in flowering plants. Because fungi are not plants and mushrooms are not fruits, technically it is incorrect to refer to fruiting of mushrooms. However, because fungi were long thought to be plants, many botanical terms, such as fruiting, fruitbodies, and stem, have been applied to them. Similarly, the mushrooms in an area often are referred to as its mycoflora or mushroom flora. Although it is recognized that these terms ideally should not be applied to fungi, it has been difficult to develop simple workable alternatives.

The onset of the fall mushroom season comes on the heels of the first substantial rains, which can occur any time beginning in mid- to late August. One predictor of how good the mushroom season will be is how the general public is talking about the late August–September weather. If most people think the weather has been great (clear, sunny, warm, and rain-free), it is not likely to be a good mushroom season. On the other hand, if folks are complaining about the early onset of winter because of gray skies and frequent rains, then a good mushroom year could be in store. However, the rains should not come too soon, as there is evidence to suggest that warm summer weather is an important pre-condition for a good mushroom season. The peak of the mushroom season at different places along the Pacific Coast can be approximated by the dates on which the local mushroom club holds its annual mushroom fair, exhibit, or foray. Generally speaking, the seasonal peak progresses from north to south:

Southeast Alaska: late August–September
Southern B.C.: early September–late October
Washington and northern to central Oregon: October–early November
Southern Oregon and northern California: mid–late November
Central California: early December–early January
Southern California: late January–early March

Mycena griseoviridis, a common snowbank mushroom.

Thus, by traveling north to south (and then back again for the April–May morels and June montane boletes in the PNW), you can extend your mushroom season over much of the year. In the PNW, mushroom season usually is brought to an end by the arrival of freezing nights. Although some species can tolerate cold weather, the drop-off in fruiting from one week to the next brought about by even one hard freeze can be quite striking. However, even in the absence of hard freezes, fruiting drops off significantly as November progresses in most of the PNW. Farther south and at the immediate coast, the critical factor is the onset of warm dry weather.

Mushrooms usually are most abundant and diverse where there are trees. There are good ecological reasons for this, and if you aspire to become a proficient mushroom-hunter, you must learn to recognize the principal forest trees. Since many mushrooms occur only with particular trees, knowing which ones you are collecting near can be a useful clue as to the identity of the mushrooms, and also can help you focus your search for particular mushrooms in areas where they are likely to occur. For instance, if you wish to find *Suillus cavipes*, you must locate a forest containing larch.

Although broadleaved, or "hardwood," trees such as black cottonwood and red alder can dominate streamside areas, and oak woodlands occur in some areas, most PNW forests are dominated by conifers. Near the coast, Sitka spruce and western hemlock typically are the most abundant species and are joined by Douglas-fir, western redcedar, red alder, and bigleaf maple. At the immediate coast, especially on sandy soils, shore pine–Sitka spruce woodlands are a charac-teristic sight. Sitka spruce becomes much less abundant away from the coast, and the lowland and lower montane forests comprise mostly Douglas-fir, western hemlock, and western redcedar, with grand fir, western white pine, red alder, and bigleaf maple. With increasing elevation, grand fir is replaced by silver or noble fir, western hemlock by mountain hemlock, and the other lower elevation trees gradually drop out, while Engelmann spruce, subalpine fir, and whitebark pine join mountain hemlock. East of the Cascade crest, and in some drier westside sites, ponderosa pine is very common, along with western larch, Douglas-fir, and grand fir. Other eastside areas support abundant lodgepole pine and groves of aspen. In central to southern Oregon, additional trees such as oaks, sugar pine and other pines, and incense cedar bring an increasingly Californian aspect to the forests, marking the southern limit of the main PNW biological region and the beginning of a broad transition zone. Not surprisingly, parallel changes are evident in the mushrooms that occur there.

Access to Collecting Areas— Permits and Other Legalities

Several popular edible mushrooms, notably chanterelles, matsutake, morels, and king boletes, grow in great abundance in the PNW and because of our usually cool spring and autumn temperatures, they remain in edible condition longer than mushrooms do in areas where the rains come during warm weather. Thus, commercial collecting of mushrooms has become a major enterprise here and this has led to discussion, sometimes heated, concerning who has the right to pick mushrooms, where, and in what quantity. In order to control access to mushrooms and hopefully provide for their continued existence, collection limits and permit programs have been instituted by the State of Washington and a number of public lands agencies such as the USDA Forest Service.

Although there has been talk and some progress toward standardizing collection limits and permit requirements across jurisdictions, the state of the current situation still can be summarized as "confus-

In some areas, permits are required for picking mushrooms.

In other areas, no mushroom-picking is allowed.

ing." The requirements differ from place to place, they are not well advertised, even on agency Web sites, and there is no official clearinghouse where a law-abiding mushroom-picker can go for the necessary information. What is more, even if the requirements for an area in which you want to collect can be ascertained, the administrative offices that issue the permits often are closed on weekends, which is when most recreational mushroom-hunters head for the woods. Although enforcement budgets are meager, the consequences of getting caught without a permit or collecting in an unauthorized area can be severe, as evidenced by two fines that have come to our attention—$250 for a single mushroom in a "no-picking" area, and $475 for not having a permit in a state park! So do your homework, get your picking and parking permits, and stay within the bag limits.

Guidelines for Collecting Mushrooms

Identification of mushrooms is much easier when you have specimens of good quality and quantity. Even someone with many years of experience may find it impossible to identify a single ratty, over-the-hill mushroom. So to make your life as simple as possible, follow these tips whenever possible.

- Collect only mushrooms that are fresh and in good condition. Use the same sensory criteria that you would when selecting produce at your local market.
- Collect a number of specimens to show the range of variation, especially representatives of young to mature mushrooms to show developmental changes. That said, always collect conservatively to promote the long-term health of the

fungus populations. Take only what you really need and leave the rest behind, ideally undisturbed. Unfortunately, many mushroomers, especially those who carry pointed sticks, make a habit of tipping over every mushroom they encounter and then leaving the corpses behind as forest litter. If you pick a mushroom that you decide not to collect, please "replant" it if possible (it will not continue to grow, but at least the woods will look better) or toss it into the underbrush where it will be hidden from sight.

- Carry a small notebook and use it liberally. Some features of the mushrooms, such as odors and bruising reactions, are ephemeral and might not be observable by the time you return home and begin working on them. In addition, our memories are never as reliable as we would like. Record such things as the date, your location, the current and recent weather (especially whether raining or hot and dry), the type(s) of trees growing near each collection of mushrooms you make, whether the mushrooms are growing on soil or wood, or among mosses or other substrate, a tentative name for the mushrooms, other mushrooms currently fruiting, and color of spores that have been deposited on adjacent leaves, mushrooms, or soil ("natural spore-prints").
- Collect one species at a time, from a limited area—say, within a 1-m (3-ft.) radius—and keep those mushrooms (which constitute a "collection") separate from your other collections. Assign each collection a unique number and record it in your notebook. If you are taking photographs with a digital camera, the collection number can also be used when assigning filenames to your photographs.

Any format you like will work. One of us uses a combination of initials, last two digits of the year, sequential day of the year (Julian day), and sequential collection; for instance, SAT-09-276-03 would be assigned to Steve's third collection on 3 October 2009. It also is helpful to write the collection number on a small slip of waterproof paper and include it with the mushrooms in their bag, wrapping, or utility-box compartment.

- Do not collect too many species on a single hunt. Identification takes time, even after you have become a gray-haired veteran of the process, and this limits the number of collections that you can realistically deal with, especially if you return from the field on Sunday evening and have to work the next day. If you are able to dry your mushrooms for archiving in your own or an institutional herbarium, you can collect somewhat more material, as the actual identification process (but not your note-taking) can be undertaken at a later time if you have taken photos and appropriately detailed notes. However, even then, it takes real willpower to avoid bringing home too many mushrooms and having them wind up unstudied and nameless on the compost heap.
- Use waxed paper, waxed-paper bags, aluminum foil, plastic tackle or utility boxes with divided compartments, or other containers to transport your mushrooms from the field to your home. These materials provide physical support to prevent crushing, and retain moisture while still allowing the mushrooms to "breathe," as their cells remain alive for some time after you pick them. Plastic bags retain too much moisture and heat, which leads to rapid deterioration; do not use them!

- If wrapping your mushrooms in waxed paper or foil, carry the packets in a rigid, preferably shallow, container to reduce crushing and allow you to find a particular collection without emptying everything. A broad shallow woven basket is

Plastic utility boxes are great for small and medium-sized mushrooms.

the traditional tool of choice, but many other types have been devised by inventive mushroom-hunters.
- If the sun is out, or it is at all warm, do not leave your mushrooms in the trunk (or sometimes even the interior) of your car for extended periods. They will spoil rapidly. An ice-chest can be handy in such weather.
- When you return home, keep your mushrooms refrigerated. Tackle boxes with their tight-fitting lids come in handy here, as they prevent the ubiquitous "worms" (actually the larvae of fungus gnats) from escaping and causing consternation among squeamish housemates.

The color of the spores, in mass, is a key feature for identification in many mushroom groups and so preparation of a spore-print should be one of your first steps. To

A typical mushroom-hunter's basket and equipment.

do this, cut the cap off a mature but still fresh mushroom leaving a short stump for support; place it gills-down on a piece of heavy white paper or card stock (such as index cards), and cover the whole affair with a glass or bowl to slow drying and reduce air movement. If decapitating mushrooms is not to your liking, you can cut a hole in the white card, pass the stipe through the hole, and then support the card with mush-room on the rim of a glass or bowl. Leave the set-up in a cool place for several hours or even overnight. If the mushroom was fresh and discharging spores, gradually piles will form as the spores fall from the gills and collect on the paper. Assuming you used a gilled mushroom, this will appear as a pattern of radiating lines, more or less like spokes in a wheel, that correspond to the spaces between the gills. Some people

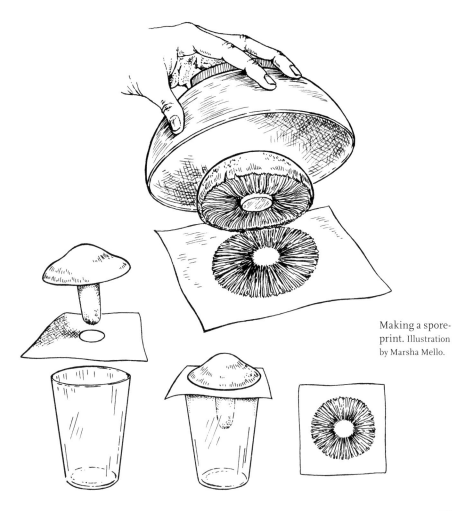

Making a spore-print. Illustration by Marsha Mello.

advocate placing half the cap on white paper and the other half on black paper to help in visualizing white spore-prints. However, white is the standard background for color comparisons, and if the print is held at an angle to the light, the texture of the deposit will make it readily visible, even if it is white. These procedures also work with boletes and spine-fungi with stipes. For clubs and corals, simply lay the fruitbody on its side on the paper. To save time, spore-prints can be started in the field. Place the specimen and card in a waxed-paper bag, fold the open end closed, and place the set-up flat in your basket so that it will remain properly oriented. Often you will have a good print by the time you get home.

Hazards of Northwest Mushroom-Hunting

For many city-dwellers, a trip to the forest can cause considerable anxiety over possible woodland dangers. However, the hazards likeliest to affect mushroom-hunters are not necessarily the ones you might expect. Yes, bears and cougars do inhabit many of our forests, but, in most of the PNW, they are not abundant, and usually have little interest in mushroom-hunters. If you are visiting public lands, such as a national forest or state park, where bear or cougar activity is high, warning signs often will be posted with tips on how to behave in the event you encounter one of these large animals. It is usually said that there are no poisonous snakes west of the Cascade crest. However, rattlesnakes are present on the east side (and probably in local areas on the west, as well), and you should keep that in mind, but their period of greatest activity lies outside the main mushroom-hunting times. The same also applies

to the smaller critters such as biting flies, mosquitoes, wasps and hornets, and ticks. Although these little creatures are merely annoyances for most people, some mosquitoes and ticks carry serious diseases, and wasp stings can be life-threatening for sensitive individuals. Use of insect repellants is a good idea when hunting in the spring and summer. Poison oak and poison ivy also are present in certain parts of the PNW, but most of our forests are free of these hazardous plants. Poison oak is, however, a major issue for sensitive individuals in southern Oregon and California.

However, for most people, the greatest danger of a mushroom trip is the drive to and from the hunting site. Our highways are not the safest of places, plus many drivers are not used to the off-pavement driving on forest roads that mushrooming often entails. Another consideration, especially on weekdays, is encounters with log trucks. Many log-truck drivers are justifiably notorious for driving at high speeds, occupying the whole road, and expecting everyone else to get out of their way. Meeting one of them on a blind curve can be a memorable experience.

In addition to the four-, six-, and eight-legged forest organisms, you should be aware of the two-legged ones. Much of the fall mushroom season overlaps with hunting season, as evidenced by signs on the sides of taverns welcoming hunters to the woods. Rifles and 12-packs are a combination to be wary of! Consider wearing a blaze orange vest, jacket, or hat, and minimize your time crawling under salal in search of one more chanterelle. Making your presence known by talking with your fellow forayers or giving an occasional toot of your whistle also is a good idea.

Once in the woods, slipping or tripping on a log can easily sprain or break an ankle. Be especially cautious with logs that have just lost their bark and support a thin layer of algae, and large well-rotted logs that may no longer have wood in the middle. And, of course, there is always the danger of getting lost. Practically every year, there are news reports of someone getting lost while looking for mushrooms. Walking in an unfamiliar area with head down and visions of morels in cream sauce occupying your thoughts is a recipe for trouble. To avoid spending a cold miserable night in the woods, or worse, stick to trails unless you know the area well. Carry a GPS unit or compass and map, if you have and know how to use them. Do not forget to take a compass bearing or GPS reading before leaving your vehicle to provide a reference point to return to. While walking, be sure to look up regularly to maintain your bearings and check landmarks.

Often it is recommended that you carry such things as a space blanket, two-way radio, cellphone (although they often do not get good signals in the woods), water, and energy bars or other food. Certainly all these things can come in handy, but carrying too much stuff is not going to be practicable, especially when you find that mother lode of large prime boletes. So, the best advice we can offer is to know your outdoor capabilities and limitations and stay within them. Always hunting with one or two companions is also a good idea.

Ecology of the Mushroom-Fungi

If you have taken a biology class, or read a general biology or botany textbook, you doubtless learned that fungi are the "great

In certain areas, extra caution is called for.

Although less of a health hazard in the Pacific Northwest, disease-carrying ticks are a serious concern for mushroom-hunters in other parts of North America.

Mushrooming during deer season calls for increased awareness and caution.

decomposers" and that, without them, we would be buried by huge piles of leaves, branches, and logs, not to mention animal carcasses and other even less appealing organic materials. Certainly this is true. The fungi, along with bacteria and many tiny soil animals, do indeed reduce organic materials to simple chemical forms, making them available for recycling into new live organisms. Mostly they do this by releasing digestive enzymes from their hyphae as they grow through their substrates. The enzymes break down organic matter into smaller component bits that can be absorbed by the hyphae, providing food for the fungus. However, not all fungi are strictly decomposers and, without the activity of the so-called mycorrhizal fungi, there would be little, or no, plant and animal life and, therefore, little needing to be decomposed. In fact, we would not exist, so burial by plant matter would hardly be an issue. The word "mycorrhiza" comes from two Greek words meaning "fungus" and "root." Thus, mycorrhizas are "fungus-roots."

What are mycorrhizas?

Mycorrhizas are mutualistic symbiotic associations between fungi and the roots of plants. Symbiotic means that the two partners live in intimate association, while mutualistic means that both of the partners benefit from the association. The benefits each partner receives are different—fungi receive sugars ("food") from the plant, and the plant receives from the fungi nutrients such as nitrogen, phosphorus, and potassium (the principal constituents of most commercial fertilizers), water, and, in some cases, protection against pathogens as well as other benefits. Mycorrhizas are diverse, ubiquitous, ancient, and essential to natural terrestrial ecosystems and, therefore, to us.

There are seven or eight main types of mycorrhiza—of these, arbuscular mycorrhizas (AM), ectomycorrhizas (EcM), and ericoid mycorrhizas (ErM) are by far the most important ecologically. There are many different fungi and many different plants involved in each type, and there are very many different fungus-plant combinations. Some of the associations are very specific, such as that between *Suillus cavipes* and larch; others not so specific. For instance, *Amanita muscaria* and *Boletus edulis* grow with a variety of trees.

Arbuscular mycorrhizas

The presence of arbuscular mycorrhizal (AM) fungi in a handful of excavated roots cannot be determined by looking at macroscopic features. The roots must be chemically treated, stained, and then examined under a microscope in order to visualize the fungal structures. The fungi involved comprise approximately 150 species known collectively as glomeromycetes. They produce extremely large spores (some visible with the naked eye), but not mushrooms. The plant partners in AM are extraordinarily diverse. Worldwide, perhaps 80–90% of the more than 300,000 species of plants form them. Redwoods, western redcedar, Alaska yellowcedar, maples, tropical rainforest trees, strawberries, corn, grasses, ferns, and liverworts are examples of the diversity of AM plants. AM is the dominant form of mycorrhiza in tropical forests, some temperate forests, grasslands, and deserts. They are present in PNW forests, but usually do not predominate.

A mycorrhizal association,
this an ectomycorrhizal
one, between *Amanita
muscaria* and a spruce tree.
Illustration by Marsha Mello.

Ectomycorrhizas

In contrast to AM, ectomycorrhizas (EcM) can be recognized with the naked eye or with a handlens. They are formed by basidiomycetes (many) and ascomycetes (far fewer), and many are mushroom-formers. In fact, a large percentage of the larger mushrooms in PNW forests are formed by EcM fungi. There may be over 10,000 species of EcM fungi, whereas there are only about 7500 species of EcM plants. Most of these are trees in the pine, oak, birch, and willow families, plus the genus *Eucalyptus*. These are dominant trees in temperate and boreal forests, and include Douglas-fir, western hemlock, the pines, the true firs, spruces, oaks, beeches, birches, aspen, and willows.

Ericoid mycorrhizas

Ericoid mycorrhizas (ErM) are formed by relatively small numbers of fungi (about 25 species, mostly ascomycetes) and plants (perhaps 1000 species in the heath family and other families closely related to it). ErM plants in the PNW include rhododendrons, huckleberries, cranberries, and salal. Other ericaceous plants, such as madrone and manzanitas, form arbutoid mycorrhizas, which are similar to ectomycorrhizas. Despite the low diversity, ErM are very important understory plants in temperate and boreal forests and in non-forest habitats at high latitudes where soils are cold, wet, and very acidic.

Ecology and physiology of mycorrhizas

The world distribution of AM, EcM, and ErM correlates very closely with climate and soil type, and these patterns probably reflect cause and effect. To have achieved such widespread distribution, mycorrhizas must be ancient. Indeed, the oldest land plant fossils (about 400 to 450 million years old) contain typical AM structures, and the subsequent history of plant evolution is closely intertwined with that of the fungi. Nowadays, mycorrhizal ecology is being found to be more complex than ever imagined. For instance, girdling (removing a strip of bark, including the active food transport tissue, from around a tree) experiments have shown that substantial portions of the abundant sugars delivered to EcM fungi by the trees are later released into the soil and provide an important foundation for the entire soil food web. Other evidence suggests the existence of "wood-wide webs" in which forest trees could be tied together into large networks by fungal hyphae connecting their roots.

On a smaller scale, it is known that EcM fungi can access various nutrients from sources heretofore not suspected to be available to plants, including rocks, proteins, nucleic acids, pollen, nematodes, and insects. The ability of mycorrhizal fungi to access these nutrients shows that traditional notions of nutrient cycling and plant nutrition (developed mostly with herbaceous plants in agricultural settings) are insufficient to explain the complexity of these processes in natural ecosystems. It also shows that the critical ecosystem importance of fungi has been grossly underestimated.

Lichens

Another mutualistic symbiosis involving fungi and photosynthetic partners is that of lichens. In these organisms, the fungus

Peltigera membranacea, a foliose lichen common in the Pacific Northwest.

Alectoria sarmentosa, a fruticose lichen common in the Pacific Northwest.

(the mycobiont) forms most of the body and its partner (the photobiont) lives within the fungal framework. The photobiont can be either a green alga or a cyanobacterium (once called "blue-green algae") and, in some lichens, both types of photobiont are present. For classification purposes, lichens are considered to be fungi; however, the overwhelming majority of them are ascomycetes that produce rather small fruitbodies; only a few are basidiomycetes that produce mushrooms for fungal reproduction. Lichens are abundant in forests and many other habitats and play important roles in those ecosystems.

An assortment of rock-dwelling crustose lichens.

Cladonia is a widespread genus of squamulose lichens.

Parasitic fungi

Another type of symbiosis is parasitism —where two organisms live intimately together, but one benefits from the relationship to the detriment of the other. Typically the benefitting organism (the parasite) is much smaller than its partner (the host). Most fungal parasites are microfungi, but several examples are found among the mushroom-fungi. Most of these, such as many honey mushrooms (the genus *Armillaria*) and polypores (such as *Heterobasidion annosum* and *Phaeolus schweinitzii*) are parasitic on trees and are important forest pathogens. Others attack insects, while still others, such as *Asterophora lycoperdoides*, *Collybia cirrhata*, *Cordyceps capitata*, and *Hypomyces lactifluorum*, attack mushroom-fungi.

Is Mushroom-Picking Sustainable?

With the advent of large-scale commercial collecting of chanterelles and matsutake in the PNW, concern arose over the effect that the picking might have on future fruiting. By far the biggest adverse impact on mushrooms has been loss or alteration of habitat. Where our homes, highways, universities, grocery coops, and mobile-phone stores now stand was once prime mushroom habitat. Best estimates suggest that, at most, only 10% of the PNW's original forest cover remains intact. Although much of the 90% that was logged now is in second- or third-growth plantation or forest, a considerable portion is forest no more. Compared with this lost or highly altered area, any impact on fungus populations caused by mushroom-picking must be small. Nonetheless, even a small impact on what remains should not be ignored, if we are to prevent further loss.

Thus, careless and/or gluttonous picking should be discouraged, especially practices such as raking moss beds to expose matsutake buttons. This directly disrupts the mycelium and interferes not only with future fruiting but possibly with the mycorrhizal connections with nearby trees. Such disruption of mycelium during harvesting is probably a bigger impact than removal of the mushroom itself. But what about careful harvesting of a small number of mushrooms? In theory, if all mushrooms were picked before releasing spores, the reproductive potential of the fungi would be seriously impacted. However, we actually know very little about the extent to which the fungal populations rely on spores for establishment versus the importance of vegetative growth and expansion. What evidence there is suggests that different mushroom species do things differently. For instance, *Laccaria bicolor* establishes new mycelia each year from the previous year's spores. Species of *Suillus* on the other hand appear to have longer-lived mycelia and less frequent establishment from spores. So it is not clear what the impact of spore "loss" would be. In a related vein, some mushroom-pickers justify their harvesting by claiming that they are helping to disperse the species because spores are released from the mushrooms in their baskets, or special mesh morel bags, as they walk through the woods. Not only is there no evidence to support this, we know of no reason to believe that such Johnny Appleseed activities make any difference to the fungal populations, given the huge numbers of highly mobile spores that mushrooms release.

Questions have also been asked about whether mushrooms should be cut off or pulled from the substrate. If the mushroom is one you do not know, by all means collect the whole thing, including any deeply rooted stipe. Do not cut it off as you might be leaving behind a critical clue to its identity. But if you are collecting an edible mushroom you know well, such as chanterelles or morels, cutting them above the soil line will minimize the amount of dirt and debris you have to deal with when you get home. As for impact on the mycelium, or effect on future fruiting, there is no firm empirical evidence one way or the other. In general, to minimize your impact on the habitat, remain aware of what you are doing, harvest in moderation, and try your best to tread lightly, picking up a few discarded beer cans, water bottles, and other bits of litter as you go.

Mushroom Poisoning— Occupational Hazard or Unfounded Fear?

Ask most Americans or Canadians what proportion of mushrooms are poisonous and likely they will say it is high. This leads to the common perception that eating wild mushrooms is a risky business on par with being a movie stunt-person or jumping motorcycles over large canyons. Although it is certainly true that mushrooms can, and do, kill people, the data show that such occurrences are both rare and nearly always preventable.

How common is poisoning and death by mushrooms?

Nationwide, of the many calls to poison control centers in the U.S., only about one in 200 involves mushrooms and, of these, the vast majority involve incidents where there are no symptoms—usually a child was found chewing, handling, or even just looking at a mushroom and the parents panicked. On average, the North American Mycological Association (NAMA) receives about 70 well-documented reports of human poisoning and 30 cases of animal poisoning per year from throughout North America. Undoubtedly, there are far more cases where the illness was mild enough or passed quickly enough that emergency treatment and/or formal reporting was not considered necessary.

The NAMA data suggest that about 1% of the people made ill by mushrooms die as a result. However, because virtually every fatality that occurs is widely publicized while large numbers of mild poisonings go unreported, 1% undoubtedly is a gross overestimate. While 50% often is quoted as the death rate for those who eat the deadliest mushrooms, those in the destroying angel group, the database, although small, suggests a death rate of 10% or less, as well as a low (less than 5%) rate for liver transplants. Perhaps the lower rate observed recently is due to greater public awareness leading to victims seeking treatment earlier and more emergency rooms knowing what treatment to provide. Overall, although deaths often occur in groups, on average about one person per year dies of mushroom poisoning in North America, devastating for those close to the persons involved and important to keep in mind for those who eat wild mushrooms, but hardly a cause for considering mushroom-hunting to be an inherently risky endeavor.

Who gets poisoned and why?

First of all, in order to get poisoned by mushrooms, one must eat them. Although some mushrooms, such as several species of *Suillus*, can cause contact dermatitis, touching mushrooms will not cause poisoning. Likewise, some individuals experience allergic reactions when they inhale large quantities of mushroom spores, such as might be found in a room containing a wild mushroom exhibit or where mushrooms are being dried, but such exposure will not cause poisoning. Thus, one need not fear handling even the deadliest of mushrooms, such as *Amanita phalloides*. If this does not completely allay your fears, consider simple precautions like washing your hands after handling mushrooms.

So who gets poisoned and why? The simplest answer is "people who don't know what they are doing eat mushrooms that they shouldn't." Contrary to hearsay and newspaper headlines, there is no evidence that professional mycologists or even moderately experienced mushroom-hunters "make fatal mistakes." In 1995, mushroomer and pathologist Dr. Denis Benjamin stated in his excellent book, *Mushrooms: Poisons and Panaceas*, "To date, I am unaware of a single fatal poisoning of any member of an amateur mycological society" and, to our knowledge, that statement remains true in 2009. Of course, many mycophagists (those who eat mushrooms) experience occasional cases of poisoning when trying new species that were correctly identified. However, these usually consist of digestive upset that resolves itself in a few hours or overnight.

According to Dr. Benjamin, accidental poisoning usually involves two categories of people—the vulnerable (primarily the young, the elderly, and recent immigrants) and the reckless (teenagers, psychoactivity seekers, and the mycologically naïve). Ingestion of mushrooms by children, usually from their yards, may result from toddlers grazing or from games such as "playing house" or "dares." However, most of these incidents produce no symptoms, much less serious poisonings, and, in many cases, the patient suffers more unpleasant effects from the treatment than from the mushrooms. Elderly individuals who are prone to confusion or suffering from failing memory have been known to make seemingly inexplicable misidentifications. Many of the most tragic mistakes have been made by recent immigrants to the Pacific Coast, for a variety of reasons. First, they are hunting in an unfamiliar environment, where many things may not be as they were in their native land. Second, their knowledge of which species are safe to eat probably was passed down from parents or grandparents and did not include training in how to critically observe and identify all sorts of mushrooms. Third, they may not have access to field guides or other identification aids because of limited finances or command of English.

The other main category is the reckless —those who eat wild mushrooms without taking time to learn about them and the necessary precautions to observe. One such group is teenagers intentionally experimenting with something with which they may have only a vague familiarity. A case from several years ago illustrates this point. Members of a high-school music group were returning home from a competition and stopped at a hamburger stand for lunch. Seeing some large mushrooms under nearby trees, they decided to add them to their burgers, with unfortunate results. The mushrooms were *Amanita pantherina* and, instead of arriving home, the students spent an unpleasant night in the local hospital. Another group that includes a high percentage of ill-prepared individuals is the magic-mushroom hunters—those who are seeking psychoactive *Psilocybe* species. Beyond these two groups, there are many other mycologically naïve individuals who rely on hearsay and proceed without knowing what they are doing.

It is easy to learn to recognize the most commonly eaten mushrooms and, no doubt, that is an important reason for their popularity. The same is true of the most dangerous mushrooms, which are rather few in number. Thus, if one invests a bit of time learning some basic mushroom identification and maintains a conservative attitude in deciding what to eat, mushroom-hunting and -eating (mycophagy) can be a perfectly safe and rewarding pastime.

How to avoid becoming a poisoning statistic

Although more complete reporting of mushroom poisonings would provide us with a more detailed understanding of the issue, it is clear that mushroom-eating need not entail high risk. Nonetheless, here are some guidelines that, along with a modicum of common sense, will help you avoid the dark side of mushrooming.

- There are no simple "rules of thumb" for recognizing poisonous mushrooms. The only reliable approach is to identify the mushroom species and see what the history of human consumption indicates about its edibility.
- Do not pick mushrooms from places where they could have become contaminated by garden chemicals, fallout from vehicle exhaust, or other pollution sources. Fungi often concentrate substances from the environment and these can be dangerous. For instance, in the wake of the Chernobyl nuclear power plant accident, mushrooms from many parts of Europe were found to contain high levels of radioactive cesium.
- Inspect every one of your mushrooms carefully to be certain they all are of the same kind and that they are in good fresh condition. Start this process in the field to avoid mixing collections or bringing home over-the-hill mushrooms. Many cases of "mushroom poisoning" in fact are food poisoning caused by bacteria on spoiled mushrooms. Save two or three good-condition specimens in the refrigerator for later inspection by experienced identifiers in the event of adverse effects ("one for the pot, one for the doctor").
- Never eat a mushroom unless it is positively identified as edible by you or someone whose judgment you have good reason to trust. Remember that to one who knows little, nearly anyone can appear to be an expert. Maintain an attitude of healthy skepticism and use the same discerning approach for identifying experts that you would for identifying mushrooms.
- Never eat mushrooms raw (for nutritional, as well as toxicity, reasons). Some contain toxins that are degraded by heat, plus cooking breaks down the cell walls and makes the nutritious cell contents available to our digestive systems.
- When trying a new species, eat only that one species and only a small amount, and then wait 24 to 48 hours before eating other mushrooms. Idiosyncratic

reactions are possible with what are, for most people, good edible mushrooms. Keep this in mind when serving wild mushrooms to guests.

- Eat wild mushrooms in moderation. Some contain toxins that appear to accumulate in our bodies over time to a point where adverse effects manifest themselves. In addition, overeating of even good edible species can make you sick, because mushrooms can be difficult to digest.
- Use extra caution when collecting outside your usual hunting grounds, especially when you are far from home. What you think is the same mushroom might, in fact, not be.
- Above all, remember that no meal is worth ending your life. When in doubt, throw it out (or seek help from someone with more experience).

Should you become a statistic . . .

If you are unfortunate enough to fall victim to mushroom poisoning, help others benefit from your experience by compiling good notes and filing a report with the North American Mycological Association's mushroom poisoning case registry. Reports can be submitted electronically or a mail-in form downloaded at http://www.namyco.org/toxicology/.

Types of mushroom poisoning

There are a number of different types of mushroom poisoning ranging from mild digestive upset to allergic reactions to death by kidney and liver failure. The major groups of mushroom toxins, examples of the mushrooms that contain them, and summaries of the symptoms they produce are provided in Appendix 1.

Tasting mushrooms for identification

For many mushrooms, taste can furnish an important clue to their identity. For instance, some russulas and lactariuses have very hot peppery tastes while others are mild. To taste a mushroom, nibble a small bit (perhaps the size of a small corn kernel) from the edge of the cap and, using your front teeth, chew it on the tip of your tongue. In some cases, the taste will be immediately obvious but, in others, you will need to wait 30 to 60 seconds for it to develop. When finished with your observation, rid yourself of the remnants in a socially acceptable manner. Note that tasting in this manner is not dangerous. In order to be poisoned, one must swallow a much larger amount of mushroom.

What's Its Name?—How to Identify Your Mushrooms

The goal of this book is to provide you with an effective tool for identifying a large number of mushrooms found in the Pacific Northwest (PNW). Be forewarned, however, that you will find many mushrooms in the woods that you will not find in this book. Although we describe and picture more than 450 species in the Mushrooms section, that is a relatively small proportion of those that live in our fungally diverse region. Just how small a proportion is hard to tell. Much work remains to be done before we will have anything approximating an accurate census of PNW mushrooms; however, the total certainly exceeds 5000 species, perhaps by a wide margin. Thus, this is a selective assemblage of species and so you might ask how we did the selecting.

We began by listing the species for which we had good-quality photographs taken in the PNW. From those candidates, we established a working list designed to include

- a wide variety of mushroom types and species;
- the more common characteristic PNW species, especially good edibles and notorious poisoners;
- species that occur only, or mainly, in the PNW;
- species mentioned, but not illustrated, in other field guides;
- unusual or rare species not covered in most other field guides.

Now, concerning our selection of which names to use—mushroom systematics (their naming, classifying, and evolutionary study) is in a state of tremendous flux. The astronomical increase in generation of DNA and other molecular data is producing major changes in how we view the evolutionary relationships among mushroom-fungi and, consequently, in their classification and names. After much deliberation, we chose to take a moderately liberal approach to using the most recent names, even though we are aware that name changes represent probably the number-one source of frustration for many mushroomers. Consequently, where the names we use might be unfamiliar to PNW mushroomers, we have also included the older, probably more familiar, names in our comments and the index.

Another problem in choosing which names to use comes from not knowing whether the PNW fungi to which European names have been applied really do represent the same species. Few mycologists have spent sufficient time on both continents to have first-hand knowledge of their mycofloras, and few critical studies have been done to evaluate our use of European names. The studies that have been done suggest that many of our species indeed are virtually identical to European material but that, for many others, our fungi do not quite fit the European concept and thus might require new names. Although this is confusing to everyone, in most cases it reflects the fact that mycologists are developing better understandings of the relationships within the mushroom-fungi, and we view this as a good thing. In our species accounts we have tried to make clear the cases where this issue has been recognized.

Suggested Approach for Identifying Mushrooms

You have returned from your foray with a basketful of prime fungi, rolls of film or a memory card containing their images, and a notebook packed with keen observations. Now what do you do? If you did not start spore-prints in the field, then that is a good place to start. As you go through your mushrooms setting up prints, organize the collections as best you can, keeping multiple collections of the same species together (but do not "lump" them into one), all the boletes or cup-fungi together, and so forth. If you have more than a few collections, get most of them re-wrapped or back in their boxes and into the refrigerator right away to keep them fresh. That done, you can proceed to "work up" your collections, as mycologists say. Your first step should be to choose one collection and carefully inspect each mushroom in it. Think about what you are seeing, paying attention to shapes, proportions, colors, textures, odors, and tastes, and then record your observations on paper. This can be done on blank paper, or on a pre-printed standardized form (or forms, because no single form of reasonable length will work equally well for all types of mushroom). In Appendix 2, we have included a list of information that should be helpful in guiding your observations and note-taking.

You will find that making drawings of the features you observe is very helpful, even if you claim no artistic talent. With a little care, anyone can make a recognizable rendering of a mushroom, but the drawing itself is actually of secondary importance. The greatest value comes from the fact that drawing something forces you to look at it more closely than you otherwise might. Committing the results of your critical examinations to paper will prove indispensable when you go on to identify the mushrooms. Once you have spore-prints, digital photos (film-users will have to wait for their images to be processed), notes, and drawings in hand, you will be ready to determine the name of your mushroom.

Finding Your Mushroom's Name

When we teach mushroom identification, we emphasize the use of keys—analytical winnowing devices that require you to make observations of and decisions about the features of your mushrooms, in the process, gradually zeroing in on what is hopefully the correct name. Successful keying requires command of a large specialized vocabulary and the ability to form accurate mental images of mushrooms based on those terms. Over the years, we have come to realize that the ability to translate technical terms into mental pictures is a skill that takes considerable time to develop. On the other hand, it takes much less time to learn to compare a collection of mushrooms with a good-quality color image. We also have found that the "comments" section of most mushroom descriptions often is more useful than the "just-the-facts" technical information when a good image is available. Thus, we have chosen to emphasize the images and comments in this guide, keep the keys simple and few in number, and minimize the amount of purely descriptive facts and figures.

That said, we also recognize that those

with limited experience can make some pretty amazing mistakes when picture-matching. Thus, we cannot overemphasize the need to critically observe and record the detailed features of each mushroom collection before attempting to use picture-matching, keys, or any other identification approach.

How to Use Keys

The most common keys have a dichotomous structure. The keys in this book are mostly dichotomous but, in places, present more than two simultaneous alternatives. In a dichotomous key, you are presented with a pair of contrasting descriptive statements (a "couplet") and you must decide which of the "leads" better describes the mushrooms you are trying to identify. If you have closely studied your mushrooms and recorded notes about their features before starting to key, you will be much better able to come to your own conclusions about their features and run a much lower risk of being biased by the words and pictures in the books.When you have chosen one lead or the other, it will direct you to another couplet where you will repeat the process. Eventually you will reach a point where, instead of another couplet, you will be directed to another key or given the name of a species, genus, or larger group of mushrooms. Often you must work through a series of keys that cover smaller and smaller groups before you arrive at a tentative species name. Once you have a tentative name, you must carefully compare descriptive information about, and images of, that species with your mushrooms to be sure you have a match. This step is absolutely crucial, because you can almost always arrive at a name when keying, regardless of whether the mushroom in question

is included in the key. That is why we chose not to include keys to species in this guide. You will encounter more species that are not in this book than those that are, and we feel that having species keys could lead to more misidentifications than correct ones.

The keys to the higher groups, however, are intended to be generally useful, regardless of which books you use to identify species. Be aware, though, that in our attempt to make these keys short and simple to use, we had to sacrifice some potential effectiveness. So keep an open mind when you reach a name and be prepared to admit you might have been wrong. Whenever you are keying, keep these tips in mind:

- Learn the jargon. Things go much quicker when you do not have to look up every word used in the key lead.

- Start with complete material that is in good condition. It can be very difficult to identify a collection unless you have good-quality specimens and both young and mature individuals.

- Write out a description of your collection before looking at the key. That way your observations are less likely to be biased by the words in the key.

- Do not start out assuming you will succeed; often you will not. Try not to become frustrated if you do not succeed; it might not be your fault (see below).

- Keep track of your history of lead choices, so that you can retrace your steps if necessary.

- If you cannot decide which of the leads to choose, mark your place and try one. If it does not lead to a convincing answer, go back and try the other lead.

- After you have reached a tentative identification using a key, always confirm it by critically comparing your material with a written description and/or available illustrations.
- Practice by keying backward. Take a mushroom whose name you know and work backward to see how it would have keyed-out.

Some reasons you might not succeed:

- You goofed somewhere. Don't worry, it happens to all of us.
- Your material is atypical or incomplete.
- The key is less than perfectly constructed and/or written. Like most things in life, there is a vast range of quality and user-friendliness in keys.
- The specimen you have selected is not a species that is included in the key you are using. This is an important reason for always checking your tentative identifications against descriptions and illustrations.

Organization of This Book

The major breakdown of the Mushrooms section reflects, more or less, a traditional classification scheme based on macromorphological features, those you can see with your naked eye or a handlens. Thus, there are gilled mushrooms (further divided by spore color); boletes; spine-fungi; club-, coral-, and fan-like fungi; polypores and crust-fungi; puffballs, earthballs, and earthstars; jelly-like fungi; morels, false morels, and elfin saddles; cup-fungi; truffles and false truffles; and odds and ends, for things that do not fit

comfortably into the other groups. Each of these groups has been assigned a color to facilitate locating it in the species accounts by finding the pages with the appropriate colored edge. This is an arrangement of convenience and does not accurately reflect evolutionary relationships as they are currently understood. Some of these major groups are further divided by genus, groups of similar genera, or by appearance. Within a genus or other group, the species usually are arranged alphabetically.

How to Use This Book

Start with a key to major groups of mushrooms, either the shortcut visual version inside the front cover, or the textual key that opens the Mushrooms section. Work your way through the key until you arrive at a group name and then go to that group's subsection. In some cases, you will have an additional key, or keys, to work through to narrow the possibilities further. Once you have run out of keys, go to the species accounts and see if you can find a close match to your fungus. The most important factor in making this, or any other identification approach, work is you taking time to make careful observations and record them. Always keep in mind that your mushroom might not be included in the book, so do not try to force a match, especially if you are considering eating the fungus in question. Whenever possible, compare your mushrooms to additional descriptions and illustrations from other books or the World Wide Web. Be wary of the latter, however, as anyone can post anything, and inaccurately identified images are commonplace.

So have at it! We wish you luck.

Concerning the Photographs and Collections

Except as noted otherwise, all the photographs were taken by Steve Trudell, using a Nikon FE2, 55-mm macro lens, and 35-mm transparency film, mostly Kodak Ektachrome and Elite 100 ASA. The camera was mounted on a tripod with legs that open to nearly flat, and ambient light provided the primary illumination, augmented with fill flash and a small collapsible reflector. Small apertures (mostly f32 and f22) were used to provide maximum depth of field so as to show the mushrooms in the context of their habitat. Those photographs for which a voucher collection exists are indicated in the caption by the collection number, such as SAT-99-296-15 for *Cantharellus cibarius* var. *roseocanus*. These collections are archived at the University of Washington (Seattle) Herbarium (WTU) and are available for study and research purposes.

The MUSHROOMS

Key to Major Morphologic Groups

1. Mushroom has a cap with an obvious top and underside, although in some cases the underside merges gradually into the stipe; stipe usually present, but it may be short and off-center 2
1. Mushroom has no cap, or cap has no obvious top and underside; stipe may or may not be present 6

2. Cap has gills on its underside, either radiating plates as in the grocery store button mushroom or blunt ridges. 3
2. Cap has pores, spines, or is smooth on its underside 4

3. Spores in mass white, cream, yellowish, lilac, or other pale color; gills of mature individuals often similarly pale-colored . . . . **Light-Spored Gilled Mushrooms** (page 40)
3. Spores in mass salmon-pink to brownish pink; gills of mature individuals usually similarly colored . . . . **Pink-Spored Gilled Mushrooms** (page 140)
3. Spores in mass dull brown, yellow-brown, orange-brown, cinnamon, rusty red-brown; gills of mature individuals usually similarly colored; if color is deep chocolate or purple-brown, see next choice . . . . **Brown-Spored Gilled Mushrooms** (page 145)
3. Spores in mass dark chocolate or purple-brown to black; gills of mature individuals similarly colored . . . . **Dark-Spored Gilled Mushrooms** (page 187)

4. Underside of cap bears icicle-like spines; stipe may or may not be present. . . . . **Spine-Fungi** (page 229)
4. Underside of cap smooth or, more often, bears a layer of closely packed tubes whose mouths appear as pores; stipe may or may not be present. 5

5. Mushroom has a fleshy cap, a more or less central stipe, and the tube layer is rather soft and spongy. . . . . **Boletes** (page 212)
5. Mushroom is tough, leathery or woody, and usually lacks a well-defined stipe; usually growing shelf-like, hoof-like, or crust-like on wood, less often on the ground . . . . **Polypores and Crust-Fungi** (page 254)

6. Mushroom has a cap and stipe; cap is brain-like, saddle-shaped, thimble-like, cup-shaped, or honeycombed with pits and ridges. . . . . **Morels, False Morels, and Elfin Saddles** (page 276)
6. Mushroom lacks a stipe and cap, or cap is differently shaped 7

7. Mushroom is erect and club-like (unbranched), coral-like (branched), or fan-like with smooth to slightly wrinkled surfaces but without a well-defined cap . . . . **Club-, Coral-, and Fan-like Fungi** (page 236) ▬▬▬

7. Mushroom is not club-like, coral-like, or fan-like; may or may not have well-defined cap 8

8. Mushroom cup-shaped, sometimes spherical and hollow when young; stipe lacking or, at most, rudimentary . . . . **Cup-Fungi** (page 285) ▬▬▬

8. Mushroom more or less spherical, interior solid when young; stipe usually lacking 9

8. Mushroom shaped differently; stipe usually lacking 10

9. Mushroom solid inside when young and filled with powdery spores when mature; may be mounted on a stipe or set of expanded rays; growing on the ground or sometimes on wood; odor usually mild at most. . . . . **Puffballs, Earthballs, and Earthstars** (page 267) ▬▬▬

9. Mushroom remains more or less solid as it matures, although it may become somewhat jelly-like; never mounted on a stipe or set of expanded rays; growing underground or partially exposed; odor of mature specimens often strong and penetrating . . . . **Truffles and False Truffles** (page 297) ▬▬▬

10. Mushroom's texture soft and jelly-like; usually growing on wood . . . . **Jelly-like Fungi** (page 272) ▬▬▬

10. Mushroom's texture not jelly-like 11

11. Mushroom is tough, leathery or woody, and usually lacks a well-defined stipe; usually growing crust-like on wood . . . . **Polypores and Crust-Fungi** (page 254) ▬▬▬

11. Mushroom more or less a branching mass of down-hanging, icicle-like spines . . . . **Spine-Fungi** (page 229) ▬▬▬

11. Mushroom different from above choices . . . . **Odds and Ends** (page 302) ▬▬▬

Light-Spored Gilled Mushrooms

Key to Light-Spored Gilled Mushroom Groups

1. Mushroom with more or less distinct cap and stipe; gills thin and plate-like, separate from one another, either attached to stipe to various degrees or not attached 2
1. Mushroom often vase- or funnel-shaped without distinct cap and stipe; gills thick and vein- or wrinkle-like, often merging together and/or with cross-veins, extending down stipe . . . . **Chanterelles** (page 42)
1. Mushroom shelf-like or bracket-shaped; stipe lacking or very reduced, sometimes centrally attached but more often attached at the edge of the cap; gills thin and plate-like, extending down stipe when one is present . . . .
. . . .**Genus *Pleurotus* and similar mushrooms** (page 134)

2. Gills thick, often widely spaced, and with a waxy appearance; many species small and brightly colored (especially red, orange, or yellow), others larger and duller-colored (mostly white, brown, or gray). . . . .**Wax-Caps** (page 62)
2. Gills usually thinner and more closely spaced without a waxy appearance; mushroom size and color varied 3

3. Mushrooms mostly medium- to large-sized; stipe (when present) not particularly slender relative to cap diameter, texture of stipe similar to that of cap 4
3. Mushrooms mostly small, stipe rather slender relative to cap diameter, texture of stipe different from that of cap (stipe usually tougher and more pliable). 9

4. Gills free; stipe often cleanly separable from cap (like a ball and socket joint) 5
4. Gills attached to stipe; stipe not cleanly separable from cap 6

5. Young mushroom completely enveloped by a veil, the remnants of which remain as a volva (cup, collar, or rings of tissue) at the base of the stipe and/or a superficial patch or warts on the cap, cap surface (beneath any patch or warts) smooth but outer edge may be grooved. . . . .**Genus** *Amanita* (page 80)

5. Young mushroom not completely enveloped by a veil (but gills may be covered by a partial veil that remains as a ring on the stipe), thus no volva, patch, or warts present, cap surface may be smooth, powdery, or innately scaly, outer edge not grooved. . . . . . .
. . . . **Lepiotas and similar mushrooms** (page 71)

6. Texture of cap, gills, and stipe brittle, fresh mushroom shattering (like automobile safety glass) when thrown against a tree and stipe snapping cleanly like a piece of chalk when broken 7

6. Texture fibrous, not behaving as above 8

7. Fresh mushroom (especially the gills) exuding a watery, milky, or colored liquid when cut or broken; color of cap usually dull, color of stipe usually similar to that of cap . . . .
. . . . **Genus** *Lactarius* (page 54)

7. Mushroom not exuding liquid when cut or broken; color of cap often bright (red, green, yellow, purple, etc.), color of stipe usually white, sometimes with reddish or purplish blush. . . . . **Genus** *Russula* (page 48)

8. Gills usually decurrent, although sometimes merely attached, cap often vase- or funnel-shaped, colors usually drab (white, brown, or gray). . . . .
. . . .**Genus** *Clitocybe* **and similar mushrooms** (page 89)

8. Gills attached, often only slightly, but not decurrent, cap usually convex to flat, colors may be dull or fairly bright. . . . . . . **Genus** *Tricholoma* **and similar mushrooms** (page 99)

9. Caps usually thin-fleshed and often quite fragile, edge of cap not inrolled when young, cap often conical, at least when young, gills vary from attached to decurrent, those with decurrent gills often exhibit a vase- or funnel-shaped cap, dried specimens not reviving when moistened . . . . **Genus** *Mycena* **and similar mushrooms** (page 122)

9. Cap usually somewhat thicker-fleshed and tougher, edge of cap often inrolled when young, cap usually convex to flat, not conical (although a central hump often is present), gills attached, but not decurrent, dried specimens often reviving when moistened. . . . . **Genus** *Collybia* **and similar mushrooms** (page 115)

Cantharellus formosus

CHANTERELLES

The chanterelles include a variety of mushrooms belonging to four genera (*Cantharellus, Craterellus, Gomphus,* and *Polyozellus*) that are similar in bearing their spores on ridges instead of plate-like gills. The fruit-bodies range from small to large and have a cap and stalk, although there is not always a clear distinction between them; in many cases, they are more or less vase-, funnel-, or trumpet-shaped with the fertile ridges extending down the stipe. They are brittle, fleshy, or leathery in texture, never woody. The stipe can be fleshy or hollow. The fertile surface often has a waxy luster and comprises an anastomosing system of thick, shallow folds with blunt edges and cross-veins. The fertile surface is nearly smooth in some species of *Craterellus* and *Canthar-*ellus, but only one of these, *Craterellus cornucopioides,* occurs (uncommonly) in the PNW. The chanterelles are strictly woodland fungi, as they are ectomycorrhizal with a variety of trees. Thus, they are found on soil or sometimes on well-rotted wood.

Our current understanding of evolutionary relationships among the fungi suggests that the chanterelles are more closely related to some of the spine-, club-, and coral-fungi than they are to the gilled mushrooms. Despite their similar appearance, the different chanterelles are not all closely related to one another. *Cantharellus* and *Craterellus* indeed are closely related to each other, as well as to the spine-fungus *Hydnum repandum* and its relatives. On the other hand, *Gomphus* is closely related to stinkhorns (and their truffle-like relatives), earthstars, and coral-fungi such as ramarias. *Polyozellus* appears related to the thelephoras and spine-fungi in the genera *Hydnellum* and *Sarcodon*.

Cantharellus formosus Corner
PACIFIC GOLDEN CHANTERELLE

Although nearly all the golden chanterelles in North America have been referred to as *Cantharellus cibarius*, recent studies have confirmed that there actually are several, if not many, different species. The species epithet *formosus* ("finely formed," "beautiful") is certainly descriptive of many of our golden chanterelles. The fruitbodies are often large for a chanterelle, and have a dull orange to brownish orange cap that readily bruises brownish and often is finely scaly. The fertile ridges often are deep and relatively thin; they are usually pale orange-yellow but may have a pinkish cast. The

Cantharellus formosus

Ridged hymenium of *Cantharellus formosus*
SAT-00-251-13

Golden chanterelles for sale at Pike Place Market in Seattle

Cantharellus formosus and two non-edible lookalikes—*Chroogomphus tomentosus*, left, and *Hygrophoropsis aurantiaca*, right

stipe usually is fairly slender and tapered downward. *Cantharellus formosus* fruits abundantly throughout moist portions of the PNW and is the species most commonly found for sale in produce markets and grocery stores, as well as on restaurant menus.

Gilled mushrooms that could be confused with golden chanterelles include *Hygrophoropsis aurantiaca*, *Chroogomphus tomentosus*, and, in California, *Omphalotus oliva-*

Cantharellus cascadensis

Cantharellus cibarius var. *roseocanus*
SAT-99-296-15

scens. All three have sharp, blade-like gills (although those of *H. aurantiaca* can be deceivingly chanterelle-like), none of these is worth eating, and the latter is poisonous. *Gomphus floccosus* and *G. kauffmanii* both have blunt fold-like gills like chanterelles; however, both are generally more vase-like and have coarse scales on the cap. Dark individuals of the white chanterelle (*Cantharellus subalbidus*) and individuals of other golden chanterelle species such as *C. cascadensis* can be hard to differentiate from Pacific golden chanterelles, but seeing as how all are good edibles, the consequences of misidentification are negligible.

Cantharellus cascadensis Dunham, O'Dell, and R. Molina

Both this golden chanterelle and *Cantharellus cibarius* var. *roseocanus* Redhead, Norvell, and Danell (rainbow chanterelle) first passed as *C. cibarius*, and then as *C. formosus*, but now are recognized as separate entities in large part as a result of molecular analyses. They are very similar to *C. formosus* in most respects, differing primarily in sometimes subtle details of coloration, bruising reaction, scaliness, and habitat. The cap of *C. cascadensis* usually exhibits bright yellow hues and a smooth or slightly wooly surface. The stipe often is clavate or bulbous. This species has only recently been recognized, so its distribution has not yet been well worked out, although it can occur in at least some of the same places as other PNW chanterelles. The cap of *C. cibarius* var. *roseocanus* is smooth, bright yellow-orange, often has a pinkish blush near its edge, and bruises less than the other two golden chanterelles. It seems to be associated primarily with spruce, occurring with

Sitka spruce and shore pine near the coast and with Engelmann spruce in the mountains. All three of the golden chanterelles discussed here appear to be pretty much restricted to the PNW.

Cantharellus subalbidus A. H. Smith and Morse
WHITE CHANTERELLE

Cantharellus subalbidus differs from the golden chanterelles primarily by its cream to ivory color. It darkens to yellow-orange with age and so older specimens sometimes can be difficult to distinguish from golden chanterelles. Although it occurs in a variety of forests containing Douglas-fir and hemlock, it seems to have a greater affinity for old forests than do C. formosus and C. cascadensis.

Craterellus tubaeformis (Fries) Quélet
WINTER CHANTERELLE

Craterellus tubaeformis is a small, slender, trumpet-shaped chanterelle with a brownish or orange-brown cap, hollow stipe, and penchant for growing on mossy rotten wood. It has a long fruiting season although, in most of the PNW, it is not common in winter (it is in California, though). Previously it was known as Cantharellus tubaeformis and also, incorrectly, as Cantharellus/Craterellus infundibuliformis. Results of the molecular analysis that supported Craterellus as the appropriate genus for C. tubaeformis also suggest that the winter chanterelle of the PNW is not that species. Thus, we may need a new name for our fungus, and C. neotubaeformis has been suggested, although not yet formally proposed. Despite its size, C. tubaeformis is edible and considered choice by some. Its tendency to grow in large troops allows

it to be gathered in sufficient quantity to be worthwhile.

Gomphus clavatus (Persoon) S. F. Gray
PIG'S EAR

According to Alexander Smith, "This is the fungus usually referred to when someone asks about 'that funny-looking thing which is purplish underneath' . . . It is a most peculiar fungus to say the least." The purplish, veined fertile surface combined with

Cantharellus subalbidus SAT-05-259-05

Craterellus tubaeformis SAT-01-276-14

LIGHT-SPORED GILLED MUSHROOMS **45**

the flat to funnel-like tan cap and growth in clusters make it distinctive. *Polyozellus multiplex* also is clustered and has a veined fertile surface, but is entirely dark purplish, blue, or black. *Gomphus clavatus* is less abundant than many mycophagists would like, but is not rare, occurring throughout the conifer forests of western and northern North America. Many consider it a choice edible but, unlike the other chanterelles, it often is insect-infested unless you find it very young.

Gomphus floccosus (Schweinitz) Singer
WOOLY CHANTERELLE

Not truly wooly, *Gomphus floccosus* is more accurately characterized by the coarse scales that usually line its deeply vase-shaped cap; however, it is a highly variable fungus, and the degree of scaliness is by no means constant. In its common form, the cap when fresh is a deep reddish orange but fades with age, and old pale specimens can be found that might seem to be a different fungus. The fertile surface is whitish to pale yellowish and highly wrinkled and forked, with portions appearing almost like pores in older specimens. The size of the fruitbodies varies from small-medium to fairly large, and the shape can be tall and slender or short and squatty with the vase shape being more or less developed. It is common throughout the conifer forests of western and northern North America. *Gomphus bonarii* has been said to differ by being smaller, having blocklike yellow-orange scales with red tips, and a tendency to grow in clusters. However, in practice, it is very difficult to distinguish two species, and many mycologists do not recognize *G. bonarii* as a separate species. Although some people consider *G. floccosus* delicious, others find the taste poor, and still others have reported gastric discomfort after eating it. Thus, we recommend that it be avoided. Based on results of DNA analyses, *G. floccosus* seems less closely related to *G. clavatus* than had been thought, so some mycologists feel the former species should be called *Turbinellus floccosus* instead.

Gomphus clavatus SAT-00-250-13

Gomphus floccosus

Gomphus kauffmanii (A. H. Smith)
R. H. Petersen

Gomphus kauffmanii is similar to *G. floccosus*, but in its typical form usually can be recognized by the lack of orange hues in the cap, more abundant and coarser scales, often larger size, and more substantial stocky appearance. It is not prone to growing in clusters. In the PNW, it seems to be found most commonly in old-growth conifer forests, but it also occurs in other conifer forests here and throughout most of western North America. It is encountered less often than *G. floccosus*. The edibility of *G. kauffmanii* is questionable, so we recommend it be avoided. It is very closely related to *G. floccosus* and so may also be transferred to the genus *Turbinellus*.

Gomphus kauffmanii SAT-98-260-06

Polyozellus multiplex (Underwood)
Murrill

BLUE CHANTERELLE, BLACK CHANTERELLE

The purplish to blackish color, veined fertile surface, and tendency to grow in tight-packed clusters make *Polyozellus multiplex* easy to identify. If confirmation is necessary, the warty white spores and blackish green reaction of the flesh when potassium hydroxide is applied will cinch the identification. In the PNW, it is an uncommon to somewhat rare species that occurs most frequently in old-growth forests. It also occurs in conifer forests throughout western and northern North America and in Japan and Korea. *Polyozellus multiplex* is thought by many to be a good edible species, but because of its rarity we recommend restraint when collecting it for the table.

Polyozellus multiplex SAT-99-296-13

Polyozellus multiplex, ridged hymenium SAT-05-265-16

Russula adusta SAT-01-264-50

GENUS *RUSSULA*

Russula is a particularly easy genus to recognize, and many of its species also can be identified readily. However, most species are difficult to identify both because of the nature of variation within the genus and because its taxonomy is a nightmare. Most russulas are medium to large woodland mushrooms with colorful caps, white stipes, and a characteristic squatty appearance resulting from the width of the caps being about the same as the height of the stipes. They are very clean-looking in part because they lack veils; thus they do not have rings or volvas (at least the species in North America do not). The other distinctive characteristic is their brittle texture—a fresh russula thrown against a tree will shatter like automobile safety glass with relatively clean edges on the fragments (we

recommend that everyone try this once, but not make a habit of destroying russulas as, when intact and in place, they are a very attractive visual element in our forests). Other than in *Lactarius* (close relatives of russulas, in which it is less well developed), this brittle texture is very rare in mushrooms. A less violent means of experiencing it is to break a fresh stipe in half—it will break cleanly, like a piece of chalk. The reason for this texture can be seen under the microscope—the flesh includes nests of spherical cells that look much like soap suds in a sink of dishwater. These cells can move fairly freely past one another, unlike long slender hyphae that are intertangled like a mass of spaghetti. Another characteristic microscopic feature is the spores, which are mostly ellipsoid to nearly globose, with warts or ridges or networks of ridges that stain bluish black in Melzer's reagent. The spores vary from pure white, through shades of cream and yellow, to fairly dark ocher. The flesh of many species is acrid either immediately or delayed, and it has led some San Francisco Bay Area mushroomers to refer to "russula mouth." The members of *Russula* and *Lactarius* are closely related, usually being separated by the presence of latex in *Lactarius*. In addition, the more brittle flesh of the russulas, their tendency to have more brightly colored caps, and their characteristic stature make recognition of the two genera fairly easy in most cases.

In recent years, molecular and morphological studies have shown that the russulas and lactariuses form an evolutionary line distinct from that of the other gilled mushrooms. The molecular analyses also have added to the confusion of *Russula* taxonomy by suggesting that *Russula* and *Lactarius*, as currently configured, do not represent natural evolutionary groups. Instead many species of *Lactarius* are included among the russulas. As with other aspects of mushroom taxonomy, time will tell how things shake out. For now, we will maintain the traditional arrangement. Russulas and lactariuses are ectomycorrhizal and hence are found in forests and other areas where suitable host trees are present.

Ben Woo, an ardent student of russulas, characterized the edibility of the genus as follows: "Russulas are so abundant that the question of their edibility is always raised by beginners. The answer is usually a wry, 'Well, if they taste mild, you can try eating them.' The implication is that they are not particularly choice. It's the plain truth that, given the availability of almost any other edible mushrooms, russulas come off a dis-

tant second. Most are either of poor quality or unpalatable." The only species our good friend recommended are *Russula olivacea* and *R. xerampelina*.

Russula adusta (Persoon: Fries) Fries

Russula adusta is a member of the subgenus *Compactae*, which includes relatively large, dense, hard-fleshed mushrooms that are white to brownish and often blacken in age. *Russula adusta* blackens only slightly, and the flesh pinkens lightly when cut. The cap is brownish to grayish (*adust* is Latin for "burned" or "tanned"), relatively shiny, and the odor is said to approximate that of empty wine barrels (although this odor has not been noticed in PNW collections). The spores are white and the taste is mild. It grows with conifers. *Russula densifolia* is very similar, with more white in the cap, reddening flesh, perhaps a more acrid taste, and perhaps slightly yellowish spores. *Russula albonigra* is whiter at first, and then turns black without reddening, with the gills often the last part to blacken.

Russula amoenolens Romagnesi

Russula amoenolens is the name we have chosen for a medium-sized, yellow-brown to gray-brown fungus with a spermatic odor, hot taste, and pale creamy yellow spores, that is both widespread and abundant in natural habitats and, especially, under trees in parks and landscaped settings. There may be more than one species involved, but sorting out the different concepts in the literature is extremely difficult. Many original descriptions are skimpy at best, and interpretations vary from author to author. Other names that have been used for this fungus, or similar species, include *R. insignis, R.*

pectinata, R. pectinatoides, R. cerolens, and *R. sororia.* They appear related to the group exemplified by *R. laurocerasi,* but differ in their smaller size, less yellowish cap color, more finely ornamented spores, and different odors.

Russula brevipes Peck

Russula brevipes is one of the more common mushrooms in the PNW as well as being one of David Arora's leading candidates for "most boring mushroom." It is a usually large white member of subgenus

Russula amoenolens SAT-06-301-03

Russula brevipes SAT-00-264-01

Compactae that does not redden or blacken, although it may develop brownish stains. As its epithet suggests, the stipe (*-pes,* Latin for "foot") is short (Latin, *brevi*) compared to the cap diameter, so it often has difficulty getting its cap above the soil surface. Often it is found as "mushrumps," particularly along the edges of trails and unpaved forest roads. The cap usually is somewhat to markedly vase-shaped, the spores are white, and the taste is mild to variably acrid. *Russula cascadensis* is a supposedly separate species, differentiated by its smaller size, cap with buffy tones, smaller spores, and very acrid taste. However, many collections fall uncomfortably between the two concepts, so it remains to be seen whether there is more than one species here or not. *Russula brevipes* is very similar to *R. delica* and *R. chloroides* of Europe, the latter perhaps corresponding to *R. brevipes* var. *acrior,* which is acrid and has a narrow greenish band around the stipe apex adjacent to the gills.

Russula crassotunicata Singer

Russula crassotunicata is a mostly white fungus often found growing on well-rotted wood. Its cap may be somewhat creamy or yellowish, and the gills and stipe often develop brownish stains. Its most distinctive characteristic is its thick, tough, rubbery cap cuticle that often can be completely peeled away from the cap flesh. It is most often found in old-growth forests and can be rather common. The spores are white and the taste is bitter to acrid.

Russula crenulata Burlingham

Russula crenulata, R. raoultii Quélet, and *R. cremoricolor* are three very similar species that cannot be confidently separated by macroscopic features, and not easily even with microscopic features. All are medium-sized, with whitish to pale yellowish to yellow caps, white spores, and acrid taste, and all grow in a variety of forests with both conifers and hardwoods. *Russula crenulata* has the largest spores (8–10.5 × 6.5–7.5 µm), numerous cystidia in the cap cuticle, cap cuticle that peels easily at least halfway to the center, and finely serrated gill edges (often need a handlens to see it clearly). *Russula raoultii* has the smallest spores (5.7–9 × 5.5–7.5 µm), best developed network of spore ornamentation, less numerous cystidia in the cap cuticle, and moderately peelable cap. *Russula cremoricolor* has mid-sized spores (7.5–9.5 × 5.7–8 µm) and less prominent spore ornamentation, and lacks partial gills between the full gills.

Russula fragilis (Persoon: Fries) Fries

Russula fragilis is a small to small-medium species with very fragile flesh that becomes water-soaked very quickly. The cap color is generally a mix of watery purple, pink, and olivaceous green on a whitish to grayish background, and the cap edge is translucent-

Russula crassotunicata

Russula crenulata

Russula fragilis SAT-00-298-36

Russula raoultii SAT-04-304-05

striate. The spores are white, the odor mild or pleasantly fruity, and the taste very acrid. It occurs singly or in small groups, often on or near well-rotted wood.

Russula laurocerasi Melzer

Russula laurocerasi is one of our larger russulas. It has a viscid yellowish brown cap with a grooved margin, whitish to brown-stained stipe, and strong, but generally pleasant, odor of almond extract or maraschino cherries. The spores are cream to pale yellow and the taste is very acrid. Microscopically, the spores have much more prominent warts (1.5–2.5 μm high) than the many similar species. These include R. foetens, very similar except for the strongly fetid odor, R. subfoetens with fetid odor and flesh that yellows when cut, R. fragrantissima with odor similar to R. laurocerasi or anise-like but persisting after the fruitbodies have been dried, and edge of the cap smooth or short-striate, and R. illota, gill edge and stipe with blackish brown dots and odor like R. laurocerasi, but with a very noticeable fetid component. Various of these have been synonymized or made varieties of one another, and the question of which of them occur in the PNW remains largely open.

Russula laurocerasi

Russula nigricans Bulliard: Fries

Russula nigricans is another species in subgenus Compactae. It is a large, hard mushroom, with brownish or blackish brown cap and flesh that turns red when bruised; it blackens almost completely in age. The spores are white and the taste is mild to slightly acrid. It is distinguished from similar species, such as R. adusta and R. densifolia by its widely spaced gills. Russula dissimulans was described based on collections from North America, but the concept is very close to that of R. nigricans and so the name has not been applied frequently. Russula nigricans is widespread in the Northern Hemisphere.

Russula occidentalis Singer

Russula occidentalis is a common species under conifers in the Washington Cascades and, like many russulas, causes a great deal of confusion. It is a medium-sized or larger mushroom, with a variably colored cap—

Russula nigricans

usually it is purplish with a yellow-green center, but it can appear in many shades of purplish, olive-green, and browns, usually in mixtures. The gills are cream to pale yellowish, and the stipe is white and often turns grayish in age or when handled, sometimes with a reddish phase. The flesh is white and turns reddish to grayish to black when exposed. The spores are cream-colored.

Russula queletii Fries

Russula queletii is the name usually applied to specimens with a purplish cap, purple-blushed stipe, cream or pale yellow spores, pleasant fruity odor, acrid taste, and association with spruce. The color of the illustrated collection is brighter and less reddish than most illustrations of European material, so we could have a closely related species and not the real thing. Similar species include *R. sardonia* (= *R. drimeia*), with bright yellow gills and spores with bands rather than mostly isolated warts, and *R. torulosa*, with less acrid flesh, spores similar to those of *R. sardonia*, and association with pine. The occurrence of these species in the PNW has not been established.

Russula rosacea (Persoon) S. F. Gray

Russula rosacea (= *R. sanguinea*, *R. sanguinaria*) is easily recognized by the bright red cap, usually red or pink-tinged stipe, creamy yellow spores and gills, acrid taste, and growth in often large groups under pines. Collections from other conifer habitats could represent *R. americana*, which has larger spores (9–11 × 8–11 vs. 7.5–9.5 × 7–8 μm) and more fragile flesh but, otherwise, is virtually identical. Because it is often said that the acrid taste disappears

Russula occidentalis

Russula queletii SAT-01-279-05

Russula rosacea SAT-04-018-09

during cooking, several *R. rosacea* were sautéed at an Oregon Mycological Society foray. The acrid taste did disappear, but the resulting flavor was disgusting and no one could manage to swallow a bite.

Russula stuntzii Grund

Russula stuntzii is characterized by its small to medium fruitbodies with a viscid pale grayish cap, white to pale yellowish spores and gills, white stipe, and acrid taste. It occurs singly or in small groups in conifer forests, often on or near rotting wood. The

Russula stuntzii SAT-07-268-11

Russula xerampelina SAT-00-261-57

epithet honors Dr. Daniel E. Stuntz, longtime mycologist and teacher at the University of Washington. As far as is known *R. stuntzii* occurs only along the Pacific Coast, from B.C. to California.

Russula xerampelina (Schaeffer) Fries

Russula xerampelina produces generally large stout fruitbodies with a fishy or crabby odor, whitish stipes that stain brown when handled, pale yellow spores and gills, and mild taste. The typical form has a bright red, maroon, or deep purple cap and various degrees of pink tinge on the stipe. Either *R. xerampelina* exhibits an extraordinary range of cap colors, or there are a large number of very similar species that differ primarily in cap color; thus, many varieties of *R. xerampelina* and separate species have been described. Among the better known of these are *R. elaeodes* (= *R. x.* var. *elaeodes*), with green to olive to dark brown or blackish cap colors, singly or in mixtures, and *R. graveolens*, with brownish purple to vinaceous or vinaceous-brown colors. *Russula xerampelina*, in the broad sense, is very widely distributed in a variety of forest types. It is probably the most frequently eaten russula.

GENUS *LACTARIUS*

MILK-CAPS

Lactarius is characterized by exuding a watery to milky or colored fluid when broken or cut, best seen in the gills or flesh of the stipe apex. Only a few other mushrooms (for example, certain mycenas and hydropuses) produce similar latex, and all these species are small and fragile compared to lactariuses. The texture of most lactariuses is brittle, like that of russulas, because they contain similar

Lactarius deliciosus group

clusters of round cells in their flesh. Also like russulas, lactariuses have white to yellowish spores with striking patterns of ornamentation (dark blue to bluish black in Melzer's reagent). Lactariuses come in a variety of colors and have a number of easily recognized features that, when combined with the color of the latex and color changes, make many of them relatively easy to identify to species. While there are some smaller species, such as *L. occidentalis*, most are medium-sized or larger. Many lactariuses have a relatively broad cap relative to the stipe length, and the cap often has an incurved edge and is depressed in the center when mature. Lactariuses are ectomycorrhizal, and some are host-specific—for example, *L. torminosus* occurs only with birches—while others occur with a variety of trees. Some species, such as *L. deliciosus* and

L. rubrilacteus, are collected for food. The acrid species, such as *L. torminosus* and *L. piperatus*, generally are said to be poisonous; however, in Finland, Russia, and other areas, such species are regularly eaten, after proper preparation.

Lactarius deliciosus (Fries) S. F. Gray Group

The name *Lactarius deliciosus* has been applied, in both North America and Europe, to a widespread group of common mushrooms that have in common an overall orange to salmon coloration, zonate caps, a tendency to discolor greenish when bruised or in age, and orange to reddish orange latex. In western North America, several varieties of *L. deliciosus* have been recognized; however, recent studies show that, although these are closely related to the "real" *L. deliciosus*, they probably should not be considered the same

Lactarius deliciosus group (the drops on the gills are water, not latex) SAT-99-301-11

species. One of our orange milk-caps has an orange, moist to subviscid cap with a slight whitish bloom, subtle zonation, and orange spots when fresh. The stipe has a whitish bloom and often watery orange spots over a light orange background. The gills are light orange with paler edges, the scant bright orange latex stains the flesh reddish on exposure, and the fruitbodies develop moderate to complete green-staining in age. Another type occurs later in the season in coastal forests, often under spruce. It has caps with strong grayish green colors mixed with brownish orange, orangish gills and stipe, and extensive green staining. The orange latex is scant and does not change or stain the flesh. Work is under way to clarify species concepts for our orange milk-caps and their relationships with similar species elsewhere. All are gathered for food; however, the interior of a fresh-looking specimen may be home to numerous larvae and, even when larva-free, they are not generally considered deserving of their species name.

Lactarius fallax A. H. Smith and Hesler

Lactarius fallax is commonly encountered on litter in spruce and mixed conifer forests along the coast and in the interior mountains. It is a medium-sized species with a dry, velvety, brown to blackish brown cap with a distinct pointed umbo. The stipe is dry, velvety, often wrinkled at the top, and similar in color to the cap, except for the whitish base. The gills are white with either white or gray-brown to dark brown edges. The spacing of the gills ranges from crowded to distant in some forms, and the gills often extend a bit onto the stipe apex. The latex is white and unchanging, often scanty, and after some time broken flesh becomes pinkish to vinaceous. *Lactarius fallax* can occasionally be abundant but most often occurs as one or a few fruitbodies. The taste and odor are mild, but pleasant. *Lactarius lignyotus* of eastern North America and Europe is a close relative.

Lactarius glyciosmus (Fries: Fries) Fries

Lactarius glyciosmus occurs primarily in areas where birch has been planted, especially parks and grassy roadsides. In natural habitats, it occurs in moist areas, primarily in sphagnum under birch, but also with alder and willow in both boreal and montane habitats. It is a small to medium-sized mushroom with a fruity smell like coconut and a slightly acrid taste. The cap surface is dry, somewhat velvety to finely scaly and pinkish buff or pinkish gray, with clay to cinnamon tones usually in concentric zones. The gills are crowded, light pinkish buff, and run onto the stipe apex. The stipe is dry, slightly pruinose at the apex and glabrous below, similar in color to the cap but

Lactarius fallax SAT-00-284-55

Lactarius glyciosmus SAT-04-278-02

Lactarius kauffmanii SAT-05-265-12

often paler, has a white felty base, and may be compressed. The latex is white and usually abundant.

Lactarius kauffmanii Hesler and A. H. Smith

In the past, *Lactarius kauffmanii* was often misidentified as *L. trivialis*, a species that occurs with spruce and birch in Europe. The two are similar in size and stature; however, *L. kauffmanii* has white latex that dries grayish green and a viscid cap that is brown to dark brown with grayish or vinaceous tones, but not zoned. The gills are typically pale orange to light orange and stain brownish when cut or bruised. The stipe is viscid and light grayish orange or tan to vinaceous cinnamon, with distinctive dots. The taste is decidedly acrid. *Lactarius trivialis* differs primarily by its lighter color and pale cream latex that turns white paper yellow.

Lactarius occidentalis A. H. Smith

Lactarius occidentalis is a small fragile species that occurs with alders. The cap is smooth to wrinkled, dry to moist, dark brown to brown with olive colors when fresh, sometimes developing orange-brown tones, non-zoned, and translucent-striate along the edge when fresh. The gills are pinkish cinnamon to pinkish tan, narrow, and close. The stipe is dry and dark brown to brownish orange or grayish brown. The latex is white to whey-like, mild, and may be scanty or absent, especially in older mushrooms. Cut or broken surfaces slowly become reddish brown. *Lactarius obscuratus* is a closely related species that grows with alder in Europe.

Lactarius olympianus Hesler and A. H. Smith

Lactarius olympianus is common in conifer forests throughout the PNW and Rocky

Lactarius occidentalis SAT-01-279-40

Lactarius olympianus SAT-00-263-03

Mountains. It is sometimes confused with species in the *L. deliciosus* group because of the viscid cap with concentric zones of orange tones. However, breaking any part of the mushroom produces abundant white unchanging latex that is extremely acrid. The gills are whitish or yellowish and discolor orange-brown when bruised or in age. The stipe is usually whitish at first, and becomes ochraceous in age. The European species *L. zonarioides* is similar.

Lactarius pallescens Hesler and A. H. Smith

Lactarius pallescens is a close relative of *L. uvidus*. Both species are medium-sized to large, produce copious white latex, and their flesh stains lilac when injured. *Lactarius pallescens* has a viscid to slimy, white to grayish or grayish vinaceous cap, whitish gills that may be slightly decurrent, and viscid to slimy white stipe that is shiny when dry. All parts develop ochraceous to pale rusty stains in age. It can be found commonly in conifer forests throughout the PNW. *Lactarius uvidus* var. *montanus* (= *L. montanus*) is darker-colored and occurs from the southern Rockies to Alaska.

Lactarius plumbeus (Bulliard: Fries) S. F. Gray

Lactarius plumbeus (= *L. necator*, *L. turpis*) is a medium-sized to large species, with cap and stipe that have strong olivaceous tones usually mixed with yellow at first and brown or green when mature. The cap becomes broadly depressed when mature, with a somewhat sticky surface that is velvety to hairy or somewhat scaly, and the edge often appears veined from above. The gills are crowded, usually forked near the stipe, and whitish with pale orange to pale yellow tints when fresh. The stipe is slightly sticky, cylindrical to barrel-shaped, and sometimes has dark spots. The mushrooms exude copious white acrid latex. The flesh is firm and the taste mild at first but then very acrid. All parts of the mushroom darken with age or when broken or bruised. In the PNW, *L. plumbeus* occurs frequently under planted birch trees and often persists into late fall as dry black specimens. In Europe, it is reported from birch and spruce forests.

In PNW conifer forests, we have a related species, *Lactarius olivaceo-umbrinus* Hesler and A. H. Smith. It is very similar in appearance and coloration to *L. plumbeus* but with somewhat stronger olive-brown cap and stipe and dark spots on the stipe. It is most frequent in the coastal Sitka spruce forests, but also extends into interior montane forests. It is rarely abundant, most often being found as single fruitbodies.

Lactarius pseudomucidus Hesler and A. H. Smith

Lactarius pseudomucidus is entirely gray to grayish brown or brownish except for the

Lactarius pallescens SAT-05-266-11

Lactarius plumbeus

Lactarius pseudomucidus SAT-99-300-09

Lactarius olivaceo-umbrinus

whitish stipe base. Older or water-soaked fruitbodies are often faded and may develop more brownish colors. Both cap and stipe are viscid to slimy. The gills are strikingly white with a grayish or yellowish tint and stain brownish when cut or bruised. The latex is white to whey-like, and dries yellowish. Both the latex and flesh are acrid. *Lactarius pseudomucidus* is frequently found in coastal and mid-elevation conifer forests, and eastward at least as far as Idaho and southward into California. In the past, it was misidentified as *L. mucidus*, an eastern species.

Lactarius rubrilacteus Hesler and A. H. Smith

Lactarius rubrilacteus is related to the *L. deliciosus* group but differs by the light orange to brownish orange, obscurely to distinctly zonate cap, which often is broadly vase-shaped when mature, the light orange to grayish orange gills, and a light orange to brownish orange or somewhat reddish stipe, which often has a whitish bloom at first and develops distinct spots when mature. The latex is reddish brown and does not change color on exposure; however, bruised, dam-

aged, or aged mushrooms often have grayish to greenish colors, and sometimes even unexpanded mushrooms are greenish. It occurs in a variety of habitats, often in young stands of pine and Douglas-fir. In North America, *L. rubrilacteus* has mistakenly been called *L. sanguifluus*, a similar species that occurs under pine in Europe and is related to *L. vinosus*. Both of the latter species also have reddish brown to wine-red latex. *Lactarius rubrilacteus* is perhaps the most widely eaten lactarius in the PNW, although that is not saying much.

Lactarius rufus (Scopoli: Fries) Fries

Lactarius rufus has a reddish brown to brick-colored or orange-brown, dry, non-zoned cap that sometimes wrinkles in age. The gills are pale orange; the stipe is pinkish brown to brownish orange or reddish orange, but often its lower and upper areas are pale. The latex is copious, white, and unchanging, and the taste is exceedingly, but slowly, acrid. *Lactarius rufus* commonly occurs with spruce and pine, often in abundance, for example, near the edge of bogs or in other moist mossy areas where spruce occurs. It is very common in northern conifer forests around the world.

Lactarius scrobiculatus var. *canadensis* (A. H. Smith) Hesler and A. H. Smith

Lactarius scrobiculatus is one of a number of lactariuses that have a bearded cap margin. They come in various colors, often have concentrically zoned caps, and frequently are viscid when fresh. The cap color, latex color and color changes, and habitat are helpful in identifying them. *Lactarius scrobiculatus* is typically a large mushroom with whit-

Lactarius rubrilacteus

ish to yellow or ochraceous caps. The gills are crowded, often forked near the stipe, whitish to yellowish, and develop brownish stains. The copious latex is white and quickly turns yellow. The stipe is dry, white to yellowish with large glazed spots (scrobiculae), and eventually develops yellowish to rusty brown discolorations. *Lactarius scrobiculatus* is common in our conifer forests. Other bearded species include *L. alnicola* with a pale yellow cap and white latex that slowly becomes yellow or stains white paper yellow; it occurs in mixed conifer-hardwood forests. *Lactarius repraesentaneus* has a rich yellow cap, white to pale yellow latex that becomes lilac after drying, and flesh that when broken stains lilac; it occurs with birch and conifers such as spruce. *Lactarius controversus* is a whitish to vinaceous species with pink gills and copious white unchanging latex; it grows with cottonwoods, aspen, and willows. *Lactarius torminosus* is a pinkish to light pinkish orange species with copious white latex that is unchanging or slowly changes to yellowish; it occurs with planted birches in urban settings. Many of these species have an acrid to bitter taste. *Lactarius plumbeus* is another member of this group.

Lactarius rufus SAT-03-308-04

Lactarius scrobiculatus var. *canadensis* SAT-97-263-11

Lactarius subflammeus Hesler and A. H. Smith

Orange to brownish orange to reddish brown lactariuses are common in our coastal conifer forests. Certain species such as *Lactarius rufus* are relatively easy to identify, but many others require careful observation of the latex, taste, and spore color, plus microscopic study of the cap structure and spore size and ornamentation. But, even after all that, sometimes the identity of your lactarius

Lactarius subflammeus SAT-00-313-04

still is uncertain. *Lactarius subflammeus* is a common, small to medium-sized species with orange to reddish brown caps that are moist to subviscid and short-striate on the margin. The gills are whitish to pale pinkish buff, sometimes tinted with the cap color, and the stipe is about the same color as the cap. The latex is milk-white and unchanging, and the taste is slightly acrid. Similar species with acrid taste are *L. substriatus* and *L. subviscidus*, both of which have white latex that changes to yellow on exposure. *Lactarius luculentus* var. *laetus* has white unchanging latex and apparently a mild taste.

WAX-CAPS

The wax-caps are fungi that, at one time, were together in the large genus *Hygrophorus*. The wax-caps can be difficult for beginners to recognize as they include a variety of different-looking fungi, in much the same way that the large brown-spored genus *Cortinarius* does. The difficulty arises from the fact that the most important character, the lustrous waxy look and feel of the gills, is not easy to recognize until one has gained some experience. As in *Cortinarius*, however, a little field experience enables one to recognize on sight most of the species as being wax-caps. In general, they have attractive, often colorful, small to medium fruitbodies, white spores, fleshy stipes, and waxy, usually wide-spaced, gills. The waxiness, which leads to a very clean look, comes from abundant, long, narrow basidia. To test for "waxiness," rub a piece of gill between your fingers. Aside from the waxy gills, there is little to separate many of them from genera such as *Clitocybe*, *Mycena*, *Omphalina*, and *Marasmius*. To further complicate matters, other gilled fungi possess waxy gills, and species of *Gomphidius* and *Laccaria* are especially likely to be misidentified as wax-caps at first glance.

Most wax-caps occur in the later part of the mushroom season after the onset of colder weather. Most seem to have broad dis-

Hygrocybe ceracea SAT-04-317-02

tributions, and many North American wax-caps fit European species concepts rather well. Nonetheless, much critical comparative study remains to be done to confirm these initial impressions.

Opinion among taxonomic mycologists is divided over whether the genus should be interpreted broadly, with all wax-caps placed in *Hygrophorus*, or in a narrower sense, with many species being shifted into a number of smaller genera. The commonest approach is a middle of the road one, with three genera being recognized. Each of them, in turn, is subdivided into groups that some mycologists would consider separate genera. Unfortunately, even this fairly conservative differentiation of genera is based mostly on microscopic characteristics, such as the arrangement of the gill trama, as seen in cross-section. Species of *Hygrophorus* in the narrow sense have hyphae that diverge downward and outward from a central strand, in *Hygrocybe* they are more or less parallel, and in *Camarophyllus* the hyphae are intricately interwoven. With practice, one can accurately assign most collections to one of these genera without microscopic examination based on the following suites of characters; however, even with a microscope it sometimes can be difficult.

- *Hygrophorus* (in the narrow sense): mostly medium to fairly large fruitbodies, white to dull tan or gray, or occasionally brightly colored, gills adnate to decurrent, veil lacking or present, sometimes viscid to gelatinous, causing the cap and/or stipe to be very slimy, other times leaving a fairly well formed ring. Ectomycorrhizal fungi, found predominantly in forests; uncommonly with urban trees.
- *Hygrocybe*: small to medium fruitbodies mostly with relatively slender stipes, colors typically very bright, cap dry to moist or viscid, gills adnexed to adnate to occasionally decurrent, veil lacking, some with very slimy or viscid stipes (but not caused by a veil, rather by gelatinous hyphae that project from the surface of the stipe). Saprotrophic fungi, found commonly in forests on leaf litter; several species also can be found in town, usually in mossy, unfertilized lawns.
- *Camarophyllus*: mostly small (to medium) dull-colored (white, tan, gray) fruitbodies, cap dry to viscid, stipe dry, veil lacking, gills usually decurrent. Often included in *Hygrocybe*. Mostly found in forests, sometimes in grass, occasionally as urban fungi. Probably saprotrophic, but not well characterized.

Neohygrophorus is a fourth genus erected for a single hygrophorus-like species described from Washington's Olympic Peninsula. We treat it with the clitocybe-like mushrooms based on its overall appearance. Recent molecular analyses suggest that some small club-fungi (*Typhula*) and several small, clitocybe-like species in *Chromosera*, *Chrysomphalina*, *Lichenomphalia*, and *Xeromphalina* are closely related to the wax caps.

It is probable that most wax-caps are edible; however, very few are sought-after by mycophagists. As David Arora wrote, "I have yet to find one to my liking. By and large they are too bland or too watery or too bland *and* too watery to be worth eating."

Hygrocybe ceracea (Fries: Fries)
P. Kummer

Hygrocybe ceracea is distinguished by the small, yellow to golden orange fruitbodies, caps that are viscid at first, gills that are adnate to slightly decurrent, and dry stipe colored like the cap or paler. Although not emphasized in most descriptions, our collections were markedly hygrophanous. We have collected this species repeatedly at one site in Seattle in a mossy lawn. It is widespread in Europe but not well known in North America.

Hygrocybe conica (Schaeffer: Fries) P. Kummer
WITCH'S HAT

Hygrocybe conica is one of the easier mushrooms to identify. Its fruitbodies are medium-sized with moist to viscid, yellow, orange, or red conical caps, and pale yellowish gills and stipe; all parts blacken in age or when handled. It is perhaps the most widely distributed species in the genus, and occurs in a wide range of habitats, including forests, woodlands, and unfertilized, often mossy, grasslands or lawns. As would be expected with a highly variable fungus, several varieties have been described, differing in details of stature and color. *Hygrocybe singeri* was described from collections with particularly viscid stipes, but otherwise it seems identical to *H. conica*. Although normally a fall fungus, *H. conica* occasionally is found in spring.

Hygrocybe conica SAT-05-306-02

Hygrocybe flavescens (Kauffman) Singer

Hygrocybe flavescens is a widespread species recognized by its medium size, bright yellow-orange colors, and viscid, convex to plane cap. The cap can be orange when young, but is usually bright lemon-yellow when expanded. The stipe is about the same color as the cap, and the gills are generally a paler shade of yellow. It occurs in a wide range of forest and woodland habitats. Many mycologists differentiate *H. flavescens* and *H. chlorophana* by the moistness of the stipe, with the latter being viscid and the former merely dry to moist. However, in Europe, *H. chlorophana* is widely accepted as having stipes dry to moist to viscid, so it is hard to know whether these are distinct species, especially in the absence of additional correlated characters. We have used the North American name here but, if only one species is involved, then *H. chlorophana* would have priority.

Hygrocybe flavescens

Hygrocybe laeta (Persoon: Fries)
P. Kummer

Hygrocybe laeta is a smallish, viscid, hygrophanous species that can be difficult to pick because of the heavy slime layer on the stipe. The translucent-striate cap varies greatly in color, from orange-brown to yellow-orange to pinkish red, the stipe is similar or a bit paler, and the decurrent gills are whitish to grayish to orange-pinkish, sometimes with a violet tinge. The odor, when present, is variously described as burnt rubber, fishy, skunk-like, or pleasantly herbaceous. The variation in color has led to description of a number of different varieties. *Hygrocybe laeta* is common in the redwood forests of north-coastal California, but less so throughout the PNW. It has been reported from many parts of the Northern Hemisphere.

Hygrocybe laeta

Hygrocybe miniata (Fries: Fries)
P. Kummer

Hygrocybe miniata is one of a large number of small red hygrocybes. It is distinguished from the others by having a dry, convex to plane, hygrophanous cap beset with small scales (check with a handlens), reddish to yellow, broadly attached to slightly decurrent gills, reddish stipe, and bean-, corn-, or pear-shaped spores. Even using these features, it can be difficult to sort the many similar species out, and many mycologists consider various of them (*H. mollis*, *H. moseri*, *H. strangulata*) to be synonyms. *Hygrocybe miniata* occurs in small groups in a wide variety of habitats, including forests, grasslands, and mossy lawns.

Hygrocybe miniata SAT-07-329-01

Hygrocybe virescens Hesler and
A. H. Smith

Hygrocybe virescens is a rarely collected, medium-sized, green to greenish yellow

Hygrocybe virescens SAT-07-328-05

species that is hard to confuse with any other. The cap and stipe may be moist, but are not viscid to glutinous, and the gills are whitish or tinged with lime green. *Hygrocybe virescens* was described from the redwood forests of northern California, and our one collection was made under redwood in a Seattle park. It is very similar to *H. citrinovirens* of Europe and might be synonymous with it.

Camarophyllus pratensis (Persoon: Fries) P. Kummer

As the abundance of names indicates, *Camarophyllus pratensis* (= *Hygrocybe pratensis*,

Camarophyllus pratensis

Camarophyllus virgineus SAT-98-332-15

Hygrophorus pratensis, Cuphophyllus pratensis) has been a very difficult fungus to classify. Fortunately, it is easier to identify. The fruitbodies typically are medium-sized and stocky, with a dry, dome-shaped, dull orangish cap, creamy decurrent gills, and orangish to whitish stipe. The stature and color vary somewhat, and so several varieties have been named. It occurs widely in the Northern Hemisphere in a variety of forest and non-forest habitats. *Camarophyllus pratensis* is edible, although we are not aware of it being popular.

Camarophyllus virgineus (Wulfen: Fries) P. Kummer

Camarophyllus virgineus (= *C. niveus, C. borealis*) is a small to medium-sized species, white or slightly yellowish overall, sometimes with pinkish tints on the stipe base, and with a viscid cap and dry stipe. The taste is often bitter to acrid. It is widespread and common in grass and bare soil around trees in urban areas, in open grassy areas, and in conifer and hardwood forests. Other PNW camarophylluses include *C. russocoriaceus*, an ivory to cream-colored species with the odor of cedar wood, and *C. lacmus* (= *C. subviolaceus*), with a gray, violet-gray or brownish violet, striate, viscid cap, smoky violaceous gills, and a dry stipe that is white or tinted with cap colors.

Hygrophorus agathosmus (Fries) Fries

Hygrophorus agathosmus fruitbodies exhibit grayish to gray-brownish viscid caps, white gills, white to pale gray dry stipes, and an odor of almond extract (or sometimes said to be of anise or celery). It grows in conifer forests, particularly with spruce, and is fairly common in the PNW, northern California, and the Rocky Mountains. It is less common elsewhere in North America and also occurs in Europe and Asia. *Hygrophorus odoratus* is a very similar species with the same odor; it differs by being smaller and more slender with larger spores (11–14 × 6.5–8 vs. 8–10.5 × 4.5–5.5 μm). *Hygrophorus agathosmus* is edible, but reported to be bland and unappealing.

Hygrophorus bakerensis A. H. Smith and Hesler

Hygrophorus bakerensis is characterized by its medium to large, relatively slender-statured fruitbodies with a pleasant almond odor, and growth often on or near rotting conifer wood. The viscid cap is brown in the center and cream to white near its incurved edge, the gills and stipe are white, and the latter often appears somewhat powdery or dandruffy in the upper portion. It is common throughout the PNW and extends into northern California but is not as common there. *Hygrophorus variicolor* differs only in having a stipe made slimy by a gelatinous veil. If the two taxa actually represent a single species, then *H. variicolor* would have priority. *Hygrophorus bakerensis* is another edible but low-quality fungus.

Hygrophorus chrysodon (Batsch: Fries) P. Kummer

The epithet (Greek for "golden tooth") refers to the most distinctive feature of this species, the golden yellow granules or minute hairs on the cap (especially the edge), stipe, and gills. Otherwise, the fruitbodies are white, or sometimes very pale yellow, small to medium-sized, and variable in stature from rather slender to fairly stocky. *Hygroph-*

Hygrophorus agathosmus SAT-04-018-01

Hygrophorus bakerensis SAT-00-285-28

Hygrophorus chrysodon SAT-00-298-19

orus chrysodon is widespread throughout much of the Northern Hemisphere.

Hygrophorus eburneus (Bulliard: Fries) Fries

Hygrophorus eburneus is a medium-sized, pure white, often remarkably slimy fungus that is common in a variety of forest types throughout the PNW and elsewhere in the Northern Hemisphere. The closest look-alike is *H. piceae*, which differs by having a less slimy cap, dry to slightly viscid stipe, and frequent association with spruce; it also

Hygrophorus eburneus SAT-00-296-70

Hygrophorus erubescens SAT-05-229-01

is widely distributed, but is less common than *H. eburneus* in many areas.

Hygrophorus erubescens (Fries: Fries) Fries

The fruitbodies of this pink-splashed forest fungus are medium-sized or slightly larger, whitish with various degrees of purplish pink streaks on the cap and stipe and similarly colored spots or splotches on the mature gills, and usually develop yellow stains in age. The cap edge usually is inrolled, the gills somewhat widely spaced and decurrent, and the odor is mild to somewhat pleasant. *Hygrophorus erubescens* is a late summer and fall-fruiting species that occurs widely in conifer forests of the Northern Hemisphere, especially with spruce and pine. In the PNW, it is neither rare nor particularly common. The very similar *H. purpurascens* (Albertini and Schweinitz: Fries) Fries usually is stockier, has an often faint ring and more closely spaced gills, does not develop yellow stains, and occurs in the spring and early summer. It also is widespread in montane conifer forests. *Hygrophorus capreolaris* is a more evenly colored species with an overall wine-red appearance without yellow stains. Another similar species, *H. amarus*, is distinguished by the bitter taste of its cap surface and slightly yellowish gills. Given the gradational nature of the distinguishing traits, it is not surprising that deciding which species one has found is often extremely difficult.

Hygrophorus goetzii Hesler and A. H. Smith

Hygrophorus goetzii is one of the species that make up the so-called snowbank fungi of our western mountains. These mushrooms appear near, or even in, snow as it melts in the late spring and early summer. *Hygrophorus goetzii* produces smallish, slender, pale pink fruitbodies with viscid cap and dry stipe. Although the habitat, color, and waxy gills make it hard to confuse with anything else, its large spores (10–15 × 7–10.5 µm) furnish an additional diagnostic character. It is not encountered very often. Two other snowbank hygrophoruses are the rare blue fungus, *H. caeruleus*, and *H. subalpinus*. *Hygrophorus goetzii* was named in honor of Donald and Christel Goetz, pioneering members of the Oregon Mycological Society and Pacific Northwest Key Council.

Hygrophorus purpurascens SAT-07-125-05

Hygrophorus hypothejus (Fries: Fries) Fries

Hygrophorus hypothejus is a pine forest fungus that generally does not appear until late fall. It is recognized by its yellowish or olivaceous brown (darkest in the center), highly viscid cap, whitish to yellowish decurrent gills, and whitish to yellow viscid stipe. The fruitbodies usually develop yellowish to golden orange stains in age, a feature that allows it to be distinguished readily from other viscid, brown-capped hygrophoruses. *Hygrophorus hypothejus* often fruits in large groups, both singly and in loose clusters. When old, water-soaked, and frostbitten, it can be a downright unattractive fungus.

Hygrophorus goetzii SAT-97-176-01

Hygrophorus olivaceoalbus (Fries: Fries) Fries

The name *Hygrophorus olivaceoalbus* has been applied differently by various mycologists both in Europe and North America. However, typically it is considered a fungus with a streaky, olivaceous brown or grayish brown, viscid cap (darkest in the center),

Hygrophorus hypothejus

Hygrophorus olivaceoalbus SAT-01-321-15

white clean-looking gills, long white stipe with bands of grayish brown fibrils overlaid by a slime layer below the ring-zone, large ellipsoid spores (10–15 × 6.5–9 µm), and association with spruce. When fresh, it is a most attractive fungus. *Hygrophorus persoonii* is a very similar species that associates with broadleaved trees in Europe; it has been reported from California, but under spruce. A smaller species with dry stipe, *H. inocybiformis*, is often reported from Idaho and the Rockies, and rarely from west of the Cascades.

Hygrophorus sordidus Peck

Hygrophorus sordidus is distinctive because of its large size and all-white coloration, but little else. Its caps are up to 20 cm (8 in.) in diameter and viscid, the gills attached to decurrent, and the stipe dry. The waxy gills set it apart from several clitocybes and leucopaxilluses which it otherwise resembles. *Hygrophorus sordidus* is fairly common under oaks in California, but much less common in the PNW. The collection in the photograph was found near the coast in Oregon's Tillamook County, with nary an

Hygrophorus cf. *sordidus* SAT-04-304-12

Hygrophorus speciosus

Hygrophorus subalpinus SAT-07-140-06

oak in sight and may represent a different species, although we were unable to find any likely candidates among those that have been described. In an amusing story, David Arora likens the *H. sordidus* he once used in a curry to overfed and undercooked banana slugs, hardly an image to whet one's appetite!

Hygrophorus speciosus Peck
LARCH WAX-CAP
Hygrophorus speciosus is perhaps the most picturesque species in the genus and, when found in its typical habitat, is easily identified. When fresh, it has a brilliant reddish orange cap and white to yellow stipe, both of which are slimy. As the fruitbodies age, they become less slimy, and the cap color usually fades to orange or yellow. The decurrent gills are whitish to pale yellow. *Hygrophorus speciosus* is found most commonly in the inland portion of the PNW, where larch is locally abundant. Other than the color scheme and tree preference, *H. speciosus* and *H. hypothejus* are quite similar.

Hygrophorus subalpinus A. H. Smith
Hygrophorus subalpinus is a very common member of the western montane spring snowbank fungi, although it usually does not appear until after the snow has receded from its fruiting sites, in contrast to species like *H. goetzii* and *Clitocybe glacialis*, which often can be found poking their caps right through the snow. It is a pure white, short, stocky fungus that can easily be mistaken for a small *Russula brevipes* at first glance. The waxy gills and fibrous not-so-brittle flesh distinguish it. Among the hygrophoruses, it is recognized by its fruiting season, habitat, tendency to remain partly bur-

ied, and presence of a veil that, at times, can form a slight ring low on the stipe. Opinions vary as to the desirability of its texture, but all are unanimous in declaring it tasteless at best. Nonetheless, we have seen it for sale at Seattle-area farmers' markets.

LEPIOTAS AND SIMILAR MUSHROOMS
Historically the genus *Lepiota* included a large number of species with considerable variation in size and appearance. Over time, many species have been transferred to genera such as *Chlorophyllum*, *Macrolepiota*, *Leucocoprinus*, *Leucoagaricus*, and *Cystolepiota*, and these have gradually gained acceptance. Recent work by Else Vellinga has shown that the lepiotas are closely related to a varied group of saprotrophic fungi, including *Agaricus*, *Coprinus comatus*, *Melanophyllum*, *Battarrea phalloides*, puffballs such as *Lycoperdon* and *Tulostoma*, and secotioid fungi such as *Podaxis* and *Endoptychum*.

The lepiotas range from small to large. The caps are mostly umbonate, campanulate to broadly convex or parasol-shaped when expanded. The cap surface often is broken into concentric patches or scales, but may also be smooth, granular, or powdery. The gills are free and usually whitish, but sometimes yellow, green, or pinkish. The stipes vary in shape, the interior is hollow, and the surface smooth, wooly, granular, or powdery. In some species, a ring is present. Microscopically, there is considerable variation in spore features and structure of the cap surface, and these are important characters in the identification of genera and species. *Lepiota*, *Leucocoprinus*, and

Chlorophyllum olivieri SAT-07-282-02

Leucoagaricus, however, overlap in many features so that identification of species and separation of genera can be difficult even with a microscope.

Lepiotas are decomposers, usually occurring on the ground in association with plant litter. A few species grow on woody material, sawdust, or manure; others such as *Leucoagaricus leucothites* grow in lawns and other grassy areas. In temperate areas, greenhouses and houseplants often harbor warmer-climate species such as the yellow *Leucocoprinus birnbaumii* and the compost-dwelling *L. cepistipes*. Because most lepiotas dislike cold weather, in the PNW, many species occur near the coast or inland at lower elevations.

Only a few lepiotas commonly make it onto the dinner table. Macrolepiotas, *Chlorophyllum rachodes, C. brunneum,* and *C. oli-*

vieri are the ones most frequently mentioned as edibles. However, caution is in order with chlorophyllums: several individuals have experienced severe gastrointestinal symptoms after eating them. The toxic *C. molybdites*, which has not been reported in the PNW, routinely causes such poisoning. Macrolepiotas are known to accumulate heavy metals, which emphasizes the importance of not eating mushrooms collected from roadsides, areas where pesticides and herbicides are used, or other possibly contaminated areas. The most dangerous lepiotas are in the section *Ovisporae* of the genus *Lepiota* (in the narrow sense), such as *L. subincarnata*. These mushrooms contain amatoxins and have caused a number of fatalities. Thus, it is wise to avoid eating all small lepiotas.

Chlorophyllum Massee

The once monotypic genus *Chlorophyllum* ("green leaves," from the color of the mature gills) has been redefined in recent years to include not just the green-spored *C. molybdites* but additional species including the secotioid *Endoptychum agaricoides*. Now typical chlorophyllums are large, the caps have large more or less flattened, pale brown or grayish to olivaceous scales, the smooth stipes have a distinct ring, the gills are free, and the spores are white or green. The species are often widespread and frequently found in areas such as parks, edges of woods, and compost heaps.

Chlorophyllum rachodes (Vittadini) Vellinga, *C. brunneum* (Farlow and Burt) Vellinga, and *C. olivieri* (Barla) Vellinga occur in our area, and all have been called "*Lepiota rachodes*" because of difficulty in distinguishing one from another. All have whitish spores, and the flesh of fresh specimens when bruised turns orange and then more brownish over time. *Chlorophyllum olivieri* can be distinguished from *C. brunneum* and *C. rachodes* by the nearly uniform color of the cap, as the color of both the scales and background is grayish brown to olivaceous brown. *Chlorophyllum olivieri* can be common in the fall in urban areas as well as at the edges of woods. *Chlorophyllum brunneum* and *C. rachodes* are very similar. Both have caps with brownish patches and scales over a whitish background except for the center, which usually is smooth and brownish; they frequently grow in clusters. *Chlorophyllum brunneum* has a distinct, often abrupt-rimmed bulbous stipe base and a single ring with a brownish underside. *Chlorophyllum rachodes* has a bulbous, but not rimmed, stipe base, and the ring

has two distinct layers. Both species occur on plant debris in gardens, compost piles, and other disturbed areas. All three species are commonly collected for the table, but be aware that some individuals are severely poisoned by them. The toxic *C. molybdites* has not been reported in the PNW, but it is common in central and southern California and other warm parts of the U.S. It has green spores and the gills are greenish when mature, but otherwise it is quite similar to the other chlorophyllums.

Chlorophyllum brunneum

Chlorophyllum rachodes

Lepiota felina (Persoon) P. Karsten

Lepiota felina is generally similar to several other small to medium-sized lepiotas for which microscopic examination of the spores and structure of the cap cuticle is important for determination of species. It has a broadly convex cream-white cap with a very dark brown center, concentric zones of small brown patches, and radially arranged matted squamules at the margin. The gills are white to faintly pinkish, the cap flesh is white and non-staining, and the odor is like cedar wood or somewhat unpleasant and

Lepiota felina SAT-05-303-02

Lepiota magnispora

rubbery. The stipe is whitish to pale brownish above the ring and pinkish brown to grayish brown with zones of brownish squamules below. The ring is cuff-like and typically is adorned with brownish squamulose patches. The spores are ellipsoid to oblong, and the cap cuticle is composed of tufts of long erect elements that arise from clavate cells. *Lepiota felina* is not common in the PNW.

Lepiota magnispora Murrill

Lepiota magnispora (= *L. ventriosospora*, *L. fusispora*) is one of several lepiotas collected near Seattle by W. A. Murrill in the early 1900s. However, this name was largely ignored for nearly a century, and our mushrooms all were called *L. clypeolaria*. While the latter species does occur in the PNW, it is much less common than *L. magnispora*. The two are very similar in size and overall shaggy appearance and both often have an unpleasant odor. *Lepiota magnispora* is the more variable—most often the center of the cap is distinctly brown, while the edge is whitish, but sometimes it is more uniformly brownish overall. The stipe usually is cloaked with ragged white to yellowish veil remnants. *Lepiota clypeolaria* has a less contrasty cap, with a pale brown center that gradually fades toward the edge, and the veil remnants on the stipe are white, never yellow. The surest way to separate the two is by spore shape—those of *L. magnispora* look a bit like penguins (Else Vellinga's apt term) in profile, or fat bellies (according to Kew mycologist Derek Reid). In contrast, those of *L. clypeolaria* are somewhat almond-shaped or like segments of an orange. The spores are large in both species, but more so in *L. magnispora* (15–21 vs. 11–18.5 µm in length). *Lepiota cortinarius* has somewhat the appearance of these two species but is pinkish brown to pinkish orange-brown and has short, narrow, cylindrical spores.

Lepiota subincarnata J. Lange

Lepiota subincarnata (= *L. helveola*, *L. josserandii*) is medium-sized and somewhat stocky, with caps that are pinkish red to reddish brown at the center and cream to pinkish cream toward the margin, which typically bears concentric rings of small pinkish red to reddish brown patches. The gills are whitish and the cap flesh is white to slightly pink under the cap surface. The stipes are cylindrical or slightly enlarged at the base, cream to pinkish in the upper part, and, below the ring-zone, cream with small zones or incomplete bands colored like the cap. The odor is slightly fruity and the taste is unpleasant. The spores are oblong and the cap surface is composed of long, vertical elements that do not have clavate cells at their base. *Lepiota subincarnata* and its close relatives contain amatoxins, the same deadly substances found in *Amanita phalloides* and the other destroying angels, so make a point of avoiding all small lepiotas when collecting for the table. *Lepiota subincarnata* is widespread in summer and fall in wooded areas, but also occurs frequently in rich soil in parks and gardens.

Leucoagaricus barssii (Zeller) Vellinga

Leucoagaricus translates to "white agaricus" and, accordingly, many species in this genus have the aspect of an agaricus, but with whitish rather than brown spores. One of the first mycologists to come to the PNW, plant pathologist S. M. Zeller did research

on mushrooms as well. He named *Leucoagaricus barssii* (as *Lepiota barssii*) from collections made on agricultural lands in Oregon. It is a medium to large mushroom characterized by a conspicuously hairy to fibrillose gray to gray-brown cap, with a whitish margin and fringe when young. The whitish gills are crowded, and the stipe is stout, tapered toward the base, whitish, and discolors brownish when handled. The veil is somewhat fragile and may leave a ring or remain attached to the edge of the cap. When formed, the ring is whitish above

Lepiota subincarnata SAT-95-283-02

Leucoagaricus barssii SAT-92-312-01

and brownish below. *Leucoagaricus barssii* is widespread but not particularly common, occurring in sandy or loamy soils.

Leucoagaricus leucothites (Vittadini) Wasser

Leucoagaricus leucothites (long called *Lepiota naucinus* in North America) is a widespread mushroom that occurs mostly in grassy areas, gardens, and other human-influenced habitats, but also occasionally in forests. It has the aspect of an agaricus, but its white to pale pink spores distinguish it. The cap often has a fine granular texture and in the typical form is white at first, then often develops grayish colors. The gills are crowded and white at first, then may become grayish or pinkish. The stipe is whitish to grayish brown and may discolor yellowish or pinkish. A distinct whitish to grayish ring is usually present. When bruised, the flesh may turn yellowish and the gills may redden. *Leucoagaricus leucothites* is eaten by many people but is not considered choice by most. Its similarity to the white destroying angels causes us to recommend avoiding it as an edible.

Leucoagaricus leucothites, white form

Leucoagaricus rubrotinctoides Murrill

Leucoagaricus rubrotinctoides is a very common and conspicuous species of our coastal and lower elevation forests. It is medium-sized and has a convex to more broadly expanded cap that is some shade of reddish

Leucoagaricus rubrotinctoides

Leucoagaricus leucothites, gray form

brown to pinkish brown; the margin soon splits and exposes the whitish flesh so that it has radiating lines of reddish to pinkish brown color. The gills are white and do not stain or discolor. The stipe is whitish, club-shaped or enlarged at the base, and typically has a thin, fragile, movable ring that is white with pinkish tints on the underside. *Leucoagaricus rubrotinctoides* generally has been called *L. rubrotinctus*, a species from eastern North America.

Leucocoprinus brebissonii (Godey)
Locquin

Leucocoprinuses typically are thin-fleshed with a radially pleated cap and tendency to look collapsed with age, as if partially deliquescent. The mushrooms are mostly small to medium-sized and, in cooler climates such as ours, mostly occur in greenhouses, compost piles, and indoor plants. *Leucocoprinus brebissonii*, however, is a woodland species. The center of its cap is very dark gray-brown to almost black and the margin is white but decorated with small gray-brown to blackish scales. The gills are crowded and white and the stipe is slender and clavate, white with pinkish brown in the lower part, and bearing a white somewhat fragile ring that often is lost with age. The spores are thick-walled with a distinct germ pore. *Leucocoprinus brebissonii* often appears in late spring but is most abundant in summer, often occurring in large groups on forest litter. It has been very common in recent years, seemingly appearing overnight, especially in second-growth forests in the Puget Sound lowlands, and it is hard to understand how such an abundant species could have been overlooked in the past. Perhaps its summer occurrence caused it to go unnoticed. Another possibility is that it has been misidentified as the somewhat similar *Lepiota atrodisca*, a species described from Oregon and also reported from California. Clearly more work is needed to solve this puzzle.

Leucocoprinus ianthinus (Cooke)
Locquin

In the PNW, we have at least four greenhouse or compost leucocoprinuses—one is a yellow species related to *Leucocoprinus birnbaumii*, the second is *L. cepistipes*, the third

Leucocoprinus brebissonii SAT-07-204-04

Leucocoprinus ianthinus occurs in potted plants

Leucocoprinus ianthinus SAT-99-198-01

is *L. heinemannii*, and the fourth is *L. ianthinus* (= *L. lilacinogranulosus*). The cap has a finely scaly, purplish to reddish brown center and white margin, often with small purplish fibrils. The gills are white with a slight lilac tint, and the stipe is club-shaped and white to yellowish with purplish fibrils on the lower portion. The ring is white with a purplish edge, and it may disappear in age.

Cystoderma Fayod

Historically, species in the small genus *Cystoderma* were considered closely related to lepiotas and, in fact, some cystodermas originally were placed in *Lepiota*. Cystodermas are small to medium-sized mushrooms characterized by dry, granular or powdery veil remnants covering the cap and lower portion of the stipe, and often leaving small tooth-like fragments on the edge of the cap. For such a small group of mushrooms there is a lot of variation in color, from whitish to pinkish or vinaceous brown to ocher-brown or orange-brown to brick-red. The gills are pale and only slightly attached to the stipe, often appearing almost free. A well-defined

ring or less distinct ring-zone is often present. The spores are white, those of some species are amyloid, and a few species produce crystal-covered, harpoon-shaped cheilocystidia. Cystodermas occur in forests, often among grasses and mosses, and can be very abundant in some seasons. The mushrooms often persist for a long time after they mature. It seems unlikely that the cystodermas form a natural evolutionary group, and their relationships to other mushrooms are not yet clear. *Phaeolepiota aurea* is larger and has a yellowish brown spore-print, but otherwise is very similar. The cystodermas with non-amyloid spores are placed in the genus *Cystodermella* by some mycologists.

Cystoderma amianthinum (Scopoli) Fayod

Cystoderma amianthinum is a widespread species found in moss along road edges and open grassy areas. The color of the finely granular cap and the covering below the poorly defined ring varies from yellow-ocher and yellow-orange to brownish yellow or more ochraceous to olivaceous. Some forms have a highly wrinkled cap surface; others have white to pale yellow coloration. The gills are white to pale yellowish, the odor is disagreeable or somewhat like freshly husked corn, and the spores are amyloid.

Cystoderma fallax A. H. Smith and Singer

Cystoderma fallax is distinctive because of its large, flaring, membranous ring. The color of the cap and lower stipe is cinnamon-brown or rusty orange-brown and the gills are white, often with a pinkish tint. It occurs in a variety of habitats, including

Cystoderma amianthinum

Cystoderma fallax

Cystoderma granulosum SAT-00-296-07

conifer, mixed, and hardwood forests on litter, humus, rotting wood, and in mosses. *Cystoderma fallax* apparently occurs only in western North America but is similar to *C. granosum* of eastern North America. Both species have amyloid spores.

Cystoderma granulosum (Batsch) Fayod

Cystoderma granulosum is common, widespread, and highly variable. The cap ranges from dark red-brown to orange-brown, sometimes with a paler margin, and the gills are white to pale yellowish. It is very similar to *C. amianthinum* and similar to *C. terreyi*; however, it lacks the harpoon-shaped cheilocystidia of *C. terreyi*. Both *C. granulosum* and *C. terreyi* can be distinguished from *C. amianthinum* by their non-amyloid spores.

Cystoderma terreyi (Berkeley and Broome) Harmaja

Cystoderma terreyi (= *C. cinnabarinum*) has an orange-red to bright brick-red cap that sometimes becomes darker red when handled. The gills are thin, white to creamy, and often crowded, and the ring-zone is faint. The flesh has a strong pungent or farinaceous odor. *Cystoderma terreyi* is fairly common, occurring on litter in conifer and hardwood forests, often in moss beds. With-

Cystoderma terreyi SAT-05-282-08

out a microscope to check for its harpoon-shaped cheilocystidia, it can be difficult to separate from *C. granulosum*.

GENUS *AMANITA*

Amanitas arguably are the best-known gilled mushrooms for a number of reasons. They are mostly large and conspicuous; many, such as *Amanita muscaria*, are brightly colored; some, such as *A. caesarea*, are good edibles; the destroying angels, such as *A. phalloides*, contain deadly poisons; and nearly all have a distinctive elegant look. *Amanita* is a widely distributed genus and occurs in a variety of forested and urban habitats, open areas with scattered trees and shrubs, and alpine and arctic habitats. Nearly all the PNW species appear to be ectomycorrhizal.

The genus is characterized by having white (usually) spores, free or nearly free gills, a universal veil that leaves remnants on the stipe base and often on the cap, and often a partial veil that often leaves a ring. The remnants of the universal veil, either those on the lower stipe (the volva) or those

on the cap (as warts or a patch), constitute one of the critical characters used for species identification. When membranous and fairly tough, the veil can leave large patches of tissue on the cap and a well-formed sac-like volva around the stipe base. However, the veil often is more fragile and almost powdery and, in this case, may leave behind only small bits of tissue or a powdery covering on the cap, and bands or patches of tissue or a powdery covering on the lower stipe, sometimes with a free rim or collar at the top of a bulbous stipe base. Because of the importance of the volva for identification of amanitas, the fact that the volva often is quite fragile and easily overlooked, and the possibility of a fatal mistake, it is vitally important to always excavate the entire mushroom when collecting and carefully inspect the residual soil for fragments of the stipe or volva. The spores are smooth, usually ellipsoid to nearly globose, and may be amyloid or non-amyloid. Cystidia typically are lacking or hard to distinguish.

Amanitas often are confused with a number of larger mushrooms—for instance *Amanita ocreata* or *A. bisporigera* (white destroying angels) with *Agaricus silvicola*, *Amanita phalloides* with *Tricholoma flavovirens*, and *A. smithiana* with *T. magnivelare*. However, carefully noting the (usually) white gills and spores, remnants of partial (usually) and universal veils, and, especially, the elegant amanita look, which is easily recognized with a modicum of experience, in most cases will avoid confusion. In addition, young unopened amanita buttons sometimes are confused with puffballs; however, cutting a "puffball" in half to look for the outline of a developing mushroom versus uniformly marshmallow-like tissue will allow them to be told apart easily. The

Amanita aprica SAT-07-161-02

PNW has far fewer amanitas than eastern North America; however, most of the subgroups within the genus are represented by at least one species here.

Amanita aprica Lindgren and Tulloss
JAN'S YELLOW FRIEND

In the PNW, we have several species in the *Amanita muscaria* group, and often they fruit in abundance. In early spring, two species in this group appear—*A. aprica* and *A. pantherina*. Later in spring and summer, *A. gemmata* joins them and often persists with *A. pantherina* until much later in the season, while *A. aprica* declines. *Amanita aprica* has a bright yellow to yellow-orange or orange cap decorated with remnants of the thin, frosty whitish universal veil, either as warts or larger patches. In dry weather, these patches present a sense of butter being spread too thinly over a slice of toast. The gills are whitish and the stipe is equal or somewhat enlarged at the base and colored like the gills. The volva is pressed tightly to the stipe base, usually forming zones, and sometimes has a free margin. The partial veil often leaves a whitish, fragile, skirt-like ring that may disappear with age. *Amanita aprica* can be locally abundant in mixed conifer forests, particularly with Douglas-fir, and occasionally occurs with conifers in urban areas.

Amanita constricta Thiers and Ammirati

Amanita constricta, described from California, is a member of the *A. vaginata* group. In the vaginatas, the cap varies from white to various shades of brown and gray to, occasionally, brighter colors such as salmon-orange. Usually the edge of the cap has long deep striations, and the center may bear a membranous patch. The universal veil also forms a slender sac-like, often reddish-stained, volva around the base of the stipe. The vaginatas lack a partial veil, so there is no ring, and usually have equal, rather than bulbous, stipes. The gills are white but may be grayish, or with edges that are grayish or more darkly colored. The spores are non-amyloid. The group contains a number of edible species but, given the difficulties in their identification, we do not recommend them for the table.

Identification of species in the vaginata group is challenging because there are few well-understood species concepts. All too often, European names have been applied to our fungi based on superficial comparisons, and no detailed study of the PNW vaginatas has been undertaken. Thus, we no doubt have several undescribed species here and, while one can assign collections to the vaginata group, getting to a species name is difficult or impossible, even with technical literature and access to a microscope.

Amanita constricta is characterized by a gray-brown to brown cap, white to grayish or gray-brown-tinged gills, small white to buff or grayish patches on the cap, and a delicate sac-like volva, the lower portion of which is attached to the stipe base and is constricted above before flaring outward at the upper edge. The volva may or may not develop reddish stains. *Amanita constricta* has been reported from both hardwood and conifer forests but, given the identification difficulties, its habitat preferences remain to be clarified.

Amanita constricta SAT-99-296-03

Amanita franchetii (Boudier) Fayod

Historically, the name *Amanita aspera* has been used for this species. More recently, it has been called *A. franchetii*, but that name too might be incorrect—we could have an undescribed species here in the PNW. Whatever its name, our mushroom is easily recognized. It first appears in early summer and fruits well into fall. It produces medium-sized to larger fruitbodies with a brown to gray-brown or yellowish brown cap with mealy warts that are yellow then grayish and flattened in age. The gills are white to yellowish and closely spaced. The stipe is relatively thick, enlarged at the base, and white to yellowish. The volva forms zones of loose bits of yellow veil on the stipe base, which often drop off into the surrounding soil. The partial veil leaves an ample ring that is white above and yellow below and on the edge. *Amanita franchetii* often occurs with *A. porphyria* and *A. gemmata* in mature forests. It has been reported as toxic when eaten raw or only partially cooked.

Amanita gemmata (Fries) Bertillon

The use of the name *Amanita gemmata* for our PNW representative(s) of this group has long been debated, and likely will continue to be. In this region, *A. gemmata* appears in late spring or early summer and continues into fall. In addition to occurring in forests, it can be found under trees in suburban and urban areas, similar to *A. aprica*, *A. pantherina*, and *A. muscaria*. *Amanita gemmata* is a medium-sized species with a creamy, pale yellow or darker yellow cap with striations at the edge. The outer veil leaves whitish patches or warts on the cap and a short, close-fitting volva with a collar or free rim, and sometimes loose patches around the basal bulb. The gills are closely spaced and white. The stipe is more or less fleshy, white to pale cream and usually floccose on the lower surface. The partial veil is white and leaves a somewhat fragile, white, skirt-like ring that may be lost by maturity. Some forms of this species are small and slender while others are large and robust.

Amanita lanei (Murrill) Saccardo and Trotter

COCCOLI

Amanita lanei (= *A. calyptrata*, *A. calyptroderma*) is most common in California but extends along the coast northward into the PNW. It occurs in mixed conifer-hardwood forest, often occurring with madrone and oak, and can be abundant in years with early fall rains. The fruitbodies typically are large with orange to brown and yellow caps with a large, thick, white cottony patch over the center, and striations along the margin. The

Amanita franchetii

Amanita gemmata

Amanita lanei

Amanita phalloides, on the left, is deadly poisonous, whereas A. lanei, on the right, is a good edible. Thus, being sure of your identifications is critical.

gills are white to creamy yellow and close. The stipe is similar in color to the gills, with a delicate, skirt-like ring, and a large, thick, cottony to felty (sometimes double) sac-like volva around the base. The buttons can be quite large and reminiscent of cottony eggs. The spores are non-amyloid. *Amanita lanei* is closely related to *A. caesarea* and, like it, is edible and quite good in the opinion of many mycophagists. But beware! The deadly *A. phalloides* produces fruitbodies that often are similar in size, stature, and color to *A. lanei*, and the two species can occur in the same forests at the same time, so be absolutely positive of your identification if you decide to gather *A. lanei* for the table. A mistake could be your last!

Amanita muscaria (Linnaeus: Fries) Lamarck
FLY AGARIC

With its bright red cap and white "polka dots," the typical *Amanita muscaria* no doubt is the most widely recognized mushroom in the world. However, it is highly variable and different forms have received names that have never quite caught on. These are based primarily on two variables—first, the color of the cap, which ranges from white to yellows and oranges, to deep red and even brown, and second, whether the universal veil is white or yellowish. Different combinations of these two features have produced a number of forms that usually are referred to as varieties. The names and distributions of these varieties, as well as other forms of *A. muscaria*, are currently being studied. We have illustrated three color forms that occur in the PNW—var. *flavivolvata*, the commonest one in natural habitats, with red cap and yellowish veil remnants; a paler form common with planted birches and under spruce and pine, with orange cap and white veil remnants; and a rather uncommon one, with white cap and veil remnants. Variety *muscaria*, with red cap and pure white veil remnants, has been reported from Alaska, but not from more southerly portions of the PNW.

All the forms have striate cap margins, rings that may or may not persist into maturity, and volvas in the form of rings of loose tissue that extend part way up the stipe from a bulbous base. Along with *Amanita gemmata*, *A. pantherina*, and *A. aprica*, all contain ibotenic acid. Thus, they cause accidental poisonings but also are sought-after by some who seek their psychoactive effects, and *A. muscaria* has been used ritualistically in areas such as Siberia. *Amanita regalis* is a related brownish to ocher species that has a boreal distribution, including Alaska.

Amanita pachycolea D. E. Stuntz in Thiers and Ammirati

Amanita pachycolea, a very large species in the vaginata group, can be one of the more spectacular amanitas in the PNW. Its cap is large, brown to very dark brown, sometimes paler near the margin, and always with long striations at the margin. The gills are white with distinct gray to brown edges, and develop orange-brown stains in age. The stipe is long and thick, with a white to brownish fibrillose-scaly surface. The base is surrounded by a large, thick, felty volva, that is white at first but soon develops rust to brown or yellow colors, and in age can be entirely rust-colored. There is no ring.

Amanita pantherina (Candolle: Fries) Krombholz

Like clockwork in late winter to early spring, an amanita in the *Amanita pantherina* complex appears, especially in urban areas. Other members of this group fruit

Amanita muscaria var. *flavivolvata*

Amanita muscaria, orange-capped form

Amanita pachycolea SAT-00-251-35

Amanita muscaria, white-capped form

Amanita pantherina, dark brown form
SAT-00-076-01

Amanita pantherina, medium brown form
SAT-99-139-02

Amanita phalloides SAT-99-276-01

through summer and fall in a variety of habitats. They come in a variety of color forms, from pale yellowish tan ones that are similar to *A. gemmata* to dark brown ones that are more like classical European *A. pantherina*. The mushrooms are medium-sized or larger, the cap has striations on the margin, and the universal veil leaves conspicuous whitish warts and patches on the cap and a close-fitting volva with a distinct free rim (like slightly rolling back the top of a sock) around the bulbous stipe base. The gills are white and closely spaced, and the partial veil is white and leaves a skirt-like ring on the stipe. *Amanita pantherina* causes a number of accidental human and dog poisonings, especially puppies, and also is consumed intentionally for its psychoactive effects. Typically the ibotenic acid concentrations are higher in this species than in *A. muscaria*, and are highest in the dark brown forms. Here, again, applying a European name to a western North American mushroom might be incorrect. Our mushrooms may well not be "real" *A. pantherina*.

Amanita phalloides (Fries: Fries) Link
DEATH CAP

Amanita phalloides and its relative *A. ocreata* Peck, both members of the destroying angel group, definitely occur in the PNW. A third relative, *A. verna*, has been reported twice from the PNW, but these collections may well have been *A. ocreata*, as there is a question over whether *A. verna* occurs anywhere in North America. All these species can cause deadly poisoning, and it is important to keep them in mind when collecting for the table. The destroying angels have the following features in common—fleshy medium-sized to large fruitbodies, non-striate cap margin, white gills that may be slightly attached or free, a membranous outer veil that leaves a sac-like volva on the enlarged stipe base and sometimes a patch on the cap, and a partial veil that typically forms a ring that often disappears in age. All have white amyloid spores.

Amanita phalloides usually has an olive to greenish yellow or yellowish brown to bronze cap, often with darker streaks, but not striations, on the margin; occasionally it occurs in a white form. It has been introduced into North America and has become naturalized in the forests of the San Francisco Bay region. It typically occurs in fall. In urban areas, A. phalloides occurs with a variety of trees including oak; it also is found in hazel (filbert) orchards and may well become established in natural forested areas of the PNW. Amanita ocreata is similar in size and stature to A. phalloides, but is an all-white species, sometimes with pinkish tan overtones. In the PNW, it is found in spring in mixed woods, especially with oak, hazel, and cottonwood. Before collecting mushrooms for the table learn the distinguishing features of these deadly amanitas, and remember to be particularly careful when collecting white mushrooms and those that have olive, greenish, or yellowish colors.

Amanita porphyria Albertini and
Schweinitz: Fries

Amanita porphyria can be found in our conifer forests during the latter part of summer and into fall. It is medium-sized with a gray to gray-brown cap with violet or reddish gray tones. Usually there are small, grayish warts or patches of veil tissue on the cap surface and around the margin of the distinctly bulbous stipe base. The gills are white to grayish and darken when bruised,

and the stipe is whitish above the ring and below it covered with grayish or grayish violet fibrils. The partial veil leaves a thin gray ring that may collapse onto the stipe. The odor is said to resemble that of raw potatoes or radish. Amanita porphyria often can be found in mid-August with A. gemmata and A. franchetii in established conifer forests.

Amanita ocreata SAT-98-046-02

Amanita porphyria SAT-97-263-12

Amanita silvicola Kauffman

Amanita silvicola, a small to medium-sized species with a short, stout stipe in relation to the cap diameter, is one of two chalk-white amanitas in our region that have a

Amanita silvicola

Amanita smithiana

soft, white, cottony outer veil. The other, *A. smithiana*, is a usually larger species with a long rooting stipe that tapers upward from a spindle-shaped base. *Amanita silvicola* usually pushes up the litter or soil from a deep-seated, club-shaped or rimmed stipe base. The outer veil covers the cap and leaves a slight rim of tissue around the stipe base. The partial veil also is soft and fragile and leaves a floccose zone on the upper stipe when the cap expands; typically the surface of the stipe has a soft powdery to cottony covering. The gills are white, close, and have floccose edges. The edibility of *A. silvicola* is uncertain, but its close relationship to *A. smithiana* should preclude anyone from eating it.

Amanita smithiana Bas (= *A. solitaria*) features a small to medium-sized cap and long rooting stipe that is enlarged at the point where it enters the substrate (either soil or well-rotted wood). The outer veil leaves a coating on the cap, sometimes on the cap edge, and around the enlarged portion of the stipe. The gills are close to crowded, whitish or slightly pinkish. As in *A. silvicola* the lower stipe is coated with a soft white covering that comes off if you touch it. The partial veil is fragile and leaves a ragged, floccose zone on the upper stipe. If you are a matsutake enthusiast, be sure to learn *A. smithiana* because it contains a toxin that damages the kidneys, and has been involved in several severe poisonings (see Appendix 1). It occurs in conifer and mixed woods and has been reported with a variety of tree hosts including alder. The species epithet honors Alexander Smith.

Clitocybe albirhiza SAT-98-172-01

GENUS *CLITOCYBE* AND SIMILAR MUSHROOMS

In its original sense, *Clitocybe* included a diverse group of white- to yellowish-spored mushrooms with adnate to decurrent gills and funnel-shaped fruitbodies. It included both small and large species, all typically with a central, slender to fleshy stipe, no veils, and saprotrophic on soil, litter, or sometimes decaying wood. Omphalinas—represented by small, thin-fleshed, rather brittle funnel-caps—often have been included in *Clitocybe*. For convenience, we treat them with the similarly small mycenas. Recent molecular data have shown that the typical clitocybe stature occurs in several evolutionary lines, and so several new genera have been created including *Clitocybula*, *Cleistocybe*, *Infundibulicybe*, and *Ampulloclitocybe*. Usually microscopic examination is required to distinguish these from one

Well-developed white rhizomorphs at the base of the stipe of *Clitocybe albirhiza*

another. Most mushroomers rightfully consider clitocybes to be a challenging group taxonomically. In addition, they include several toxic species and few with any culinary value, and so rarely receive much attention.

Clitocybe albirhiza H. E. Bigelow and A. H. Smith

Clitocybe albirhiza is one of the western snowbank mushrooms and typically occurs in the spring and early summer following snowmelt, often at the same time as *C. glacialis*. It occurs in clusters or is scattered in conifer litter in montane forests and at times is abundant. Its species epithet refers to the abundant white mycelial strands that extend from the stipe base. The mushrooms are generally small to medium-sized but can become robust. The caps often have a whitish bloom at first, and the underlying color varies from pale buff to pinkish buff, or more brownish; moist caps are typically darker-colored and often have concentric color-zones, while drier caps are usually paler and opaque. Mature caps are broadly depressed to funnel-shaped with an elevated margin. The gills are short decurrent to adnate, close, and pale buff to pinkish buff. The stipes are fibrous and tough, and colored like the cap surface. The taste is bitter. *Clitocybe ramigena* is a similar species that occurs in spring and summer on wood and debris. It is somewhat smaller and apparently does not have a bitter taste.

Clitocybe avellaneialba Murrill

Clitocybe avellaneialba (=*Ampulloclitocybe avellaneialba*) is a western species that occurs from northern California northward in the coastal forests and east to Idaho. It is associated with conifers, typically on very decayed logs or woody debris, usually appearing in fall and extending late into the season. *Clitocybe avellaneialba* is usually a medium-sized species but can be smaller or rather robust. It has a dark brown to olive-brown, funnel-shaped cap with inrolled edge and dark radial lines (not striations) on the margin which are distinctive in fresh specimens. In age, the cap often fades and the margin becomes paler and less noticeably lined. The stipe is relatively long and fleshy, typically the same color as the cap, usually with a pattern of longitudinal fibrils, and equal or somewhat enlarged below. The gills are whitish and long decurrent, close to subdistant. The spores are long, narrow, and fusoid.

Clitocybe avellaneialba SAT-05-274-02

Clitocybe clavipes (Persoon: Fries) P. Kummer

Clitocybe clavipes (= *Ampulloclitocybe clavipes*) is a common widespread species that occurs in conifer and mixed woods as well

Clitocybe clavipes SAT-98-311-02

as other habitats. It typically produces gray to gray-brown or slightly olive-tinted caps that are darker in the center, usually moist, and often coated with fine matted fibrils. The stipe is club-shaped (hence the epithet), whitish with a coating of fibrils colored like the cap, and covered at the base with tomentum. The gills are often forked, whitish to pale yellowish, and close to more widely spaced. When fresh the fruitbodies smell like grape bubble gum. *Clitocybe clavipes* zoomed into fame some years ago when it was reported that, similar to *Coprinopsis atramentaria* (see Appendix 1), it can be toxic when consumed with alcohol.

Clitocybe connata (Schumacher) Gillet

Large clusters of this conspicuous white mushroom are encountered commonly along roadsides, ski slopes, edges of woods, and similar areas in bare soil or low vegetation. Often gray when young, the caps of this medium-sized mushroom soon become whitish with watery buff areas in wet weather, and fade to chalky white when dry. The gills are whitish to yellowish or somewhat pinkish buff, close to crowded, and adnate to moderately decurrent. The stipes are whitish then discolored in age, fibrillose to minutely scaly below, and often fused into clusters at their bases. A drop of iron sulfate turns the cap and gills violet in one to two minutes. *Clitocybe connata* has been known by several names, the most common being *Lyophyllum connatum* in Europe and *C. dilatata* in the PNW; it has also been interpreted as *C. cerussata* var. *difformis*. *Clitocybe connata* has been thought to contain muscarine and other bioactive compounds, but also has been reported as a good edible in western Montana, with a flavor like aspar-

agus. Given this uncertainty, we do not recommend it for the table.

Clitocybe diatreta (Fries: Fries) P. Kummer

There are a number of smaller clitocybes that fruit in abundance on litter under trees. Their identification is challenging because they have few distinctive features to use in separating similar species. *Clitocybe diatreta* has shallowly depressed caps, with striate edge and a somewhat pruinose surface at first, pinkish to pinkish brown or vina-

Clitocybe connata

Clitocybe diatreta SAT-97-264-01

ceous buff and darkest in the center when moist, then fading to very pale colors on drying. The gills are white then pinkish or buff, close and usually short decurrent. The stipe is colored like the cap, equal or slightly enlarged downward, with tomentum on the base that often is entangled in needles. *Clitocybe diatreta* occurs from our area across northern North America and Europe in needle beds under various conifers.

Clitocybe epichysium (Persoon) H. E. Bigelow

This small, dark funnel-cap (recently transferred to the genus *Arrhenia*) is common on conifer and hardwood logs and stumps in North America and Europe. It has a small, watery dark brown to blackish cap that is finely translucent-striate when fresh, then fades to pale gray or gray-brown. The gills are narrow, gray to gray-brown, decurrent, and often end at a collar around the stipe apex. The stipe is usually equal, colored like the cap, and with white or pale tomentum where attached to the substrate. This mushroom has the appearance of an omphalina and has been placed in that genus by some mycologists. The similarly shaped *Lichenomphalia umbellifera* also frequents logs and stumps but is paler in color.

Clitocybe epichysium

Clitocybe glacialis Redhead, Ammirati, Norvell, and Seidl

When fresh, this common western snow-bank mushroom (until recently *Lyophyllum montanum*) has a pale gray to silvery gray cap, but older specimens develop gray-brown or yellow-brown colors, changing so much as to appear to be a different mushroom. The gills are close and grayish, and darken somewhat with age. The stipe is equal, colored like the cap, somewhat fibrillose below and with a dense covering of white strands at the base. *Clitocybe glacialis* often can be found with *C. albirhiza* and *Melanoleuca angelesiana* and is easily confused with the latter when mature. However, melanoleucas have spores with amyloid ornamentation while those of *C. glacialis* are smooth and non-amyloid.

Clitocybe glacialis SAT-03-153-06

Clitocybe nebularis (Fries) P. Kummer

Clitocybe nebularis occurs in a variety of forests, often appearing along woodland trails late in fall. The cap is broad with an incurved edge, and is grayish to brownish gray with radiating fibrils on the margin. The gills are whitish, adnate to short-decurrent, close, and often forked. The stipe is large, fleshy, and enlarged at the base, with a whitish surface that is coated with light gray-brown fibrils. *Clitocybe nebularis* usually has an unpleasant odor, described as like skunk cabbage or rodent cages, or just strongly farinaceous; however, sometimes an odor is lacking. It is among the largest of clitocybe-like mushrooms, another being *Leucopaxillus giganteus*, which differs primarily by its whiter color and amyloid spores, and *C. geotropa*, which has a buff to pale pinkish brown cap.

Clitocybe nuda (Bulliard: Fries) H. E. Bigelow and A. H. Smith
BLEWIT

Because of its tricholoma-like stature and pale pinkish roughened spores, the blewit (from "blue hat") has been classified both as a tricholoma and a lepista; however, recent studies suggest it is most closely related to species of *Clitocybe*. Whatever its scientific name, the blewit is well known to mushroomers because of its widespread occurrence, abundance, and edibility. It is typically medium-sized or larger with a convex, smooth, almost waxy-appearing cap, adnate to slightly decurrent, close gills, and stout, fleshy stipe that often is enlarged at the base. The color typically includes violet, purple, lavender, or bluish colors, although the caps and stipes can develop gray to tan or brownish tones at times and often are watery tan in age. The odor is pleasant. Blewits can

occur in forests but more often are found in lawns, gardens, and parks, sometimes in compost heaps or other yard waste. The name *C. glaucocana* is used for a form that occurs in the mountains. *Clitocybe tarda* is similar in color, but smaller and more slender and usually grows in grass.

Clitocybe sinopica (Fries) P. Kummer

This small mushroom can be found at almost any time of year, often on bare soil. It has a shallow depressed orange-brown to brown cap that becomes finely scaly with

Clitocybe nebularis

Clitocybe nuda SAT-04-324-01

Clitocybe sinopica

Clitocybe squamulosa

Clitocybe subditopoda SAT-00-313-49

age, close whitish, short-decurrent gills that are somewhat fragile, and an equal to tapered stipe that is colored like the cap and has white tomentum and mycelial strands at the base. The odor is farinaceous. *Clitocybe sinopica* is similar to *C. squamulosa* and *C. mitis*; however, the latter has a mild odor.

Clitocybe squamulosa (Persoon: Fries) P. Kummer

Clitocybe squamulosa (= *Infundibulicybe sinopicoides*) is a widespread, often common, and variable species. The mushrooms are small to somewhat larger, broadly funnel-shaped, and usually watery brown to tan usually with some cinnamon or pink mixed in, and paler pinkish buff in age. The specific epithet refers to the small, often obscure scales that occur in the center of the cap, sometimes extending to the margin. The stipe is colored like the cap, with tomentum at the base and a few white strands. The gills are decurrent, often forked, and whitish to pinkish buff in contrast to the darker cap and stipe. The odor is fungoid to farinaceous. In western North America vars. *montana* and *sicca* have been described, but these are difficult to separate from one another and from var. *squamulosa*. *Clitocybe squamulosa* occurs on needles under conifers and in mixed woods with alder, but can be found along roads in open areas as well.

Clitocybe subditopoda Peck

Clitocybe subditopoda is a small to medium-sized species that is relatively widespread in North America and most common in Pacific Coast conifer forests. It can be abundant locally and can occur late into the fall. The extremely hygrophanous caps are rich watery gray-brown with a vinaceous tint when fresh, but fade to pale gray as they dry. Fresh caps are finely striate on the margin, but this feature also is lost in age. The gills are grayish to slightly vinaceous buff, adnate to moderately decurrent, close, and may form a slight collar at the stipe apex. The stipe typically is equal or somewhat enlarged below, colored like the cap, often thinly coated with silvery fibrils, and the base has a watery gray tomentum. The odor is persistently farinaceous.

Clitocybe tarda Peck

Clitocybe tarda (= *Lepista tarda*), a slender relative of *C. nuda*, typically occurs in groups or clusters in cultivated or grassy areas but occasionally can be found in wooded places. The fruitbodies range from small to medium-sized with expanded caps that are somewhat raised in the center and often have an incurved edge. The flesh is thin and brittle. The cap is watery and shiny when fresh, often faintly striate at the edge, and usually a shade of violaceous or vinaceous brown, fading to paler shades especially on the margin. The gills tend to become somewhat decurrent as the caps expand and usually are violaceous to pinkish or paler, sometimes fading to dull buff in age. The stipes are colored like the cap, often coated with thin whitish fibrils, and commonly the base has tufts of whitish to lilac tomentum. The pinkish buff spores are smooth to ornamented.

Cleistocybe vernalis Ammirati, Parker, and Matheny

In the mid-1900s *Clitocybe subvelosa* and *C. gomphidioides* were described from western North America. They differed from other clitocybes by having a partial veil. Species of this sort were not recorded again until Drew Parker found another veiled clitocybe fruit-

ing in spring near Metaline Falls, Washington. New analyses, including DNA data, led to a new genus, *Cleistocybe*, being created for this mushroom, and it was given the epithet *vernalis* to reflect its spring occurrence. The cap has a covering of vinaceous brown fibrils, like kidskin, over a pale pinkish gray background when fresh, and becomes more ochraceous brown in age. The surface turns greenish when a drop of 3% potassium hydroxide is applied. The gills are pale pinkish gray, close, and decurrent. The stipe is enlarged below and colored like the cap. The

Clitocybe tarda

Cleistocybe vernalis Photograph by Andrew D. Parker

veil leaves a thin, pale, pinkish gray ring on the upper stipe and coarse patches of veil tissue on the lower stipe and margin of the cap. In some instances, the ring is quite faint, so careful observation of a range of specimens is required. As far as is known it occurs only in spring following snowmelt. Discovery of *C. vernalis* also led to renewed study of *Clitocybe gomphidioides* and *C. subvelosa*, and they were determined to represent only one species, with the earlier name *C. gomphidioides* having priority. This species has been found occasionally in conifer forests of Washington, Idaho, and Colorado, and fruits in September and October. Both *Cleistocybe vernalis* and *Clitocybe gomphidioides* are related to *Catathelasma*, but they are much smaller and do not have amyloid spores.

Cantharellula umbonata (Gmelin: Fries) Singer

Cantharellula umbonata has the aspect of a slender clitocybe. The cap is grayish, minutely tomentose, and radially wrinkled with a small central papilla. The stipe is minutely tomentose, and similar in color to the cap. The gills are decurrent, forked, and whitish. The gills and flesh turn reddish to reddish brown when bruised or in age. The spores are white and amyloid. *Cantharellula umbonata* is primarily a northern species and is not common in our area, compared to the Great Lakes region and elsewhere. It occurs in conifer forests on acidic soils and grows in association with *Dicranum*, *Polytrichum*, and other mosses.

Cantharellula umbonata

Catathelasma ventricosum SAT-99-296-14

Catathelasma ventricosum (Peck) Singer

Catathelasma is an easy genus to recognize because of its large size, strongly inrolled cap margin, tough texture, long decurrent, crowded, narrow gills, and especially the presence of two veils, an inner one that leaves a conspicuous ring on the upper stipe, and an outer one that leaves an additional narrow ring or ring-zone and patches of tissue below the upper ring. In addition, the flesh has a strong farinaceous odor and taste and the spores are white and amyloid. Catathelasmas usually occur on calcareous soils in conifer forests, often in large local populations, forming arcs or rings of fruitbodies. There are two species, and both occur in our region. *Catathelasma ventrico-*

sum has a pale to grayish cap, and *C. imperiale* has a brownish cap and is somewhat larger; however, intermediate-sized mushrooms with grayish brown caps are not uncommon.

Clitocybula atrialba (Murrill) Singer

Clitocybula is a genus of small to larger clitocybe- or collybia-like mushrooms that occur on wood or woody debris and have whitish amyloid spores. Some of the species, such as *C. abundans*, grow in clusters and have adnate to slightly decurrent gills. *Clitocybula atrialba* is a western species that occurs singly on the (sometimes buried) wood of alder and perhaps other hardwoods. It can be very common in some years, but virtually absent in others. It is an elegant slender-stiped mushroom with a funnel-shaped, dark smoky to blackish brown, matted fibrillose to furfuraceous cap, distant, decurrent, pale grayish gills that end at a collar-like line on the stipe apex, and a scaly to furfuraceous stipe that is colored like the cap, enlarged below, and often bears white strands at its base.

Hygrophoropsis aurantiaca (Wulfen: Fries) J. Schröter
FALSE CHANTERELLE

Hygrophoropsis aurantiaca is a characteristic fall species of our western conifer forests. It comes in several color forms and sizes, occurs in soils rich in decayed wood and woody litter, and can be relatively common in drier years when many other mushrooms cannot be found. It is typically medium-sized, and has a dry, somewhat velvety, irregular, funnel-shaped cap, thin, narrow, forked, decurrent gills that are rather soft, and central or off-center stipe. The cap, gills, and stipe are often some shade of orange, but the colors vary from yellow-orange to

orange to brownish orange or almost blackish orange; the colors fade in age, occasionally to pale yellowish or even whitish. Although *H. aurantiaca* has the general form of a clitocybe and often is confused with chanterelles, it is more closely related to the genus *Paxillus* and many boletes.

Hygrophoropsis morganii (Peck) H. E. Bigelow

This small fungus is easy to identify but only occasionally encountered. All parts typically are rose to pinkish, but fade in

Clitocybula atrialba SAT-04-316-02

Hygrophoropsis aurantiaca SAT-05-301-01

Hygrophoropsis morganii SAT-00-298-11

age, the stipe is centrally attached or some-what off-center and has pink tomentum at its base. The gills are decurrent on a more or less funnel-shaped cap with an arched, often lobed, narrowly inrolled margin. The fragrant, fruity odor of cinnamon candy or grape soda is distinctive. It occurs in coni-fer forests on needles and litter from June to October. *Hygrophoropsis olida* appears to be the same species.

Myxomphalia maura (Fries) Hora

Myxomphalia maura (= *Fayodia maura*) has the aspect of an omphalina because of its small size, decurrent gills, and dark color-ation. The caps have a shallowly to deeply depressed center, feel gelatinous, have dis-tinct fine, long striations and typically are blackish brown to dark gray-brown and hygrophanous. The fruitbodies are thin-fleshed, with adnate to short decurrent, whit-ish to faintly grayish gills. The stipes are thin and brittle, have a viscid surface, and are col-ored like the caps. The spores are white, smooth to roughened, and amyloid. *Myxom-phalia maura* occurs on charred earth or burned wood under conifers or in fire pits,

Myxomphalia maura SAT-06-237-16

Neohygrophorus angelesianus SAT-07-147-09

Neolentinus lepideus

appearing from early summer late into fall. It often is found with *Lyophyllum atratum*, a small blackish brown collybia-like species.

Neohygrophorus angelesianus
(A. H. Smith and Hesler) Singer

Neohygrophorus angelesianus is most commonly found in the mountains near melting snow but also can appear on bare soil, in meadows, or even at lower elevations under conifers, far from any snow. The entire mushroom is about the same color, purple, violet, or vinaceous when fresh, usually with a mix of brown; the cap fades greatly in age. The gills are fairly distant and waxy, giving it the appearance of a wax-cap. It has two distinctive microscopic features—amyloid spores and gill tissue which is vinaceous to brownish pink when mounted in 3% potassium hydroxide. It occurs primarily in spring, but sometimes can be found in summer and fall as well. It is most peculiar that such a distinctive fungus traveled for a long time under two names, *N. angelesianus* (or *Hygrophorus angelesianus*, its original name) and *Clitocybe mutabilis*.

Neolentinus lepideus (Fries: Fries)
Redhead and Ginns

Neolentinus lepideus (= *Lentinus lepideus*) is a tough-fleshed mushroom that probably is more closely related to polypores than to most gilled mushrooms. It has a whitish to pale yellowish depressed cap with large brown, often flattened, scales. The gills are whitish and have saw-toothed edges. The white stipes are tough and thick, often with a ring, and the lower portions bear small brownish scales. Both gills and stipe may become rusty to reddish brown in age. The odor of fresh specimens is fragrant, sometimes anise-like. *Neolentinus lepideus* is

not common in natural habitats but can be found on conifer logs and stumps in some areas. It is a brown-rot fungus and is more commonly encountered on construction timbers, railroad ties, and, in the past, on automobile frames when they were made of wood. It can occur almost any time but is most common in summer and fall. *Neolentinus ponderosus* is a similar tan to yellowish brown species commonly found on conifer wood such as pine stumps during late spring and summer at higher elevations. It lacks a partial veil and therefore has no ring.

GENUS *TRICHOLOMA* AND SIMILAR MUSHROOMS

In its original sense, *Tricholoma* included all mushrooms with white spores, central fleshy stipes, adnexed to sinuate gills, and no ring or volva. Although the universe of tricholomas has shrunk over time with the transfer of many species to other genera, the remaining species are true to the original description (except for the "no ring" part, as a few species with faint rings are included). The fruitbodies are mostly medium to large and fibrous-fleshy, the cap surface varies— viscid or dry, smooth, fibrillose, or scaly— the gills are narrowly attached, the stipe fleshy, central, and usually whitish, the veil, when present, is usually fibrillose and disappears, but occasionally a small ring lingers. The spores are smooth and ellipsoid to subglobose, and cystidia are usually lacking; thus, there are very few distinctive microscopic characters, and species concepts are based mainly on the macrocharacters. However, most of these are gradational, making differentiation among species difficult in many of the subgroups.

Tricholoma atroviolaceum SAT-00-284-49

Many of the fleshy entolomas and hebelomas share the same stature as tricholomas, but are easily distinguished by their pink and dull brown spores, respectively. Armillarias and tricholomopsises also are very similar but occur on wood; leucopaxilluses, lyophyllums, and melanoleucas differ microscopically. Representatives of these five genera are treated here, after the tricholomas. Collybias have cartilaginous stipes, hygrophoruses waxy gills, and clitocybes and catathelasmas decurrent (or at least adnate) gills. Floccularias are very similar but have rings and usually abundant veil remnants as wooly scales on the cap and stipe; none are included here.

In *Mushrooms in Their Natural Habitats* (1949), Alexander Smith called *Tricholoma* species "difficult to recognize" and wrote that particularly those that occurred in North America were "badly in need of a critical study based on fresh material." More than half a century later, Alex's assessment remains true. Until such studies have been published, we will not know whether the practice of applying European names to many North American tricholomas is justified or not. Tricholomas are terrestrial woodland fungi, ectomycorrhizal with both conifer and broadleaved trees. Some, such as the matsutake, are good edibles and are highly sought-after, many are of unknown edibility and quality, and still others present a significant hazard, even death, so accurate identification is essential if one wants to partake of them.

Tricholoma atroviolaceum A. H. Smith

Tricholoma atroviolaceum is characterized by medium-sized to large hard-textured fruitbodies with a broadly convex to plane cap, densely covered with small blackish violet to violaceous gray-brown fibrillose scales, and often with the edge split radially in age. The flesh of the cap often stains reddish gray when cut, the gills are cinnamon- or pinkish gray-tinged, and the stipe is thick, brownish in age, and sometimes has an enlarged base. The flesh has a mildly to strongly farinaceous odor and somewhat bitter taste. *Tricholoma atroviolaceum* occurs in northern California and the PNW under conifers, but usually not in large numbers. Apparently it is restricted to the Pacific Coast.

Tricholoma caligatum (Viviani) Ricken

Tricholoma caligatum is a medium-sized, slender fungus with an attractive mix of light and dark coloration. Typical forms are white, with a dense covering of dark brown fibrils that become increasingly isolated as scales or patches as the cap expands. The cap edge is inrolled and often bears slight cottony remnants of the partial veil, most of which remains as a ring. The gills and upper stipe are white (the gills often become reddish brown-spotted in age), and the stipe below the ring often bears brown fibrils like those of the cap, giving the mushroom the appearance of wearing a boot (*caligatum* is Latin for "boot"). *Tricholoma caligatum* formerly was classified in the genus *Armillaria* (as *A. caligata*), along with *T. focale*, *T. magnivelare*, and other tricholomas that differ from the rest of the genus by having a ring, albeit one that is not always well developed. *Tricholoma caligatum* is encountered in the PNW less frequently than its nearest look-alike, *T. magnivelare* (which is stockier, with fewer and paler fibrils, and nearly always with a pleasant cinnamon-spicy odor), but is widepread and sometimes abundant in other parts of North America, Europe, and Asia. There are conflicting reports about its edibility—PNW collections often have an unpleasant odor and taste, yet in the Rockies and northeastern U.S., it is reported as good. Perhaps the odor and taste of populations vary (it often is reported as being pleasantly spicy), collections of *T. magnivelare* are being misidentified, or more than one species is involved.

Tricholoma flavovirens (Persoon: Fries) S. Lundell

Tricholoma flavovirens is a distinctly colored fungus and one of the easier tricholomas

Tricholoma caligatum

Tricholoma flavovirens SAT-00-308-05

to identify. Its stipe and gills are bright yellow; the cap also is yellow, at least near the edge, and usually grades to orange-brownish in the center. The cap may be viscid at first but, if so, soon becomes dry, so a quick touch with the tip of your tongue may be necessary to detect the stickiness. *Tricholoma flavovirens* occurs scattered to gregarious, most often under pine but with other conifers, cottonwood, and aspen as well. It is one of the commonest species in

Tricholoma focale, a form with strong orange coloration

Tricholoma focale, a form with little orange color
SAT-01-278-08

the shore pine stands on old sand dunes along the Oregon coast. Molecular data suggest to some mycologists that we have more than one species going by the name *T. flavovirens* along the West Coast, but no directed studies have been conducted to follow up that notion. *Tricholoma sejunctum* and *T. sulphureum* are other yellow tricholomas that could be confused with *T. flavovirens*—the former has black or dark brown radiating fibrils on its cap, and the latter has an unpleasant coal gas or heavy floral odor. *Tricholoma flavovirens* generally is considered a good edible species in North America, but reports of fatal poisonings by *T. equestre*, a very similar (or possibly the same) species in France, suggest caution is in order.

Tricholoma focale (Fries) Ricken
Tricholoma focale, more often known in the PNW as *Armillaria zelleri* or *T. zelleri*, is a common fungus that varies widely in its size and coloration. Typical forms are stout, with a rounded cap, downward tapering stipe, very firm flesh, cottony ring, strong farinaceous odor, and very bitter taste. The odor is even present in the soil from which the fruitbodies arise, due to large amounts of mat-forming mycelium. The color varies from a mix of orange and olivaceous green to tans and browns with merely a hint of orange. The gills are whitish at first, but develop rusty orange stains fairly quickly. The stipe usually is scaly below the ring and colored somewhat like the cap. Dull-colored fruitbodies could be mistaken for *T. magnivelare*, although the strong farinaceous odor of *T. focale* quickly separates the two. Brighter orange fruitbodies are distinguished from *T. aurantium* by the presence of the veil; in the latter species, there usually is a sharp contrast in color of the

stipe where a ring would otherwise occur, but no actual remnants of a veil. *Tricholoma focale* is very common in the PNW, occurring under conifers in low-nutrient soils. The strong unpleasant odor and taste make it inedible.

Tricholoma imbricatum (Fries: Fries)
P. Kummer

Tricholoma imbricatum is one of a large number of reddish brown tricholomas that are notoriously difficult to identify. It usually can be separated from the others by its dull brown, dry cap, which often is broken up into small scales, especially in the center, and often has short grooves along its edge, medium to large firm fruitbodies, lack of a veil, and growth under pines. Most of the similar species, such as *T. muricatum*, *T. ustale*, and *T. populinum*, have viscid caps and grow in different habitats. Probably the species with which *T. imbricatum* is most easily confused is *T. vaccinum*, which also is dry-capped. In comparison, the latter is usually smaller, softer with an often hollow stipe, scalier, a bit more brightly colored, and is more common, most often under spruce rather than pine. *Tricholoma imbricatum* may be edible, but its tough texture argues against it being very desirable.

Tricholoma inamoenum (Fries: Fries)
Gillet

Tricholoma inamoenum and *T. sulphureum* (Bulliard: Fries) P. Kummer are two small to medium-sized fungi with wide-spaced, broad gills and a coal gas odor. Other than the sulfur-yellow color of the latter (often with brownish colors in the cap), there is little to separate them and, occasionally, pale yellow fruitbodies are found that are difficult to place in one or the other species.

Tricholoma imbricatum

Tricholoma inamoenum SAT-00-285-01

Tricholoma sulphureum SAT-00-324-03

Tricholoma platyphyllum, described from near Seattle, seems to be the same as *T. inamoenum*. Coal gas is not something many people get an opportunity to smell nowadays but the odor of these mushrooms is strong and unpleasant for most people; some liken it to a heavy floral odor, such as that of *Narcissus*. Both species are widely distributed in the Northern Hemisphere, *T. inamoenum* under conifers and *T. sulphureum* under both hardwoods and conifers. Neither is edible.

Tricholoma magnivelare SAT-00-283-55

Tricholoma muricatum SAT-04-304-11

Tricholoma magnivelare (Peck)
Redhead
PINE MUSHROOM, AMERICAN MATSUTAKE

Tricholoma magnivelare (= *Armillaria ponderosa*) is one of the more widely sought-after fungi in the PNW, including as a commercial commodity. It is recognized by the stocky stature, overall white color, often with brown fibrils or scales on cap and lower stipe, thick stipe that usually tapers to a pointed base and bears a large cottony ring, and firm flesh with a characteristic spicy odor. It occurs throughout much of North America, but is most abundant on the West Coast, usually appearing scattered to gregarious under conifers on nutrient-poor soils such as dune sands. It is edible and choice according to many, but considered mediocre by others. The very similar *T. matsutake* is enormously popular in Japan, and large quantities of American matsutake collected in the PNW are imported to satisfy the demand, creating an important conservation and sociological issue. The volatile spicy odor (famously described by David Arora as a cross between cinnamon candy and dirty socks) demands that the mushroom be used in simple dishes and not overcooked. Matsutake is most likely to be confused with *T. caligatum*, or *Catathelasma imperiale* and *C. ventricosum*, all three of which are pale-colored, and have white spores, prominent rings, and pointed stipe bases. However, both of the latter species lack the matsutake's spicy odor and have an overall coloration with more gray than brown tones. *Amanita smithiana* is a dangerously poisonous species that also is white with an often slender rooting stipe base. It too lacks the spicy odor, usually is more slender in stature, and has softer flesh than matsutake. Many other large whitish mushrooms have been mistaken for matsutake, including *Russula brevipes* and *Tricholoma apium*. The mycelium of *T. magnivelare* apparently is parasitized by *Allotropa virgata* (candystick), a red and white plant that lacks chlorophyll and cannot make its own food as most plants do.

Tricholoma muricatum Shanks

Tricholoma muricatum is one of a confusing bunch of reddish brown-capped, viscid tricholomas, distinguished from the others by its radially fibrillose cap with short grooves at the edge, orange-white gills, brownish orange stipe, and growth with pine. It is very similar to the European *T. pessundatum*, differing only in minor microscopic details, and is one of the characteristic fungi of the coastal Oregon shore pine woodlands. When found in this habitat, it is fairly easy to identify, but away from coastal pines, identifications in this group become extremely difficult. Other look-alike species include *T. fracticum* (= *T. batschii*) with conifers and a sharp color change in the ringzone like that in *T. aurantium*, *T. manzanitae* with manzanita, *T. nictitans* (= *T. flavobrunneum*) and possibly *T. fulvum* with conifers or in mixed woods and with some yellow tones in the stipe and gills, *T. populinum* with cottonwoods and aspen, *T. ustale* with oaks, and *T. stans* with pines. This whole group is sorely in need of critical study worldwide, as it seems there must be more names than there are taxa! Until that happens it will be difficult to assess the presence of the different species in the PNW. None of these species is edible, and some or all are probably somewhat toxic.

Tricholoma nigrum Shanks and Ovrebo

Tricholoma nigrum is a little-known species, described in 1996 from a single collection made along the Oregon coast. Its fruitbodies are medium-sized or larger, and reminiscent of those of *T. atroviolaceum*, *T. atrosquamosum*, and *T. luteomaculosum*. The cap is moist to somewhat sticky and densely covered with dark gray fibrils and small scales in the center, less so near the edge, the gills whitish to grayish, the stipe whitish, coated with silky fibrils, and sometimes with scattered blackish scales in its upper portion. Microscopically, the key characters are the layer of inflated cells that underlies the cap cuticle and presence of (often inconspicuous) cheilocystidia. The odor and taste are strongly farinaceous. The type collection was made in a shore pine woodland, whereas our collections came from an old-growth, mixed conifer forest dominated by Douglas-fir and western hemlock, with occasional western white pines on nutrient-poor soil. The edibility of *T. nigrum* is unknown, but the odor and taste and reputation of similar species suggest it isn't.

Tricholoma nigrum SAT-00-314-38

Tricholoma pardinum (Persoon) Quélet

One of the larger species in the genus, *Tricholoma pardinum* is also notable for causing severe gastrointestinal problems when eaten. The fruitbodies are whitish overall, and the dry caps are covered with small brownish gray to blackish fibrillose scales, giving it a spotted appearance (*pard* is Greek for "leopard"). The odor is farinaceous. Microscopically, the abundant clamp connections set it apart from most tricholomas. Other medium-sized, grayish, farinaceous tricholomas, such as *T. nigrum* and *T. virgatum*, can be distinguished by their caps appearing streaky rather than spotted with scales. The little-known *T. venenatum* is similar in size and general appearance, but the cap scales are pale tan. *Tricholoma pardinum* occurs throughout the cooler parts of the Northern Hemisphere, but usually is not abundant.

Tricholoma pardinum SAT-01-292-12+13

Tricholoma saponaceum (Fries: Fries) P. Kummer

Tricholoma saponaceum is a common and confusingly variable fungus. The principal characters used to distinguish it are the somewhat greasy look of the cap, the often faint or lacking soapy odor (from which the species got its name), and the pinkish orange color of the flesh in the base of the stipe, another character that unfortunately is not always well developed. The cap ranges in color from greenish yellow to olivaceous to grayish brown to pale brown or whitish, and often develops cracks in dry weather. The gills are broad and thick, giving somewhat the appearance of a wax-cap; they and the stipe are whitish, but often show flushes of color similar to that of the cap. The flesh sometimes stains pinkish orange, but often does not. Microscopically, similar to *T. pardinum*, it has abundant clamp connections. *Tricholoma saponaceum* is widespread in the Northern Hemisphere in a variety of forest types, often occurring in large numbers.

Tricholoma saponaceum

Tricholoma sejunctum (Sowerby: Fries) Quélet

Tricholoma sejunctum is a medium-sized fungus with a greenish brownish yellow, slightly viscid cap adorned with abundant, well-defined, blackish fibrils that radiate from the dark center, and whitish to pale yellow gills and stipe. The odor is mild to far-inaceous and the taste mild to unpleasant. Because of its yellowish colors, *T. sejunctum* often is mistaken for *T. flavovirens*; however, the latter usually is larger and fleshier, has a yellow to brownish cap with only a faintly fibrillose appearance, and the even yellow color of the gills and stipe is deeper than the often splotchy yellow of *T. sejunctum*. What constitutes the "real" *T. sejunctum* has been subject to differences of opinion and consensus has not yet been reached. Many illustrations and descriptions of European material suggest a fungus with white (but often yellow-tinged) gills and stipe; some suggest growth with oaks and beech, others with conifers, and a variety of forms, and even new names such as *T. arvernense* and *T. viridilutescens*, have been erected for different variants. Although clearly similar to the European species (whether singular or plural), our fungus could be a distinct entity. Until the necessary critical studies have been done, however, we will use the name *T. sejunctum* for it. It should not be eaten.

Tricholoma vaccinum (Schaeffer: Fries) P. Kummer

Tricholoma vaccinum is perhaps the most distinctive of the brown tricholomas by virtue of its medium size, warm brown colors, dry wooly-scaly cap and fibrillose-scaly stipe that often is spindle-shaped and hollow, and growth with conifers, especially spruce. The cap edge usually is inrolled with a thin weakly developed veil, the center retains an umbo, and the gills are white to cream, but may spot reddish or turn orangish red entirely in age. The odor is mild to farinaceous and the taste mild to bitter. *Tricholoma vaccinum* is widely distributed in the northern portion of the Northern Hemi-sphere and is especially common in the Rockies and PNW. It is said to be edible but of low quality; in light of this, and given the toxic nature of most brown tricholomas, we recommend avoidance. The epithet means "pertaining to cows," presumably in reference to the color rather than to its occurrence in large herds.

Tricholoma virgatum (Fries: Fries) P. Kummer

Tricholoma virgatum is characterized by its small-medium size, dry, silvery gray, some-

Tricholoma sejunctum

Tricholoma vaccinum SAT-97-278-07

Tricholoma virgatum SAT-00-263-26

what shiny, streaky-fibrillose, pointed conical cap, very peppery or bitter taste, and growth with conifers. The radially streaky (virgate) nature of the cap surface sets it apart from most of the small to medium gray tricholomas, as they tend to have scaly caps. The closest look-alike probably is *T. sciodes*, described as having pinkish to violaceous tones, less pointed cap, bitter but not peppery taste, and growth with beech and perhaps other broad-leaved trees. It has been collected in California by Orson and Hope Miller, but we are unaware of reports from the PNW. *Tricholoma virgatum* is another species that should be avoided by mycophagists.

Armillaria nabsnona T. J. Volk and Burdsall

HONEY MUSHROOM

Once upon a time, there was a single honey mushroom, *Armillaria mellea* (= *Armillariella mellea*) that was considered a good edible species in some places and a poisonous one in others. Although it was acknowledged as highly variable, and several mycologists suggested that it actually encompassed multiple species, proposals for recognizing more than one species did not gain widespread acceptance. Because of its importance as a forest pathogen, *A. mellea* was one of the few fungi for which research funding was relatively abundant, and a series of studies in the 1970s and 1980s provided convincing evidence that more than one honey mushroom exists. The key studies were tests of the ability of mycelia derived from spores of different honey mushrooms to fuse in a manner that would allow mating to occur (a prerequisite for formation of mushrooms). In North America, 11 so-called biological species were identified in these studies and the possibility for more to exist was noted. Subsequent work has focused on confirming the biological species and linking them to species concepts based on the characteristics of the mushrooms, so-called morphological species. Currently, it is generally accepted that we have 10 biological species of honey mushroom in North America, and 8 of them have been given names linked to morphological characteristics.

At least 4 of the 8 named North American honey mushrooms occur in the PNW—*Armillaria nabsnona*, *A. ostoyae*, *A. gallica*, and *A. sinapina*—plus the still unnamed North American biological species X and XI. The true *A. mellea* has not been reported from our region, although it does occur in California.

Armillaria nabsnona was named only in 1996, and so is not widely recognized by mushroom-hunters; thus, it is probably more common than we think. It has a reddish brown smooth cap, stipe that is pale in the upper portion and gradually darkens downward, and grows singly or in groups, but not clusters, in fall or spring on the wood of broadleaved trees, especially alder. It is thought to be restricted to the Pacific Coast and little is known about its edibility.

Armillaria ostoyae (Romagnesi) Herink probably is our most common honey mushroom. It usually grows in clusters, mostly on conifers, but also on broadleaved trees and shrubs such as willow and salmonberry; both the clusters and the individual mushrooms can be quite large. The caps are brown and usually covered with dark scales, a fairly well defined brownish ring is present on most fuitbodies, and the stipes often taper to pointed bases where they fuse in clusters. At other times, the bases may be somewhat enlarged. *Armillaria sinapina* differs only slightly in appearance, with a cobwebby veil and slightly smaller cap scales, grows singly or in clusters of only a few individuals, and in the PNW appears to also grow primarily on conifers. Its most distinctive feature in eastern North Amer-

ica, the bright yellow color of its veil, is lacking, or at least inconsistent, in PNW specimens. Thus, this species often cannot be distinguished from *A. ostoyae*. *Armillaria ostoyae* is a virulent pathogen of conifers, and, although edible when young, is considered worth collecting by relatively few mycophagists.

Armillaria gallica, probably the most common honey mushroom east of the Rockies, appears to occur only rarely in the PNW. It has a white cobwebby veil, pinkish brown coloration, and bulbous-based stipe, and

Armillaria nabsnona SAT-00-313-84

Armillaria ostoyae often fruits in large numbers on logs and snags

Armillaria ostoyae, fruiting from a buried root

occurs singly or in groups, not clusters, on or near logs, stumps, or bases of broad-leaved trees such as willow.

Calocybe onychina (Fries) Donk

Calocybes are small to medium fungi that look very much like tricholomas. The cap is white or brightly colored, the odor often far-inaceous, and the basidia contain small sid-erophilous granules (they turn blackish vio-let when heated with iron in the chemical reagent acetocarmine). *Calocybe onychina* is a not commonly collected, high-moun-tain species that occurs with conifers such as Engelmann spruce, subalpine fir, and Douglas-fir. When fresh, it has a beautiful, velvety, burgundy-colored cap that contrasts with the creamy yellow gills and the purple-flushed white stipe. The texture of the cap and unusual color combination separate it from the tricholomas which it otherwise resembles closely. We have found it in the spring in the Cascades and summer in the southern Rockies. In Europe, it is said to be edible; but the odor suggests it would not be particularly tasty, and a conservation ethic would argue against collecting it unless found in abundance.

Calocybe onychina

Laccaria amethysteo-occidentalis
G. M. Mueller

Laccarias range from quite small to medium-large, and have fairly thick, waxy-looking gills that may be whitish to sordid pinkish to strikingly purple in color, an often long, slender, shaggy-fibrillose stipe, and spores that are globose to ellipsoid, bear more or less conspicuous spines, and are non-amyloid. The overall color of many of the species is a distinctive orange-brown that one learns to recognize with experi-ence. The laccarias are ectomycorrhizal and are a common element of our forests; sev-eral species also occur abundantly in parks or yards where appropriate trees have been planted. Some species, such as *Laccaria lac-cata*, are considered edible.

Laccaria amethysteo-occidentalis is one of the more stunning members of our PNW mushroom community. When fresh, the whole mushroom is rich purple, but the color fades to a purplish tan as the mush-room ages. It is large for a laccaria and could be confused with *Cortinarius viola-ceus*; however, the latter usually is a darker blackish purple and has brown spores and a much less fibrillose hairy stipe. While *L. amethysteo-occidentalis* is restricted to, or at least is most common along, the Pacific Coast, neither of the other two North Amer-ican purple laccarias is known to occur in the PNW; *L. amethystina* is an eastern and European species that occurs with oak and beech, and *L. vinaceobrunnea* is a Gulf Coast species found under oak.

Laccaria bicolor (Maire) P. D. Orton is smaller and more slender than *L. amethys-teo-occidentalis*, and much less purple. The cap and stipe are orange-brown, and the gills are purplish when fresh, but then fade. The mycelium that cloaks the base of the stipes is purplish, in contrast to similar-looking species, such as *L. laccata*, in which it is whitish. *Laccaria bicolor* is common and abundant in the PNW, occurs throughout most of the north temperate and boreal conifer forests, and has been used extensively in mycorrhiza research. It probably is edible, but we have little information on how widely it is collected for the table.

Leucopaxillus albissimus (Peck) Singer

Leucopaxillus is a fairly small genus of medium to large dry mushrooms with dense firm flesh that decomposes very slowly, overall chalky white or dull brownish coloration, inrolled cap edge, adnate to decurrent gills, no veils, masses of cottony white mycelium which cloak the base of the stipe and extend into and bind the surrounding leaf litter, and spores with strongly amyloid warts. They typically occur in fall in forested areas and can be locally common in parks and other urban settings.

Leucopaxillus albissimus is a large, all-white (*albissimus* means "whitest" in Latin), widespread though not especially common fungus that grows with conifers. Several varieties have been described based on spore characteristics, cap color, and taste, but the concepts are not always easy to apply to collected specimens. The refusal to rot is probably the most distinctive characteristic of *L. albissimus*; however, the biological basis for this trait is not yet understood. The tough texture, combined with the unpleasant odor and taste, make it inedible.

More common in the PNW is *Leucopaxillus gentianeus* (Quélet) Kotlaba (= *L. amarus*), with a dull brownish cap, white gills and stipe, and intensely bitter taste. The mycelial mat formed by the vegetative body

Laccaria amethysteo-occidentalis SAT-97-289-01

Laccaria bicolor SAT-97-278-19

Leucopaxillus albissimus

Leucopaxillus gentianeus SAT-99-232-01

Lyophyllum decastes, young moist specimens

Lyophyllum decastes, drier, more typical specimens SAT-05-266-10

of the fungus is well developed and easy to observe when the mushrooms are collected. This characteristic, along with the dry cap, white gills that do not develop red spots in age, and very bitter taste distinguish *L. gentianeus* from the brown-capped tricholomas. It is too tough and bitter to be edible.

Lyophyllum decastes (Fries: Fries) Singer

Most lyophyllums are small mushrooms, but the better known species are the larger ones, particularly those that occur in large clusters. Regardless of size, all share a dull gray and brown overall coloration, whitish to grayish, attached to decurrent gills, an often greasy lustrous cap surface, lack of veils, and basidia with siderophilous granules. Many stain black, but spore shape and ornamentation vary, and lyophyllums occur in many types of habitats.

Lyophyllum decastes occurs in large dense clusters and is rather common, occurring primarily in disturbed areas such as campgrounds and along roadsides and trailsides in conifer forests. The cap is smooth and has a consistently slippery feel, but is highly variable in color, ranging from whitish to pale watery tan to grayish brown or almost black. These different color forms are considered separate species (e.g., *L. fumosum* and *L. loricatum*) by some mycologists, but the lack of distinct breakpoints in the color range and consistent correlated features make this view difficult to apply. The stipe is fairly thick and whitish or flushed brownish gray. The spores are broadly ellipsoid to nearly globose, $5–7 \times 5–6.5$ μm. *Lyophyllum decastes* is edible and considered quite good by some mycophagists, but only mediocre by others. Because many possibly poisonous entolomas can be quite similar in stature and coloration, be sure to collect only specimens growing in large clusters and having white spores (entolomas have sordid-pink spores and do not grow in large clusters).

Lyophyllum semitale (Fries) Kühner is similar in color to the common brown forms of *L. decastes*, but is somewhat smaller, grows singly, in groups, or small clusters, and turns black in age or when bruised, although often the change is slow. It also has larger, narrowly ellipsoid spores, 6.5–9 × 3–4.5 μm. *Lyophyllum infumatum* is very similar with larger spores (9–11 × 5–6 μm) and white, instead of cream to grayish, gills. *Lyophyllum semitale* is widely distributed in conifer forests and generally considered inedible.

Lyophyllum semitale SAT-07-278-03

Marasmius oreades (Bolton: Fries) Fries
FAIRY-RING MUSHROOM

Marasmiuses are generally small, tough mushrooms, with mostly convex caps, narrowly attached gills, thin rigid stipes, no veils, and the characteristic of reviving from the dry state when moistened. They are much more common and diverse in eastern North America than they are in the West. Mushrooms with which they can be confused include species of *Collybia*, *Micromphale*, *Strobilurus*, and *Marasmiellus*; usually microscopic examination is necessary for confident identification.

Marasmius oreades

The most common species in the PNW, *Marasmius oreades*, occurs in many parts of the world in lawns, parks, pastures, and other grassy areas, where it often grows in arcs or circles known as fairy rings. Although a small mushroom, it nonetheless is large, stocky, and fleshy for a marasmius. The cap is light to medium reddish brown, bright tan, or warm buff, with a central umbo. The gills are similar in color,

A fairy ring of *Marasmius oreades*

though paler, and are thick and widely spaced, looking a bit like wax-cap gills; they have a faint but recognizable odor of cyanide. The stipe is similar in color to the cap and rather tough. *Marasmius oreades* can be found almost any time of year, but is most abundant in warmer weather after rains or where lawns are watered regularly. A somewhat similar poisonous species that occurs in the same habitats and can also form rings is *Clitocybe dealbata*. It is about the same size, but is duller and whiter, has close, narrow decurrent gills, and lacks the pleasant odor. Fairy rings and arcs form as the mycelium of a fungus grows outward from its point of origin, exhausting its food supply as it spreads, forming a ring if soil conditions are relatively uniform and arcs if they are not or if obstructions are present. The growth of the fungus temporarily disrupts the growth of the grass so the rings can be seen as brown areas when the fruitbodies are not present. *Marasmius oreades* is an excellent edible mushroom, but be sure of your identification and take care not to collect it from places where lawn chemicals have been applied. Most people use only the caps as the stipes are rather tough.

Melanoleuca cognata (Fries) Konrad and Maublanc

Melanoleucas are medium-sized fleshy mushrooms with a distinctive stature— usually the cap is broad in relation to the length of the stipe and usually it retains at least a small umbo well into maturity. The cap usually is some shade of grayish brown and hygrophanous, the gills whitish to cream, the stipe longitudinally striate and slender, and veils are lacking. Microscopically, the spores are roughened with amyloid warts, and large, encrusted, pointy cystidia are present in many species. As far as is known, melanoleucas are saprotrophic; they occur in a wide variety of forest and non-forest habitats.

Melanoleuca cognata is characterized by its medium to large fruitbodies, smooth, orange to red-brown, somewhat viscid cap that fades to pale tan or pale golden brown, deep ocher gills, and large spores (7.5–10 × 4.5–6.5 µm). It often is tall for the genus. The odor is mild or sometimes sweetish with unpleasant undertones. *Melanoleuca cognata* is widely distributed, but not common, in forested areas, meadows, parks, and gardens, fruiting from spring into fall. Its often tall stature and golden tones distinguish it from other species in the genus, most of which are poorly known, as no comprehensive study of melanoleucas has been carried out for North America. *Melanoleuca cognata* is probably edible, but is not highly regarded, is not common, and without a microscope can be hard to identify with certainty, so we do not recommend it.

Melanoleuca cognata

Tricholomopsis rutilans (Schaeffer: Fries) Singer
PLUMS AND CUSTARD

The species in *Tricholomopsis* closely resemble tricholomas in stature, but differ by their saprotrophic growth on wood, abundant large cheilocystidia, and overall bright yellow coloration, often with dark contrasting fibrils and/or scales on the cap. Veils are lacking.

Tricholomopsis rutilans is the most distinctive species of the genus in the PNW and is readily recognized by its relatively large size and stocky stature, bright yellow fruitbodies that are overlaid with reddish purple fibrils and small scales, and its growth at the base of trees, especially pines. It is widespread in the Northern Hemisphere. Although edible, an informant of David Arora claims it tastes like rotting wood. The somewhat smaller *T. decora* (Fries: Fries) Singer tends to grow on conifer logs rather than at the base of trees; it too is bright yellow, but the fibrillose scales are olivaceous to dark brownish or almost black, rather than bright reddish purple. It is likewise widespread but inedible.

Tricholomopsis rutilans SAT-04-304-09

Tricholomopsis decora SAT-06-301-17

GENUS *COLLYBIA* AND SIMILAR MUSHROOMS

Originally the genus *Collybia* contained species of minute to medium-sized woodland mushrooms with convex caps with incurved margin, attached but not decurrent gills, cartilaginous to fleshy stipe, usually relatively slender in comparison to the diameter of the cap, no veils, and whitish, smooth, non-amyloid spores. The large species are similar to tricholomas or melanoleucas as well as several pink-, brown-, and dark-spored mushrooms of similar stature.

Over time, these fungi have been divided into a number of smaller genera, and this has reduced the genus *Collybia* to a few very small mushrooms with thin stipes that grow from a sclerotium (small hard structure composed of close-packed hyphae) or blackened mushroom remains. The genus *Dendrocollybia* consists of a single species that differs in having branches on the stipe. Many of the original *Collybia* species have been transferred to *Gymnopus*, for thinner

Collybia cirrhata SAT-02-285-06

fleshed, white- to yellowish- or buff-spored species, and *Rhodocollybia*, for pinkish-spored species that tend to be fleshier and somewhat larger than gymnopuses.

Collybia cirrhata (Persoon) P. Kummer

The residual *Collybia* is made up of three very small (caps up to about 2 cm, 0.8 in.) species: *C. cirrhata* without sclerotia, usually associated with decaying mushrooms; *C. cookei*, arising from yellow, irregularly shaped sclerotia, sometimes with decaying mushrooms but also in soil and litter; and *C. tuberosa*, with reddish brown, apple-seed-like sclerotia, usually associated with decaying mushrooms. All have minute to small, whitish, convex to flattened caps, narrow white gills, and thin whitish stipes that are often hairy below or have white strands

associated with the sclerotia or substrate. The spores are white, small, smooth, and non-amyloid. These fungi are common, often in large troops, throughout western forests. Species of *Strobilurus* and *Baeospora myosura* are similar in appearance to these small collybias.

Gymnopus acervatus (Fries) Murrill

A number of *Gymnopus* species form clusters with stipes fused together at their bases, making it possible to excavate the entire unit from the substrate. *Gymnopus acervatus* has caps that are reddish brown with paler edges, narrow, pale pinkish gills, and red to red-brown, hollow, shiny stipes with whitish hairs and narrow strands at the base. Young, unexpanded clusters often are a characteristic reddish purple color. It is a common inhabitant of conifer forests, occurring on rotting logs and stumps, and other woody debris.

Gymnopus confluens (Persoon: Fries)
Antonín, Halling, and Noordeloos

Gymnopus confluens is among our more common species in mixed woods with heavy litter accumulations. It most often is in clusters or occurs as a few to many closely associated fruitbodies. The mushrooms are thin-fleshed and marcescent, so that the clusters can remain in the forest for a long time. Usually they begin to appear in late spring or early summer and continue through fall. The gills are crowded, very narrow and pale to whitish. The caps are reddish brown when fresh but soon fade to pinkish buff or whitish, and the stipes are long, narrow, enlarged at the base, tough, similar in color to the cap, but becoming darker in age, and often covered with fine small hairs. The taste and odor are usually mild, but occasionally reported as onion-like.

Gymnopus dryophilus (Bulliard: Fries) Murrill

Gymnopus dryophilus is a well-known and widely distributed species in all sorts of forests. In the PNW it occurs from spring into fall during moist periods, but its abundance varies considerably from year to year. It is a medium-sized or sometimes smaller species that occurs scattered or in crowded groups or clusters. The caps, when fresh and moist, have a buttery appearance, and are reddish brown; however, they fade readily on drying and become tan to yellow-brown, pinkish buff, or paler. The fruit-bodies are long-lived, and with age the caps

Gymnopus acervatus SAT-00-285-35

Gymnopus confluens

Gymnopus dryophilus

may become irregular and lobed. The gills are close and white to buff, usually attached but can pull free in age, and the edges are even at first but eroded with age. The stipes are slender, often enlarged below, hollow, rather tough, colored like the cap or paler, sometimes with longitudinal striations, and the base often with white strands extending into the substrate. The whitish to pale yellow spores are smooth and do not react in Melzer's reagent. The taste is pleasant. In some areas this species carries a fungus parasite, *Syzygospora mycetophila*, which produces small, pale irregular growths on the surface of the mushrooms. *Gymnopus dryophilus* sometimes is confused with *Rhodocollybia butyracea*, but the latter fungus has a pinkish spore deposit and at least some of the spores turn reddish brown (dextrinoid reaction) in Melzer's reagent.

Gymnopus erythropus (Persoon: Fries) Antonín, Halling, and Noordeloos

Gymnopus erythropus is a small to medium-sized mushroom usually found in tight clusters. The caps are rounded, brown to reddish brown and striate when fresh, then become flattened and fade to lighter brown, brownish orange, or buff. The gills are attached, sometimes forked, rather broad, close, and whitish. The stipes are fibrous and somewhat elastic, hollow, equal, pallid to pale orangish above and dark reddish to orange-brown or brown below, and usually with reddish to orange-brown hairs at the base. The mushrooms are long-lived; the caps fade to whitish with age, but the red color of the stipes persists. *Gymnopus erythropus* is often abundant in gardens and landscaped areas on soil, wood chips, or woody litter. Whether it has become naturalized in our forests is unclear, but we have collected it in one of Seattle's forested parks. It has been reported from both eastern and western North America and is known from Europe and other parts of the world, sometimes under the name *Collybia marasmioides*. *Gymnopus erythropus* was not included in Joanne Williams-Lennox's 1975 PhD dissertation on collybioid fungi, which could indicate it has been introduced here since then. It could be confused with *G. acervatus*, but the latter is found in forested areas, its caps and stipes both are purplish when young, the caps are much narrower in relation to the stipe length, and it occurs in larger, tighter clusters.

Gymnopus luxurians (Peck) Murrill

Gymnopus luxurians is an attractive mushroom with reddish brown caps that fade to pale brownish with age, cream-colored, close to crowded gills, and fleshy-fibrous, whitish to pale brownish stipes that have a twisted striate appearance, split lengthwise in age, and have cottony material over the lower surface and white strands attached to the base. Although solitary fruitbodies or small groups can occur, it usually forms

Gymnopus erythropus SAT-07-285-04

large conspicuous clusters. *Gymnopus luxurians* is large and fleshy for a gymnopus and may reach 10 cm (4 in.) in diameter, the expanded caps becoming irregularly shaped and splitting from mutual pressure. It occurs in a variety of urban and suburban habitats including flower beds with wood chips and in lawns around the roots of trees. It can appear in summer, when few other species are fruiting, if sufficient moisture is available, such as from yard-watering. Like *G. erythropus* and *G. peronatus*, it seemingly has become common in recent years.

Gymnopus peronatus (Bolton: Fries) Antonín, Halling, and Noordeloos

Gymnopus peronatus is a medium-sized collybia with a brownish to ochraceous rounded cap with a small central umbo, radiating streaks, and a usually paler margin. The free gills are yellowish to light brownish, the stipe is tough, slender, yellowish to yellowish brown and darker in age, longitudinally fibrillose, and its base is enlarged, and covered with hairs and strands connected to an abundant whitish to yellowish mycelium that permeates the leaf litter. The taste is mild for a short time then peppery hot, and the odor is often pleasant and spicy. The spores are long and narrow, and the edges of the gills have long, slender cheilocystidia. *Gymnopus peronatus* is a widespread and often extremely abundant species at lower elevations in the PNW, occurring in mixed woods on leaf litter and woody debris. It usually appears first in early summer and then is present well into fall. The mushrooms are tough and persistent, rehydrate when moistened, and hang around a long time, often looking discolored and tattered in old age. The mycelium at times so impregnates the litter that one can lift up

an entire section of the forest floor when attempting to pick some of the mushrooms. For the past several years this species has been widespread and extremely common in the Puget Sound area. However, despite its current abundance, there are no earlier records of it occurring here. The reasons for this phenomenon remain a mystery.

Rhodocollybia butyracea (Bulliard: Fries) Lennox

In the PNW, we have several species in the *Rhodocollybia butyracea* complex, named

Gymnopus luxurians SAT-07-204-06

Gymnopus peronatus SAT-05-199-01

for their buttery-looking caps—*R. unakensis* (= *Collybia extuberans*), *R. badiialba*, and *R. butyracea* f. *butyracea* primarily in conifer forests, plus *R. b.* f. *asema* in hardwood forests. The various taxa are difficult to distinguish without a microscope and can be confused with *Gymnopus dryophilus*. When fresh and young, the cap of *R. b.* f. *butyracea* is red-brown to violet-brown, and then fades to lighter browns. The gills are crowded, thin, and white, developing a slight pinkish tint, and the edges are even and then serrulate in age. The stipe is clavate, tinted with colors of the cap, and has a tough rind and soft white spongy interior. The gill edges have a variety of different-shaped cheilocystidia, and the spores are pale pinkish buff, relatively large (mostly 7–9 × 3.5–4 µm) and tear-shaped, almond-shaped, or ellipsoid. *Rhodocollybia badiialba* is similar in color to *R. b.* f. *butyracea* and can be separated from other species in this group by its spherical spores. *Rhodocollybia butyracea* f. *asema* has a gray-brown to grayish cap when fresh. *Rhodocollybia unakensis* can be similar in color to *R. b.* f. *butyracea*, but has a somewhat rooting stipe base, is associated with rotting wood, and has smaller (5.5–7 × 3–4.5 µm) spores.

Rhodocollybia butyracea f. *butyracea*
SAT-00-297-40

Rhodocollybia maculata

Rhodocollybia maculata (Albertini and Schweinitz: Fries) Singer

Rhodocollybia maculata produces medium-sized to larger fruitbodies that are relatively thick-fleshed and not unlike tricholomas in appearance. Close observation of the cap reveals red-brown spots (hence *maculata*, "spotted"), which contrast with the usually cream to whitish cap. The edge of the cap remains inrolled for a long time. The gills are narrow, crowded, thin, and whitish to cream, yellowish white or pinkish, and become red-brown spotted with age. The stipe is relatively long, tapers downward, and often is deeply buried in the substrate; it is similar to the cap in color, including the spots, the interior is hollow, and the flesh tough and elastic. *Rhodocollybia maculata* is very common in the PNW, often fruiting in large numbers, in clusters on or near rotting conifer wood. It occurs from late spring until fall, and can be found even in dry years. Specimens with yellowish gills and sometimes yellowish stipes have been referred to as var. *scorzonerea*.

Baeospora myriadophylla (Peck)
Singer

Baeospora myriadophylla typically occurs on hardwood logs and stumps, and less often on conifer wood and forest floor litter. Fresh specimens are quite striking when plucked from a log and turned over to reveal the crowded, narrow, lilac gills. The thin-fleshed caps and the stipes are usually brownish, occasionally with lilac tones, and they, as well as the gills, develop grayish or paler tones with age or loss of moisture. The tough, hollow stipe is usually somewhat pruinose above and has white short hairs on the base. Baeospora myriadophylla is an uncommon fungus and usually occurs in small numbers in fall or spring.

Strobilurus trullisatus (Murrill)
Lennox

Strobilurus trullisatus is probably the most common cone-dwelling gilled fungus in the PNW, overwhelmingly favoring Douglas-fir cones that are fairly well rotted. The fruitbodies often arise from buried cones, so a little excavation may be required to make the substrate apparent. Like other members of the small genus Strobilurus, it forms small, dull-colored fruitbodies with broadly convex to flat caps, cap cuticle composed of club-shaped cells, and no clamp connections. In addition, the cap is whitish, often with pink tones, the gills are closely spaced, and the stipe is thin, grades from whitish at the apex to yellowish to brown in its lower portion, and bears yellow-brown or orangish wooly hairs at the base. Important microscopic features include the small (3–6 × 1.5–3.5 µm) non-amyloid spores and abundant, relatively thin-walled, pleurocystidia whose tips usually bear a mass of granular material that leaves a bit of a ridge when it

disappears. The less common S. occidentalis is very similar, usually differentiated by its darker cap that lacks pinkish tones, thicker-walled pleurocystidia that lack the granular material, and occurrence on spruce cones; Baeospora myosura (Fries) Singer also

Baeospora myriadophylla

Strobilurus trullisatus

occurs on spruce (mostly) and Douglas-fir cones, but has a brownish cap often with a pale edge that fades to pale tan, even more crowded buff gills, light brown, somewhat hairy stipe with whitish strands on the base, smaller (3–4.5 × 2–3 µm) weakly amyloid spores, clamp connections, and cap cuticle with mostly thin, flat-lying hyphae. *Strobilurus albipilatus* is a litter-inhabiting species that grows in scattered groups, usually at high elevation, often in the spring near melting snow. Despite its epithet (Latin for "white cap"), the cap color usually is some shade of medium to dark brown.

Baeospora myosura SAT-97-284-05

Callistosporium luteo-olivaceum SAT-07-285-10

Callistosporium luteo-olivaceum

(Berkeley and M. A. Curtis) Singer

Callistosporium luteo-olivaceum is a distinctively colored, smallish mushroom that grows on well-rotted, often mossy, wood any time from spring through fall. It prefers conifer logs and stumps (often associated with the bark) and fruits singly, as scattered individuals, or in small clusters. Typically the caps are yellow-brown to liver brown, with thin, close, yellow to ocher or olive-tinted gills, and hollow, fibrillose stipe that is similar in color to the cap and has yellowish tomentum at the base. The taste is farinaceous-bitter, and the flesh turns violet when dabbed with 3% potassium hydroxide. The spores are colorless, with yellow contents when mounted in ammonia.

GENUS *MYCENA* AND SIMILAR MUSHROOMS

Mycena is a large genus of small mushrooms, many of which fit the common name, fairy bonnets, quite well. In terms of numbers of fruitbodies, they are the most abundant mushrooms in the PNW. The fruitbodies are tiny to small to (occasionally) medium-sized, fragile and soft (but a few are fleshy), and often produced in large numbers (troops) over large areas of forest floor, especially on conifer needles. Typically the cap is conic or has a conic umbo, but it can also be bell-shaped or convex at first; the edge is often translucent-striate and not incurved or inrolled, the gills attached but usually not decurrent, the stipe usually thin and fragile, hollow, and without veils. Mycenas are decomposers of a wide variety of plant materials—leaves, humus, wood, sometimes grass—but not dung. Dry fruitbodies do not revive when moistened. Micro-

Mycenas often occur in large troops on conifer needle litter

scopically, a layer of inflated cells usually is present below the surface layer of the cap, the spores are smooth, and cheilocystidia are usually present. Microscopic characters, such as the size and shape of the cheilocystidia, are critical for identification and one cannot hope to identify more than a handful of species without a microscope and technical literature. The hordes of brown and gray mycenas are especially difficult to identify, but the more brightly colored species often can be distinguished with some success. There are no important edible species, most being tiny and fleshless, and some could be poisonous.

Mycenas could be confused with several other small mushrooms, including many of the collybias. A few representatives of other genera, many differing by having decurrent gills (omphalina-like species), also are

treated in this section. Still other similar genera, which are not covered here, include *Delicatula, Fayodia, Gamundia, Gerronema, Haasiella, Hemimycena, Hydropus, Mycenella,* and *Resinomycena*. They are separated from one another primarily by microscopic characteristics and, with the exception of *Hemimycena*, are all very small genera.

Mycena amicta (Fries) Quélet

When fresh, *Mycena amicta* is unmistakable by its typical mycena stature and blue color; however, in age, the blue fades to brownish and it becomes considerably more mistakable. When only faded specimens are available, they can be recognized by the powdery-hairy stipe, thick peelable cap cuticle, close gills, ellipsoid spores (6–10 × 3.5–5.5 μm), and simple, narrow cheilocystidia. *Mycena amicta* usually is found in groups of

Mycena amicta

Mycena aurantiidisca SAT-92-251-25

Mycena aurantiomarginata SAT-07-292-05

a few fruitbodies, often on or near well-rotted conifer wood in the PNW, and elsewhere on the wood of broadleaved trees.

Mycena aurantiidisca (Murrill)
Murrill

Mycena aurantiidisca is brilliant orange at first, but gradually fades, usually at the edge of the cap first, to yellowish or almost whitish. Typically, specimens are found that are yellowish around the edge and still bright orange in the center. The gills are whitish at first, then become somewhat yellowish, and the stipe is whitish with a yellowish base. *Mycena aurantiidisca* is common on needle litter in moist conifer forests, but usually occurs in relatively small numbers. It is very similar to *M. adonis* and *M. amabilissima* (itself considered a synonym of *M. adonis* by some mycologists), differing primarily in color, as these species are brilliant pink before fading.

Mycena aurantiomarginata (Fries)
Quélet

This distinctively colored species occurs widely in conifer forests along the Pacific Coast. The cap is dark olive-brown with smoky tints and orangish shades near the margin. It is not markedly hygrophanous. The gills are pallid to grayish orange on their faces and have bright orange edges. The stipe is colored somewhat like the cap. The spores are ellipsoid, 7–9 × 4–5 μm, smooth and amyloid, and the cheilocystidia are club-shaped with numerous short projections, somewhat like a mace. *Mycena aurantiomarginata* also is known from Europe.

Mycena citrinomarginata Gillet

Mycena citrinomarginata is a variable species that occurs in a wide variety of habitats, including under trees in forests and parks, among fallen leaves and mosses, on rotting tree bark, and in city-dwellers' lawns. The cap and stipe can be anything from pale yellowish to olivaceous to date brown, the gills from whitish to yellow-gray usually with a lemon-yellow edge (hence the epithet). Alexander Smith noted a distinct correlation between the amount of light in the habitat and the color of the fruitbodies: "Out in the open, [they] are very dark brown and have sordid-brown gill edges. In the deep shade of conifer thickets, a very pale delicate yellow to whitish form is found. The majority of [those] collected in moderately open stands are intermediate between the extremes." The odor and taste of *M. citrinomarginata* are not distinctive. Its spores are 8–12 × 4–5.5 µm, and the cheilocystidia varied, often with complex, branching, finger-like protrusions, especially in older fruitbodies.

Mycena clavicularis (Fries) Gillet

Mycena clavicularis is a common widespread species that often fruits in troops on conifer needles in late summer or early fall with the onset of the rain. The cap is dry to moist or greasy, dark gray to dark brown in the center, and fading somewhat with loss of moisture. The gills are pale grayish or brownish and attached to somewhat decurrent, and the stipe is about the same color as the cap and, in wet weather, is distinctly sticky or slimy, making the mushrooms hard to pick. The spores are medium-sized (7–10 × 3–5.5 µm) and cheilocystidia club-shaped with numerous short, thick, spine-like projections. *Mycena vulgaris*, a similar brownish species that also occurs in large troops on conifer litter, differs by fruiting later in the season, after the onset of colder weather,

and by having differently shaped cheilocystidia, much more slender and branched, appearing almost shrub-like.

Mycena epipterygia (Scopoli: Fries) S. F. Gray

Mycena epipterygia is another variable species that can be recognized easily in some forms and not so easily in others. The not-soon-forgotten sight of a line of brilliant yellow, glistening fairy bonnets marching along an arching, moss-draped maple branch evokes the essence of our wet old-

Mycena citrinomarginata SAT-03-291-01

Mycena clavicularis SAT-00-250-04

growth forests. The cap varies from mustard-yellow, often with a faint greenish tone and whitish edge, to shades of pale gray and brown with or without yellowish tinges, to dark brown in one variety. The cap is viscid in wet weather and its gelatinous skin completely peelable. The gills are white to buff and somewhat widely spaced, and the stipe is smooth, white to lemon-yellow, viscid when wet, and shiny when dry. The spores measure 8–11 × 5–6 µm, and the cheilocystidia are club-shaped with short projections, like those of *M. clavicularis*. In

Mycena epipterygia SAT-97-297-03

Mycena griseoviridis

the PNW, *M. epipterygia* occurs in small to somewhat larger groups in needle litter, or on twigs or wood. It also occurs widely in northern North America, Europe, and Asia, and numerous varieties (12! in Maas Geesteranus's Northern Hemisphere compilation) have been described based primarily on differences in fruitbody color, substrate, presence of clamp connections, and small differences in other microscopic features. Certain varieties are elevated to species status by some mycologists; but the key characters are gradational, and the existence of consistent discrete entities remains to be convincingly demonstrated.

Variety *griseoviridis*, one of the varieties recognized by Maas Geesteranus, was originally described as *Mycena griseoviridis* A. H. Smith, a name that in the western U.S. has been applied to a common montane snowbank mycena with dark olive-brown viscid caps, yellow to olivaceous viscid stipe, and tendency to stain reddish brown in age. Careful comparison suggests that this snowbank mycena differs sufficiently from *M. griseoviridis* to be considered a separate species. Although no formal proposal has been made to date, the name *M. nivicola* has been suggested as appropriate for our western fungus.

Mycena haematopus (Persoon: Fries) P. Kummer

Mycena haematopus is one of a group of mycenas characterized by containing a colored latex that is exuded when the fruitbodies are broken or cut. The fluid in *M. haematopus* is dark blood-red in color and is most easily seen by breaking the stipe near its base (hence the epithet: *haem-* is "blood" and *-pus* is "foot" in Greek). The fruitbod-

Mycena sanguinolenta SAT-99-129-01

Mycena haematopus SAT-01-321-13

Mycena maculata

ies grow in groups, often in loose clusters, on both hardwood and conifer logs and can get quite large (for a mycena). The edge of the cap often is finely scalloped, the spores are broadly ellipsoid, 7–12 × 4–7 μm, and the cheilocystidia are somewhat fat with extended necks that sometimes are branched. *Mycena sanguinolenta* (Albertini and Schweinitz: Fries) P. Kummer similarly exudes a red latex, but is smaller and more slender, consistently has red-edged gills (those of *M. haematopus* sometimes are and sometimes are not), and grows scattered on needle litter.

Mycena maculata P. Karsten

Mycena maculata is characterized by its conic or bell-shaped to convex, smooth to greasy caps, which are blackish brown to dark brown when young, then fade to brown-

ish gray, usually retaining an umbo, often wrinkled or slightly grooved and with reddish brown spots in age or after being cut or bruised. The gills are whitish to pale gray, spotted or almost wholly reddish in age, and the stipe is long and fairly stout, sometimes

Mycena galericulata SAT-07-285-02

Mycena oregonensis

with a rooting base when growing in soft well-rotted wood, its base densely covered with long coarse whitish hairs and staining reddish in age. Unfortunately for identifiers, the staining of the fruitbodies does not always develop. Microscopically, the spores are ellipsoid, 7–10 × 4–6 μm, and, although not conspicuous, the cheilocystidia are of varied shape and often bear projections. *Mycena maculata* grows in groups or clusters on wood of both hardwoods and conifers in North America and Europe, mostly on conifers in the PNW. In the absence of the reddish spotting, *M. maculata* is almost indistinguishable macroscopically from *M. galericulata* (Scopoli: Fries) S. F. Gray, which also grows in groups or clusters on wood, but has somewhat larger spores (8–12 × 5.5–9 μm).

Mycena oregonensis A. H. Smith

This tiny species, with caps no more than 1 cm (0.4 in.) across, is noticeable primarily because of its color. All parts are brilliant yellow, and this allows it to stand out in the litter under Douglas-fir and other conifers. It also occurs in Europe.

Mycena overholtsii

Densely hairy lower stipes of *Mycena overholtsii*

Mycena overholtsii A. H. Smith and W. Solheim

Mycena overholtsii is a large brown species ("a most un-*Mycena*-like member of the genus," according to Dutch mycologist R. A. Maas Geesteranus) that grows in clusters on wood, in much the same manner that *M. maculata* and *M. galericulata* do. However, *M. overholtsii* appears in the mountains in late spring to early summer on wet rotting stumps and logs recently exposed by, or still partially covered with, melting snow. Also, compared to the other two species, the gills are more distinctly gray and the lower portions of the stipes are densely covered with long white hairs. The spores measure 5–8 × 3.5–4 µm, and the sometimes hard-to-see cheilocystidia are smooth, slender, and cylindrical or sometimes a bit club-shaped. *Mycena overholtsii* apparently is restricted to the mountains of western North America.

Mycena stipata Maas Geesteranus and Schwöbel

Mycena stipata is another wood-inhabiting, cluster-forming, brown fairy bonnet, but of more typical mycena proportions. It is characterized by the dark brownish bell-shaped caps that are covered by a whitish powdery bloom when young and fade to pale grayish brown in age, the whitish to pale gray-brown gills that may stain reddish in age, pale grayish brown stipe, and bleach-like odor. The odor varies in strength from nearly absent to relatively strong, so it often is necessary to crush a cap in order to detect it. The spores measure 7.5–11 × 4.5–7 µm, and flask-shaped cheilocystidia with long necks are abundant; pleurocystidia of similar shape were said by Orson Miller to be abundant, but in the original description they are said to be absent or rare. *Mycena*

stipata has long been called *M. alcalina*, a name that has been rejected because of difficulties in interpreting it. *Mycena stipata* occurs most commonly in spring and early summer on logs and stumps in conifer forests, not necessarily associated with melting snow.

Mycena strobilinoides Peck

Even though it usually is smallish, *Mycena strobilinoides* can, in Alexander Smith's words, "add considerable color to the often otherwise dull needle carpet under conifers"

Mycena stipata SAT-07-154-01

Mycena strobilinoides

when it is present in troops of hundreds of fruitbodies. The fruitbodies are brilliant orange overall, even more intense orange on the edge of the gills, and are covered with long orange hairs at the base of the stipe. The spores are 7–9 × 4–5 µm, and the abundant cheilocystidia and pleurocystidia are variably flask-shaped with short necks to clavate and in all cases with abundant short knobby projections; they often contain pale to bright orange contents. *Mycena strobilinoides* seems to be most common at mid-elevations in the mountains, often in association with pines. It occurs less commonly elsewhere in northern North America and also in Europe.

Omphalina-like species

The following species, although now arrayed among six genera, at one time were all classified in the genus *Omphalina* (or *Omphalia*). Omphalina-like mushrooms are those that are small and have decurrent gills, cartilaginous stipe, broadly convex to slightly vase-shaped cap (*omphalina* is Greek for "small navel"), and no veils. In general, they look like small clitocybes and, in fact, many of them have been placed in *Clitocybe* at one time or another (we include them with the mycenas because of their small size and relatively dainty appearance). Based mostly on microscopic and chemical differences, a number of new, mostly quite small, genera have been created for many of these morphologically similar fungi. Although the ranks of *Omphalina* have been depleted by these removals, a number remain; however, none are included here.

Chromosera cyanophylla (Fries)
Redhead, Ammirati, and Norvell

Long known as *Mycena lilacifolia* in North America and as *Omphalina cyanophylla* in Europe, *Chromosera cyanophylla* is a beautiful, not uncommon but often overlooked fungus. The cap and stipe are bright golden yellow and slimy, the yellow contrasting with the lilac color of the young gills. The colors fade quickly to pale yellow or whitish, so young fruitbodies must be found to fully appreciate the beauty of this fungus. *Chromosera cyanophylla* usually grows in small groups and can be found in fall on rain-soaked conifer logs, as well as spring and early summer on wet conifer logs exposed by melting snow. It is the only member of the genus.

Chrysomphalina aurantiaca (Peck)
Redhead

Chrysomphalina aurantiaca (= *Omphalina luteicolor*) is a common bright orange species that often can be found in large groups on rotting conifer logs and stumps. The color fades considerably in age, although usually retaining vestiges of orange, and is difficult to capture accurately on film. *Chrysomphalina aurantiaca* was described from a collection made near Seattle and is a typical fall

Chromosera cyanophylla SAT-07-126-02

species in the PNW, but also can be found in spring. Apparently it is restricted to the PNW and northern California. Molecular analyses suggest that the other two chrysomphalinas are related relatively closely to the hygrocybes and *Chromosera*, so presumably *C. aurantiaca* is too.

Contumyces rosella (Moser) Redhead, Moncalvo, Vilgalys, and Lutzoni

Contumyces rosella (known briefly in the PNW as *Omphalina rosella* var. *vinacea*) is a velvety-capped, variably salmon-pink to somewhat wine-red fungus. Its most distinctive microscopic features are the presence of abundant hair-like cheilocystidia and fat-necked cystidia on the cap and stipe surfaces. Molecular analyses currently place it close to *Rickenella* in a group of fungi that contains a variety of morphologic forms, but predominantly polypores (many in the genus *Phellinus*) and crust-fungi. *Contumyces rosella* is a rarely collected spring-fruiting fungus, appearing on mossy soil, such as along trailsides, from late March to early June apparently with a peak in the first half of April.

Lichenomphalia umbellifera
(Linnaeus: Fries) Redhead, Lutzoni, Moncalvo, and Vilgalys

Most lichens involve ascomycetes; only a handful of them involve basidiomycetes, and *Lichenomphalia umbellifera* is one of those. It is an orangish tan or yellowish tan, translucent-striate and hygrophanous fungus that occurs pretty much throughout the year, mostly on rotting logs and stumps, but also on damp soil. The fruitbodies arise from a dark green film that coats the surface of the wood or soil. *Lichenomphalia umbellifera* (better known as *Omphalina ericetorum* and also as *Phytoconis ericetorum*)

Chrysomphalina aurantiaca

Contumyces rosella SAT-03-112-01

Lichenomphalia umbellifera

is common throughout the PNW and much of the Northern Hemisphere, being particularly abundant northward into the Arctic.

Rickenella fibula (Bulliard: Fries)
Raithelhuber

Rickenella fibula is a small, long-stiped, bright orange to yellowish fungus that occurs very widely on, or buried among, mosses. Microscopically, it is characterized by its conspicuous, large, long-necked cystidia on the gill edges and faces, stipe apex, and cap. It occurs in mossy forest habitats but also is a common urban mushroom, occurring in small to large groups in mossy lawns of homes, parks, and similar habitats. Molecular analyses suggest that *R. fibula* is not closely related to most other gilled mushrooms, instead it falls within a heterogeneous group that includes mostly polypores and crust-fungi. *Rickenella swartzii* is a similar, but less colorful, woodland species.

Xeromphalina campanella (Batsch: Fries) Kühner and Maire

Xeromphalinas differ from the other omphalina-like mushrooms in their bright yellowish brown to orangish brown cap with yellowish gills, and tough wiry stipe with rusty red hairs at the base. Microscopically, the spores are amyloid, and the dried fruitbodies can revive when moistened. All the species are saprotrophic on wood and leaf litter, some occurring in large masses on logs and stumps, others in dispersed fashion on small twigs and conifer needles.

Xeromphalina campanella is an example of the former type; it is very common on conifer wood in the PNW and elsewhere throughout the Northern Hemisphere. *Xeromphalina brunneola* is a very similar conifer-dwelling species described from Idaho and reported to occur in Washington; it is somewhat darker, has smaller, more elongated spores (5–6.5 × 2–3 vs. 5–9 × 3–4 µm), and a disagreeable taste. *Xeromphalina campanelloides* also resembles *X. campanella* in the field, but differs in certain microscopic characters—the hyphae of the flesh turn red in potassium hydroxide, and irregularly shaped cystidia are present on the stipe; it is a little-known species, described on the basis of two collections from Washington and one each from Vancouver Island, Québec, and

Rickenella fibula SAT-03-297-02

Xeromphalina campanella SAT-07-125-09

New York. Another very similar species, *X. kauffmanii*, has a yellower cap, yellowish hairs at the base of the stipe, smaller spores (4–6 × 3–4 μm), and occurs on hardwood in the central and eastern U.S.

Xeromphalina cornui (Quélet) J. Favre, an example of the latter type, occurs as single fruitbodies on conifer needles and small bits of woody debris, although often in troops; it also is found in sphagnum bogs. Contrary to general belief, it appears to be more common than the very similar *X. cauticinalis*, which differs in microscopic details, such as the type of pigmentation of the hyphae at the cap edge. *Xeromphalina fulvipes* is another similar species that is common along the Pacific Coast; it has fully to slightly attached gills (as opposed to at least somewhat decurrent in the former two species) and cap flesh with an upper gelatinous layer when mounted in potassium hydroxide and viewed under the microscope.

Marasmiellus candidus (Bolton) Singer

Strictly speaking, *Marasmiellus candidus* is more similar to the collybias than it is to the mycenas; however, its smallish size and fairly dainty stature cause us to include it here. Its bright white cap and tendency to grow in large groups make it an attention-grabber in our dark forests where it occurs on berry canes and twigs of both conifers and hardwoods. Up close it is exquisite. The cap is broadly convex, usually with a navel-like central depression, and nearly flesh-less, and the gills are thin, very widely spaced, and usually with blunt vein-like connections between them. Both cap and gills often stain pinkish or reddish in age. The stipe is mostly blackish, but usually grades upward to almost white at the

apex. Microscopically, the spores are shaped somewhat like elongated teardrops (11–15 × 3.5–5.5 μm), the cheilocystidia are smooth, quite slender, and sometimes wavy, with a swollen base. *Marasmiellus candidus* occurs throughout much of the Northern Hemisphere, but probably reaches its peak abundance in the PNW and northern California. Several species of pure white mycenas, placed in the genus *Hemimycena* by many mycologists, could be confused with *M. candidus*; however, they typically are smaller, do not have dark stipes, more often grow in

Xeromphalina cornui SAT-00-251-16

Marasmiellus candidus SAT-07-285-03

litter or on herbaceous plant remains, and occur in smaller groups.

Micromphale perforans (G. F.
Hoffmann: Fries) S. F. Gray

Micromphale perforans is another dainty mushroom with features that resemble collybias or marasmiuses more than mycenas. It has a fading, brown, wrinkled-furrowed cap with a depressed center, thin, wide-spaced, beige, somewhat wavy gills, and a long, dark brown to almost black, hairy, elastic stipe. The odor is unpleasant, resembling rotting cabbage or broccoli. It has oblong to elongated tear-shaped spores (6–9.5 × 3–5.5 µm) and smooth, cylindrical to slightly clavate, cheilo- and pleurocystidia that often are rare or missing. *Micromphale perforans* typically occurs in groups on conifer litter, often that of spruce, and is widely distributed in the northern Northern Hemisphere. Several similar-looking species occur in northern California and the PNW, but these differ from *M. perforans* in their garlic or onion odor and, usually, substrate. These include *M. sequoiae* with a mild odor and occurrence on coast redwood needles, *M. arbutic-*

Micromphale perforans

ola on shed pieces of madrone bark, *Marasmiellus filopes* on conifer needles, *Marasmius salalis* on Oregon grape or salal leaves, and *M. copelandii* on oak, tanbark oak, or chinquapin leaves.

GENUS *PLEUROTUS* AND SIMILAR MUSHROOMS

The shelf-like gilled mushrooms are referred to as pleurotoid, after the genus *Pleurotus*, the most conspicuous such fungi. Pleurotoid mushrooms typically are wood-inhabiting, grow in clusters, and have laterally attached stipes, or no stipe at all, and adnate to decurrent gills. Only rarely do they have a veil. They range from very small to quite large and usually are fairly fleshy but can be tough and pliable as well. Spores vary from white to pink, brown, and nearly black. We include a few of the light-spored pleurotoid mushrooms here. Other light-spored pleurotoid genera include *Tectella* and *Hohenbuehelia*. Pleurotoid mushrooms with darker spores can be found in genera such as *Claudopus* (pink), *Crepidotus* (brown), and *Melanotus* (purple-brown).

Pleurotus pulmonarius (Fries) Quélet
OYSTER MUSHROOM

Oyster mushroom is the name used for species of *Pleurotus*. The status of the PNW's oyster mushrooms is unclear beyond the fact that they definitely do occur here, often in spring, and are widely sought-after by mycophagists. The name applied to most North American oysters, *Pleurotus ostreatus*, is European in origin and refers to a species with dark, often blue-gray, caps. It does occur in eastern North America but is not known to grow in the PNW. Our oysters usually have whitish to brown caps and

Pleurotus pulmonarius SAT-05-232-04

likely represent *P. pulmonarius* and *P. populinus* O. Hilber and O. K. Miller ex O. Hilber. These two species are virtually identical morphologically and are best identified by substrate—*P. populinus* grows primarily on the wood of cottonwoods and aspen, whereas *P. pulmonarius* grows on the wood of a range of other conifers and hardwoods. All the oysters are variable in size, forming small to large, fan-shaped to broadly convex, often lobed caps, without a stipe or with a short lateral or off-center one with copious white hairs at the base. The gills are whitish, and decurrent if a stipe is present. In age the fruitbodies may turn yellowish and, if carefully examined when first found, small beetles often can be observed among the gills of mature fruitbodies. The spores are white, pale lilac, or somewhat grayish. The odor is pleasant, anise-like at times. When growing

Pleurotus populinus SAT-97-253-01

Pleurotus populinus SAT-06-290-11

Species of *Pleurotus* are easily cultivated. This home-kit features a beautiful pink strain of *P. djamor.*

Pleurotus populinus SAT-97-253-01

Pleurocybella porrigens

on the top of a log, the stipe can be central and then the mushroom has the aspect of a clitocybe. Caution should be used when collecting such forms for eating, as many clitocybes are poisonous.

Pleurocybella porrigens (Persoon: Fries) Singer
ANGEL WINGS

Pleurocybella porrigens can be found on conifer (especially hemlock) logs and stumps throughout the PNW, often occurring in large, exquisite, imbricate masses. It has spoon- to conch-shaped caps that are translucent-striate when fresh and develop a wavy margin when expanded. It is white to ivory, has no stipe, thin, rather tough, elastic flesh, and crowded narrow gills. In comparison, oyster mushrooms are fleshier and usually darker-colored, and the thin flesh makes *P. porrigens* less desirable than oysters as an edible. In addition, it recently was responsible for the deaths of several elderly Japanese, so caution is in order.

Panellus longinquus (Berkeley) Singer
In our area, we have three common species that have been placed in the genus *Panellus* but which when compared with one another are not very much alike, beyond the fact that all have a pleurotoid stature and small, white, amyloid spores. These are *P. stypticus*, a small ochraceous brown, tough, astringent-tasting species; *P. serotinus*, a tough, rather large, often viscid, yellowish green to olivaceous brown, late-fall (its common name is winter oyster) species; and *P. longinquus* (= *Pleurotopsis longinquus*),

Pleurocybella porrigens

Panellus longinquus

a small, viscid to slimy species with a pink to white or sometimes purplish brown, distinctly striate cap that is attached by a small stipe, and white to pinkish gills. It is a fairly common species, most abundant in cool wet falls, but also present at other times, on a variety of hardwood trees including alder and maple.

Lentinellus montanus O. K. Miller

Lentinellus montanus has fan- to kidney-shaped, rounded to lobed, buff to tan or brownish caps that are hairy to tomentose near the short stipe or point of attachment. The gills radiate from the point of attachment, are whitish to tan, and have saw-toothed edges. The fruitbodies are fleshy to tough and pliable and often have a slowly developing acrid taste. The spores are white, amyloid, and faintly ornamented. *Lentinellus montanus* is most common in higher elevation forests on conifer logs following snow-melt. The similar *L. ursinus* also occurs in our region, on hardwood and conifer logs at lower elevations, and can be found throughout the fruiting season but especially in moist cool weather.

Lentinellus montanus SAT-97-166-09

Lentinus strigosus (Schweinitz) Fries

Lentinus strigosus (commonly *Panus rudis*) is one of several mushrooms with a short, lateral hairy stipe that is usually about the same color as the cap. The epithet is descriptive of the dense covering of stiff hairs over the cap. The cap, when expanded, is somewhat vase-shaped with the edge inrolled, the color is often purple at first, but soon fades to reddish brown, pinkish brown, orangish brown, or tan, and the flesh is white, thin, and rather tough. The gills are close, narrow, colored like the cap at first and then

Lentinus strigosus

fading to whitish, and have even edges. The taste can be somewhat bitter. The spores are white, smooth, and non-amyloid. *Lentinus strigosus* is a widely distributed species, occurring on logs and stumps of hardwoods whenever temperature and moisture conditions are suitable. *Phyllotopsis nidulans* is another hairy-capped pleurotoid species, but it is orange-yellow, has a very disagreeable odor, and is rare in the PNW.

Neolentinus kauffmanii (A. H. Smith) Redhead and Ginns

Neolentinus kauffmanii can appear either pleurotoid or collybia-like, depending on the orientation of the stipe. Usually it is off-center and curved, so we have included it here. When mature, the pale tan to pinkish tan or vinaceous tinged caps are nearly flat, with lobed margins. The crowded, adnate to decurrent gills are irregular or saw-toothed and vary from whitish to pinkish buff. The taste is slightly peppery at times. The spores are white, small, and non-amyloid. *Neolentinus kauffmanii* is primarily a fall species and causes a brown rot of conifer logs and stumps, usually Sitka spruce. *Neolentinus adhaerens*, a rare brownish species with amber resin spots on the cap, occurs in the same habitats.

Ossicaulis lignatilis (Persoon) Redhead and Ginns

Ossicaulis lignatilis is a usually refrigerator-white mushroom with the habit of fruiting inside hollowed-out branches, trunks, and stumps of trees, making it difficult to find. The caps are medium-sized and may exhibit tinges of rose to vinaceous pink, the gills are typically crowded, adnate to decurrent, and the stipes are variable in length,

Neolentinus kauffmanii SAT-97-284-07

Ossicaulis lignatilis SAT-98-332-18

often curved, usually off-center, often in fascicles with small aborted caps, and with white strands at the base. Fresh-cut specimens have a farinaceous odor. *Ossicaulis lignatilis* causes brown rot of hardwoods, especially maple and cottonwood, and, less commonly, conifers. It is known from elsewhere in North America, as well as Japan and Europe, but is not commonly recorded. The tough texture and unpleasant odor argue against it being a worthwhile edible.

Pink-Spored Gilled Mushrooms

Several groups of mushrooms from different evolutionary lines have spores that can be described as pink although, in most cases, the color is more accurately salmon-pink, reddish pink, brownish pink, or even pinkish brown. The principal genera in the pink-spored group, as traditionally defined, are characterized here. In addition to these, some species in genera such as *Rhodocollybia*, *Lepista*, *Leucoagaricus*, and *Pleurotus* have spores with pinkish colors but, because they have close relatives with non-pink spores they usually are not considered part of the "pink-spored" group and we include them in the light-spored section. Similarly some species of brown- or dark-spored genera such as *Hebeloma* and *Psathyrella* can have spores with a reddish or pinkish cast.

- *Clitopilus* is a small genus whose species have central to lateral stipes or are bracket-like and look like small oyster mushrooms. The elongated spores have longitudinal ridges and are angular in end-view only. All the species appear to be saprotrophs.

- *Entoloma*, as increasingly accepted, is a very large genus encompassing a broad range of morphological forms, including species that look like tricholomas, collybias, clitocybes, omphalinas, mycenas, and pleurotuses. These are tied together by their spores, whose outline is angular in all views. There have been two different approaches to the classification of entolomas—one is to put all the species into a single genus *Entoloma*, which we have adopted here, the other is to recognize several other genera in addition to *Entoloma*, such as *Alboleptonia*, *Claudopus*, *Leptonia*, and *Nolanea*. The larger fleshy species are ectomycorrhizal, many of the small slender ones are saprotrophs, and for many others, the lifestyle has not been determined.

- *Pluteus* is characterized by its free gills and stipe that can be cleanly detached from the cap, lack of veils (so no ring, warts, or volva), soft watery flesh, smooth subglobose to globose spores, and growth on wood or woody debris, mostly in forests, although some species also occur in urban settings.

- *Volvariella* is similar in most respects to *Pluteus*, but differs in having a well-developed volva and by growing mostly in grasses, landscaping, or cultivated areas, on substrates other than wood, although some species occur on trees or in areas with wood chips. Volvariellas are not particularly common in the PNW, and we have not included any here.

In *Mushrooms in Their Natural Habitats* (1949), Alexander Smith observed, "The species of *Rhodophyllus* [= *Entoloma*] offer a very difficult study from the standpoint of the specialist to say nothing of the novice. It is the long series of very closely related species and the intergradations which occur between them which makes units at the species level so difficult to recognize." Nothing has changed since then; it is therefore important to be very careful when identifying pink-spored mushrooms with the intention of eating them, since many species of *Entoloma* are highly toxic.

Clitopilus prunulus (Scopoli: Fries) P. Kummer
THE MILLER

Clitopilus prunulus is a medium-sized, rather fleshy mushroom with decurrent gills and an equal to tapering central or off-center stipe that may be enlarged at the base. The cap is typically plane or umbonate, dry and whitish with beige, grayish, or pinkish tones, and its margin typically is inrolled. The gills are thin, whitish, and develop pinkish tones as they mature. The

stipe is similar in color to the cap. Fresh mushrooms have a farinaceous odor (hence the common name). *Clitopilus prunulus* is widely distributed in conifer as well as deciduous hardwood forests. It is edible, but not first-rate.

Entoloma holoconiotum
Light to dark brown entolomas are common in our moist western forests, and are often among the first mushrooms to appear in spring. Most species have a watery brown,

Clitopilus prunulus SAT-06-301-01

Entoloma holoconiotum SAT-00-147-09

umbonate, silky to smooth hygrophanous cap with a striate margin. The gills are often white to pallid or brownish at first and easily separable from the stipe. The stipe is often slender and fragile, colored like the cap, and coated with longitudinal fibrils. The species are difficult, if not impossible, to name unless a microscope and technical literature are available.

Entoloma holoconiotum is characterized by a brown-orange conical cap with a lighter apex, often appearing bicolored, white gills, and pale yellow stipe that is powdery over at least the upper half (use a handlens). It is one of several species that appear in late winter and early spring and continues to occur at higher elevations through the summer and fall. It is widespread in conifer forests throughout western North America. Entoloma cuneatum is similar but has a reddish brown cap with a pale apex and somewhat colored gills at first. Entoloma holoconiotum has often been called E. vernum because of its occurrence in spring; however, the latter is a dark brown to blackish brown species that, in its typical form, occurs rarely, if at all, in the PNW. These species are placed in the genus Nolanea by many mycologists and, indeed, the current name for this species is N. holoconiota Largent and Thiers. We have included it as an entoloma in anticipation of the new combination being made in the near future.

Entoloma nitidum Quélet
This beautiful dark blue species is widespread and sometimes locally abundant in moist western conifer forests where it occurs on humus and litter. It has a medium-sized shiny, radially fibrillose cap and a slender, somewhat fragile stipe, which is blue except for the whitish to yellowish base. The gills, including the edges, are whitish at first but gradually become pinkish from the maturing spores. The odor is variable—mild to somewhat radish-like. Entoloma bloxamii (= E. madidum) is a similarly colored species but is larger and fleshier with a farinaceous odor. Some mycologists feel E. nitidum should be assigned to the genus Rhodocybe.

Entoloma sericellum (Fries: Fries) P. Kummer
Entoloma sericellum (= Alboleptonia sericella) is widespread in forests on conifer and hardwood litter or moss-covered humus, as well as in grassy areas. It is a small species with a dry white cap covered by fine fibrils, white fragile gills, and a slender white stipe that sometimes appears translucent. The cap and stipe become yellowish in age, and the gills develop a pinkish tint from the maturing spores.

Entoloma sericeum (Bulliard) Quélet
Entoloma sericeum (= Nolanea sericea) is a cosmopolitan species occurring in a variety

Entoloma nitidum SAT-00-262-12

of habitats, but particularly lawns, grassy places, and along the edges of paths, often on hard-packed soils. It can often be found in parks and yards in any month of the year. It has a blackish brown to dark gray-brown cap that is translucent-striate then opaque. The gills are dark gray-brown and become darker with pinkish tones in age. The stipe is fragile, somewhat translucent-striate, light brown and then darker with age, and with a white wooly base. It has a very strong farinaceous odor and taste.

Entoloma trachyosporum var. purpureoviolaceum Largent

Entoloma trachyosporum (= *Rhodocybe trach-yospora*) comprises a number of color forms that have been given varietal names. The caps are grayish with brown, yellow-brown, or vinaceous, purplish, or grayish brown mixed in. The stipe and gills are off-white, grayish to grayish brown, dark blue to viola-ceous, or vinaceous mixed with gray. Four varieties with different color combinations have been recognized, including var. *pur-pureoviolaceum*, which has a bluish to blu-ish gray stipe, bluish gray gills, and a deep blue to bluish gray cap. All the varieties are slender and can look a bit like *E. nitidum*. They can be found during fall in our coni-fer forests.

Macrocystidia cucumis (Persoon: Fries) Josserand

Macrocystidia cucumis has spores with a pinkish brown tint and, in the field, might be confused with entolomas. However, the overall coloration and its smooth ellip-soid spores are very different and, in the PNW, it is usually found in nutrient-rich soils among herbaceous plants in gardens and parks rather than in forests (although

Entoloma sericellum

Entoloma sericeum SAT-07-328-08

Entoloma trachyosporum var. *purpureoviolaceum* SAT-00-296-27

it can occur there, usually along trailsides). The reddish brown cap with a pale yellowish edge and blackish to red-brown velvety stipe are distinctive, as is the strong cucumber or fishy odor. Microscopically, the presence of large lance-shaped cystidia on the cap, stipe, and edge and faces of the gills clinches the identification and accounts for the genus name.

Macrocystidia cucumis

Pluteus cervinus SAT-99-292-04

Pluteus cervinus (Schaeffer) P. Kummer

Together, *Pluteus* and *Volvariella* represent a group of pink-spored mushrooms which have free gills and a stipe that is easily separated from the cap. *Pluteus* lacks veils while *Volvariella* has a well-developed, membranous universal veil that leaves a distinct volva around the stipe base. In the PNW, *V. gloiocephala* (= *V. speciosa*) is about the only species of this genus frequently encountered, occurring in gardens, pastures, and other cultivated areas, sometimes in large numbers. *Pluteus*, by comparison, is common in our forests, frequently occurring on logs and stumps or snags of conifers and hardwoods. *Pluteus cervinus* is by far the most commonly encountered pluteus. It grows on a variety of woody substrates, including sawdust and wood chips, and can be found throughout the year when temperature and moisture are conducive. It often is one of the early spring species at lower elevations. *Pluteus cervinus* usually is medium-sized but can become larger and more robust. It has a smooth, satiny, brown to blackish brown, umbonate cap that is often darkest in the center. The flesh is white and has a strong odor of radish or potato. The gills are close, white then pinkish, and the edges are white-fringed (use a handlens). The stipe is cylindrical, slightly enlarged at the base, fibrous, and white with grayish black fibrils. *Pluteus atromarginatus* is very similar to *P. cervinus*, but has dark gill edges and seems to occur only on conifer wood. Care should be taken not to confuse pluteuses with similar entolomas, many of the latter being extremely poisonous.

Brown-Spored Gilled Mushrooms

Key to Brown-Spored Gilled Mushroom Groups

1. Partial veil usually present, finely fibrillose and appearing cobweb-like in young specimens; spores (in deposit) rusty brown to cinnamon-brown; growing on ground near trees . . . . **Genus *Cortinarius*** (page 147)
1. Partial veil absent or, if present, membranous to fibrillose; spore color usually not rusty brown; growing on soil, wood, or other substrate, near trees or not 2

2. Stipe fleshy, usually with skirt-like ring; often growing in clusters on wood or woody debris 3
2. Stipe not fleshy and/or skirt-like ring lacking; growing in clusters or not, on wood, soil, or other substrate 4

3. Spores pale yellowish brown to ochraceous rusty brown; cap, underside of ring, and lower stipe golden brown with powdery to granular coating. . . . .
. . . .**Genus *Phaeolepiota*** (page 185)
3. Spores medium to dark brown; mushroom lacking powdery to granular coating . . . . .
. . . . **Genera *Pholiota*** (page 171) **and *Agrocybe*** (page 178)

4. Mushrooms small to large; stipe fleshy, skirt-like ring lacking 5
4. Mushrooms usually small, sometimes small-medium; stipe slender and more or less fragile, skirt-like ring present or lacking. 6

5. Mushroom usually more or less stocky; cap surface sticky to somewhat glutinous; growing on soil, only occasionally in clusters . . . . **Genus** *Hebeloma* (page 183)
5. Mushroom usually short and slender; cap surface usually dry and fibrillose to scaly; growing on soil (or rarely on well-rotted wood), only occasionally in clusters . . . . **Genus** *Inocybe* (page 162)
5. Mushroom slender to stocky; cap surface dry, sticky, or glutinous; usually growing on wood or woody debris, often in clusters . . . . **Genera** *Pholiota* (page 171), *Gymnopilus* (page 181), **and** *Agrocybe* (page 178)
5. Mushroom generally stocky with decurrent gills that can be peeled from the cap easily; cap surface dry; growing on soil or wood, not in clusters . . . . **Genera** *Paxillus* (page 184) **and** *Tapinella* (page 185)
5. Mushroom usually tall and slender with conical cap and root-like stipe extending deep into the soil; cap surface usually sticky to glutinous; growing on soil, often in large close-packed groups . . . . **Genus** *Phaeocollybia* (page 169)

6. Cap surface, when dry, appearing to be covered with small shiny particles; usually growing in rich soil or dung. . . . . **Genus** *Conocybe* (page 179)
6. Cap surface not as above; growing in rich soil, dung, or elsewhere 7

7. Gills extend down stipe; often growing in grass or among wood chips . . . . **Genus** *Tubaria* (page 186)
7. Gills attached to some degree, or rarely free, but do not extend down stipe; growing in various settings 8

8. Spores olive-brown; margin of young cap inrolled; growing on soil under alder or willow trees . . . . **Genus** *Naucoria* (page 184)
8. Spores ochraceous brown to rusty brown; margin of young cap not inrolled; often growing in moss, occasionally on wood or woody debris. . . . .**Genus** *Galerina* (page 180)
8. Spores dull medium brown; margin of young cap not inrolled; usually growing in grass. . . . .**Genus** *Agrocybe* (page 178)
8. Spores greenish at first, drying to reddish; margin of young cap not inrolled; gills free; usually growing in rich soil, including manure piles . . . . **Genus** *Melanophyllum* (page 183)

Cortinarius acutus SAT-05-303-10

GENUS *CORTINARIUS*

Cortinarius is by far the largest genus of mushrooms and is found throughout the world. As far as is known, all the species are ectomycorrhizal, and they are characteristic of many forest ecosystems as well as alpine and arctic habitats; they also can be found in parks and other urban settings where appropriate tree hosts occur. Forests of all types can produce an abundance of species in some years, presenting a colorful, but bewildering, array of red, yellow, orange, blue to violet, and greenish species, always accompanied by the inevitable brownish ones. They come in many sizes and shapes and, except for some smaller species, are relatively fleshy. They typically have brown spores, often somewhat rust-colored, but cinnamon-brown or medium brown as well.

The name *Cortinarius* comes from the cobwebby veil, or cortina (from the Latin for "curtain"), that at first covers the developing gills. In addition, an outer veil may be present, extending from the base of the stipe onto the surface of the cap, and sometimes leaving white or colored bands on the stipe surface and patches on the cap surface or edge. The outer veil usually is composed of thread-like fibrils but it can be much more membranous in some species, although only rarely does it form a skirt-like ring; in some instances it can be covered by or embedded in viscid or glutinous material. A cortina is lacking in only a few species. The color of the young gills, cap, and stipe is important for the identification of species, and in many cases older specimens are difficult to identify because these colors have faded or changed. Thus, it is very important to have a collection of specimens ranging from young to mature for identification. Certain cortinariuses have odors and tastes that are helpful for identification; however, most species have nondescript odors and tastes.

Microscopically, the most important features for identifying cortinariuses are the size, shape, and degree of ornamentation of the spores. Shape varies from round to almond-shaped or cylindrical, and nearly all are noticeably roughened to warty. Most species lack well-defined cystidia on the gills, so finding them (usually cheilocystidia) can be an important clue. Except for a few species in subgenus *Myxacium*, cortinariuses have clamp connections. The structure of the cap cuticle is somewhat variable and is important in some cases.

Cortinarius has been split into about a half-dozen subgenera using features such as whether there is a viscid layer on the cap and/or stipe and whether the cap is silky, covered by fibrils or scales, or moist and hygrophanous. The more commonly used subgenera are *Cortinarius*, with dark violet fruitbodies and dry tomentose-scaly caps; *Dermocybe* with slender fruitbodies and red, orange, yellow, or greenish colors and elliptical spores; *Sericeocybe* with non-hygrophanous, silky to scaly, usually thick-fleshed caps (dry to slightly viscid); *Telamonia* with small to large mostly moist hygrophanous caps; *Phlegmacium* with viscid caps and non-viscid stipes; *Myxacium* with viscid caps and viscid stipes; and *Leprocybe* with fruitbodies having olive, green, brown-olive, yellow, yel-low-brown, orange-brown, or rarely red colors, and often broadly elliptical to rounded spores. However, it now appears that some of these subgenera do not represent natural evolutionary groups, and they have been abandoned by some mycologists. Nonetheless, the subgenera remain helpful for sorting and naming species and will be indicated in the species accounts. Recent data also suggest that several secotioid and gastroid fungi, such as *Thaxterogaster pinguis* and *T. pavelekii*, are close relatives of many cortinariuses and perhaps should be added to the genus. Finally, it appears that species of *Rozites* also are closest relatives of some cortinariuses. However, in this guide we have chosen to retain *Thaxterogaster* and *Rozites* in the customary sense.

A number of other brown-spored mushrooms can resemble cortinariuses. The most easily confused genus is *Gymnopilus*, which has ornamented, bright orange-brown or bright rusty brown spores and usually occurs on wood. Hebelomas and inocybes occur in soil and litter like cortinariuses; however, they have medium brown spores and the spores of inocybes are smooth or angular to lumpy, not roughened. Hebelomas and inocybes also have abundant cheilocystidia, and inocybes often have pleurocystidia as well. Some of the terrestrial pholiotas, such as *Pholiota lubrica*, may also be confused with cortinariuses; however, their dull brown smooth spores distinguish them. Smaller cortinariuses can be confused with galerinas and naucorias. Galerinas often occur among mosses or on woody substrates, often have the stature of a mycena, and are rather fragile. Naucorias have more yellow-brown colors, a less obvious veil, and are typically found with alder or willow.

Being a huge genus, *Cortinarius* might be expected to include species with a wide range of edibility and, indeed, that seems to be the case. A small number, typified by the European species *C. orellanus* and *C. rubellus*, are deadly poisonous (see Appendix 1). Others are considered good edibles in Europe, and *Rozites caperata* (the gypsy), which is now thought to be a cortinarius, is considered choice and eaten by many mushroom-hunters. However, because the *Cortinarius* mycoflora of North America is so little known, and the species sometimes impossible to identify, we have no information on the edibility of most species. Thus, until more is known, we recommend avoiding all cortinariuses.

Cortinarius acutus (Persoon: Fries) Fries

Cortinarius acutus (subgenus *Telamonia*) is one of the smaller species in the genus, along with *C. bibulus*, a deep violet species that occurs with alder. It has somewhat the aspect of a galerina. The cap is conic to campanulate, pointed, strongly striate, hygrophanous, often fading at its tip first, and the color is light red-brown to yellowish brown fading to yellowish white. The stipe is thin and somewhat fragile and may have a thin coating of white veil fibrils. The edges of the gills are white, slightly ragged, and, microscopically, are covered with balloon-shaped cheilocystidia. The spores are ellipsoid, densely ornamented with fine warts, and 7–8 × 4–5 μm. *Cortinarius acutus* occurs in nutrient-poor conifer forests, often on moist sites in litter, and can be found throughout the north temperate region. Smaller specimens of the closely related *C. obtusus* can be quite hard to distinguish from *C. acutus*.

Cortinarius alboviolaceus (Persoon: Fries) Fries

Cortinarius alboviolaceus (subgenus *Sericeocybe*) is a medium-sized species with a broadly umbonate silky fibrillose cap that is silvery bluish to bluish white at first then develops yellowish tones and often becomes grayish white. Under moist conditions the surface can be viscid. The gills are pale grayish brown or sometimes slightly bluish at first. The stipe is usually club-shaped and colored like the cap; the white veil sometimes leaves faint zones or a thin covering over its lower portion. The flesh is whitish to pale blue-lilac, and the odor and taste are not distinctive. The spores are distinctly ornamented, ellipsoid, and 8.5–10 × 6–6.5 μm. In eastern North America and in Europe *C. alboviolaceus* is considered a species of hardwood forests. In western North America, we

Cortinarius alboviolaceus

have an essentially identical species, sometimes with a viscid stipe, in conifer forests, that has been called *C. griseoviolaceus*. *Cortinarius alboviolaceus* is sometimes confused with *C. camphoratus*, which also is sometimes common in our conifer forests; however, the latter has a penetrating, sickening odor similar to rotting potatoes. *Cortinarius malachius* also is somewhat similar to *C. alboviolaceus*, but it has a grayish white to grayish brown cap that may have lilac colors when young, and with a finely scaly surface when dry.

Cortinarius anomalus SAT-04-262-03

Cortinarius caninus SAT-03-305-04

Cortinarius anomalus (Fries: Fries) Fries

Cortinarius anomalus (subgenus *Sericeocybe*) and the related *C. caninus* (Fries) Fries occur in a variety of forests, but can be especially abundant during summer along small streams in subalpine forests with spruce. Distinguishing them is difficult because of their variation in color. *Cortinarius anomalus* has a light blue-gray cap that develops brown to red-brown tones in age and retains a bit of lilac along the edge. The cap is fibrillose and dry at first and then somewhat finely scaly in age. The gills are gray-violet when young. The stipe is light blue-gray with buff to pale ochraceous zones on the surface; sometimes these are thin and pale, making them difficult to see. *Cortinarius caninus* differs by its cap being browner when young and having browner and more strongly developed veil remnants on the stipe. Both species have nearly round spores and a cap cuticle with a layer of enlarged, isodiametric cells just beneath the surface layer of radially arranged hyphae. There is a difficulty with these species in that the concepts have not been well defined. Thus, it is hard to know if our species are the "real thing."

Cortinarius aurantiobasis Ammirati and A. H. Smith

Cortinarius aurantiobasis (subgenus *Dermocybe*) appears to represent a complex of forms that are related to *C. croceus* and *C. cinnamomeus*. In *C. aurantiobasis*, the cap is distinctly orange-brown to red-brown, sometimes with a darker brown center, usually has a distinct umbo, and the margin is finely fibrillose-scaly. The gills are rich yellow to orange-yellow with yellow edges, and they develop strong orange to brownish tones with age. The stipe is equal but often tapered at the base, with a yellowish surface above, and the lower portion and particularly the base is a rich watery orange. The flesh of the cap is yellowish, and that of the stipe grades from yellowish in the upper portion to orangish at the base. The cortina is yellow; however, the veil fibrils on the stipe are often reddish to olive. The odor and taste are not distinctive or slightly radish-like. Microscopically, a distinguishing feature is the distinctly ornamented ellipsoid spores that often are up to 10–11 µm long, significantly larger than those of *C. croceus* or *C. cinnamomeus*. *Cortinarius aurantiobasis* tends to occur in wetter habitats with conifers, often near western hemlock and/or Sitka spruce, and frequently among sphagnum or other mosses. In Northern Europe two species have been recognized that are similar to it, *C. bataillei* and *C. croceoconus*.

Cortinarius brunneus (Persoon: Fries) Fries

Cortinarius brunneus (subgenus *Telamonia*) has relatively large, fleshy fruitbodies, with dome-shaped caps that reach 8 cm (3 in.) in diameter, are watery red-brown to umber in color, sometimes with bluish tones, and have a striate margin when fresh. The gills are subdistant to distant, relatively thick and wide, and dark brown, sometimes with bluish or reddish brown tints. The stipe is fleshy, equal to clavate, pale brown, sometimes with bluish tints, and darkens with age or when bruised. The veil leaves a white to brownish zone on the stipe. The flesh of the fruitbody is whitish brown to grayish brown or slightly bluish. On drying the entire fruitbody becomes grayish black. The spores are ovoid and coarsely ornamented. *Cortinarius brunneus* and its rela-

tives are common in moist conifer forests of North America, Europe, and likely elsewhere in the Northern Hemisphere. At times, *C. brunneus* can be exceedingly abundant in PNW forests with Sitka spruce and other conifers, especially near the coast. *Cortinarius glandicolor* is similar, but has more slender fruitbodies and is less likely to have a distinct ring-zone on the stipe. It appears to be more widely distributed than *C. brunneus*, in both moist and dry conifer forests.

Cortinarius aurantiobasis SAT-03-305-08

Cortinarius brunneus SAT-00-285-17

Cortinarius clandestinus Kauffman

Cortinarius clandestinus (subgenus *Leprocybe*) typically is medium-sized with thin and somewhat fragile flesh, and slender equal or slightly clavate stipe. The golden olive cap is dry and covered with small dark brown to dark olive-brown, fibrillose scales, and the edge may be yellowish olive from veil fibrils at first. The flesh of the cap and stipe is yellowish to olive-yellow or somewhat darker when fresh, and usually has a radish odor. The gills are close, pale to yellowish or olive-tinted, and become orange-

brown when mature. The stipe typically is covered with light greenish yellow to yellowish veil fibrils and often has a slight ringzone. *Cortinarius clandestinus* was described from Douglas-fir and western hemlock forests of western Washington. While it has been reported from New York state, it seems primarily a species of western conifer forests, extending from lower elevations into the higher mountains. *Cortinarius melanotus* is a similar European species that differs by having a brownish veil on the stipe. *Cortinarius cotoneus*, a species of hardwood forests, is more robust and has olive-brown veil fibrils and zones on the stipe. *Cortinarius venetus* var. *montanus* can be found in our region with conifers; its color is more olive-green to yellow-green, the cap is finely tomentose when fresh, and it has a sulfuryellow veil when young. All these species have rounded, finely ornamented spores and fluoresce bright yellow in ultraviolet light.

Cortinarius clandestinus SAT-00-285-18

Cortinarius croceus SAT-04-304-06

Cortinarius croceus (Schaeffer) S. F. Gray

Cortinarius croceus (subgenus *Dermocybe*) is generally a medium-sized species with caps that are dry and finely fibrillose to fibrillose-scaly, with yellow-brown to red-brown colors, and often more yellowish on the margin. The veil usually is yellow but can be brownish red to olive, and sometimes leaves distinct fibrils or zones and patches on the stipe. The gills are close to crowded, rich yellow, sometimes with olive, orange, or red tones. The stipe is slender, typically cylindrical, yellowish, with a whitish yellow, yellow, or even reddish-tinted base. The flesh is yellowish or sometimes olive-tinted or grayish, and typically has a radish odor. The spores are ellipsoid, distinctly ornamented, and up to about 9 μm long. *Cortinarius croceus* is one of the more common and widespread cortinariuses, occurring throughout north temperate forests and into alpine and arctic areas. It grows with various conifers, as well as hardwoods including beech, birch, and willow. Often large numbers can be found in open areas, along roadsides and banks, among mosses and lichens, or on bare soil. It is a common mushroom of drier conifer forests and, in our region, can be found from spring through fall. A number of species are similar to *C. croceus*, the closest being *C. cinnamomeus*, which differs by its orange gills, and *C. cinnamomeoluteus*, a yellow-gilled species that occurs with willows. Species in this group are commonly used for dyeing wool.

Cortinarius riederi (Weinmann) Fries

Cortinarius riederi (= *C. fulvo-ochrascens*, *C. pseudoarquatus*) is a medium-sized to larger species of the subgenus *Phlegmacium* characterisitc of conifer forests across the Northern Hemisphere and is common and widespread in the PNW. The caps are various shades of brown, often with light grayish to bluish tones mixed in toward the margin, and the inrolled margin often bears patches or streaks of veil fibrils. The gills are persistently bluish and the cortina is pale bluish at first. The stipe, at least when young, has some bluish gray tones above and, in age, it develops strong bronze to yellowish or brownish discolorations. The bulb at the base of the stipe often is turnip-shaped, without a distinct rim. The spores are broad and nearly ellipsoid, 11–14 × 6–8 μm. The coloration of *C. riederi* is quite variable but to date trying to define distinct varieties has been a fruitless endeavor.

Cortinarius gentilis (Fries) Fries

Cortinarius gentilis (subgenus *Telamonia*) is easily recognized when fresh by its bright brownish yellow colors and long, slender, often root-like stipe, with bright yellow veil remnants in the lower part. The cap typically is umbonate, slightly striate on the edge when moist, and fades quickly to yellowish or paler on drying. The flesh is usually brownish yellow, and the odor is often strongly of raw potatoes. The gills are distant, brownish yellow then dark reddish and sometimes with grayish to violet tints. The

Cortinarius riederi SAT-07-268-10

Cortinarius gentilis SAT-00-298-06

spores are more or less rounded and distinctly ornamented. Historically *C. gentilis* has been classified in subgenus *Leprocybe*, and reported as containing orellanine (a dangerous kidney toxin found in some leprocybes; see Appendix 1), which appears not to be true. Recent studies suggest that it better fits in subgenus *Telamonia*, close to the *C. brunneus* group. *Cortinarius gentilis* has a broad ecological range, occurring in moist environments as well as drier, upland conifer sites. During the summer in the western mountains it can be very common, often fruiting in groups, sometimes from well-rotted woody debris.

Cortinarius laniger Fries

Cortinarius laniger (subgenus *Telamonia*) is medium-sized to large and rather fleshy. The cap is dome-shaped with an umbo, bright brown to cinnamon-brown or deep red-brown, and often wrinkled, streaked, and covered with whitish veil remnants along the edge when fresh. The odor is strongly of radish, and the flesh of the cap and stipe is whitish, usually with cinnamon-brown or yellow-brown areas. The gills are vivid cinnamon-brown to rust-brown, and close to crowded. Usually the stipe is club-shaped to bulbous, rather thick, white to brownish, and has a heavy white veil that leaves bands and patches below the ring-zone. The spores are large, rather broad (8–11 × 5–6.5 µm), and densely ornamented. *Cortinarius laniger* is characteristic of boreal and montane conifer forests, and is rather widespread, but variable in its fruiting, in some years being rather common and in others being absent. It and related species come in a variety of forms. Some have lilac colors in the stipe apex when young, and might be closer to *C. solis-occasus*. *Cortinarius bivelus* is somewhat similar but grows with birch.

Cortinarius magnivelatus Dearness ex Fogel

Cortinarius magnivelatus (subgenus *Phlegmacium*) is one of several cortinariuses that develop more or less beneath the soil surface and often remain partially buried at maturity. They vary in color and other features but have in common a heavy, membranous, more or less persistent veil; all actively release their spores and give a spore deposit, unlike secotioid fungi such as thaxterogasters. The species with heavy veils apparently have evolved this feature independently, and do not form a natural group. They are found in the mountains of western North America, especially higher elevation dry conifer forests of fir, pine, and spruce. *Cortinarius magnivelatus* appears to be one of the more widespread species. It is rather thick-fleshed and tough, and at first white overall because of the heavy veil that covers the stipe and gills. In age the cap develops yellowish to brownish colors. The gills are white to grayish then brown from the spores, and often forked near the stipe.

Cortinarius laniger SAT-01-292-05

The stipe is rather long and bulbous with a slightly tapered base. The veil is persistent, often covers much of the stipe, and is firmly attached to the edge of the cap. The flesh is white, and the odor is not distinctive. The spores are rather large, up to 14 µm long, and strongly ornamented. *Cortinarius wiebeae* is similar in many features, and it remains to be seen if it is a distinct species. *Cortinarius verrucisporus* is somewhat similar but develops stronger yellow colors on the cap and has yellowish flesh. *Cortinarius saxamontanus* is even more strongly yellow to brownish orange, has a light yellow cortina, and yellow-brown to brownish orange gills; its fruitbodies turn wine-red after drying and storage, probably due to the presence of anthraquinone pigments.

Cortinarius montanus Kauffman

Cortinarius montanus (subgenus *Phlegmacium*) varies in color but is usually fairly easy to recognize. It is medium-sized to large and rather fleshy with a distinct bulbous base that is covered at first by a pale yellow-green veil and basal mycelium. Typically the cap is viscid, variegated and spotted hazel-brown to deep brown with light yellowish olive colors on the margin, and typically becomes more brownish in older specimens. The flesh is whitish or tinged with the colors of the cap, and in the stipe is whitish in the center and bluish near the surface; the odor is not distinctive. The gills are close, rather narrow and light yellowish olive to olive at first, eventually becoming more brownish. The stipe is bluish to grayish blue beneath white silky fibrils when fresh and sometimes discolors purplish when handled. The spores are elliptical and distinctly ornamented. *Cortinarius montanus* was described from west-

ern North America, where it is common in older, cool, moist conifer forests. It can be very common and widespread, but often occurs as one or a few fruitbodies at a time. It is closely related to *C. scaurus*, which has been divided into various taxa and ecological forms in Europe; further work is needed to better define the species concepts in this group. *Cortinarius albobrunnoides* (similar to *C. napus*) is another species with pale yellow mycelium beneath the base of the stipe. It has a brownish cap, light brown gills, a pale violet stipe that soon fades to whitish,

Cortinarius magnivelatus SAT-91-152-01

Cortinarius montanus SAT-01-293-35

and either a whitish or violet veil. It occurs from the Rocky Mountains into the Cascades, often with spruce.

Cortinarius muscigenus Peck

Cortinarius muscigenus (subgenus *Myxacium*) is a cylindrical-stiped species with a viscid cap and stipe. The myxaciums have a universal veil composed of patches and fibrils which is covered with gelatinous material when fresh and that, in most species, breaks into bands and patches as the stipe elongates. These species can be split into two groups based on the presence or absence of clamp connections. *Cortinarius muscigenus* is a member of the former group, which is related to the secotioid species *Thaxterogaster pinguis*. It is a medium to large species with a strongly gelatinous, brownish orange to brownish red or ochraceous brown cap, which often is darkest in the center and striate near the edge. The flesh is fibrous, white to yellowish, and typically turns brownish in the lower stipe. The gills are grayish white or grayish brown then cinnamon in age. The stipe is whitish, except for the inner veil which is typically bluish violet, sometimes very faintly so. The spores are almond-shaped and coarsely ornamented. *Cortinarius muscigenus* varies in abundance from year to year, and in some seasons can be very common in mid- to high elevation conifer forests. *Cortinarius muscigenus* was described from conifer forests in eastern North America. In our area, it can be confused with *C. trivialis*, which is a species associated with cottonwoods and aspen, and *C. mucosus*, a species with a white stipe that most frequently occurs with pines. *Cortinarius vernicosus* is another conifer associate that differs by fruiting in spring. Although rather widespread, it is relatively rare. Members of this group that occur in subalpine forests include *C. absarokensis* and *C. favrei*, both of which are associated with willow. The myxaciums that lack clamp connections on the hyphae are represented in our area by *C. vanduzerensis* and a form of *C. mucifluus*, both of which are relatively common in moist conifer forests. The rare secotioid species *T. pavelekii* also lacks clamps and is related to these species. The European species *C. collinitus* has been considered the same as *C. muscigenus*, but the larger spore size characteristic of collections from North America suggests the matter could use more study.

Cortinarius mutabilis A. H. Smith

Cortinarius mutabilis (subgenus *Phlegmacium*) is one of a handful of viscid-capped species that stain purple when bruised or cut. It is medium-sized, violet to violet-gray, and has a club-shaped stipe. In age it develops grayish and brownish colors. The flesh is pale to darker violaceous and the odor is not distinctive. It occurs in a variety of habitats with different conifers and is more frequent in moist areas. *Cortinarius porphy-*

Cortinarius muscigenus SAT-00-296-61

ropus is another purple-staining species that occurs in our area in mixed woods; it is more slender than *C. mutabilis*, its cap is often pale grayish to brownish, without distinct lilac colors, and it has a narrow, clavate stipe base. *Cortinarius purpurascens* has a viscid ocher-brown to red-brown or darker brown cap with a violet stipe and gills, and a bulbous base with a rim; in our region, it is most commonly found along the coast, especially with Sitka spruce.

Cortinarius obtusus (Fries: Fries) Fries

To some mycologists, *Cortinarius obtusus* (subgenus *Telamonia*) represents a species complex that is easy to recognize but difficult to separate into distinct taxa. To others, it is merely a highly variable species. Regardless of one's viewpoint, the cap is red-brown to yellow-brown and striate on the margin when fresh; it then fades dramatically in streaky fashion. The margin of the cap is covered with white veil fibrils when young, and the stipe frequently is thinly coated by the veil or bears a few patches. The stipe is hollow, pale yellowish brown to pale orange-brown beneath the veil, and pinched off and frequently curved at the base. The flesh is orange-brown to yellow-brown, and fresh specimens can have a faint odor of iodine. The gills are close to crowded, yellowish brown to brown with pale edges. The spores are distinctly and coarsely ornamented. *Cortinarius obtusus* can fruit extensively in groups and troops in both spring and fall. It is a widespread species found in a variety of habitats including pine forests and alpine areas with dwarf birch and sometimes is one of the more common species in our moist conifer forests. The closest look-alike is *C. acutus*, which is smaller and has a more sharply pointed umbo.

Cortinarius olympianus A. H. Smith

Cortinarius olympianus (subgenus *Phlegmacium*) is a spectacular medium-sized, glutinous-capped, pale lilac to pale pinkish lilac species. At times, however, it is merely whitish lilac or, in age, slightly yellowish on the center of the cap and then it is much less spectacular. The close to crowded gills are pale pinkish lilac and become brownish lilac in age. The base of the stipe has a broad, distinct bulb with a raised rim. It occurs in low to mid-elevation conifer forests and varies in abundance from year to year. *Cortinarius*

Cortinarius mutabilis SAT-03-303-01

Cortinarius obtusus SAT-00-313-28

Cortinarius olympianus SAT-00-312-38

Cortinarius phoeniceus var. *occidentalis*
SAT-05-302-05

Cortinarius salor SAT-01-301-12

olympianus can sometimes be found in groups, but not uncommonly is scattered across the forest floor as single fruitbodies. A drop of potassium hydroxide or ammonia turns the flesh brilliant red.

Cortinarius phoeniceus var. occidentalis A. H. Smith

Cortinarius phoeniceus var. *occidentalis* (subgenus *Dermocybe*) features a medium-sized, blood-red cap, deep, dark red gills, and a pale yellowish stipe with a coating of yellowish fibrils, and yellow or vinaceous red base. It is a common species in our conifer forests and often can be found in large numbers. The epithet *phoeniceus* is no longer used in Europe, so the closest relatives of our mushroom probably are *C. purpureus* and *C. fervidus*. *Cortinarius semisanguineus* is similar to these species but in its typical form has a yellow-brown to olive-brown cap. In our region there are populations of *C. semisanguineus* with red caps, and these are best separated from *C. p.* var. *occidentalis* by their fluorescence in 360-nm ultraviolet light. The lower stipe glows a rich orange-yellow. All these species are highly sought-after for dyeing wool because they can yield hard-to-get red colors.

Cortinarius salor Fries

Cortinarius salor, a small to medium-sized species, is found fairly frequently in conifer forests of our region. When it is fresh and young it is a most spectacular species, featuring a deep blue-lilac cap, gills, and stipe. In age the cap and the stipe often become ochraceous to yellow and the blue-lilac colors fade. The blue-lilac veil often leaves a slight zone near the stipe apex. Because of the viscid stipe and cap, *C. salor* has been considered a myxacium, but this is likely to change because its round spores and cap structure are similar to those of *C. anomalus* and a possible relationship has been supported by molecular data. *Cortinarius salor* is found in a wide range of forest types and comes in forms that quickly change to olive-yellow or ochraceous brown. Other myxaciums are discussed under *C. muscigenus*.

Cortinarius talus Fries

Cortinarius talus (subgenus *Phlegmacium*) and *C. multiformis* are closely related medium-sized species that, in Europe, are distinguished ecologically, the former occurring in hardwood forests as well as arctic and alpine habitats with dwarf birch, and the latter in acidic conifer forests. In PNW conifer forests, *C. multiformis* is the more common species, and is abundant in some years. It has dark ochraceous yellow to orange-brown or reddish brown caps, and its paler forms closely resemble *C. talus*. The latter typically has an ochraceous yellow to whitish yellow cap and pale stipe with a distinct basal bulb, and is not common, sometimes occurring in moist areas in subalpine forests. Both species have pale gills, bulbous white stipe base that sometimes has a slight rim, sparse white veil, white flesh, and a faint honey-like odor.

Cortinarius traganus (Fries: Fries) Fries

Given time, every PNW mushroom-hunter will find *Cortinarius traganus* (subgenus *Sericeocybe*) in our conifer forests. It is widespread and often abundant in the far-western montane and boreal regions but is much less frequent in the Rocky Mountains. Its

Cortinarius talus SAT-00-261-63

Cortinarius traganus, strongly lilac specimens SAT-01-278-30

Cortinarius traganus, rather pale specimens

coloration is peculiar in that the cap and stipe are pale lilac to blue-lilac, as is the veil, however, the gills are brown-yellow and the flesh is mottled saffron to brown-yellow. It has a fruity odor, although for some people this is hard to detect. Sometimes the cap develops white sectors, and *C. t. f. ochraceus* completely lacks lilac colors. *Cortinarius traganus* is similar to *C. camphoratus*, a completely blue-violet species with a very strong disagreeable odor, not unlike rotting potatoes.

Cortinarius vanduzerensis SAT-05-303-09

Cortinarius variosimilis SAT-00-312-43

Cortinarius vanduzerensis A. H. Smith and Trappe

Cortinarius vanduzerensis (subgenus *Myxacium*) was described from Oregon and is a very common species in coastal conifer forests from northern California to southern Canada. For many years, it was called by a European name, *C. elatior*. When fresh, it has an extremely glutinous cap and stipe. The cap is blackish brown to dark brown at first, then the margin fades to brown or yellow-brown and becomes wrinkled and deeply striate. The gills are pale brownish or rarely slightly lilac or gray-tinted, becoming brown and often wrinkled in age. The stipe is cylindrical to slightly spindle-shaped, white to yellowish brown, especially toward the base, and sometimes lilac at the apex, and the veil is typically lilac beneath the gluten. *Cortinarius vanduzerensis* is closely related to *C. stillatitius*, which is found in conifer and sometimes hardwood forests in Europe. Other myxaciums are discussed under *C. muscigenus*.

Cortinarius variosimilis M. M. Moser and Ammirati

Cortinarius variosimilis (subgenus *Phlegmacium*) is a close, but distinct, relative of *C. varius* of Europe. In many ways, it is a pale form of the latter, lacking the distinctly bright lilac-blue gills and the strong yellow-brown to orange-brown colors of the cap. *Cortinarius variosimilis* has a yellow-brown cap often with white veil remnants along the edge, the gills are pale lilac or almost lack lilac color, and become gray-brown. The stipe is clavate, white or pale pinkish buff, and often coated with wooly white veil material. Potassium hydroxide turns the white flesh bright yellow. *Cortinarius variosimilis* is one of the more common phlegmaciums in western North America, occurring both in Rocky Mountain spruce-fir forests and the forests of the Cascade and Coast ranges.

Cortinarius vibratilis (Fries: Fries) Fries

Cortinarius vibratilis has been classified in the subgenus *Myxacium*; however, recent studies suggest that it is not closely related to typical myxaciums, but instead forms a separate group with species such as *C. causticus* and *C. pluvius*. All these share a bitter taste, easily discovered by licking the viscid cap, and have medium-sized to small, rather fragile fruitbodies that feature red-brown, orange-brown, and yellow-brown caps with a whitish edge. The gills are whitish to pale ochraceous, and the stipe is usually cylindrical to narrowly clavate, and often tapered at the base, soft and white becoming yellowish, and glutinous. The veil is white. The spores are more or less elliptical, small, and finely ornamented. *Cortinarius vibratilis* is common in our conifer forests and can be particularly abundant in some areas.

Cortinarius violaceus (Linnaeus: Fries) S. F. Gray

Cortinarius violaceus (subgenus *Cortinarius*) is perhaps the most distinctive species in the genus. It has a dark violet, dry, scaly to tomentose cap with a somewhat metallic sheen. The close gills are deep violet, and the stipe is typically broadly club-shaped, dry and violet, with a bluish color on the base at times, and a veil that appears somewhat grayish. The flesh is violet with white mottling and the odor is distinctly of cedar wood. Often the stipe base darkens when handled. In Europe, two very similar species are recognized, *C. violaceus* in hardwood forests and *C. hercynicus* in conifer

Cortinarius vibratilis SAT-00-285-09

Cortinarius violaceus

Cortinarius violaceus

forests. The latter has almond-shaped to ellipsoid spores that are slightly narrower than those of the former. The form occurring in western North America may well represent a separate species, but that is yet to be determined. *Cortinarius violaceus* is widespread in older forests in our region, but much less common in the interior mountains than nearer the coast. In some years it is difficult to find, but in general it is commonly encountered, but usually in small numbers.

Rozites caperata (Persoon: Fries) P. Karsten
THE GYPSY

Traditionally, the genus *Rozites* was separated from *Cortinarius* because its species have membranous partial veils that form skirt-like rings rather than fibrillose cortinas. However, recent studies suggest that *Rozites* species nest within *Cortinarius*, so *C. caperatus* probably is a better name for this mushroom. *Rozites caperata* is distinctive among brown-spored mushrooms because of the persistent white membranous ring, and the white universal veil that often

Rozites caperata SAT-07-268-07

leaves a thin whitish coating on the cap and a slight membranous rim around the base of the stipe. The cap is brownish to brownish ocher, sometimes with whitish veil remnants at the center. The gills are pale brown to darker brown with pale edges and often appear crisped or wavy. The stipe is whitish to creamy or pale yellow-brown and fibrillose, especially below the ring. Sometimes the veil on the cap or the stipe apex has slight violet tones. *Rozites caperata* is commonly collected for food and it is very abundant to the north of us. It also is common in certain years in the PNW, but becomes less abundant inland and to the south.

GENUS *INOCYBE*

Inocybes are small to medium-sized, fleshy, terrestrial mushrooms. Most species are some shade of dull brown but some exhibit colors such as reddish brown, golden yellow, lilac, or white. A few undergo pronounced color changes when handled or upon aging. The cap usually is conical at first, expanding to bell-shaped or nearly plane, but even then an umbo usually persists. Its surface typically is dry, radially fibrillose, silky, wooly, or scaly and the edge often splits at maturity. The odor often is distinctive—spermatic, fishy, like green corn husks, even fruity at times—but not often radish-like. The gills are attached, usually pale cream, grayish, or tan at first and darker brown at maturity; the edges often are whitish and finely fringed (as a result of the abundant large cheilocystidia). The stipe often is powdery, at least at the apex; non-powdery portions are usually fibrillose or even wooly. There is no ring; if a veil is present (check the youngest individuals), then it will be fibrillose or cobwebby

Inocybe albodisca SAT-04-274-06

and usually disappears early. In some the stipe flares abruptly into a bulb. The spores are smooth, coarse-warty, angular, or with large lumps; they lack a germ pore. The edges of the gills usually are lined with large cystidia (cheilocystidia), and similar (pleuro)cystidia may occur on the face of the gills. The spore-print is dull medium brown, tobacco brown, or yellow-brown.

Inocybes differ from cortinariuses by the dull brown color of the spores, less obvious partial veil, and the smooth to lumpy (not roughened) spores. Although the stature of many of the smaller cortinariuses can be similar to that of inocybes, their colors are usually darker with red, purple, and black tones rather than the yellow-brown colors of inocybes. Inocybes differ from pholiotas by their terrestrial habit, lack of scales on the stipe, and by not growing in clusters. Hebelomas usually are larger and fleshier, have viscid caps, roughened spores, and often a radish-like odor. Other small brown mushrooms are less fleshy, and many grow on wood.

The limits of the genus *Inocybe* are fairly easy to draw, and even a novice mushroom hunter will soon be able to recognize an inocybe in the field. However, identifying them to species is another matter. Although, with experience, many species can be recognized, inocybes are generally not identifiable without microscopic examination. As Alexander Smith wrote, "Long ago mycologists despaired of classifying them on macroscopic characters because so many have the same dull brown to yellow-brown color, fibrillose and subconic pilei and the same stature. The characters of the spores and to some extent the cystidia, however, were found to be very contrasting and the species are now delimited largely on these in addition to the more striking macroscopic differences." These include the odor, color changes, extent of powderiness on the stipe, and presence of an abrupt bulb at the base of the stipe. Recent studies by Brandon Matheny, including DNA analyses, have led him to believe that the genus *Inocybe* should be elevated to the level of family, and several groups within the existing genus be elevated to genera in their own right. Fortunately the bulk of the species would remain in the genus *Inocybe*, which would reduce the need for name changes.

As far as is known, all inocybes are ectomycorrhizal and thus will be found near trees such as hemlock, spruce, fir, oak, and especially Douglas-fir. In our experience, they occur most frequently in young forests and are less prevalent in old-growth. For instance, *Inocybe lacera* can be exceedingly abundant in Douglas-fir plantations. Direct evidence about edibility is lacking, probably because inocybes are small, hard to identify, and usually do not occur in large numbers. Thus, they are not good targets for pot-hunters. However, it is thought that most, if not all, are poisonous (see Appendix 1).

Inocybe albodisca Peck

Inocybe albodisca's most distinctive feature is its two-toned, cream-on-brown coloration; the cap is smooth to silky-fibrillose, sometimes slightly moist, and pale grayish brown to pinkish brown (sometimes with a slight lilac tint) except at the center, which has a persistent creamy white superficial layer. The odor is spermatic. The gills are whitish when young, then become dingy pinkish or ashy brown with age, except for the edges which remain whitish. The stipe is similar in color to the brown or gray tones in the cap, sometimes paler and often with a slight pinkish tint; it is powdery over its entire length and has an abrupt white bulb at the base. The spores are elliptical to almost rectangular, lumpy with seven to nine small warts, and roughly 6–9 × 4.5–6 µm. Both cheilocystidia and pleurocystidia are abundant; they are thick-walled with the narrowed apex often encrusted; mixed among the cheilocystidia are thin-walled club-shaped cells (paracystidia). *Inocybe albodisca* has been reported from throughout the forested PNW, south to California, and east to New England. Some mycologists consider it to be synonymous with *I. grammata* (which name would have priority).

Inocybe assimilata (Britzelmayr) Saccardo

Inocybe assimilata (= *I. umbrina*) has a fibrillose umber cap that often bears faint grayish veil remnants. The odor is mild. The gills are creamy beige at first and later become grayish to reddish brown. The stipe is reddish brown, powdery at most at the apex, fibrillose over most of its length, and has a rounded bulb at its base. The spores are 6.5–9.5 × 4.5–6.5 µm and weakly nodulose; cheilocystidia and pleurocystidia are slender to slightly ovate with thick walls, slightly narrowed necks, and crystals on the apices. *Inocybe assimilata* is widespread in North America, Europe, and temperate Asia.

Inocybe chelanensis D. E. Stuntz

Inocybe chelanensis is a basic brown inocybe not obviously different from many others. However, it occurs in the mountains in spring and early summer, often near melting snow, and has large, distinctive bullet-shaped spores. The cap is yellowish brown and fibrillose, often with cracks on the margin. Sometimes the center is somewhat whitish. The stipe is powdery only at the apex, or not at all, and the odor is faint and has been variously described as spermatic, fungoid, and *Pelargonium*-like. The spores are 13–19 × 5–8 µm, with up to five nodules at the widened end of the bullet. *Inocybe chelanensis* occurs widely in the mountains of western North America.

Inocybe hirsuta var. *maxima* A. H. Smith

Often identified as *Inocybe calamistrata*, *I. hirsuta* var. *maxima* is a medium to large robust (for an inocybe), shaggy-scaly mushroom with reddish brown coloration; the flesh, stipe, and gills bruise reddish, and the base of the stipe is usually greenish blue. The odor usually is strong, a mix of fish and conifer resin. *Inocybe calamistrata* is very similar, but generally is smaller, less robust, lacks the reddish tints and bruising reaction, and more reliably has a green stipe base. Because of the similarities, some mycologists include *I. hirsuta* in *I. calamistrata*. The spores are smooth and elliptical to somewhat bean-shaped, 8–12 × 4.5–6 µm; cheilocystidia are simple, somewhat cylindric to slightly club-shaped, and occasionally somewhat capitate; pleurocystidia are lacking. The distribution of *I. hirsuta* is uncertain because of confusion with *I. calamistrata*. It is said to be common in the western U.S. and, in our experience, is more common than the latter species in the PNW. An association with hemlock has been noted, but it remains to be seen whether this is an obligate relationship.

Inocybe assimilata SAT-00-147-02

Inocybe chelanensis SAT-07-125-07

Inocybe hirsuta var. *maxima*

Inocybe lanuginosa (Bulliard: Fries)
P. Kummer

Although the photograph illustrates *Inocybe lanuginosa*, it could just as well be used for *I. leptophylla*, which is indistinguishable based on macroscopic characteristics. Both are rather small, densely scaly and, unusual for inocybes, usually are found on rotting wood. The odor varies from mild to unpleasant to spermatic. The two species are distinguished easily using microscopic characteristics. *Inocybe lanuginosa* has spores 8–10 µm long, with eight to 12 warts, and ovate, thick-walled, encrusted cheilocystidia and pleurocystidia. *Inocybe leptophylla* has spores 8.5–12 µm long, with 12 to 20 warts, thin-walled, slender cheilocystidia, and no pleurocystidia. The form of *I. lanuginosa* typically found in the PNW also is known as *I. ovatocystis*. Both *I. lanuginosa* and *I. leptophylla* are fairly common in the PNW, with the former occurring more frequently west of the Cascade crest and the latter more frequently on the east side.

Inocybe lanuginosa SAT-00-261-25

Inocybe mixtilis SAT-98-332-01

Inocybe mixtilis (Britzelmayr) Saccardo

Inocybe mixtilis has an ocher or honey-yellow cap that, when wet, is slightly slippery or greasy to the touch; the edge of the cap usually is not split or tattered. The odor is mild or faintly spermatic. The gills are grayish white at first and later become olivaceous brown. There is no veil. The stipe is whitish to pale yellowish, powdery along its entire length, and has an abrupt bulb at its base. The spores are 7.5–10 × 5.5–7 µm, with eight to 12 warts; cheilocystidia and pleurocystidia are ovate with thick walls, narrowed necks, and crystals on the apices; thin-walled, clavate cystidia are mixed among the cheilocystidia. This is one of the commoner inocybes on the Pacific Coast. It also occurs in Montana, eastern North America, and Europe.

Inocybe olympiana A. H. Smith

The most striking feature of *Inocybe olympiana* is a microscopic one. It has abundant huge pleurocystidia that turn bright yellow in potassium hydroxide—they look like mountain-islands emerging from a sea of basidia on the gill face. Macroscopically, *I. olympiana* is a fairly robust, shaggy-scaly, yellow-brown to tawny mushroom. The odor, if present, is faintly farinaceous. The stipe is powdery only at the apex, and has a rounded, often whitish, bulb at the base. The spores are smooth, somewhat irregularly shaped, and 7–9 × 4–5 µm; the cheilocystidia and pleurocystidia are thick-walled and the narrowed apices are encrusted with crystals. *Inocybe olympiana* appears to be restricted to west-side old-growth forests, where it is fairly common. It has also been reported from California. The eastern species *I. subochracea* is smaller, but otherwise very similar, and critical study is needed to assess the relationship between the two species; if only one species is involved, then *I. subochracea* would have priority.

Inocybe pusio P. Karsten

Inocybe pusio (= *I. obscura* var. *obscurissima*) is one of a small number of inocybes in which the stipes are lilac, at least in part (and then at the apex). This color can fade quickly, so having young fruitbodies is essential for a correct identification. The cap is relatively dark brown and coarsely fibrillose to somewhat scaly. Gills are light gray to slightly lilac-tinged when young, and become darker brown with age. The stipe is fibrillose, lilac when young (at least the upper part), brownish in the lower part with age, and the upper part powdery and often remaining whitish. The odor is faintly spermatic. The spores are smooth and somewhat almond-shaped, 7.5–11 × 4.5–6 µm; cheilocystidia and pleurocystidia are thick-walled with narrow, crystal-encrusted necks, and the cheilocystidia are interspersed with thin-walled, club- or pear-shaped cells. Similar species include *I. cincinnata* (= *I. cincinnatula*, *I. obscura*, *I. obscuroides*, *I. phaeocomis*), with red or brown fibrillose-scaly stipe, *I. lilacina*, lilac all over, at least when young, and *I. griseolilacina*, with a more grayish or slightly lilac overall color, *Pelargonium*-like odor, and non-powdery stipe. *Inocybe pusio* is said to be a hardwood associate in Europe; however, given the paucity of ectomycorrhizal hardwoods in the PNW (alder, cottonwood/aspen, and birch), it seems likely to also associate with conifers. The distributions of *I. pusio* and the other lilac-stiped species are not well known, in part because of the differing interpretations of the taxa.

Inocybe olympiana SAT-00-297-44

Inocybe pusio SAT-04-310-01

Inocybe rimosa SAT-00-251-26

Inocybe vaccina SAT-00-261-19

Inocybe xanthomelas SAT-99-328-01

Inocybe rimosa (Bulliard: Fries) P. Kummer

Inocybe rimosa is a highly variable species that has gone by many different names, including *I. fastigiata*. Its size ranges from fairly small to, more commonly, medium to large (for an inocybe) and it is relatively robust. The cap is cone-shaped at first and then expands, usually retaining a prominent broad umbo; color is (rarely) whitish to (usually) yellowish brown or tawny with the center remaining darker and somewhat reddish and the edges being more yellowish; the surface is rather silky, strongly fibrillose, and prone to extensive radial splitting (so it is rimose, hence the epithet). The odor is usually spermatic. The gills are pale grayish when young and eventually become dull coffee-brown. The stipe is whitish to pale yellowish, somewhat fibrillose, powdery at the apex, and has a slightly enlarged base, but not an abrupt bulb. The spores are smooth, elliptical or somewhat bean-shaped, 9–15 × 5–8.5 µm; the cheilocystidia are thin-walled and cylindrical to somewhat club-shaped; pleurocystidia are lacking. *Inocybe sororia* is very similar but has brighter yellow coloration and an odor of green corn. *Inocybe rimosa* occurs widely with a broad assortment of trees and often is common.

Inocybe vaccina Kühner

Inocybe vaccina is distinctive because of the rusty orange or bright orange tints in the cap. Such tones are unusual in *Inocybe*. The cap is small to medium-sized, smooth to finely scaly, and often with a wavy paler-colored margin. Odor is lacking or faintly spermatic. Gills are pale grayish when young and darken to olivaceous brown. The stipe is whitish at first, then darkens to yellow-brown, powdery over almost its entire length, and has a slightly thickened base. The spores are smooth, almond- to orange-seed-shaped, 8.5–11.5 × 4.5–6.5 µm; cheilocystidia and pleurocystidia are thick-walled, with crystals encrusting the narrowed tips. *Inocybe vaccina* is said to be rare in Europe and appears to be rare, or at least not often recognized, in the PNW.

Inocybe xanthomelas Boursier and Kühner

Inocybe xanthomelas has a light yellowish brown cap that may be slightly cracked at the edge. The odor is somewhat oily and, unusual for an inocybe, radish-like. The gills are ocher to slightly grayish violet at first and later become grayish brown. There is no veil. The stipe is light yellowish brown, powdery along its entire length, has an abrupt bulb at its base, and darkens to gray or blackish upon drying. The spores are 9–11.5 × 7.5–9 µm, with eight to 12 warts; cheilocystidia and pleurocystidia are ovate with thick walls, narrowed necks, and crystals on the apices. *Inocybe xanthomelas* also occurs in Europe.

GENUS *PHAEOCOLLYBIA*

If the entire mushroom is excavated and the spore color noted, then *Phaeocollybia* is one of the easier mushroom genera to recognize. Phaeocollybias are medium-sized to large, terrestrial, forest mushrooms that often grow in large troops or close-packed groups. The cap usually is viscid or glutinous when moist, conic with an inrolled or strongly incurved margin at first, and

Phaeocollybia attenuata SAT-00-262-06

retains an umbo as it expands. Typical colors include bright orange-brown, rusty brown, liver brown, or olivaceous brown to greenish, but most become uniformly rusty brown with age. Typically both cap and stipe have brittle cartilaginous flesh. The gills are narrowly attached, pallid, pale orangish, or lilac at first, and rusty brown or cinnamon at maturity. The stipe has a cartilaginous rind, making it rather brittle or sometimes pliable, and a very long tapered base that extends well down into the soil. As much as 90% of the stipe can be below-ground. Most other gilled mushrooms with root-like stipes have white spores. Neither partial nor universal veils are present. The spores are cinnamon to rusty brown, somewhat spherical or lemon-shaped to elliptical to almond-shaped, roughened, and lack both a germ pore and plage. Cystidia are present, at least on the gill edges.

Phaeocollybias are ectomycorrhizal, associating primarily or exclusively with conifers such as Sitka spruce, especially in old-growth forests. They are rare or lacking in many parts of the world, but are diverse and fairly abundant in the PNW. Until recently, they have received little study but work by Lorelei Norvell is leading to a better understanding of the different species and their ecological occurrence. Identification of many species, however, requires young specimens and microscopic examination and, even then, often is difficult. Little is known about their edibility.

Phaeocollybia attenuata (A. H. Smith) Singer

Phaeocollybia attenuata is one of the smaller phaeocollybias and, at first glance, the small conical caps might be mistaken for a mycena or galerina. However, the extremely long slender stipe and the relatively tough fleshy cap with no sign of translucent-striation clearly identify it as a phaeocollybia. The cap is orangish brown to tawny when young and darkens with age; the surface is smooth and moist to viscid. It has a distinctive odor said by Lorelei Norvell to be a combination of potato, pansy, and burnt hair. The stipe is very slender at the apex and thins to a hair-like "root" that is tough and pliable; it is smooth and dark-colored, from brownish above to black below. The spores are somewhat lemon-shaped, distinctly roughened, and 7–9 µm long; the cheilocystidia are thin-walled and club-shaped; clamp connections are absent. *Phaeocollybia attenuata* often occurs in large troops, especially in lower-elevation spruce-rich forests. It apparently is restricted to the Pacific Coast, being most abundant from B.C. to central Oregon and less abundant in southern Oregon and northern California.

Phaeocollybia lilacifolia A. H. Smith

Phaeocollybia lilacifolia is generally larger than *P. attenuata*, but does not reach the large size attained by species such as *P. ammiratii* and *P. kauffmanii*. The young cap is dark brown and glutinous with an odor that is penetrating but hard to characterize. The gills are lilac when young, a feature shared by only a few other phaeocollybias. The stipe gradually narrows downward, but does not become hair-like as in *P. attenuata*; it is purplish or pale brownish and shiny when young, and becomes stuffed with cottony to fibrillose pith when mature. The spores are lemon-shaped, distinctly roughened, and about 8.5 µm long; the cheilocystidia are thin-walled and broadly club-shaped; clamp connections are absent. It is not a common species, occurring as solitary or scattered individuals in old-growth forests. *Phaeocollybia fallax* is very similar but has greenish tones in the young caps; it has been suggested that it might represent a color variant of *P. lilacifolia*. *Phaeocollybia rifflipes* also is very similar, but generally smaller with a floral odor and slightly smaller (about 7–7.5 µm long) spores. Other generally similar species lack the lilac gill coloration.

Phaeocollybia piceae A. H. Smith and Trappe

Phaeocollybia piceae is similar in size, stature, and habit to *P. lilacifolia*, but differs in coloration and other less obvious features. The cap is bright orange to red-orange and moist to viscid when young; the young gills are pale orange. The odor is mild or somewhat penetrating. The stipe gradually narrows downward but does not become hair-like; it is orangish when young, longitudinally lined, sometimes shiny, and becomes stuffed with cottony pith when mature. The spores are lemon-shaped, distinctly roughened, and about 9.5 µm long; the cheilocystidia thin-walled and cylindrical to slightly club-shaped; clamp connections are absent. It is somewhat common in southern B.C., occurring as solitary individuals or groups in old-growth forests with abundant Sitka spruce (hence the epithet, from *Picea*, spruce). Southward, it becomes progressively less abundant, more scattered, and can occur in forests lacking spruce. The modest size, bright coloration, lack of growth in large dense groups, and frequent occurrence with spruce help distinguish *P. piceae* from otherwise similar phaeocollybias.

Phaeocollybia lilacifolia SAT-01-293-32

Phaeocollybia piceae SAT-00-284-60

GENUS *PHOLIOTA*

Pholiota is the largest genus of brown-spored, wood-inhabiting gilled mushrooms and so pholiotas are frequently encountered in PNW forests. They are mostly medium-sized to large mushrooms usually found on snags (or sometimes living trees), logs, or woody debris. However, a few species typically occur on soil and others can appear terrestrial when they grow on buried wood. Fruitbodies range in color from pale or

Pholiota alnicola SAT-00-284-56

bright yellowish to golden, rusty yellow, or rusty brown. The stipe is centrally attached, either slender or stout, but always fleshy. The cap often is viscid to glutinous and the cap and stipe often are scaly. A partial veil is present in young specimens but only infrequently does a skirt-like ring persist on the stipe. More typically a slight ring-zone of collapsed fibrils will remain, sometimes colored brownish by accumulating spores. The spores are dull brown, sometimes with a rusty tinge, but never purple-brown, chocolate, or blackish. Microscopically, the spores are mostly elliptical and smooth, and usually have a germ pore. Cheilocystidia are present and usually pleurocystidia are too. Sometimes the latter have golden yellow contents and then they are referred to as chrysocystidia.

Pholiotas can be distinguished (sometimes with difficulty) from other brown-spored wood-rotters as follows.

- Gymnopiluses have dry caps, brighter rusty to orangish brown spores, usually bitter-tasting flesh, and ornamented spores without a germ pore.
- Galerinas and tubarias are usually smaller and much less fleshy, and their caps typically are translucent-striate and hygrophanous.
- Crepidotuses are shelf-like with very reduced, laterally attached stipes and have no veil.
- Hypholomas and stropharias often are similar in stature to pholiotas but have darker spores, usually with purplish or chocolate tints.

- Psathyrellas also have dark spores and most have hygrophanous caps and relatively fragile, non-fleshy stipes.

Other medium to large brown-spored mushrooms can be distinguished from pholiotas by their growth primarily on soil and/or in leaf litter. In addition, cortinariuses have often brighter rusty brown spores that are rough-surfaced, mostly (but not always) lack the yellowish colors, and do not often grow in clusters with their bases clearly joined. Hebelomas usually are stockier, with mostly pale, dull brown colors lacking yellow components, and often have earthy radish-like odors. Their spores, like those of cortinariuses, are rough-surfaced. Inocybes only rarely occur on wood, are small (at most medium-sized), and usually have umbonate caps that are fibrillose or fibrillose-scaly with ragged splitting edges. Many of them have lumpy-warty spores. Phaeocollybias have long root-like stipes and caps that often are glutinous and retain their conical shape well into maturity. The larger species of *Agrocybe* are similar to some pholiotas but differ in having a cap cuticle made up of club-shaped cells rather than interwoven hyphae.

Although none of the pholiotas are known to be dangerously toxic, several have been reported to cause digestive upset, and we are unaware of any PNW species that are highly sought-after edibles.

Pholiota alnicola (Fries) Singer
Pholiota alnicola is a medium-sized to sometimes large species that grows in small to large groups or clusters on rotting wood or on soil containing woody debris. It is usually yellow when young and becomes more brownish yellow or olivaceous with age,

especially the stipes. The caps are smooth and moist to viscid, but typically not glutinous, and may be somewhat hygrophanous, especially near the margin. The stipes may have a somewhat fibrillose shaggy appearance but are not scaly. Some collections exhibit a fragrant odor, somewhat reminiscent of grapefruit or tangerine, while others have no distinct odor. Taste is mild, contrary to the concept formed by some mycologists. Recent studies in Europe have shown *P. alnicola* to be a highly variable species and so several other species, including *P. malicola*, may merely be variants of it. *Pholiota flavida*, in its original sense, probably is the same species; however, various authors have used the latter name for seemingly different entities, so use of *P. alnicola* in its place has been recommended. *Pholiota alnicola* in a broad sense is widely distributed in the temperate and boreal areas of the Northern Hemisphere.

Pholiota astragalina (Fries) Singer
Pholiota astragalina is easy to recognize by the distinctive pinkish orange color of its cap, which is unique among pholiotas and

Pholiota astragalina SAT-01-293-21

not at all common among other mushrooms. It is relatively small and usually grows singly or in small groups (two to four mushrooms) or clusters on conifer logs. The cap flesh is orange, turns blackish in age, and is bitter-tasting. It looks very much like a hypholoma, but its brown spore color causes it to be placed in *Pholiota*. It grows throughout the PNW and is fairly common, although usually not abundant. It occurs widely in the temperate and boreal areas of the Northern Hemisphere.

Pholiota aurivella SAT-99-229-19

Pholiota decorata SAT-99-292-03

Pholiota aurivella (Batsch: Fries) P. Kummer

Pholiota aurivella is perhaps the most noticeable of the pholiotas. It is large, bright yellow to golden yellow-orange when young, and grows in large clusters on live trees, snags, and logs of conifers and hardwoods. The cap is viscid when young, and bears dark brown or reddish brown scales that contrast with the yellow cap color. The stipe is whitish, or somewhat yellowish, and scaly below the ring-zone. *Pholiota adiposa* is another name for the same fungus and some mycologists feel it is preferable. To further confuse matters, *P. limonella* is virtually identical in appearance, but has somewhat smaller spores and is incompatible in laboratory mating studies. Many other species have been named in North America; several (*P. abietis*, *P. connata*, *P. subvelutipes*) have been shown to be variants of *P. limonella*, and it remains to be seen whether the others merit species status or are variants of *P. aurivella* or *P. limonella*. Mating studies and close attention to ecological occurrence would help clarify the matter. Given the difficulties in assigning species names, it is difficult to know the distributions of these species. However, these large yellow pholiotas are a common feature of the northern temperate and boreal forests. *Pholiota aurivella* has been listed as edible, but David Arora reported that several people had experienced gastric upsets and that the taste of the mushrooms resembled "marshmallows without the sugar."

Pholiota decorata (Murrill) A. H. Smith and Hesler

Pholiota decorata is characterized by its small to medium-sized, variably brownish colors, and growth singly or in small to large groups on conifer (or sometimes hardwood) debris such as twigs and small branches. Although highly variable, the color of the cap usually is much paler, sometimes almost white, near the margin, and overall colors seem to be paler during wet weather than when conditions are dry. The cap usually is moist to viscid and streaky-fibrillose or scaly, at least when young, as the scales often disappear with age. *Pholiota decorata* is very common in the PNW and occurs widely in the conifer forests of western North America. Whether it occurs elsewhere remains to be seen.

Pholiota flammans (Fries) P. Kummer

Pholiota flammans is distinguished easily by its overall brilliant yellow to orange-yellow color and rough scaly texture; even the scales are yellow. It is a small to medium-sized mushroom that grows singly or in small clusters on logs, particularly western hemlock in the PNW. Other yellow species such as *P. aurivella*, are not quite so bright, are larger, less scaly with dark scales, and have whitish or pale yellowish stipes. *Pholiota flammans* grows throughout the PNW and is fairly common, though usually not abundant. It occurs widely in the temperate and boreal areas of the Northern Hemisphere.

Pholiota highlandensis (Peck)

Quadraccia

Pholiota highlandensis is one of several mushrooms that occur on burnt ground, often in or around campfire sites. It is small to medium-sized, with a viscid to glutinous cinnamon-brown, brick-brown, or orange-brown cap with paler margin. The stipe is somewhat wooly or scaly, whitish at first, and later yellowish to almost rusty brown,

partly due to the accumulation of spores. It is rather variable in size, cap color, and the color and degree of development of the veil. Thus, several other species have been described, including *P. carbonaria*, *P. fulvozonata*, and *P. luteobadia*; however, they differ only slightly from *P. highlandensis* and may merely represent variants of it. *Pholiota highlandensis* has a long fruiting season and

Pholiota flammans

Pholiota highlandensis

Pholiota lignicola SAT-07-159-05

Pholiota mutabilis, note the scaly stipe
SAT-92-210-07

Pholiota mutabilis, note the clustered habit

occurs in both spring and fall. It is common in the PNW and occurs widely in North America, Europe, Japan, and no doubt elsewhere.

Pholiota lignicola (Peck) Jacobsson

Both *Pholiota lignicola* (= *P. vernalis*) and *P. mutabilis* (Scopoli: Fries) P. Kummer usually grow in large clusters on logs or snags—typically on conifers in the PNW, but they also can occur on hardwoods. *Pholiota lignicola* most often fruits in the spring and early summer, often in the mountains near melting snow. It does not have a ring, but may have a fibrillose ring-zone on an otherwise fairly smooth stipe. *Pholiota mutabilis* generally fruits in fall, has a ring, at least when young, and scales on the stipe below the ring. Both of these differ from most pholiotas by being translucent-striate when young, hygrophanous, and dull brown without obvious yellowish or rusty tones. In addition, their spores are truncate and have larger germ pores than those of other pholiotas. For these reasons, many mycologists place them in the genus *Kuehneromyces*. Both occur widely in the temperate and boreal areas of the Northern Hemisphere and are fairly common in the PNW and Rocky Mountains; elsewhere *P. mutabilis* is the more common of the two. Both are said to be edible, but neither is particularly popular to our knowledge. The possibility of confusing them with the deadly poisonous *Galerina marginata* is good reason to avoid them.

Pholiota populnea (Persoon: Fries) Kuyper and Tjallingii-Beukers

Pholiota populnea (= *P. destruens*) is a relatively large, bulky, distinctive species found singly or, more often, in clusters on cottonwood logs along streams and rivers or in urban and suburban settings. The entire mushroom is very fleshy and has a rather hard texture, especially the stipe. If the brown color of the spores and the substrate are recognized, this species can hardly be confused with any other. It occurs widely throughout the temperate and boreal areas of the Northern Hemisphere and is said to be edible, but with a poor flavor.

Pholiota spumosa (Fries) Singer

Pholiota spumosa is small to medium-sized, rather slender with a stipe that is often long relative to the size of the cap, and has a viscid, more or less two-toned cap, yellow-brown or red-brown in the center and bright yellow or greenish yellow near the margin. The stipe and gills also are bright yellow when young, and the stipe remains more or less smooth. The gills gelatinize in age and can be stretched like a rubber band. Some forms have a strong fungusy or green-corn odor, while others are mild. *Pholiota spumosa* grows in often very large groups on the ground, usually among wood chips, bark chips, or other woody debris. We have seen it fruit abundantly near slash piles at logging sites, as well as among wood or bark chips in landscaped areas. It is common in the PNW and widespread throughout the temperate and boreal areas of the Northern Hemisphere.

Pholiota terrestris Overholts

As its name indicates, *Pholiota terrestris* usually grows on the ground, not obviously on wood. Despite the terrestrial occurrence, its growth in often dense clusters, brownish coloration, overall scaliness, presence of a veil when young, and dull brown spores readily identify it as a pholiota and, in fact,

Pholiota populnea SAT-06-290-10

Pholiota spumosa SAT-06-287-05

Pholiota terrestris SAT-99-301-21

it is the only species of mushroom to regularly combine all those characteristics. Several psathyrellas grow in clusters on soil, but they have darker spores, are less fleshy, and generally are not scaly. *Pholiota terrestris* is common in the PNW and California, often occurring among grasses at the edges of roads or parking areas in hard-packed soil. It also occurs in the Great Lakes area and Japan. Whether it occurs elsewhere remains to be seen. It is reported to be edible, but we know of no one who seeks it out.

OTHER BROWN-SPORED GILLED MUSHROOMS

Agrocybe praecox (Persoon: Fries)
Fayod

The genus *Agrocybe* includes small to medium-sized, dull-colored, generally fleshy mushrooms, characterized by rusty brown, tobacco brown, or dark earthy brown spores and smooth caps when young (but often cracking like dry mud as they age). Microscopically, the spores are smooth and have a large germ pore, and the cap cuticle is composed of close-packed, inflated hyphal ends. Stropharias and pholiotas have a range of spore colors which can be similar to those of some agrocybes; however, both stropharias and pholiotas have a filamentous cap cuticle. Thus, without a microscope, it can sometimes be very difficult to tell the yellowish brown stropharias apart from agrocybes. Psathyrellas have a similar cuticle but generally have much more fragile flesh and darker, often purplish, spores.

Agrocybe praecox typically is a medium-sized fleshy mushroom that frequently grows in dense groups of single fruitbodies or small clusters. It is very common in

Agrocybe praecox SAT-07-114-01

newly landscaped areas containing mulch or wood chips and, as its name indicates, appears in spring or early summer (*praecox* is Latin for "early"). The cap is pale yellowish brown to buff, smooth, and may have slight veil remnants on its edge when young; in age it often cracks especially when the weather is dry. The stipe is whitish, longitudinally lined, often bears a fragile, disappearing ring, and usually connects to thick white mycelial cords in the soil. *Agrocybe praecox* is edible but often has a somewhat bitter taste. Several other agrocybes are hard to distinguish from *A. praecox*; *A. acericola* has a dark yellow cap, better developed persistent ring, and is found on logs and buried wood. *Agrocybe dura* has larger spores ($10–14 \times 6.5–7.5$ vs. $8.5–10.5 \times 5.5–6.5$ µm) and somewhat fatter cheilocystidia and pleurocystidia. *Agrocybe smithii* also has larger spores ($11–13 \times 5–7$ µm) and lacks a partial veil.

Agrocybe semiorbicularis (Bulliard: Saint-Amans) Fayod

Probably better known as *Agrocybe pediades*, *A. semiorbicularis* is a small variable mushroom that grows in grass, often in the company of species such as *Panaeolus foenisecii*. It has a hemispherical, slightly viscid cap that may crack somewhat in age and occasionally bears slight whitish veil remnants. The veil does not form a ring. Although several very similar species have been described, the wide variation that occurs prevents them from being clearly separable from each other, and so it seems better to apply one name and accept the variability associated with it. *Agrocybe semiorbicularis* is said by some to be edible, but there seems to be little point in eating it, and we are not aware of anyone who does.

Conocybe filaris (Fries) Kühner

Conocybes are small delicate mushrooms with slender stipes, often conical caps, and bright rusty brown spores, and they often occur on dung or rich soil. Many of the defining features are microscopic—cap cuticle composed of hyphae with the appearance of soap bubbles (a cellular cuticle); smooth, thick-walled spores with germ pore; and capitate or flask-shaped cheilocystidia. Thus, as Alexander Smith wrote, "The species are difficult to identify and the distinctions are often made on microscopic

Agrocybe semiorbicularis SAT-07-149-01

Conocybe filaris SAT-98-044-03

characters so that it is not practical for the amateur to attempt to do more than recognize the genus." To add to the difficulty, the genus has been little studied in North America. *Conocybe filaris* is representative of a number of conocybes that have membranous rings and flask-shaped cheilocystidia and are placed in a separate genus, *Pholiotina*, by some mycologists. *Conocybe filaris* is distinguished by the relatively small size of its cap (3–12 mm) and spores (6.5–9.5 × 4–5 μm). All the ringed conocybes are thought to contain the same lethal toxins as *Amanita phalloides* and the other destroying angels (see Appendix 1) and, thus, pose a serious hazard to consumers of little brown mushrooms for their psychoactive properties.

Conocybe aurea (J. Schaeffer) Hongo

Conocybe aurea is representative of the mainstream conocybes and is related to the widespread and common *C. tenera* complex. It has vivid apricot-yellow, orange-yellow, or pale orange, relatively large (up to 5 cm, 2 in., or more) caps that are often shiny at first. The stipe is cream to pale yellow-brown and pruinose, the gills cream-colored and becoming rust-brown in age. The large (10–13 × 6–7.5 μm) smooth spores are somewhat almond-shaped. *Conocybe aurea* can occur abundantly in commercial compost applied in home landscaping. The most commonly encountered conocybe in our experience is *C. lactea* (= *C. apala*); it has a narrower, more conical, whitish cap, is extremely fragile, and grows in lawns.

Galerina marginata (Batsch) Kühner

The genus *Galerina* comprises an array of very small to medium-sized brown species that are notoriously difficult to identify without a microscope. Many are mycena-like, but larger species have dome-shaped caps and somewhat thicker stipes and are more collybia-like. The species are often uniformly colored yellow-brown to darker brown, often the cap edge is translucent-striate when fresh, and in age the cap fades to tan or brownish buff from the loss of moisture. Most species have a veil, but it is often lost as the fruitbody matures, and only in certain species leaves patches or zones on the stipe. All galerinas have rich brown to rust-brown spores. Many are associated with mosses; others occur on wood or wood chips or coarse litter. Galerinas occupy a variety of habitats including forests, sphagnum bogs, arctic and alpine tundra, parks and gardens on wood chips, and lawns where grasses and mosses co-mingle.

Galerina marginata is a medium-sized species with a dome-shaped, brown to yellow-brown cap that is smooth, slightly viscid to moist, striate along the edge when fresh, and fades to tan or buff. The gills and stipe are brown, and the veil sometimes leaves a fibrillose ring-zone on the stipe. The fruitbodies often occur in clusters or

Conocybe aurea SAT-01-289-01

groups but can be scattered or solitary as well, occurring on stumps and logs of conifers and hardwoods, or growing from pieces of buried wood, wood chips, or other woody debris. Several names have been applied to this mushroom in North America, including *G. autumnalis* (probably the most familiar name), *G. venenata*, and *G. unicolor*. By any name it is just as deadly, containing the same toxins found in *Amanita phalloides* (see Appendix 1). Thus, mushroom-hunters need to be aware of *G. marginata*, especially those in search of magic mushrooms: at least one death and several close calls have occurred in our region as a result of mistaking it for a psychoactive species such as *Psilocybe stuntzii*. It could also be mistaken for a honey mushroom, although it is usually much smaller and has brown, not white, spores.

Gymnopilus bellulus (Peck) Murrill

Gymnopilus includes small to large mushrooms that mostly are bright yellow, yellow-brown, or orange-brown, have bright orange-brown to yellow-brown spores, and occur on wood or woody debris. These types are fairly easy to recognize as gymnopiluses. However, some species are differently colored, and some occur on non-woody substrates such as among mosses or grasses. If a veil is present, it usually is a quick-disappearing fibrillose one, but occasionally is more membranous and forms a skirt-like ring. The spores usually are roughened, similar to those of cortinariuses.

Gymnopilus bellulus is a small to medium-sized species with an orange-brown to yellow-brown, smooth cap with slightly striate edge. The gills are bright yellow to dull yellow then rusty yellow as the spores mature,

and sometimes have rusty spots and brownish stains. The stipe is red-brown with a yellowish apex and whitish longitudinal fibrils on the lower portion. It does not have a noticeable veil, and the taste is somewhat bitter. *Gymnopilus bellulus* has been reported from Europe and North America on conifer logs and stumps.

Gymnopilus penetrans (Fries) Murrill

Gymnopilus penetrans is a medium-sized typical gymnopilus that is common and widespread on conifer and hardwood stumps,

Galerina marginata SAT-01-279-08

Gymnopilus bellulus SAT-97-297-09

logs, wood chips, and sawdust. The cap is smooth to slightly scaly and brownish orange-yellow to reddish yellow or pale red-brown, usually with a lighter edge when expanded. The gills are yellowish and often become red-spotted with age. The stipe is whitish to yellowish and typically becomes reddish brown below; often there are whitish veil fibrils on the surface. The veil is whitish to pale yellowish and usually disappears as the fruitbody develops, although some specimens retain a slight fibrillose ring. The flesh is very bitter, and white

Gymnopilus penetrans SAT-00-251-23

Gymnopilus ventricosus, fruiting from a stump cut off at ground level

cords often extend from the stipe base into the substrate. Some mycologists have separated several very similar species from *G. penetrans*, including *G. sapineus*, with a scalier cap, and *G. hybridus*, with a fibrillose ring and spotted gills.

Gymnopilus ventricosus (Earle) Hesler

Several very large gymnopiluses have bright yellow-orange to rusty orange, minutely fibrillose-scaly caps; thick, yellow, bitter flesh; yellow to rusty orange gills; and large, thick, orange-yellow to brownish stipes with a distinct membranous ring. These often grow in clusters and can be very spectacular, sprouting from rotting logs, snags, or stumps. Two such species occur in our region. The more common one is *Gymnopilus ventricosus*, which has caps reaching the size of dinner plates and very thick stipes that are enlarged in the middle and have a prominent, often spore-covered, membranous ring. The less common species in our region, *G. junonius* (= *G. spectabilis*), occurs on both conifer and hardwood substrates and typically is somewhat smaller with a thinner stipe. These large gymnopiluses share the common name big laughing gym, for their assumed hallucinogenic properties. *Gymnopilus ventricosus* apparently is not psychoactive, though *G. junonius* may be (specimens from Japan and eastern North America are reportedly hallucinogenic, but European populations are often inactive). More study is needed to ascertain the distribution of these species and determine their toxic properties. These large gymnopiluses could be confused with large cluster-forming pholiotas, but consideration of their yellow-orange color and bright spores should lead to the correct genus.

Hebeloma incarnatulum A. H. Smith
Hebelomas are mostly stocky, medium-sized, fleshy mushrooms (some tending toward small and others tending toward large) with cream to medium brown colors, smooth viscid caps, and often a radish-like odor. They are ectomycorrhizal and thus grow on the ground in forests, or at least near trees. They are most likely to be confused with inocybes, which have dry fibrillose to scaly caps, different odors, and differently shaped spores and cheilocystidia, or cortinariuses, which have brighter colored spores, better developed cobwebby veils, much less prominent cheilocystidia, and different overall coloration. This is another genus that, with experience, can be recognized in the field but requires microscopic examination to identify species and, even then, the task can be very difficult as only a portion of the genus has been studied critically in North America. Some species definitely are poisonous and all of them might be. Most medium-sized hebelomas get identified as *Hebeloma crustuliniforme*; however, if European experience is any indication (and it might not be), this species is much less common than usually thought. One apparently common PNW species that has been misidentified as *H. crustuliniforme* is *H. incarnatulum*. The presence of a basal bulb, spores that turn dark reddish brown when placed in Melzer's reagent under the microscope, and narrow, not club-shaped, cheilocystidia in *H. incarnatulum* and more conspicuous droplets on the edge of the gills of *H. crustuliniforme* separate them. *Hebeloma incarnatulum* seems to have a special fondness for mossy areas, sphagnum or otherwise. It occurs in northern Europe, and was described from the Great Lakes region, so probably occurs throughout much of the north temperate and boreal areas of the Northern Hemisphere.

Melanophyllum haematospermum
   (Bulliard: Fries) Kreisel
Melanophyllum is a tiny genus (with only two or three species) whose species are somewhat reminiscent of cystodermas or lepiotas both of which, however, have white spores. Melanophyllums are small mushrooms with somewhat powdery cap and lower stipe, free gills, flesh that smells like cucumber, and unusual blue-green, olive,

Hebeloma incarnatulum SAT-00-261-56

Melanophyllum haematospermum SAT-01-321-19

or green spores that dry to reddish or purplish brown. They are decomposers and are found in a variety of habitats including forests, greenhouses, and manure piles. Once the genus is recognized, the bright red gills cinch the identification of *M. haematospermum* (= *M. echinatum*). We have no information concerning its edibility.

Naucoria escharioides (Fries: Fries)
P. Kummer

Many different mushrooms have been placed in *Naucoria*, including, at one time, those now in *Phaeocollybia*. In recent years, however, *Naucoria* has been restricted to species of small, somewhat fragile, brown-spored mushrooms commonly found under alder and willow. Because there still is confusion over what a naucoria is, that name is likely to be replaced by *Alnicola*. The commonest species under red alder in our region is *N. escharioides* (= *Alnicola melinoides*). The cap is pale yellowish to yellowish brown, usually with a pale margin, the close gills are creamy white to yellowish brown, and the stipe also is yellowish brown, but often darker brown toward the base, and

Naucoria escharioides SAT-00-313-85

often with whitish veil fibrils when fresh. The flesh is watery and there is no distinct odor. The spores are rather large (over 9 μm long), ornamented, and almond-shaped with a pointed apex, and cheilocystidia are abundant, enlarged below and with a narrow extension that sometimes has a slight cap-shaped apex. Another of the several naucorias in our area is *N. salicis*, which is found in association with willow; it is dark reddish brown to chocolate-colored and has two-spored basidia.

Paxillus involutus (Batsch: Fries) Fries

Traditionally the genus *Paxillus* included brown-spored species with yellowish buff to yellow-brown spores and decurrent gills that are forked, connected by cross-veins, or pore-like near the stipe, and that are easily separated from the flesh of the cap. Currently, however, the wood-rotting species are placed in a separate genus, *Tapinella*, while the ectomycorrhizal species remain in *Paxillus*. Both genera appear to be related to some of the boletes.

Paxillus involutus is a medium to large species characterized by a yellowish brown to olive-brown or reddish brown cap that often is coated with soft matted hairs at first. The cap margin is persistently inrolled (hence the epithet). The gills are decurrent, yellowish to yellowish brown, and the stipe is similar in color to the cap. All parts of the fruitbody stain brown to reddish brown when handled or in age. *Paxillus involutus* occurs in natural forest in our region but is not common there. It is much more common and abundant in parks and landscape areas, where it is typically associated with birches, often along with *Leccinum scabrum* and *Lactarius plumbeus*. Species of

Paxillus can cause hemolysis (destruction of red blood cells) if eaten repeatedly and have been responsible for deaths in Europe. Therefore, they should be strictly avoided as edibles.

Tapinella atrotomentosa (Batsch: Fries) Šutara

Tapinella atrotomentosa grows from rotting conifer stumps, snags, and logs. The cap is dark brown and velvety when young, becomes paler and smoother in age, and can be quite large. The stipe is thick, rather short, off-center or laterally attached, and has a velvety dark brown to blackish brown surface. The gills are cream to yellowish to brownish yellow, stain brownish in age, and often are forked or form pores near the stipe. The flesh is yellowish and has an acrid taste. *Tapinella atrotomentosa* is common in our region. It first appears during early summer if we have sufficient rain and persists through fall. Also occurring in the PNW is *T. panuoides*, a smaller pleurotoid species that grows on conifer logs, wood chips, and rich accumulations of humus.

Phaeolepiota aurea (Mattuschka: Fries) P. Kummer

If there was a prize for easiest mushroom to identify, *Phaeolepiota aurea* certainly would be a contender. Its large size, golden color, powdery surface, skirt-like ring, brown spores, and tendency to grow in large groups are distinctive. It is not common, usually being found in disturbed areas of forests, such as along roadsides. When found, however, it is often present in large numbers. It is said to be edible for most people but to cause digestive upset in some. It is widely distributed in the north temperate zone.

Paxillus involutus SAT-03-271-02

Tapinella atrotomentosa SAT-05-259-03

Phaeolepiota aurea

Tubaria furfuracea SAT-98-351-01

Tubaria furfuracea (Persoon: Fries)
Gillet

Tubaria furfuracea and closely related species are differentiated from other small brown-spored mushrooms by their combination of often decurrent gills, cinnamon or reddish brown, strongly hygrophanous caps, sparse whitish veil remnants, and, microscopically, the thin-walled smooth spores that tend to collapse when mounted in potassium hydroxide. They are decomposers and occur in a variety of habitats, including wood chips and mossy lawns, often appearing later in the fall than most mushrooms, after the weather has turned cold. Some European mycologists split *T. furfuracea* into several different species based on ecology and minor differences in cheilocystidium shape and spore size. We use the name in a very broad sense here. *Tubaria confragosa* differs in often having a membranous ring and darker thicker-walled spores. It is related to the wine-red *T. punicea* and *T. vinicolor*.

Dark-Spored Gilled Mushrooms

Key to Dark-Spored Gilled Mushroom Groups

1. Spores in mass dark chocolate-brown to purple-brown 2
1. Spores in mass black 4

2. Cap surface hygrophanous, when dry, appearing to be covered with small shiny particles; stipe often whitish and usually quite fragile . . . . **Genus** *Psathyrella* (page 199)
2. Cap surface hygrophanous or not, but not with shiny particles; stipe either not whitish, not fragile, or neither 3

3. Gills free, usually whitish to pinkish when young, stipe and cap cleanly separable (like a ball and socket joint); skirt-like ring usually present on stipe; growing on soil, not often clustered or in large numbers . . . . **Genus** *Agaricus* (page 188)
3. Gills attached, stipe and cap not cleanly separable; skirt-like ring may be present, but more often a ring is lacking or present only as a fibrillose ring-zone; growing on soil, wood, or woody debris, often in clusters or large numbers . . . . **Genera** *Hypholoma, Psilocybe,* **and** *Stropharia* (page 204)

4. Gills, and sometimes cap tissue, liquefying as the mushroom matures . . . . **Ink-Caps** (page 194)
4. Gills not liquefying 5

5. Gills waxy-looking, extend down the stipe 6
5. Gills not waxy-looking, attached to some degree, but not extending down stipe. 7

6. Cap surface dry to moist; flesh yellowish to pumpkin orange. . . . .
 . . . . **Genus** *Chroogomphus* (page 192)
6. Cap surface moist, viscid, or glutinous; flesh whitish to grayish (but often bright
 yellow in the base of the stipe) . . . . **Genus** *Gomphidius* (page 192)

7. Mushroom usually hygrophanous; face of gills more or less uniformly colored; stipe
 often whitish and usually quite fragile; usually growing on soil or wood, often in
 clusters and sometimes in large numbers . . . . **Genus** *Psathyrella* (page 199)
7. Cap not strongly hygrophanous; face of gills with mottled appearance, edge of gills
 often paler than face; stipe usually brownish or grayish and not markedly fragile;
 usually growing on rich soil or dung, usually not clustered or in large numbers . . . . . .
 . . . .**Genus** *Panaeolus* (page 199)

GENUS *AGARICUS*

Members of the genus *Agaricus* are easy
to recognize if a few basic characters are
observed. The spores are some shade of
purple-brown, chocolate-brown, or blackish
brown but not rusty brown to pinkish. The
gills are free and the stipe separates from
the cap with a clean break. A skirt-like ring
is present, although it may be fragile and
easily lost, but a volva, as found in amanitas, is lacking. The fruitbodies are fleshy,
small to very large; the cap and stipe are
generally whitish, sometimes with yellowish, brownish, or reddish brown overtones.
Caps are glabrous, fibrillose, or scaly, occasionally staining yellowish or reddish when
handled. The flesh is whitish, but may stain
yellowish or reddish when exposed. The
spores are smooth, globose to ellipsoid, and
sometimes have a small germ pore; in most
species, they are approximately 4.5–8 × 3–6
µm. Cheilocystidia are present in some species, but usually are not distinctive.

Agaricuses are most easily confused with
other medium to large, free-gilled mushrooms in genera such as *Amanita*, *Lepiota*,
Leucoagaricus, *Macrolepiota*, and *Chlorophyllum*, all with pale gills and white spores
(greenish in one chlorophyllum). Some
stropharias may look similar and grow in
the same sorts of habitat, but they usually
have a viscid cap and attached gills. Agaricuses are saprotrophic and can be abundant in both fields and forests, around compost heaps and manure piles, and on heavily manured ground. They are found mostly
in the summer and fall.

Many species are edible and good, others are bland, and others cause significant digestive upset for many people. Edibility seems to correlate with odors. Species with almond, anise, or button-mush-
roomy odors are edible for most (but not all)
people, whereas those with phenolic odors
(a "chemical" odor like ink, old-fashioned
library paste, or iodine) are toxic for most
people, although others apparently are not
bothered by them. Interestingly, at least

Agaricus augustus

some of those who can eat the phenolic species apparently do not perceive the odor. The taste of the edible species is generally mild mushroomy to somewhat nutty.

Agaricus augustus Fries
THE PRINCE

The prince is a common and popular edible mushroom along the Pacific Coast, from B.C. to northern California. It is distinguished by its large size, warm brown color of the cap scales, golden yellow staining of cap and stipe, almond odor, shaggy surface of the stipe below the double ring, and growth of the stipes deeply embedded in the soil. The spores are also rather large for the genus, at 8–10 × 5–6 μm. It often appears in summer, particularly in well-watered areas under true cedars, and aborted individuals can be found when soils dry out before development is complete. Even when found in the forest, it is in disturbed areas, such as campgrounds or along trails or roads. Smaller, less shaggy specimens with less pronounced odor are sometimes found. These might represent a separate species, but critical studies have not been carried out.

Agaricus campestris Fries
MEADOW MUSHROOM

The popular edible meadow mushroom, as both its scientific and common names suggest, is usually found in fields or pastures (*campestris* means "growing in a field" in Latin), especially those rich in manure. The largest fruitings tend to occur when warm and wet weather coincide. It is a stocky,

Agaricus campestris SAT-05-228-10

Agaricus hondensis SAT-04-316-01

Agaricus moelleri SAT-07-282-04

medium-sized, clean white mushroom with bright pink gills when young (another common name is pink bottom); however, as it ages it tends to become brown overall with dark chocolate gills. The cap may be somewhat fibrillose to scaly and, typically, the cuticle extends past the margin, like an overhanging tablecloth. The ring usually is thin and not persistent, and the base of the stipe often is tapered. It occurs nearly worldwide.

Agaricus hondensis Murrill
Agaricus hondensis, described from La Honda, California, is a medium to large toxic species, with an often pink-tinged, fibrillose cap that darkens with age, solid flesh, smooth stipe, and a large thick ("felty") ring. The gills are grayish to pale pinkish when young, and the stipe base usually bruises light chrome yellow and exhibits a phenolic odor when the flesh is crushed. It is most likely to be confused with the edible *A. subrutilescens*, which, although similarly colored, is less solid and has a mild odor, shaggy stipe, and a much less substantial ring. *Agaricus hondensis* occurs primarily in forests, seems to be restricted to the Pacific Coast, and is more common in California than it is in the PNW.

Agaricus moelleri Wasser
Agaricus moelleri is another phenol-smelling, toxic species and the most common of this group in the PNW. It is a medium to medium-large species with a marshmallow-shaped cap and pallid gills when young, dark gray-brown fibrillose cap, smooth stipe, and well-developed ring. It lacks the pinkish tints and markedly solid flesh of *A. hondensis*, and the flesh in the extreme base

of the stipe stains a brighter yellow when cut or crushed. It is a fairly common mushroom in the PNW and southward into California; however, the status of its name is in question, making it difficult to assess its overall distribution. Recent studies suggest that the names *A. moelleri, A. praeclaresquamosus,* and *A. meleagris* all refer to the same taxon, which differs from *A. placomyces*, a similar species common in eastern North America. Limited analyses suggest that Pacific Coast material does not exactly fit any of these names and that more than one new species could be present here.

Agaricus silvicola (Vittadini) Saccardo

The key features of *Agaricus silvicola* are its medium-large size, overall whitish color, tendency to stain yellow on cap and stipe, pleasant (though sometimes very faint) anise odor, and occurrence in forests (*silvicola* is Latin for "forest-inhabiting"). It is probably the most frequently encountered agaricus in our woodlands. The name *A. abruptibulbus* has been applied to forms with bulbous stipe bases, but variation in stipe shape is so great that use of this name has been largely abandoned. *Agaricus arvensis* is a very similar species that is somewhat more robust, has larger spores (7–8.5 × 5–6 vs. 5–6.5 × 3.5–4.5 µm), and grows in grass. Another woodland-dweller, *A. albolutescens*, differs from *A. silvicola* in its more robust stature, stronger odor, and brighter yellow staining. Trying to decide which of these species one has found usually is a hopeless task. All are considered edible, but not for everyone. *Agaricus silvicola*, or species with similar characteristics, is very widely distributed.

Agaricus subrutilescens (Kauffman) Hotson and Stuntz

Agaricus subrutilescens is a highly esteemed edible mushroom but, like most agaricuses, it is not for everyone. It is a tall statuesque forest-dweller, with a whitish cap overlain with purplish brown fibrillose scales, shaggy white stipe, and persistent, but not especially heavy, skirt-like ring. The flesh is whitish, non-staining, and has a mild odor.

Agaricus silvicola

Agaricus subrutilescens SAT-03-287-08

The gills are whitish at first, then turn pale pinkish, and finally chocolate-brown. It is not uncommon but usually does not occur in large numbers. If not restricted to the Pacific Coast, at least it is most common here.

GENERA *CHROOGOMPHUS* AND *GOMPHIDIUS*

These two genera, which formerly were lumped in *Gomphidius*, include the only mushrooms that have both black spores and decurrent gills. The root of their names, *gomph* (Greek for "bolt" or "nail"), refers to the shape of the young mushrooms. *Gomphidius* is readily recognized by its soft, somewhat waxy, wide-spaced, decurrent gills, slimy-viscid cap, white or pallid flesh, smoky black spores, and, in most species, the brilliant yellow stipe base. The veil is usually gelatinous and disappears or remains only as a zone on the upper stipe, on which the black spores accumulate as they fall from the gills. *Chroogomphus* differs mainly in being less viscid, having orange to yellowish or pinkish flesh, and hyphae in the flesh that turn blue in Melzer's reagent. The spores in both genera are narrowly ellipsoid (fusoid, fusiform, or "boletoid") and evidence the fact that these genera are more closely related to the boletes than they are to the other gilled mushrooms. Both genera also are characterized by having large, often crystal-encrusted, pleurocystidia. Both are ectomycorrhizal and are common in the conifer forests of western North America. Some European species have been shown to parasitize the mycelia of species of the ectomycorrhizal bolete, *Suillus*. Here

Chroogomphus tomentosus

in the PNW, *Chroogomphus* and *Gomphidius* mushrooms often can be found in the company of suilluses, so it is likely that similar sorts of parasitism are at work here too. All the species are thought to be edible but they are not widely collected for the table as most are soft and tasteless, and many turn black or purple when cooked.

Chroogomphus tomentosus
(Murrill) O. K. Miller

Chroogomphus tomentosus is unusual for this group in being dry and somewhat fibrillose-wooly, rather than viscid, which makes it easy to identify once the spore color and decurrent gills have been noted. It is ochraceous orange when young, at which point it could possibly be mistaken for a golden chanterelle, and later may develop wine-reddish or purplish colors. Although it often is said that chroogomphuses associate only with pines, that is not true for *C. tomentosus* (nor for *C. helveticus* of Europe) as it often is found in mixed conifer forests that lack pines. It apparently occurs only in western North America.

Chroogomphus vinicolor (Peck) O. K. Miller

Traditionally, *Chroogomphus vinicolor*, *C. rutilus*, and *C. ochraceus* have comprised the pine spikes, a common fungal element of pine forests throughout North America. They are quite similar to each other, having ochraceous to wine-red viscid caps that are convex or umbonate in age. *Chroogomphus vinicolor* has been differentiated from the other two species primarily on the basis of having thick-walled (up to 5–7.5 µm at widest part) cystidia, whereas the other two species have been separated on the basis of color, with *C. ochraceus* character-ized by brighter colors (yellowish orange to ochraceous) than *C. rutilus* (grayish, ochraceous, vinaceous to dingy vinaceous brown). Molecular analyses by Orson Miller and Cathy Aime support recognition of the three species but suggest that *C. rutilus* occurs only in Europe, *C. ochraceus* only in North America, and that all three species vary too widely in color for it to be useful in species determination. Thus our PNW pine spikes belong to *C. vinicolor* and *C. ochraceus*. However, deciding to which species a particular collection belongs can be problematic, as cystidia often are intermediate in thickness, perhaps as a result of thickening that occurs as the mushroom ages.

Gomphidius glutinosus (Schaeffer: Fries) Fries

Both this species and *Gomphidius subroseus* Kauffman are typical members of *Gomphidius*, with viscid caps, waxy decurrent gills, black spores, soft flesh, and yellow stipe bases. *Gomphidius glutinosus* is larger (cap diameter up to 10 cm, 4 in., or larger) and duller colored, with a cap that is purplish gray to purplish brown when young.

Chroogomphus vinicolor/C. ochraceus SAT-04-304-04

Gomphidius glutinosus

Gomphidius subroseus

Gomphidius subroseus is usually somewhat smaller (maximum cap diameter only about 7 cm, 3 in.) and has a pinkish to sordid reddish cap. Both occur commonly with Douglas-fir, but may associate with other conifers as well. A handful of other species occur in the PNW. *Gomphidius oregonensis* is very similar to *G. glutinosus* and occurs in the same habitats, but has smaller spores (10–13 vs. 15–21 μm in length) and tends to grow in clusters of several mushrooms. *Gomphidius maculatus* is similar in size to

G. subroseus but has a light cinnamon to reddish brown cap, develops black stains on the stipe and cap in age, and is associated with larch. The rarely reported *G. smithii* has a grayish red cap, pinkish flesh in the lower stipe, and the stipe blackens when handled.

INK-CAPS
The ink-caps make up another easy-to-recognize group of gilled fungi. There are two characters that tie most of the species together. One is the dark-colored spores—black, reddish black, or blackish brown—and the other is the tendency for the gills to digest themselves, or deliquesce, to facilitate spore discharge by removing tissue that otherwise would obstruct release of the spores into the open air. In many species, the flesh of the cap as well as the gills deliquesces, but in others, only the gills dissolve, and in a few, little or nothing dissolves. Close inspection of a young cap shows why this is necessary. The gills are very thin with parallel faces and they are crowded quite closely together. In most other mushrooms the gills are more or less wedge-shaped in cross-section and arranged farther apart, allowing the spores to be released easily. Other features of the ink-caps include their generally dull colors—usually white, gray, ocher, or brownish—the cylindrical or bullet shape of the young caps, frequent presence of a universal veil, and whitish, fragile, hollow stipe. Microscopically, the spores are smooth, somewhat roughened, or lumpy, and have a germ pore. The nature of the tissue making up the universal veil and the degree to which the veil is developed are also important characters. Ink-caps are saprotrophs and they occur in a variety of habitats, including dung, rotting wood, com-

Coprinellus micaceus

post, lawns, and even bare hard-packed soil along roadsides. The specific habitat is important in species identification. Because the types of habitats in which they grow are widespread, so are many ink-caps. It is a large group and has not been studied critically in North America.

The deliquescing species are difficult to confuse with anything else. In some species of *Bolbitius*, the gills liquefy, but the spores are orange- or rusty brown. In psathyrellas and panaeoluses the spores are similarly dark but the gills do not deliquesce. However, some of the smaller, non-deliquescing ink-caps can be difficult to separate from psathyrellas. Several of the larger ink-caps are good edibles, with the shaggy mane, *Coprinus comatus*, probably being the most popular. However, most species

are too small to be worth collecting. A few can be poisonous if consumed with alcohol, including the common inky cap, *Coprinopsis atramentaria*.

Formerly, all the ink-caps were included in the genus *Coprinus*. However, molecular and morphological analyses suggest that most of the coprinuses are not coprinuses; instead they are much more closely related to the psathyrellas. *Coprinus comatus* and a small number of its near kin turn out to be closely related to *Agaricus* and *Lepiota* and because *C. comatus* is the species that provides the basis for the genus name, this small group of species comprises the entire genus under the recent rearrangement of the ink-caps. Species with shaggy scales that fall off easily, such as *C. atramentarius*, and many others have been transferred to

Coprinopsis; most others, such as *Coprinus micaceus*, have been moved into *Coprinellus*, and a few, including *Coprinus plicatilis*, to a newly coined genus, *Parasola*. We have chosen to use the new genus alignments for the species presented here, but have included the traditional names in *Coprinus* for convenience.

Coprinellus micaceus (Bulliard: Fries) Vilgalys, Hopple, and Johnson
MICA-CAP

Coprinellus micaceus (= *Coprinus micaceus*) is a common widespread species that can be identified readily. It grows in large groups and clusters on hardwood stumps, buried roots, and other organic debris, fruiting in spring as well as fall in our area. It is smaller than *Coprinopsis atramentaria* and

is brighter colored, with ochraceous to yellow-brown caps that usually are adorned with small glistening particles (these wash off easily in the rain, however). *Coprinellus micaceus* is a good edible species, although we do not often hear much about it.

Coprinopsis atramentaria (Bulliard: Fries) Redhead, Vilgalys, and Moncalvo
INKY CAP

Coprinopsis atramentaria (= *Coprinus atramentarius*) is a very common, large, and easily recognized species that occurs widely in many natural and disturbed habitats, including gardens and other urban settings. It has a smooth to longitudinally wrinkled or scaly, silvery gray to brown, bullet- to bell-shaped cap and usually occurs in dense clusters that may seem to be nothing but a mass of

Coprinellus micaceus, Rocky Mountain specimens with well-developed "mica" flecks

Coprinopsis atramentaria, slender smooth-capped specimens

caps until they have liquefied, leaving naked stipes behind. *Coprinopsis atramentaria* is a fairly good edible, but should not be consumed with, or even within about 48 hours of drinking, alcoholic beverages due to the presence of coprine, which causes a variety of unpleasant symptoms (see Appendix 1). Like many widespread species that exhibit wide variation in color, surface texture, and other features, there may be several species currently passing as one.

Coprinopsis friesii (Quélet) P. Karsten

Coprinopsis friesii (= *Coprinus friesii*) is a small grass-dwelling species with a gray to grayish purple cap with white veil scales and gills that liquefy only slightly, if at all. It is distinguished from similar species by its relatively large, lentil-shaped spores, 7–11 × 6–7 × 7–9 μm. Small species such as *C. friesii* are rarely noticed, much less collected. Thus, we know little about its distribution.

Coprinopsis lagopus (Fries: Fries)
Redhead, Vilgalys, and Moncalvo

Coprinopsis lagopus (= *Coprinus lagopus*) is a common, short-lived, garden mushroom, which occurs in small to large groups in soil, leaf litter, and wood or bark chips. Few last as long as a day, and most collapse only hours after emerging. It is recognized by its white to gray cap covered with coarse white veil fibrils, habitat, and tendency for the cap to remain after the gills have deliquesced. Additional microscopic characters are the hyphal nature of the veil and the spores, ellipsoid to slightly almond-shaped and 10–13.5 × 6–7 μm. *Coprinopsis lagopides* has slightly smaller lentil-shaped spores (6–9 × 4.5–6 × 5–7 μm) and is said to frequent burned sites. Both are too small and flesh-less to be of culinary interest.

Coprinopsis atramentaria, stocky scaly-capped specimens SAT-07-302-01

Coprinopsis friesii SAT-99-176-01

Coprinopsis lagopus

Coprinopsis nivea SAT-05-231-06

Coprinus comatus

Coprinopsis nivea (Persoon: Fries)
Redhead, Vilgalys, and Moncalvo

Coprinopsis nivea (= *Coprinus niveus*) is a medium to medium-large snow-white species (*nivea* comes from the Latin for "snow") that grows on dung, primarily of cattle. The white veil material is powdery due to the spherical shape of many of the cells that make it up. Other dung-loving ink-caps are either not white or are smaller, so this is an easy species to identify. Although *C. nivea* probably is edible and is substantial enough to be a candidate for the table, it rarely is found in quantity and its substrate is off-putting to many.

Coprinus comatus (O. F. Müller: Fries)
Fries

SHAGGY MANE

Clyde Christensen, longtime mycologist at the University of Minnesota, included *Coprinus comatus* as one of his "foolproof four" edible mushrooms. Although it could be argued that nothing is fully foolproof, especially when it comes to mushroom identi-cation, certainly the shaggy mane is one of the most distinctive and easily recognized mushrooms. It is usually tall and stately, with a bullet-shaped white cap covered with whitish to brown scales that are not removable. The stipe is white, usually fairly thick, and has a movable ring in its lower portion if it has not fallen off. And, of course, the caps turn to ink, from the edge upward. Shaggy manes usually occur in groups, often quite large ones, but not in clusters. They are most common in grassy areas and hard-packed soil along trails and roadsides, fruiting mostly in late summer or early fall in the PNW. *Coprinus comatus* is one of the most popular edible mushrooms, and it occurs nearly worldwide.

Parasola plicatilis SAT-05-282-07

Parasola plicatilis (M. A. Curtis: Fries) Redhead, Vilgalys, and Hopple

Parasola plicatilis (= *Coprinus plicatilis*) is strongly reminiscent of the small paper umbrellas used to decorate mai tais and other tropical drinks. It usually grows singly or in small to moderately large groups in grassy areas and among weedy plants along the edges of woodland trails and is recognized by its small size, persistent pleated papery cap, lack of a veil, and spore characters (dark brown, strongly lentil-shaped, 9.5–13 × 6–8 × 8.5–10.5 µm). Several macroscopically similar species occur in Europe, including *P. hemerobia* and *P. leiocephala*. They differ in habitat and/or spore characteristics. Whether they occur in the PNW is not clear.

GENERA *PANAEOLUS* AND *PSATHYRELLA*

Panaeolus and *Psathyrella* are two commonly encountered genera of smallish, dull-colored, saprotrophic mushrooms with cellular cap cuticles that are ignored by most mushroom-hunters, as they can be difficult to identify to species and offer little from a culinary perspective.

Panaeoluses are abundant in pastures, well-fertilized lawns, dung, and manure heaps, fruiting whenever it is moist. Often they are found with species of *Agrocybe*, *Conocybe*, and *Stropharia*. The cap usually is bell-shaped or conical when young and is dull gray to almost black, grayish brown, or brown. The gills are gray to deep brown to black when mature, their faces usually are mottled as a result of the non-synchronous maturation of spores, and the edges often appear white-fringed. They do not deliquesce. The stipe is long, slender, and fibrous to slightly tough. A veil often is present when young, but usually does not form a ring, although it may leave ragged remnants on the edge of the cap. The spores are black or, occasionally, very dark brown. The spores mostly are smooth, ellipsoid, and have a germ pore; they do not de-color rapidly in concentrated sulfuric acid. Panaeoluses are too small to warrant attention for the table, but most species have been reported to have at least tiny amounts of psilocybin and other psychoactive compounds. Only a small number of species have been reported to contain sufficient quantities to make them targets for those wishing to pursue such effects. Psilocybes and conocybes are similar and some are common in dung, but they do not have black spores. The presence of pleurocystidia in a few species has

Panaeolus foenisecii SAT-99-178-01

caused some mycologists to place those in the genera *Anellaria* and *Copelandia*. *Anellaria* has a ring and viscid cap, *Copelandia* neither.

In contrast to the occurrence of panaeoluses on dung and fertilized soils, psathyrellas are found mostly on wood, usually in the late stages of decay. The cap usually is more convex than in panaeoluses, and usually is strongly hygrophanous with a shiny-powdered surface after drying. Cap colors are dull, typically brown, buff, or gray. Although usually smooth, some are covered with fine scales or fibrils. The flesh is markedly fragile (*psathy* is Greek for "crumbling"). The gills are dark brown to black at maturity, but not mottled, and do not deliquesce. The stipe is most often white, slender, and fragile—it often snaps in half cleanly. As in *Panaeolus*, the veil, if present, usually does not leave a ring. The spores are deep brown to purple-brown, black, or sometimes brick-red; they are smooth in most species, but are roughened in a few, have a germ pore, and their color fades quickly in concentrated sulfuric acid. Most favor damp shady locations, especially along streams and trails. Several are edible, but most are unknown and few are fleshy and abundant enough to be worthwhile, even if they could be confidently identified. Recent molecular analyses suggest *Psathyrella* does not represent a natural assemblage of species and so the genus is likely to be broken up in the near future.

Panaeolus foenisecii (Persoon: Fries) J. Schröter
HAYMAKER'S MUSHROOM

Panaeolus foenisecii is perhaps the most common lawn-inhabiting mushroom in the PNW, appearing nearly any time mild or warm temperatures coincide with rainfall or lawn-watering (*foenisecii* is from the Latin for "hay-mower"). Although its stature clearly is that of a panaeolus—a generally small mushroom with conic to convex cap atop a long slender fibrous stipe— it is atypical of the genus in many respects. The cap is hygrophanous, the gills are only slightly mottled, and the spores are slightly warty (almond-shaped, 11–18 × 6–9 µm) and dark brown rather than black. Plus, it grows in grass (especially lawns, and they need not be heavily fertilized) rather than dung. Because of these differences, some mycologists feel it deserves its own genus, *Panaeolina*, while others, particularly Alexander Smith, have suggested it be placed in *Psathyrella*. Like most widespread mushrooms, its appearance varies from place to place, particularly in the cap color, ranging from dark smoky brown to pale cinnamon when fresh. The haymaker's mushroom is not considered edible. Although some populations outside the PNW have exhibited traces of psilocybin and psilocin, there is little evidence that it is psychoactive.

Panaeolus campanulatus (Bulliard: Fries) Quélet

Panaeolus campanulatus is a large (for a panaeolus) species that occurs commonly on or near cowpies and horse manure. It has a brown to grayish, rounded conical to bell-shaped cap (*campanula* is Latin for "small bell"), long slender brittle stipe, a veil that often leaves shaggy remnants on the cap edge, and gray and black mottled gills. Based on slight macroscopic differences such as wrinkling or color of the cap, some mycologists have recognized *Panaeolus sphinctrinus*, *P. retirugis*, and *P. papilionaceus*. However, we accept the argument that such differences likely are environmentally,

not genetically, caused and treat these all as members of one highly variable species. *Panaeolus campanulatus* is considered neither edible nor psychoactive.

Panaeolus subbalteatus (Berkeley and Broome) Saccardo

Panaeolus subbalteatus is typical of the genus in occurring on dung (often of horses) or dung-rich soil in gardens or lawns, its relatively small size, and having mottled gills and large, smooth black spores. It differs

Panaeolus campanulatus SAT-05-231-07

Panaeolus subbalteatus

from other panaeoluses in its tendency to grow in small clusters, its stocky stature, and convex caps that can expand to plane in maturity. The dark band that usually is present on the cap gives the species its name (*balteat* is Latin for "girdled," and *sub-* indicates "somewhat") and further separates it from most species in the genus. *Panaeolus cinctulus*, *P. rufus*, and *P. venenosus* are considered to represent the same species. *Panaeolus subbalteatus* has been spread inadvertently by use of composts that contain its spawn,

and intentionally through cultivation. It is weakly to moderately psychoactive.

Psathyrella candolleana (Fries: Fries) Maire

Psathyrella candolleana is one of the commoner psathyrellas, particularly in urban settings, and probably is the one most frequently eaten (which, however, is not saying much). The key characters are the pale honey color of the young convex caps, fragments of the veil adhering to the edge (and sometimes the center) of the cap, the white stipe, and the general stature with the cap relatively wide in relation to the length of the stipe. The veil remnants can disappear quickly and there are many species with caps that are darker when young, but similarly pale after they have dried, so young specimens are necessary for confident identification. It is found around stumps or in grassy areas in the vicinity of buried roots of hardwood trees growing in clusters, small groups, or scattered over a small area. Like many panaeoluses and psathyrellas, it occurs primarily during warm moist weather. Although edible, often abundant, and said to have good flavor, it is thin-fleshed and not always easy to identify, which limit its use for the table.

Psathyrella candolleana

Psathyrella gracilis SAT-07-282-05

Psathyrella gracilis (Fries) Quélet

Psathyrella gracilis commonly forms fungal forests among wood chips in landscaped areas; in natural settings under hardwoods such as alder and cottonwood, the fruitings are usually much smaller. It is one of many species with very long stipes and conic caps (reminiscent of many panaeoluses) that rot woody debris. It lacks a veil and the caps typically are translucent-striate when young and then fade and become opaque as they dry. The gills often are reddish-tinged and sometimes have a red line slightly above their edge. The critical microscopic characters are the ellipsoid spores, 10–13 × 5.5–7 μm, with a large apical pore, long-necked pleurocystidia, and slightly stubbier cheilocystidia. Because of *P. gracilis*'s variable characters, a large number of forms, varieties, and species have been described based mostly on rather minor differences. *Psathyrella corrugis* is a synonym of many of these and, in those cases, has priority. Regardless of what names they go by, all these mushrooms are nearly fleshless and thus have little to recommend them as edibles.

Psathyrella longistriata (Murrill) A. H. Smith

Psathyrella longistriata is distinctive because it is one of a small number of psathyrellas with a veil that persists as a membranous ring on the stipe. The cap is quite variable in color, from grayish brown to dark reddish brown; the stipe is white, very fragile, and usually clothed with a fibrillose-scaly coating below (and sometimes above) the ring, which usually is somewhat wooly on the underside and striate above. The abundant pointed pleurocystidia are an important microscopic characteristic. The name is derived from radial striations of the cap, which usually do not develop until specimens are rather old. *Psathyrella longistriata* occurs solitary to scattered to gregarious in mixed forests, often ones containing alder. It was named from a collection made near Seattle, appears to be restricted to the Pacific Coast, and is more abundant in the PNW than in California. Many of the other ringed psathyrellas were described as new by Alexander Smith in his 1972 monograph of the genus and are very poorly known.

Psathyrella longistriata

Nothing seems to be known about the edibility of *P. longistriata*, but given the thin flesh and habit of usually fruiting in small numbers it would seem to have very little culinary potential.

Psathyrella piluliformis (Bulliard: Fries) P. D. Orton

Psathyrella piluliformis is a most variable fungus characterized by its clustered growth on dead hardwood, fragile flesh, white ring-less stipe, and hygrophanous cap, which is dark red-brown when moist and yellow-brown to ocher-brown when dry. Microscopically, it can be identified by the combination of rounded to obtuse cystidia, small spores (4.5–6 × 3–4 μm), and hyphae of the cap flesh that are dark cocoa-colored when mounted in potassium hydroxide. It is common throughout the U.S., including

Psathyrella piluliformis SAT-99-291-02

Psathyrella spadicea SAT-07-341-03

tic of *P. piluliformis*. *Psathyrella multipedata* also grows in clusters, but they are much tighter and the individual mushrooms arise from a common root-like base that extends deep into the substrate; it also is duller in color and has larger spores (6.5–9 × 3.5–4.5 μm). Little information concerning the edibility of *P. piluliformis* is available; however, given the fragile texture and thin flesh of the mushrooms, they are unlikely to be good candidates for the pot, even if they can be confidently identified.

GENERA *HYPHOLOMA*, *PSILOCYBE*, AND *STROPHARIA*

These three genera are very similar to one another (and are lumped together as *Psilocybe* by some mycologists) and to the genus *Pholiota*, which differs mainly in having

the PNW. *Psathyrella hydrophila* is a probably better known name for the same species. *Psathyrella spadicea* (Schaeffer) Singer is similar, but more robust and grows in clusters of fewer individuals, not approaching the sometimes large masses characteris-

Hypholoma capnoides

dull brown, rather than purplish brown to nearly black, spores. A veil is usually present but often it is fibrillose and does not leave a ring. The gills are attached, but not decurrent, and they do not deliquesce. The cap cuticle is filamentous, not cellular, the spores are smooth or somewhat angled, and usually have a germ pore. In many species, the pleurocystidia contain material that appears yellow in potassium hydroxide— these are referred to as chrysocystidia. The three genera are usually separated (although by no means perfectly, as many species have been transferred repeatedly among them) by considering a totality of characteristics, such as those that follow.

- *Hypholoma* (= *Naematoloma*): range from small, conic-capped, and slender to stockier and fairly fleshy, with more or less pli-

ant flesh, but not reaching the size of the larger stropharias, often brightly colored— brick-red, cinnamon-brown, yellow, greenish yellow, orange-red, usually not viscid, veil absent or fibrillose and evanescent, no ring, spores smooth with germ pore, chrysocystidia usually present, inflated hyphae below cap cuticle (subcellular layer), the fleshier species usually growing in clusters on wood or woody debris, smaller species growing singly or in groups in moss or peat, or soil with abundant woody debris, partial to cold weather, some gregarious, others in bogs, under conifers in woody debris, none in dung.
- *Psilocybe*: usually small and slender with thin stipes, cap conic-campanulate, or convex in the fleshier species, often viscid, not brightly colored—brown, gray, yellow-brown, or buff, cap and stipe may

stain blue or greenish, especially when handled, veil often present but usually not leaving a membranous ring, spores mostly smooth with germ pore, but somewhat variable in shape from ellipsoid to flattened or more or less angular, cheilocystidia present and usually abundant, chrysocystidia lacking, growing in a variety of substrates including dung, rich soil, wood chips, grass, mulch, and moss beds.

- *Stropharia*: range from small to rather large, usually fairly fleshy, cap brightly colored—yellow, yellow-brown, orange, red, green, blue, or white, cap convex to plane, usually viscid, veil often forming a persistent ring, not growing in clusters, spores smooth or somewhat angular in at least one view (similar to *Psilocybe*), chrysocystidia usually present, mostly terrestrial, in humus, pastures or other grassy areas, some on dung, a few on wood or wood chips.

Although some species, such as *Hypholoma capnoides* and *Stropharia rugosoannulata* are edible and fairly good, these genera

Hypholoma fasciculare, young specimens

for the most part are unimportant for mycophagists. However, *Psilocybe* contains several blue-staining magic mushrooms that are sought-after for their psychoactive effects, similar to those produced by LSD (see Appendix 1).

Hypholoma capnoides (Fries: Fries) P. Kummer

In the PNW, *Hypholoma capnoides* probably is the most commonly eaten, for food, of the species in these three genera, although it probably is not on the top-ten list of many mycophagists. It grows in clusters on conifer logs and can be quite abundant at times. Unusual for a hypholoma, it can have a viscid cap, although most guides report it as dry to moist only. Its gills are grayish when young and the flesh has a mild taste, both of which characteristics separate it from the similar *H. fasciculare*. It occurs throughout the PNW, elsewhere in northern North America, and in Europe and Asia.

Hypholoma fasciculare (Hudson: Fries) P. Kummer

SULFUR TUFT

Hypholoma fasciculare is one of the commonest mushrooms in the PNW and one of the easiest to identify when found in its typical form. In the words of Alexander Smith, "It is a truly beautiful fungus when at its best," but often becomes sordid, watersoaked, and far less attractive. It is one of three similar-looking hypholomas that grow in clusters on logs and other large woody debris, along with *H. capnoides* and *H. sublateritium*. The latter has brick-reddish caps, and grows on hardwood in central and eastern North America, although there are a few reports of it occurring in B.C. Like *H. capnoides*, *H. fasciculare* grows in tight clusters (fascicles) on conifer wood, but it also occurs on hardwood and seems less restricted to logs, sometimes even appearing to be terrestrial. When found on the ground, it can be harder to recognize, especially if it is not in a cluster. *Hypholoma fasciculare* usually has brighter colored caps than *H. capnoides*, has bright greenish yellow gills when young (hence its common name), and is intensely bitter-tasting. This bitter taste renders it inedible, and it is reportedly poisonous.

Hypholoma marginatum (Persoon: Fries) J. Schröter

The concept of a hypholoma (or naematoloma) held by most mushroom-hunters is typified by the fleshy, clustered, wood-dwellers but, in fact, those species are in the distinct minority in the genus. The majority are small slender species with narrowly to broadly convex caps, such as *Hypholoma marginatum* (= *H. dispersum*). It grows singly, or in small to large troops on the debris or sawdust of conifers. Logged areas are a favorite habitat. Similar-appearing members of the genus occur in moss or peaty soils rather than on woody substrates. The cap color is variable, ranging from orange-tawny to tawny at first and fading slightly to yellowish and ocher tones. The gills develop olivaceous tints in age, and the stipe exhibits distinctive white fibrillose bands. Small, with thin flesh and said to have a bitter taste, it is not considered edible.

Psilocybe cyanescens Wakefield

Psilocybe cyanescens is primarily a wood-chip-dweller, being found in much the same locales as *Stropharia aurantiaca* and, like the latter species, becoming increasingly common, much to the delight of magic mushroom hunters. Normally it does not appear until relatively late in the season, typically around Halloween with the onset of cold weather. It is small, but fairly fleshy, with caramel-colored, viscid, hygrophanous caps with a wavy margin. The stipe is initially whitish, and both cap and stipe bruise blue when handled. The veil is fibrillose and rather heavy, but usually disappears without

Hypholoma fasciculare, mature specimens

Hypholoma marginatum

leaving much of a trace. It occurs in some-times large groups, either singly or in small clusters. The blue staining indicates that it is one of the psychoactive species, and is generally considered to be at least moderately active.

Psilocybe cyanescens

Psilocybe montana (Persoon: Fries)
P. Kummer

Psilocybe montana is a small, non-bluing moss-dweller, usually among species of the genus *Polytrichum*. It has a hemispheric or convex-flattened, reddish brown, translucent-striate, hygrophanous cap, and is reminiscent of a galerina in habitat and appearance. However, the dark spores clearly separate it from the galerinas. As its epithet suggests, it is most common at higher elevations and has been reported from much of the temperate Northern Hemisphere. In the PNW, it can be found beginning in late spring. It is too small to be of culinary interest and is not psychoactive.

Psilocybe montana SAT-03-136-02

Psilocybe pelliculosa (A. H. Smith)
Singer and A. H. Smith

At first glance, *Psilocybe pelliculosa* could be mistaken for a relatively large mycena, galerina, or perhaps one of the slender hypholomas. However, the combination of purplish brown spores and habitat give it away as a psilocybe. The caps are fairly dark brown, viscid, and translucent-striate when moist but fade rapidly to opaque yellowish brown or buff as they dry. The stipe is long, slender, relatively pale-colored, and coated with a thin layer of fibrils. The veil is, at most, inconspicuous. Both cap and stipe bruise bluish or greenish, although usually not strongly. *Psilocybe pelliculosa* typically grows in groups among herbaceous plants in disturbed forest settings. Thus, it often can

Psilocybe pelliculosa

be found along trails or the edges of forest roads. It apparently is confined to the Pacific Coast and is considered to be weakly to moderately psychoactive.

Psilocybe stuntzii Guzmán and Ott

The most distinctive feature of *Psilocybe stuntzii* is the membranous ring that is usually present on the stipe; this is unusual for a psilocybe. Otherwise, it is fairly typical of the genus. The cap is conical at first, then becomes convex to plane. It is dark olivaceous brown, translucent-striate, and viscid when moist, and fades to a yellowish buff as it dries. The stipe is pale at first and darkens with age. The bluing reaction typically is weak, and usually is most noticeable on the ring. *Psilocybe stuntzii* occurs frequently in well-mulched newly planted lawns, as well as in wood chips and other landscape settings. It is not often found in natural habitats. It is another species apparently confined to the Pacific Coast, particularly the PNW, and is considered weakly to moderately psychoactive. When collecting for such uses, it is imperative that one be sure of the identification and that each mushroom be checked carefully before being stuffed into the omnipresent plastic sandwich bag. Psychoactive psilocybes have a disturbing tendency to co-occur with potentially deadly galerinas and conocybes, as shown in the accompanying photograph.

Stropharia aeruginosa (M. A. Curtis: Fries) Quélet

Blue and green mushrooms are rare, so *Stropharia aeruginosa* and its close look-alike, *S. caerulea* (often incorrectly called *S. cyanea*) not only attract attention, but are reasonably easy to recognize. Both have viscid, bluish green caps that fade to yellowish, white

Psilocybe stuntzii

Psilocybe stuntzii (left) and *Conocybe vexans* (right), which probably contains amatoxins, found growing together

Stropharia aeruginosa SAT-05-305-01

stipes, typical purplish brown stropharia spores, and grow in wood chips, other landscape settings, and in disturbed portions of natural habitats such as along forest trailsides. The cap of *S. aeruginosa* usually is adorned by white veil remnants and tends to, at least partially, retain its blue color. The stipe has a persistent white ring, and usually is somewhat scaly below the ring. *Stropharia caerulea* differs by its usually incomplete veil, smoother stipe, tendency of the cap to more quickly and more completely fade to yellowish, and the presence of abundant chrysocystidia along the gill edges. Unfortunately, many collections exhibit intermediate characteristics or a mix of characters, making it impossible to decide to which species they belong. Perhaps there is only one variable species, or possibly we have a third undescribed species here. Little is known concerning the edibility of any of them.

Stropharia ambigua (Peck) Zeller

Stropharia ambigua is one of two common forest stropharias in the PNW and, when in prime condition, is one of the most elegant of mushrooms, rivaling amanitas. It is a medium to fairly large fungus, with a shiny yellowish brown to buff cap whose edge often is hung with white veil remnants. The veil also leaves shaggy scales on the stipe and, occasionally, a fragile ring. Several other stropharias, including *S. riparia*, *S. semiglobata*, and *S. coronilla*, are roughly the same color, but all are smaller, less statuesque, and occur in different habitats. *Stropharia ambigua* apparently is confined to the PNW, including northern California. Although it is known primarily from forest habitats (on soil and leaf litter), recently we have seen large fruitings among wood chips on the University of Washington campus and elsewhere in the Puget Sound area. It may be edible,

Stropharia ambigua SAT-07-332-01

but David Arora claims one source likens its taste to old leaves, and most authors recommend caution with all stropharias.

Stropharia aurantiaca (Cooke) Imai

Stropharia aurantiaca (= *Hypholoma aurantiaca, Naematoloma aurantiaca, Psilocybe aurantiaca*) is a common inhabitant of landscaped areas spread with wood chips; rarely is it encountered in natural settings. Although this fungus is easy to recognize by its habitat, bright reddish orange umbonate cap adorned with whitish veil remnants, conspicuous white cords extending from the stipe into the substrate, and growth in troops containing both single specimens and small clusters, deciding what its name should be is a problem that has not yet been satisfactorily resolved. In addition to confusion with *S. squamosa* and *S. thrausta*, and shuttling between *Stropharia*, *Hypholoma/ Naematoloma*, and *Psilocybe*, the epithet *aurantiaca*, although fitting, is now believed to apply to a different fungus. Our species is thought to have emigrated here and to Europe from Australia, where *Psilocybe ceres* (now placed in *Leratiomyces* by some) occurs and seems very similar. We have no information concerning its edibility.

Stropharia aurantiaca SAT-06-321-01

Stropharia hornemannii SAT-05-265-13

Stropharia hornemannii (Fries) S. Lundell and Nannfeldt

Stropharia hornemannii is our other common forest-dwelling stropharia. It is similar to *S. ambigua* in size and general appearance, but differs in having a cinnamon-gray to dull brown to purplish brown cap and consistently persistent ring, and in being somewhat stockier and less elegant. It sometimes occurs on intact conifer logs, but is most abundant on wood that has been more highly decomposed. It is widespread in the north temperate and boreal forests of the Northern Hemisphere. Like most stropharias, it is not recommended as an edible.

Boletes

"Bolete" means different things to different people. To some, it means the species *Boletus edulis*, the edible king bolete, cep, porcino, or steinpilz. To others, it is any member of the genus *Boletus*. We take a broader view and use bolete for mushrooms that usually have a fleshy cap and stipe, have a spongy tube layer that can be cleanly separated from the underside of the cap, and are putrescent. Putrescent means that a bolete left sitting out at room temperature overnight or longer will turn into an odorous mass of mush and fluid, seemingly alive with wriggling, feasting "worms," the larvae of small flies that lay their eggs in the mushroom. So do not leave your boletes sitting on the kitchen counter when you go to bed! The boletes, in this sense, represent a well-known group of mushrooms that are most commonly collected in forests, although some can be found in parks and other areas with appropriate trees.

Boletes range from medium-sized to large. Most of them lack a veil but in certain *Suillus* species a partial veil or veil-like material is present and may leave a ring or cottony material along the cap edge. They are ectomycorrhizal and some grow only with specific tree hosts, for example, *S. cavipes* with larch, and *Leccinum scabrum* with birch. Others are less choosy and can be found with a variety of conifers or hardwoods. Thus, it pays to take a careful look at the surrounding trees when you collect boletes, as this often will help in identifying them.

Recent and ongoing studies have shown that many close relatives do not necessarily share some features of typical boletes. For instance, secotioid forms, such as those in the genus *Gastroboletus*, often have contorted or irregular tube layers, poorly defined caps, and modified stipes that are shortened or replaced by a columella. Gastroid relatives of boletes called false truffles, such as *Rhizopogon* and *Truncocolumella*, produce underground fruitbodies. Their spore-producing tissue, or gleba, is enclosed by a tough outer skin called a peridium. Typical boletes can produce a spore-print while secotioid and gastroid forms cannot, as their spores are not forcibly discharged. There are also close bolete relatives that have gills, such as species in the genus *Phylloporus*. Other than the gills, they look strikingly like boletes such as *Boletus chrysenteron*. Other gilled mushrooms, such as species of *Paxillus*, *Gomphidius*, and *Chroogomphus* also are related to certain groups of boletes. Finally, earthballs such as *Scleroderma* and *Pisolithus*, and the earthstar *Astraeus*, all of which occur in our region, also are closely related to the boletes.

The PNW has a much smaller number of bolete species than is found in areas such as eastern North America, in part because we have far fewer ectomycorrhizal tree species to serve as hosts. However, our bolete species, particularly *Boletus edulis*, often produce in far greater abundance than those in the east, and most PNW mushroom-hunters would not consider trading our abundance of edibles for the east's greater diversity. Nonetheless, we do have fair variety, particularly in the genus *Suillus*, the species of which are almost entirely associated with conifers, particularly pines, larch, and Douglas-fir. In urban areas, we find several species that have most likely been imported into the PNW with landscape trees, including *Leccinum scabrum*, *Boletus barrowsii*, *B. rubellus*, and *Gyroporus castaneus*.

Historically, the genera have been separated in part by spore color. It ranges from brown to olive-brown in *Boletus* and *Leccinum*, olive-brown to vinaceous brown in *Suillus*, brown with reddish tints or olive in *Chalciporus*, pinkish or dark reddish brown in *Porphyrellus* and *Tylopilus*, to lemon-yellow in *Gyroporus*. Spore shape and ornamentation and various characteristics of the fruitbodies have also been used to separate the genera.

Fruitbodies of several other fungi can be mistaken for boletes. The most commonly encountered ones are species of *Albatrellus*, *Boletopsis*, and *Polyporus*. These have a cap and stipe with tubes beneath the cap as do boletes; however, they are rather tough-textured, the tubes are not easily separated from the cap, and they are not putrescent. Leave them out overnight and they look pretty much the same the next morning. In addition, the polypores are wood-rotters and nearly always are found on wood, unlike most boletes, which, with occasional exception, fruit on the ground.

GENUS *BOLETUS*

Originally, nearly all boletes were classified in *Boletus*. Bit by bit, the genus has shrunk as groups have been split out and given new names. The species that now comprise the genus are still a diverse group, and often can be recognized by ruling out other possibilities. In the PNW, if your bolete is not a suillus or leccinum, chances are good that it is a boletus. Features to observe closely when collecting and identifying them include nearby tree species, color and texture of the cap surface, color of the tubes and pores, shape, color, and nature of the surface of the stipe, and color changes, especially in the flesh when cut open and the tubes when bruised. Taste also can be important as a minority of species are bitter or peppery.

An interesting group that we were unable to include consists of species with orange to

Boletus cf. *barrowsii*, collected in Seattle SAT-03-269-01

red pores and often strong bluing reactions when bruised or cut. These include *Boletus haematinus*, a massive species similar in appearance to *B. pulcherrimus* (formerly called *B. eastwoodiae*, which appears to be a Californian version of *B. satanas*) and, occasionally, members of the *B. erythropus* group. The usual advice is that no red-pored, blue-staining boletes should be eaten and, indeed, some are known to be quite poisonous. Although claims have been made that some species are good edibles, we recommend following the usual advice to avoid them. The red-pored boletes in the PNW are very poorly known in terms of species concepts, ecological requirements, and distributions.

Boletus barrowsii Thiers and A. H. Smith

Boletus barrowsii is one of the western edulis species (see *B. edulis*). It is distinguished by its overall whitish to pale tan coloration, suede-like texture of the cap surface, strong odor when drying, and characteristic occurrence in the mountains of the southwestern U.S., most often under ponderosa pine. Generally considered to occur only in the Southwest, there have been sporadic reports of it occurring in places such as Idaho and southern California, under trees other than ponderosa pine. In Seattle, a very similar mushroom is fairly common in late spring under oaks and species of *Tilia*, such as lindens and basswood. Although it was felt that this had to be a different species, preliminary DNA analysis suggests it is very close to *B. barrowsii*. The species name honors New Mexico mushroom-hunter and artist Chuck Barrows, who claimed to be an old bold mushroom-hunter, contrary to the oft-quoted statement, "There are old mushroom-hunters, and there are bold mushroom-hunters, but there are no old, bold mushroom-hunters."

Boletus chrysenteron Bulliard

In our region, there are several dry-capped, yellow-pored boletes that have a velvety or tomentose cap surface. Many mycologists, mostly outside North America, use the genus name *Xerocomus* for these species. Two of the more common species are *Boletus chrysenteron* and *B. zelleri*; others include *B. rubellus* and *B. subtomentosus*, a larger olive-brown to yellow-brown or brown species. All these bruise bluish or bluish green, although not always strongly.

Boletus chrysenteron has a grayish brown to blackish brown cap; the surface cracks to expose the pale flesh, and often there are pinkish to reddish tints toward the cap edge in age. The tubes are yellow, the pores yellow with an irregular outline. The stipe is somewhat variable in color, often with yellow at the apex, but reddish and pallid colors occur elsewhere, and sometimes only the conspicuous longitudinal striations are reddish in color. One or more areas of the fruitbody turn bluish when cut or handled. *Boletus chrysenteron* can be found in forested areas, on the edges of woods, and in urban habitats, such as parks. *Boletus truncatus* is a common species in conifer forests and can only be separated from *B. chrysenteron* by looking at the spores, which are truncate on one end.

Boletus coniferarum Dick and Snell

Boletus coniferarum is one of the more common low- to mid-elevation conifer forest boletes. The cap is usually large and fleshy, and the surface is unpolished to somewhat velvety and dark olive-gray to gray-brown. The tubes are yellow and stain dark blue when cut or injured. The stipe is pale yellow or olivaceous to blackish in age, without red, finely reticulate at the apex, thick, and sometimes enlarged at the base. The flesh is

Boletus barrowsii, collected in New Mexico
SAT-99-231-03

Boletus chrysenteron SAT-00-251-01

Boletus coniferarum SAT-00-251-32

Boletus edulis SAT-04-262-13

Boletus edulis SAT-03-287-09

white to yellowish, stains blue quickly after cutting, and is extremely bitter, which renders the mushroom inedible. *Boletus calopus* is a very similar bitter-fleshed species that differs by its more noticeably reticulate stipe that is red in part. *Boletus frustosus*, a close relative of *B. calopus*, differs from *B. coniferarum* by its conspicuously cracked cap surface at maturity and pink to reddish color on the lower stipe. *Boletus rainisii* (formerly referred to as *B. pulverulentus*) is a medium-sized species with an olive-brown to yellow-brown, velvety cap, yellow tubes, and yellow stipe with some reddish tones near the base. It stains blue to olive-green or greenish black instantly when cut or handled, and has a mild taste. It occurs in coastal conifer forests but seems to be rare.

Boletus edulis Bulliard: Fries

Boletus edulis and its close relatives are commonly collected for food and known variously as porcini, ceps, steinpilz, and king boletes. All these species have, in common, firm whitish tubes and pores, often stuffed with white mycelium at first, that become yellow to olive and soft-gelatinous with age. The stipe is reticulate at least at the apex, typically fleshy and club-shaped, whitish at the apex and some shade of brown below. The flesh is white, unchanging or discoloring to reddish brown in some species. The cap surface is moist to viscid, may become uneven in age, and the color, depending on species, ranges from almost whitish to various shades of brown to reddish brown, often with a paler edge. *Boletus regineus* (= *B.* "aereus*") is the darkest species, with almost black caps at times, and often a whitish bloom over the surface when young. More typical *B. edulis* is often crust-brown, while the montane forms can be strongly reddish brown and when handled in large numbers can stain one's fingers a similar color. Although most of our edulis types occur with conifers, *B. regineus* is associated with oaks and madrone. Preliminary molecular studies of the western edulis group suggest that our mushrooms are sufficiently different from their European counterparts as to merit new names of their own; however, until the necessary follow-up studies have been completed, there seems no harm in continuing to use some European names. As far as edibility goes, the precise name of an edulis type is hardly important.

Boletus edulis SAT-05-301-05

Boletus fibrillosus Thiers

Boletus fibrillosus is a handsome bolete that often is mistaken for *B. edulis*. The cap color is some shade of dark brown, often with lighter areas, the cap surface is typically wrinkled and velvety to distinctly fibrillose, the tubes and pores are light yellow or somewhat darker, and the stipe is strongly reticulate, pale at the apex, dark brown below, and covered by white mycelium at the base. The overall aspect is that of a moderate to large cap on a relatively long stipe that often is pinched off at the base. It occurs locally, seldom as more than one or a few fruitbodies, but is widespread in our region in old-growth forests of fir and western hemlock as well as earlier succession forests of western hemlock and Douglas-fir and other mixed forest stands. It is edible, but inferior to *B. edulis*.

Boletus fibrillosus SAT-06-287-03

Boletus mirabilis Murrill

Boletus mirabilis is unusual for a bolete in fruiting on wood or woody debris, almost always of hemlock. Despite this habit, it is ectomycorrhizal. The distinctive cap is rough tomentose to fibrillose-scaly and

Boletus mirabilis

looks like a wine-red or reddish brown bath towel. The tubes are yellow to olive-yellow, much shorter near the stipe, with rather large, rounded to angular pores. The stipe is usually long and club-shaped, shaggy reticulate on the upper portion and ridged to uneven or smooth toward the base, brown to reddish brown with some lighter areas, and with yellow mycelium around the base. Occasionally the flesh will develop slight blue discolorations. The cap flesh is white to yellowish and typically wine-red just under the surface. Older specimens of this species, like those of *B. chrysenteron*, are often attacked by a mold, *Hypomyces chrysospermus*, which is white at first, and then bright yellow. Although not as popular as *B. edulis*, *B. mirabilis* is a good edible if you beat the hypomyces to it.

Boletus rubellus Krombholz

Boletus rubellus (= *Xerocomus rubellus*) is one of several small to somewhat larger species that have in common reddish, dry velvety caps that often crack in age, tubes and pores that are yellow to olive-yellow, stipes that are reddish but with some yellow at the apex or elsewhere, and flesh and tubes with a slight to stronger bluing reaction when cut or bruised. They are similar to *B. chrysenteron* and *B. truncatus* but are more brightly colored. The species in this group are very difficult to tell apart, and a number of different names have been used for them. *Boletus coccyginus*, described from California, fits into this group as does *B. fraternus*. There is a good chance that boletes in this group have been introduced into our area. They often occur during summer in grassy areas, mossy lawns, or along the edges of trails, always near trees such as oaks, cottonwood, willow, and basswood or linden. Several of our PNW collections fit *B. rubellus* well in occurring in a park under lindens and having bright red cap and stipe, blue staining when bruised or cut, cap cuticle composed of erect septate hyphae with tapered ends and some encrusted walls, and thick-walled spores up to 12–13 µm long.

Boletus rubellus SAT-04-263-01

Boletus rubripes SAT-05-267-11

Boletus rubripes Thiers

Boletus rubripes is medium-sized to larger, with a dry, matted tomentose to fibrillose, pale buff to olive-brown or more brownish cap; the surface sometimes cracks in dry weather, but does not develop reddish colors like *B. chrysenteron*. *Boletus rubripes* has yellow tubes and pores that readily stain blue when bruised or cut, a feature it shares with a number of similar species including *B. coniferarum* and *B. smithii*. The epithet *rubripes* ("red foot" in Latin) refers to the lower portion of the stipe, which is some shade of red. The stipe apex is yellow and it is not reticulate, unlike that of *B. coniferarum*, although the lower portion may become ridged or striate. The base usually is covered by yellow mycelium. The flesh is bitter, cream to yellow or rarely pinkish in the cap, white to yellow in the upper stipe, and red to vinaceous in the base; when cut, it instantly changes to blue. *Boletus rubripes* is widespread but not particularly common in our region. It was described from coastal conifer and mixed forests in California, but in the PNW, occurs in montane conifer forests, where one is likely to also encounter *B. calopus*. The latter is similar in coloration and bitterness, but has a reticulate stipe apex.

Boletus smithii Thiers

Boletus smithii is medium-sized with a velvety to fibrillose, dry cap that often becomes cracked in age. While the cap often has gray-brown, buff, and tan colors, especially at first, they become infused with pinkish to reddish overtones, and some caps are very reddish in age. The tubes and pores are yellow to olive-yellow but near the cap margin may be pinkish or reddish, and they stain blue where bruised. The stipe is smooth, granulose, or fibrillose to tomentose, but not reticulate; it is reddish at the apex and yellowish to pale below. The flesh is yellowish or slightly reddish beneath the cap surface, and typically turns blue when exposed, but sometimes only slightly so. The taste is mild, but it is not widely sought-after as an edible.

Boletus zelleri Murrill

Boletus zelleri (= *Xerocomus zelleri*) is very similar to *B. chrysenteron* and, although most collections of the two are easily separated, they can integrade in color. Typically *B. zelleri* has a black to blackish brown or dark brown cap, often with reddish tones near the edge. The tubes are olive-yellow and become blue when bruised. The stipe usually is some shade of red, sometimes

Boletus smithii SAT-05-302-18

Boletus zelleri SAT-01-293-14

with considerable yellow, especially at the apex, and the surface is granular to punctate. *Boletus zelleri* is a rather common species especially in coastal and low elevation conifer forests. It is usually most prevalent in fall, but it can be found at other times as well. Like *B. chrysenteron* it can be found in urban areas and parks, along trails, and in other areas where conifers occur. It is edible and a favorite of some people but, in general, is not widely collected.

Chalciporus piperatus (Bulliard: Fries) Bataille

Chalciporus piperatus (= *Boletus piperatus*) is unique among PNW boletes in its overall coloration, small to medium size, and rather slender stipe. The cap is viscid when fresh but may become somewhat fibrillose and cracked in older specimens, reddish brown to rust-brown or vinaceous brown, often with a mix of yellowish brown, and sometimes becoming more ochraceous brown in age. The tubes are yellowish to reddish yellow and the pores are angular, red to reddish brown, and darken when bruised. The stipe is rather slender and reddish brown

Chalciporus piperatus SAT-03-288-06

or colored like the cap, except for the base, which is covered with bright yellow mycelium. The flesh of the cap is yellowish buff or somewhat vinaceous to pinkish, and in the stipe brownish buff above and bright yellow in the base. The epithet refers to this species's peppery taste. It is widespread and can be rather common in some years, but usually is not abundant. It is not generally regarded as a good edible. *Chalciporus piperatoides* is similar in appearance, but the tubes stain bluish and the spore-print is olive rather than brown.

GENUS *SUILLUS*

Suillus is a prominent genus in the conifer forests of the PNW. Nearly all its species are ectomycorrhizal with conifers, especially pines, larch, and Douglas-fir. The fruitbodies usually are yellowish, although brown and reddish tones occur in many species. In addition, the following features are characteristic of many suilluses—slimy or viscid cap; angular pores, often arranged in radial lines; slimy or somewhat membranous partial veil that may leave a ring or ring-zone; and sticky dots on the stipe. A minority, which associate with larch or Douglas-fir, exhibit reddish brown, fibrillose-scaly caps and somewhat of a ring, plus they may have hollow stipes. Species that exhibit color changes when bruised or cut open are much fewer in number than those in *Boletus* and *Leccinum*. We define *Suillus* in a broad sense here, including species that often are classified in *Boletinus* and *Fuscoboletinus*. Most suilluses are edible, but few of them make many top-ten lists. If cooking the mushrooms fresh, discarding the tubes and any slimy parts will improve the texture

Suillus albivelatus

and lessen the chances of a diarrhea experience. If drying them for later use, those measures are not necessary.

Suillus albivelatus A. H. Smith, Thiers, and O. K. Miller

Suillus albivelatus has the same habit and stature as many other suilluses—a rather broad vinaceous brown to yellow-brown, viscid to shiny cap and short fleshy stipe. Careful observation will reveal that young specimens often have white veil remnants on the edge of the cap, and a slight white to vinaceous ring-zone on the stipe. The stipe is white to yellow, without glandular dots (except in age) and it discolors brown at the base. *Suillus albivelatus* occurs in mixed conifer forests and appears to be associated with pines. Similar pine-associated species with veils or cottony cap margins include *S. neoalbidipes* (= *S. albidipes*), *S. brunnescens*, *S. pseudobrevipes*, and *S. glandulosipes*.

Suillus brevipes (Peck) Kuntze

Suillus brevipes is among our most common and widespread species. The epithet (Latin for "short foot") indicates the typical short, squat stature, although some specimens do develop longer stipes. It has a slimy to viscid, dark vinaceous brown to cinnamon-brown cap when fresh and becomes streaked and yellowish in age. There is no veil or cottony tissue on the edge of the cap, and the stipe is white to yellowish with inconspicuous glandular dots that may become more apparent in age. The pores are yellow, round, and

Suillus brevipes SAT-05-302-09

Suillus caerulescens

Suillus cavipes SAT-07-271-07

usually rather small. It occurs primarily with two-needle pines during late summer and fall.

Suillus caerulescens A. H. Smith and Thiers

Suillus caerulescens is a viscid-capped species that occurs with Douglas-fir. It has a pallid veil that leaves material on the edge of the cap and a ring-zone or slight ring that is often somewhat viscid, a lack of glandular dots on the stipe, and a tendency for the flesh in the base of the stipe to discolor greenish to bluish when it is exposed. The cap is reddish brown to vinaceous brown in the center and more yellowish to ochraceous toward the margin, and often is radially streaked. The pores are yellowish, large, and rather angular, and the stipes are yellowish to brownish, often darkening with age.

Suillus cavipes (Opatowski) A. H. Smith and Thiers

Suillus cavipes is sometimes placed in the genus *Boletinus*. Like *S. ochraceoroseus* it is associated with larch, wherever it occurs in the PNW. Both these species have dry, fibrillose-scaly caps similar to that of *S. lakei*, and a veil that may leave material on the edge of the cap and a ring or ring-zone on the stipe. *Suillus cavipes* usually has a reddish brown cap although, at times, it can be pale yellowish brown. The pores are pale yellow, often angular or elongated, and sometimes decurrent. The stipe is yellowish above the ring and fibrillose and colored like the cap below it. The epithet (Latin for "hollow foot") refers to the hollow stipe, which is an important characteristic for identifying the species.

Suillus grevillei (Kotzsch) Singer

Suillus grevillei is another larch associate that can sometimes be quite abundant. It has a viscid to glutinous, typically deep reddish brown cap with a distinct yellow margin, although forms with all-yellow caps occur. The veil is rather substantial, often leaving material on the edge of the cap and a distinct ring on the stipe. The pores are angular and yellow, and may stain brownish when bruised. The stipe is rich yellow above the ring and streaked reddish brown below. The flesh is yellowish and discolors brownish.

Suillus grevillei SAT-07-271-06

Suillus lakei (Murrill) A. H. Smith and Thiers

Suillus lakei and *S. caerulescens* are among the most common fall boletes under Douglas-fir, often occurring together, and frequently in the company of gomphidiuses. *Suillus lakei* has a reddish to red-brown or orange-buff, dry to viscid, fibrillose-scaly cap, a veil that leaves a distinct ring-zone, and a stipe that is yellowish above, colored like the cap below, and without glandular dots. The tubes are rather large and angular, sometimes elongated, some shade of yellow, and typically stain reddish brown when bruised. The flesh of the stipe base sometimes turns bluish when exposed. *Suillus lakei* has sometimes been placed in the genus *Boletinus*.

Suillus grevillei

Suillus ochraceoroseus (Snell) Singer

Suillus ochraceoroseus occurs with larch in higher and interior conifer forests, mostly in late spring and summer. The cap is dry, fibrillose to scaly, often whitish at first and then rosy red. The pores are yellowish to brownish and often rather large, angular,

Suillus lakei SAT-97-278-15

Suillus ochraceoroseus SAT-05-179-02

Suillus punctatipes SAT-01-264-32

Suillus tomentosus SAT-05-302-17

and elongated. The stipe is mostly yellowish and somewhat reddish to brownish toward the base. The veil is whitish to grayish or yellowish, somewhat fibrillose-membranous, and often leaves material along the cap edge and a ring-zone or ring on the stipe. Often the interior of the stipe is hollow and the flesh stains blue-green at times when cut or bruised. *Suillus ochraceoroseus* has sometimes been placed in the genus *Fuscoboletinus* because of its reddish brown to purplish brown spores.

Suillus punctatipes (Snell and Dick) Singer

Suillus punctatipes is named for the conspicuous brownish glandular dots on the stipe. The cap is typically very viscid, some shade of brown, and often appears radially streaked on the margin. The stipe is rather short, yellow at the apex and whitish below, and darkens when handled. There is no veil. The tubes are yellowish to whitish or tan and stain brownish when bruised. The pores are large and often elongated to compound, a feature that helps to separate *S. punctatipes* from *S. granulatus*, a similar-looking species associated with pine. As it gets older, it often becomes dingy and unattractive. *Suillus punctatipes* is common in our moist conifer forests in fall, sometimes appearing in substantial numbers with true fir and western hemlock.

Suillus tomentosus (Kauffman) Singer

Like *Suillus brevipes*, *S. tomentosus* is very common and abundant in the PNW. Its cap is viscid when fresh and typically has a covering of grayish, yellowish, reddish brown, or bright red fibrils or fibrillose scales over an orange-yellow to yellowish background. The flesh is yellow and usually turns bluish on exposure. The tubes are yellow and the pores are angular, brown to yellowish, and stain blue when injured. The stipe is conspicuously glandular dotted and similar in color to the cap. There is no veil. *Suillus tomentosus* occurs primarily under lodgepole and shore pines. *Suillus variegatus* is a European kissing cousin.

Suillus umbonatus Dick and Snell

Suillus umbonatus has a viscid, distinctly umbonate cap that is yellow to olive-brown and often streaked; large, yellowish, angular, often radially aligned pores; and a slender yellowish stipe that is glandular dotted above a gelatinous ring or ring-zone and stains brown when handled. It is rather abundant at times in lodgepole pine forests in late summer and early fall, and in shore pine woodlands in fall, sometimes growing in clusters and lining the edges of moist depressions. *Suillus flavidus* is another name that has been used for *S. umbonatus*, but it is unclear if they are the same species. *Suillus sibiricus* (Singer) Singer (= *S. americanus*), a somewhat similar species, differs primarily in its brighter yellow coloration, tendency for the veil to be shaggy-membranous rather than glutinous, and being associated with five-needle pines; it is broadly distributed in the Northern Hemisphere.

Suillus viscidus (Linnaeus) Fries

Suillus viscidus (= *S. laricinus*, *S. aeruginascens*) is a larch-associated species with a viscid to slimy, gray to olive-brown or darker cap, the edge of which sometimes is adorned with bits of veil tissue. The tubes and pores are whitish to gray, not yellow as in most suilluses, and stain blue when bruised. The stipe is whitish above the slight ring or ring-zone. The lower stipe is viscid and similar

Suillus umbonatus SAT-04-304-03

Suillus sibiricus SAT-07-272-02

Suillus viscidus SAT-05-281-07

in color to the cap. The flesh is white to yellowish and stains blue when bruised or cut. Interestingly, *S. viscidus* stains waxed paper or white office paper blue. Look for it in late summer and fall. It has sometimes been placed in the genus *Fuscoboletinus*.

GENUS *LECCINUM*

Leccinum is a diverse genus, and there have been several not fully successful attempts to sort out the species in the Northern Hemisphere. Recently, however, in Europe good progress has been made in clarifying species concepts and their ecological occurrence. Leccinums are easy to identify to genus because of the brownish to grayish or blackish scabers (tufts of short stiff hyphal ends) that decorate their stipes. Although

not easy to describe, the cap colors and overall stature also are distinctive, and one soon learns to recognize them. The color and microscopic structure of the cap are important characters for identification, along with the type of tree the mushrooms were growing with. Many leccinums are ectomycorrhizal with aspens and cottonwoods or birches, a smaller proportion occurs with conifers, and others can be found with madrone and manzanita, especially along the coast of southern Oregon and northern California. Color changes of the flesh upon exposure traditionally has been an important character for defining and recognizing species; however, recent work suggests color changes are highly variable within individual species, and so this character is receiving much less emphasis. Historically, all leccinums

Leccinum insigne SAT-99-232-02

have been considered edible, although a number of severe gastrointestinal poisonings in the Rocky Mountains and Cascades indicate that at least some species should be avoided. Unfortunately, uncertainties surrounding species concepts makes it difficult to know just which species are the problem-causers. Many leccinums turn gray to black when cooked or dried and, although it does not affect the edibility, some people find it unsettling at first.

Leccinum insigne A. H. Smith, Thiers, and Watling

In our region, the larger leccinums that have conspicuous flaps of sterile tissue on the edge of the cap occur with a variety of trees and shrubs, including various conifers, aspen and cottonwood, madrone, manzanita, and, in the northern areas, birch. The characteristics of many of the larger species overlap, and identification is challenging. Several leccinums are associated with aspen in our mountains, and they have been given a variety of names. Our photo illustrates *Leccinum insigne*, a species with a reddish brown to rust-brown or orange-brown, somewhat fibrillose cap, white to olive-buff or yellowish tubes that stain brownish when bruised, a white stipe with pallid to dark brown or blackish scabers, and white flesh that may change to dark gray, and sometimes with blue in the base.

A large, often abundant, species that has been called *Leccinum aurantiacum* occurs in our conifer forests. That name, however, is incorrect since *L. aurantiacum* has been shown to be associated with hardwoods. Our species may be closer to *L. vulpinum* described from Europe. It has a red to reddish orange-brown or dark reddish brown, fibrillose cap, black scabers, a bluing stipe base, and whitish flesh that changes slightly or more distinctly to grayish or blackish, sometimes after going through a vinaceous gray phase. *Leccinum ponderosum* and *L. manzanitae*, two often massive species, are similarly colored. All these are generally considered good, but not great, edibles, although poisonings in the Rocky Mountains and PNW associated with similar-looking leccinums suggest one should adopt a cautious approach to eating them.

Leccinum scabrum (Bulliard: Fries) S. F. Gray

Leccinum scabrum is a medium-sized to large species that is very common in urban and suburban settings and less so in natural habitats. Its caps are tan to grayish brown or darker brown or olive-brown depending on age and condition; often the edge is paler. The cap surface varies from dry to viscid, may be somewhat tomentose, and can become cracked in age. The pores are cream to pale tan or olive-buff, and the tubes are whitish and darken in age. The stipe is clavate, long in relation to the diameter of the

Leccinum scabrum SAT-03-271-01

cap, whitish, and ornamented with small blackish scabers. The flesh of young specimens, which is whitish, usually does not change much, although sometimes it can become somewhat brownish after exposure. The taste is mild, but the flesh is often soft and marshmallowy, thus limiting its culinary appeal. *Leccinum scabrum* likely has been introduced into the PNW with planted birches. However, it also occurs in natural birch populations, such as in northern Idaho and Washington. In the city, *L. scabrum* often occurs with *Paxillus involutus, Lactarius plumbeus, L. glyciosmus, Amanita muscaria,* and other birch-loving mushrooms.

Porphyrellus porphyrosporus (Fries and Hök) Gilbert

Porphyrellus porphyrosporus is easy to recognize, but harder to name. The combination of a black to dark brown velvety cap, often with a paler margin, dark brown to black tubes and pores, dark brown to almost black stipe with a white base, and blue to blue-green staining reaction separates it easily from other boletes in our region. It has deep reddish brown spores, which also is helpful in identification. *Porphyrellus porphyrosporus* is widespread but not abundant in coastal and low elevation conifer forests. In western North America it also has been called *Tylopilus pseudoscaber* and elsewhere has gone by *P. pseudoscaber*. Recent studies have shown that tylopiluses are not its closest relatives. Although a few species of *Tylopilus* have been reported from California, they are uncommon there and rare at best in the PNW.

Porphyrellus porphyrosporus

Spine-Fungi

These fungi are grouped together on the basis of their producing spores on down-hanging, icicle-like spines. Although they share this feature, consideration of their other characteristics, along with molecular data, suggests that they are not all closely related to each other. Most have a stipe and cap; these often are referred to as stipitate hydnums. The odd fungus out in this case is the genus *Hericium*, in which there is no stipe and no cap, merely a series of branches that bear the spines; it also differs by growing as a saprotroph on logs and snags. The other genera represented here include the following.

- *Auriscalpium*: one species; a small, slender, dark brown, hairy, asymmetric-capped cone-dweller, spores small, amyloid, roughened.
- *Hydnellum*: fruitbodies darkly colored, stipe usually short and thick, cap wide, usually concentrically zoned, spreading irregularly, and often incorporating twigs or other debris, flesh very tough and pliable, usually zoned (like tree rings, cut a fruitbody in half lengthwise), spores small, brown, and warty.
- *Hydnum* (= *Dentinum*): fruitbodies pale-colored, stipe usually long and slender, flesh rather soft, similar to that of chanterelles, spores smooth and white.
- *Phellodon*: fruitbodies medium to darkly colored, stipe usually short and slender, cap relatively wide, spreading irregularly, and often incorporating twigs, other debris, or even its neighbors, flesh very tough and pliable, usually zoned, spores small, white, and warty; generally similar to hydnellums, but smaller and less bulky.
- *Sarcodon*: fruitbodies medium to darkly colored, stature generally intermediate between *Hydnum* and *Hydnellum*, stipe

often thick, flesh fairly tough and brittle, not zoned, not incorporating surrounding debris, spores small, brown, and warty. The genus name *Hydnum* is used for these fungi by those who use *Dentinum* for *Hydnum repandum* and similar species. Species of *Bankera* are similar to sarcodons but have white spores and often curry-like odors. They are not common.

With the exception of *Auriscalpium*, these fungi are ectomycorrhizal, especially with conifers on sandy or otherwise nutrient-poor soils, and are a characteristic element of the northern forests. Unfortunately, they have received little critical study in our region, so our knowledge of their occurrence is far from complete. Most are too tough and/or unpleasant-tasting to eat; however, *Hydnum*

repandum, H. umbilicatum, and the hericiums are good edibles. Despite their general inedibility, many of the hydnellums, phellodons, and sarcodons are eagerly sought-after for use in dyeing wool.

Auriscalpium vulgare S. F. Gray
EAR-PICK FUNGUS

Auriscalpium vulgare is an unmistakable, but usually inconspicuous, fungus found primarily on (often buried) Douglas-fir cones in the PNW. Elsewhere it can often be found on the cones of pine or occasionally spruce. It is small, dark brown, hairy, and the stipe is lateral. Current evidence suggests it is related to the gilled fungus *Lentinellus*, the coralloid *Clavicorona*, the poroid *Albatrellus*, and other relatives of the russulas, including the fellow spine-fungus *Hericium*. The epithet (*vulgare* means "common") attests to the wide distribution of the fungus in much of North America, Europe, and temperate Asia.

Hericium abietis (Weir: Hubert) K. A. Harrison

Hericium abietis is the most commonly encountered hericium in the PNW. It grows on conifer logs, especially those of fir and hemlock. The branches and spines are whitish when young, and become yellowish in age. Three other hericiums are known from North America—*H. americanum* occurs on hardwoods (rarely on conifers) in the East, *H. coralloides* (= *H. ramosum*) occurs on hardwoods throughout the continent, and *H. erinaceus* (lion's mane) occurs on hardwoods in the East and extends into California and perhaps up the Pacific Coast on oaks. The former two are difficult to distinguish from *H. abietis* by morphology; the latter differs from the others in being

Auriscalpium vulgare

Hericium abietis

unbranched and having longer (up to 5 cm, 2 in.) spines. All are edible, good, and eagerly sought by mycophagists.

Hydnellum aurantiacum (Batsch: Fries) P. Karsten

When young and bright orange, *Hydnellum aurantiacum* is easily identified; however, the fruitbodies become increasingly brown with age and harder to tell apart from old specimens of *H. caeruleum* and other species. Initially the cap has a whitish edge and orange center; at least the uppermost portion of the stipe is orange, and the remainder is brown. The spines are whitish to pale orange and do not extend much down the stipe. When cut in half, the flesh is deepest orange in the lower portion of the stipe, even in age; usually the flesh of the cap is paler, sometimes almost white. The overall appearance of the mushroom is quite

Hydnellum aurantiacum SAT-01-252-17

variable and so several varieties have been named; however, there is so much overlap in the characteristics that they appear not to represent distinct entities. *Hydnellum auratile* also has been reported from the PNW; it is smaller, has more uniformly red-

Hydnellum caeruleum

Hydnellum peckii SAT-05-265-15

Hydnellum peckii, young specimen
SAT-01-264-25

dish orange flesh in cap and stipe, and has slightly smaller spores (4.5–5.5 × 4–5 vs. 5.5–7 × 4–6 μm). *Hydnellum aurantiacum* is a widespread fungus, occurring throughout much of North America, Europe, and temperate Asia.

Hydnellum caeruleum (Hornemann: Persoon) P. Karsten

Hydnellum caeruleum differs from *H. aurantiacum* in its coloration, but otherwise is very similar. When young, the cap includes shades of blue, blue-gray, and brown, with the paler blue tones occurring near the edge. The spines are brownish, with blue overtones prominent when young, and the stipe is orange-brown to brown. The flesh of the cap is bluish to grayish to nearly black, and that of the stipe is red- to orange-brown. Most of the blue colors disappear in age, and older fruitbodies look much the same as those of *H. aurantiacum*. Another species with blue colors is *H. suaveolens*; its cap usually is yellowish brown with a whitish or very pale blue edge, the flesh is entirely blue, and the mushroom has a strong sweet anise odor. *Hydnellum caeruleum* is a widespread fungus, occurring throughout much of North America, Europe, and temperate Asia.

Hydnellum peckii Banker

When young, *Hydnellum peckii* is easily identified. At that stage, the fruitbodies are whitish lumps, usually adorned with drops of bright red liquid, which makes them look like cranberry scones according to one of our former students. In age, they become much expanded, assume an overall reddish brown color, and are much less distinctive. However, even then they can be identified by their sharp peppery taste, which "grabs" the back of your throat. *Hydnellum diabolus* of eastern

North America is very similar, but differs in having a pleasant odor when young and a distinctly rough-hairy, not matted-wooly, cap surface; some mycologists consider it synonymous with *H. peckii*. The European species *H. ferrugineum* is also very similar, but has darker flesh and a mild taste.

Hydnum repandum Linnaeus: Fries
HEDGEHOG

Hydnum repandum and the other hedgehogs are distinguished by their pale cream to creamy orangish coloration, soft icicle-like spines on the caps, and soft texture of the flesh. This combination of features, plus their occurrence in forests, makes them easy to recognize. *Hydnum umbilicatum* Peck differs in generally being smaller and having a darker orangish, distinctly umbilicate cap, longer, more slender stipe, and slightly larger spores (7.5–10 × 6–8.5 vs. 6.5–8.5 × 6–8.5 µm). *Hydnum rufescens* differs in being somewhat smaller and having more intensely colored caps and paler stipes, and *H. albidum* differs mainly in its overall pale coloration; however, many mycologists feel these are only forms of *H. repandum*. All are very popular edibles.

Phellodon atratus K. A. Harrison

Phellodon atratus is easily overlooked because of its dark purple-black cap color. It is most often noticed when growing in large troops among bright green mosses. The caps are somewhat zoned with the edges normally a bit lighter in color, the spines are very short and light gray to dark gray to purplish gray, and the flesh is purple- or blue-black. It is primarily a near-coastal species, being most common under Sitka spruce. *Phellodon melaleucus* is generally similar, but the caps are dark brown with purplish

Hydnum repandum SAT-05-266-17

Hydnum umbilicatum SAT-92-251-11

Phellodon atratus SAT-06-294-02

tints and pale edges, bruise brownish, and are easily imprinted when touched with a finger. *Phellodon atratus* appears to be confined to the Pacific Coast.

Phellodon tomentosus (Linnaeus: Fries) Banker

Phellodon tomentosus is recognized by its smallish fruitbodies with caps zoned in shades of brown, a whitish cap edge, small grayish spines, and brown flesh. No other phellodon in the PNW has this coloration. Several hydnellums have brownish zoned caps, but they usually are larger and have brown spores. Frequently, numerous individuals of *P. tomentosus* can be found together, many with the edges of their caps fused together. In this form, PNW mushroom-celebrity Maggie Rogers calls them "owl-eyes." They are quite common in PNW

conifer forests and occur elsewhere in the northern U.S., Canada, and Europe.

Sarcodon fuscoindicus (K. A. Harrison) Maas Geesteranus

The dark purple-black color of the fleshy cap and stipe, combined with the reddish-tinged spines that extend for a considerable way down the stipe make *Sarcodon fuscoindicus* easy to identify. Other PNW sarcodons are pale to medium-dark brown. It often occurs in moss near western hemlocks. Although the texture suggests it might be edible, the odor and taste are unpleasantly farinaceous.

Sarcodon imbricatus (Linnaeus: Fries) P. Karsten

Sarcodon imbricatus probably is the most common of the sarcodons and hydnellums

Phellodon tomentosus SAT-06-294-05

in the PNW and rest of North America. Its most noticeable feature is the very coarse scaly cap, with the brown scales already obvious in young individuals. In age, the scales become even more prominent, upturned, and darker. The background of the cap and stipe is usually buff to medium brown, and the short to moderately long spines are pale grayish brown and darken in age. *Sarcodon imbricatus* is commonly found in the conifer forests of the PNW and in either conifer or mixed forests in the rest of North America and much of Europe. With a mild odor and taste, it is said to be edible, but of poor quality—better in the dye pot than the soup pot.

Sarcodon scabrosus (Fries) P. Karsten

Sarcodon scabrosus is another large, stipitate hydnum that is common in the PNW, although not as common as *S. imbricatus*. It is similar in size and general appearance to the latter species, but differs by having a relatively smooth reddish brown cap when young (the scales develop with age, but do not become prominently upturned like those of *S. imbricatus*), a greenish black stipe base, and a moderate to strong farinaceous odor and strong bitter farinaceous taste. *Sarcodon scabrosus* occurs in conifer forests in the PNW, especially in second-growth stands of western hemlock and Douglas-fir with a salal understory. Similar species include *S. fennicus*, a European species whose presence in North America is uncertain, *S. rimosus*, with a cracked gray-violet cap, cinnamon stipe, and flesh that turns pinkish when cut, *S. subincarnatus*, also with flesh that turns pinkish, but with pallid spines, farinaceous odor, green stipe base, and a scaly brown cap without reddish tones, and *S. underwoodii*, with fragile spines, a milder odor, and no green on the stipe base.

Sarcodon fuscoindicus

Sarcodon imbricatus

Sarcodon scabrosus SAT-03-308-10

Club-, Coral-, and Fan-like Fungi

Historically most of the club- and coral-like basidiomycete fungi have been grouped in the large genus *Clavaria*. Over time, however, most have been transferred to other genera. These fungi produce fruitbodies that range from simple unbranched clubs to repeatedly branched coral-like or cauliflower-like forms, and with either white or colored (ocher to pale brownish) spores that range from narrowly ellipsoid to almost globose. The upright orientation separates this group from the spine-fungi, in which the spines hang downward like icicles. The flesh of the clubs and corals ranges from soft and brittle to leathery and tough. Spores are usually produced over the upper half, or sometimes the entire surface, of the club or branches and, hence, it is possible to obtain a spore-print by placing a fruitbody on its side on white paper and covering it to reduce air currents and conserve moisture. The larger, unbranched, finger-like forms (fairy clubs) belong mostly to the genera *Clavaria*, *Clavariadelphus*, and *Clavulinopsis*, and there are several other genera of mostly smaller clubs, including

Macrotyphula, *Multiclavula*, and *Typhula*. The branched forms (coral-fungi) principally include members of the large genus *Ramaria*, plus smaller genera such as *Clavulina*, *Clavicorona*, and *Ramariopsis*. We have also included a number of other fungi that produce club-like, coral-like, or fan-like fruitbodies, but that have not been associated with the genus *Clavaria*.

Despite the overall similarity in appearance that has caused them to be grouped together, recent analyses, including DNA studies, suggest that the clubs and corals do not form a natural evolutionary group. *Ramaria* and *Clavariadelphus* are most closely related to *Gomphus*, *Gautieria* (a genus of false truffles), and stinkhorns; *Clavulina* and *Multiclavula* to the chanterelles and the genus *Hydnum*; *Clavicorona* to the russulas and lactariuses; and *Clavaria*, *Clavulinopsis*, and *Typhula* to the main group of gilled mushrooms. The edibility of the small clubs is largely unknown, but the larger forms of both clubs and corals, especially certain species of *Ramaria*, are regularly collected and eaten in the PNW, although none is particularly renowned. In general the group is a relatively safe one as none of the species is thought to be dangerously toxic. However, several, such as *R. gelatinosa*, are known to cause digestive distress.

CLUB-LIKE BASIDIOMYCETES

The main club genera—*Clavaria*, *Clavariadelphus*, and *Clavulinopsis*—can be differentiated by the following characteristics.

- *Clavaria*: terrestrial, fruitbodies simple, cylindric, often clustered, sometimes sparingly branched (and then not fleshy, and often bright-colored), mostly fragile-fleshed, lacking carotenoid pigments, spores smooth and white, clamp connections usually lacking.
- *Clavariadelphus*: terrestrial, often among dense conifer needle and twig litter, fruitbodies solitary to gregarious, simple, erect, more or less club-shaped, rounded or flattened at the fertile or infertile apex, surface smooth or somewhat wrinkled, usually light yellowish or ochraceous, spores smooth, white or slightly yellowish, clamps present, iron sulfate on hymenium bright green to olive.
- *Clavulinopsis*: very similar to *Clavaria*, but clamps usually are present, the hymenium may turn green in iron sulfate, and they may have carotenoid pigments.

Calocera cornea (Batsch: Fries) Fries
Calocera cornea is a wood-inhabiting jelly-fungus. Its growth in large troops on rotting logs and small size set it apart from the other club-fungi. Microscopically, its spores are divided by a cross-wall and are produced

Calocera cornea SAT-07-204-05

on basidia that are shaped like tuning forks or wishbones. It occurs throughout much of the world. *Calocera viscosa* is closely related, but is brighter in color, coralloid, and occurs on conifer wood.

Clavaria acuta Fries

Clavaria acuta is a small pure white terrestrial club that grows as scattered individuals or fused pairs or trios. Often the clubs

Clavaria acuta SAT-02-341-01

exhibit a translucent stipe with a whiter upper fertile portion. It usually occurs on bare soil in somewhat disturbed areas. *Clavaria vermicularis* Fries is very similar (microscopically nearly identical) and more common; it too grows on soil, but in dense clusters of usually larger clubs. Its species name comes from the Latin for "worm."

Clavaria purpurea O. F. Müller: Fries

When fresh, the purple clubs of *Clavaria purpurea* are unmistakable. They are unbranched and often occur in huge masses in mossy soil under conifers, especially spruce. As they age, the clubs lose most of their purple color, becoming a dull watery tan. Current thought suggests *C. purpurea* is most closely related to omphalina-like mushrooms in an evolutionary group that includes many crust-fungi. A new genus name, *Alloclavaria*, has been proposed for it.

Clavaria vermicularis SAT-98-349-01

Clavaria purpurea

Clavariadelphus truncatus (Quélet) Donk

The species of *Clavariadelphus* can usually be told from the other clubs by their larger size, stockier stature, and characteristic ocher to yellow-orange color. *Clavariadelphus truncatus* produces rather large fruitbodies with a wide flattened cap, which makes it look something like a chanterelle, especially when the fertile surface, which runs down the upper portion beneath the "cap," is wrinkled. It occurs with conifers throughout much of the Northern Hemisphere. *Clavariadelphus truncatus* is edible, with a rather sweet taste. *Clavariadelphus pistillaris* produces similarly large fruitbodies, but they lack the wide flattened top and grow in eastern North America with hardwoods. Our western version of *C. pistillaris* is *C. occidentalis*; it occurs with both conifers and hardwoods.

Clavariadelphus sachalinensis (S. Imai) Corner

Clavariadelphus sachalinensis is one of several small slender members of the genus that are characterized by fruiting from a dense mycelial mat that permeates and binds the substrate and by having narrowly ellipsoid or sway-backed spores. Often these species can be found in large troops under conifers. All are initially pale yellow and become pinkish cinnamon to ochraceous cinnamon as they age. The entire upper portion of the club is covered with fertile tissue. *Clavariadelphus ligula* is indistinguishable from *C. sachalinensis* in the field, differing primarily by its shorter spores (12–16.5 × 3.5–4.5 vs. 18–24 × 4–6 µm). Because intermediates often can be found, it could be that only one species is involved, in which case the name *C. ligula* would have priority. *Clavariadel-*

phus lignicola is a third similar species, but has spores with average width greater than 6 µm (vs. less than 5 µm) and seems to have a smaller geographic range, reportedly only Arizona, Colorado, and Utah. *Clavariadelphus sachalinensis*, described from Sakhalin Island, is widespread in western and northern North America.

Clavulinopsis laeticolor (Berkeley and M. A. Curtis) R. H. Petersen

The small bright yellow to golden orange clubs of *Clavulinopsis laeticolor* (= *C. pulchra*,

Clavariadelphus truncatus SAT-99-296-11

Clavariadelphus sachalinensis SAT-06-228-14

Ramariopsis laeticolor) can often be found growing in scattered groups on soil among mosses. The several similar small golden clubs must be examined microscopically to identify them confidently. *Clavulinopsis laeticolor* has rather variable broadly ellipsoid to almost globose (4–7 × 3.5–5 µm) spores with a prominent apiculus that sometimes gives them an almost triangular shape. It is a widespread species, occurring across North America and in Europe and parts of Asia. *Clavulinopsis helvola* is very similar, but has coarsely warty spores, which is unusual

among these club- and coral-fungi. *Clavulinopsis fusiformis* is larger, typically bright yellow, and usually grows in dense bundles.

Typhula erythropus (Persoon: Fries) Fries

Species of *Typhula* differ from the other clubs by the presence of a sclerotium, a hard knot of hyphae, at the base of the stipe or buried in the substrate. *Typhula erythropus* is a small species, characterized by a white upper portion above a reddish brown, hairy stipe. It grows on the petioles (stalk-like portion) of the fallen leaves of hardwoods such as bigleaf maple.

Clavulinopsis laeticolor

CLUB-LIKE ASCOMYCETES

Many of these species are commonly referred to as earth-tongues. Although they vary in appearance, they differ from the club-like basidiomycetes by always having a distinct head, where the spores are produced. Ecologically, most of them are saprotophs, often on leaf litter. *Cordyceps* species, on the other hand, are parasitic on insects or, less often, other fungi.

Cordyceps capitata (Holmskjold: Fries) Link

The species of *Cordyceps* are parasitic, primarily on insects and spiders. Because the PNW climate is not conducive to the growth of lots of fat juicy insects, we have few *Cordyceps* species here. However, some species in the genus occur on truffles, which thrive in our climate, so we do get a few cordyceps. One of them is *C. capitata*, which is found on *Elaphomyces granulatus*, but only if you recognize what you are dealing with and take time to excavate the entire stipe of the cordyceps and the attached truffle.

Typhula erythropus

The dark-colored, globose head has a finely bumpy texture and sits atop a yellowish to olive-colored, often rough-textured, stipe. The spores are very long and threadlike, breaking up at maturity into 12–30 × 1.5–3 µm segments. *Cordyceps longisegmentis* (= *C. canadensis*) is very similar, but its spores have longer (30–50 µm) segments. *Cordyceps ophioglossoides* has a dark olivaceous elongated head, and dark olivaceous stipe that grades downward to a brilliant yellow base, often with yellow cords attached. Although not particularly desirable for food, many cordyceps are used in Asian medicine; however, we are not aware of *C. capitata* being used in this way.

Cudonia circinans (Persoon: Fries) Fries

Cudonia and the similar-looking *Leotia* species have well-defined heads, rather than having the head merge gradually into the stipe. Cudonias are dull-colored, fleshy, and a bit tough, while leotias are brighter-colored, with viscid surfaces and firm, but jelly-like, flesh. *Cudonia circinans* is pale brown, pinkish brown, or somewhat yellowish, and usually occurs in dense groups in conifer litter. It has long slender spores (28–46 × 2 µm) with multiple cross-walls at maturity. Our most common cudonia, it is widespread in North America, Europe, and Asia. *Cudonia monticola* is a mostly spring-fruiting, less yellowish species with shorter (18–24 µm) spores, normally with one or no cross-walls.

Heyderia abietis (Fries) Link

Heyderia abietis is an uncommon, or maybe just rarely noticed, species that occurs in scattered groups on conifer needles including, as the species name suggests, those of true firs. It rarely grows to as much as 2.5

cm (1 in.) tall, and its yellow-brown to dull brown color makes the fruitbodies difficult to spot among dead brown needles. The spores are slender cylindrical, 11–15 × 1.5–2.5 µm, and have no cross-walls. It could

Cordyceps capitata on the truffle *Elaphomyces granulatus*

Cudonia circinans SAT-05-265-09

Heyderia abietis SAT-97-297-06

Mitrula elegans SAT-07-159-06

Spathularia flavida

be confused with species of *Mitrula* (and once was placed in that genus), but the dull brownish coloration sets it apart.

Mitrula elegans (Berkeley) Fries
SWAMP BEACON

Mitrula elegans looks very much like a yellow- or golden-orange-headed wooden match. It is typically a spring-fruiter, occurring on very wet plant litter or even on litter submerged in cold, shallow, running water. *Mitrula paludosa* is a nearly identical European species; it differs primarily in having slightly broader spores (11–24 × 2–4 vs. 11–17 × 1.5–3 µm). *Mitrula borealis* is also similar; it has broad ellipsoid to ovoid spores, 10.5–18 × 2.5–5 µm, and has been reported from Alaska and western Montana, so probably occurs elsewhere in the northern portion of our region. *Mitrula lunulatospora* is another similar North American species with somewhat crescent-shaped spores, 11–19 × 2–4 µm; it is known only from the eastern part of the continent.

Spathularia flavida Persoon: Fries

Spathularia flavida is a representative of the ascomycete fungi commonly called earthtongues; the genus name is derived from the Latin for "broadsword." The stipe is whitish to yellow or yellow-brown, and usually has whitish to yellow fuzz at the base. The fertile head usually is some shade of creamy yellow. *Spathularia velutipes* differs by its darker brown hairy stipe with orangish fuzz at the base, browner fertile head, and distribution primarily in eastern North America.

Trichoglossum hirsutum (Persoon: Fries) Boudier

Trichoglossum hirsutum is one of many black earth-tongues. Its binomial roughly translates as "hairy hair tongue," and this indicates its main difference from the members of the genus *Geoglossum* ("earth-tongue"), which are also black but smooth and shiny, not velvety-hairy. The spores of *T. hirsutum* are brown, very long and narrow (80–210 × 5–7 µm), and contain about 15 cross-walls. Several other species are distinguished by spore length, number of cross-walls, and number of spores per ascus; most seem to occur primarily in eastern North America, as do most of the geoglossums.

Vibrissea truncorum (Albertini and Schweinitz: Fries) Fries

Vibrissea truncorum is another spring-fruiting fungus found on rotting pieces of wood that are very wet or submerged in cold water. Its head is usually orangish to pinkish orange and is rounder and more regularly shaped compared to the head of *Mitrula elegans*. The spores are exceedingly long and slender (125–250 × 1–1.5 µm) and usually can be seen with a handlens as they stream out from the head. When many are escaping simultaneously, the heads look as though covered with a whitish mold.

Xylaria hypoxylon (Linnaeus: Fries) Greville
CARBON ANTLERS, CANDLE-SNUFF FUNGUS

Xylaria is a large genus, whose members are well known only to a few specialists. *Xylaria hypoxylon* is an exceedingly common species that can be found year-round. The most commonly encountered form, with powdery whitish branch tips, is the asexual stage of the fungus. The sexual stage is less conspicuous as it lacks the white color; it is usually less branched (if at all) and has a rough warty surface from numerous small flask-like structures that produce the kidney-

Trichoglossum hirsutum

Vibrissea truncorum SAT-99-129-03

Xylaria hypoxylon

bean-shaped spores. Both stages occur on rotting wood.

GENUS *RAMARIA*

Ramaria, with 500 or more species worldwide, is the largest genus of club- and coral-fungi. Its fruitbodies branch multiple times from a common, usually fleshy, base, and are colored and often colorful; the spores are cream to yellowish, ocher, or pale brownish, often warty, spiny, or with longitudinal ridges, and clamps often are present. Most species are terrestrial, but some grow on wood and others in leaf litter.

Ramaria is divided into four subgenera: *Ramaria*, *Laeticolora*, *Echinoramaria*, and *Lentoramaria*. The members of *Ramaria* and *Laeticolora* occur on soil, and all seem to be ectomycorrhizal; many of the PNW

species seem particularly fond of hemlock. They are relatively large and fleshy, usually brightly colored, and can be plucked more or less cleanly from the substrate. Species in subgenus *Ramaria* are distinguished from those in *Laeticolora* by their striate (vs. smooth to warty) spores, amyloid reaction of the stipe flesh (vs. amyloid or not), often rather massive stipes, pale-colored stipe and branches contrasting with brightly colored tips (vs. more deeply colored, with or without brighter tips), basidia bearing clamps at their base (vs. clamped or not), and average spore length usually over 11 µm.

The species of subgenera *Echinoramaria* and *Lentoramaria* are saprotrophic, occurring on wood or leaf litter, which often is permeated with mycelial cords or densely matted with mycelium and pulls up with the mushroom when picked. The fruitbod-

Ramaria abietina

ies are small, usually dull-colored (brown or dingy cream to pale yellow), and have slender branches that are fairly tough or leathery, giving the mushroom a bushy look. Because the morphology and lifestyle of *Echinoramaria* and *Lentoramaria* are quite different from those of the other two subgenera, it has been suggested that they should be raised to genus level. *Echinoramaria* is distinguished from *Lentoramaria* by its more spiny (vs. more warty) spores, growth in leaf litter (vs. on wood or leaf litter), and rhizomorphs composed of a single type (vs. two types) of hypha.

Ramaria abietina (Persoon: Fries) Quélet

Ramaria abietina (= *R. ochraceovirens*), of the subgenus *Echinoramaria*, is a slender, dingy yellowish coral that develops greenish stains in age or when handled. The spores are fairly small (6–9 × 3.5–4.5 µm) and are spiny. It grows in conifer litter, often appearing in rows of fruitbodies. It occurs across the U.S. and Canada and also in Europe and Asia.

Ramaria acrisiccescens Marr and D. E. Stuntz

Ramaria acrisiccescens (subgenus *Laeticolora*) is a whitish to cream-colored, medium-sized to large, upright species with straight, elongated, crowded branches. The flesh may have pinkish or brownish tones, especially in age, and reacts with neither iron sulfate nor Melzer's reagent. If a microscope is available, check the bases of the basidia for clamp connections, as *R. acrisiccescens* is the only whitish ramaria in the PNW without basal clamps. The spores are subcylindrical, 8–14 × 4–6 µm, and have prominent warts. It occurs throughout the conifer forests of the PNW. *Ramaria velocimutans* is quite sim-

ilar but has brownish hyphae on the stipe base, a brownish band of tissue in the stipe, and clamp connections on the basidia.

Ramaria araiospora Marr and D. E. Stuntz

Ramaria araiospora (subgenus *Laeticolora*) is one of a small number of red-branched ramarias. It is distinguished from the others by having a single slender stipe, often with a bulbous base, non-amyloid flesh, slightly warty spores (8–13 × 3–4.5 µm),

Ramaria acrisiccescens SAT-07-277-03

Ramaria araiospora

and basidia without clamps. Although the branches always are red when young, the tips may be either red (in var. *rubella*) or yellow (in var. *araiospora*); in age the whole fruitbody fades to pale reddish yellow and becomes more difficult to identify by morphology alone. The other red species in the PNW are *R. stuntzii* and *R. cyaneigranosa*. Compared to *R. araiospora*, *R. stuntzii* has shorter spores (7–10 × 3–5 µm), a more massive base, reddish orange upper stipe, branches with red tips, and amyloid flesh; *R. cyaneigranosa* has wider wartier spores (8–15 × 4–6 µm), overall pinkish to salmon

Ramaria cystidiophora

Ramaria flavigelatinosa

color, and basidia with granules that appear blue in cotton blue stain. All three appear to be restricted to the PNW.

Ramaria cystidiophora Marr and D. E. Stuntz

The fruitbodies of *Ramaria cystidiophora* (subgenus *Laeticolora*) are upright, medium-sized, with distinctive yellow branches, often with brighter lemon-yellow tips, fuzzy white stipe base, often a sweet odor of anise or citrus, and clamped basidia. The species has been divided into several varieties based on differences in spore length, details of branch color (peach color in var. *anisata*), flesh consistency, odor, and bruising reactions. All these are gradational characters and thus it is not always easy to identify a collection to variety level; however, the yellow color and upright habit make the species fairly easy to recognize.

Ramaria flavigelatinosa Marr and D. E. Stuntz

Ramaria flavigelatinosa (subgenus *Laeticolora*) is a variably colored species, usually yellowish, but in some forms with more or less salmon-colored flesh that produces an orangish tint in the branches. Often very brightly colored when young, the fruitbodies often fade considerably as they age and look very different when mature. It is a small to medium-sized species and usually broader than tall. The flesh of the stipe is somewhat gelatinous (but not as much so as in *R. gelatinosa*), reacts with neither iron sulfate nor Melzer's reagent, and often has a bean-like odor. The spores are subcylindrical, 8–11 × 3.5–4.5 µm, and have prominent warts. Several varieties have been named, based on slight differences in coloration, odor, flesh consistency, and spore size.

Ramaria gelatinosa var. oregonensis Marr and D. E. Stuntz

Ramaria gelatinosa var. *oregonensis* (subgenus *Laeticolora*) is an easy species to identify if a fruitbody is cut in half. Uniquely among PNW species, the stipes are fused together and the flesh is translucent and gelatinous. Other species (*R. flavigelatinosa*, *R. gelatiniaurantia*, *R. sandaricina*) are slightly gelatinous and could be confusing to one who has not seen *R. g.* var. *oregonensis*. *Ramaria gelatinosa* var. *oregonensis* is a medium-sized orange species, with a yellow band on the upper stipe and yellow tips. It is often found close to logs or other large woody debris. It differs microscopically from *R. g.* var. *gelatinosa*, so much so that some mycologists feel it should be raised to species level. It appears to be restricted to the PNW. The gelatinous ramarias cause diarrhea in most people, and so they should be avoided.

Ramaria magnipes Marr and D. E. Stuntz

Ramaria magnipes (subgenus *Laeticolora*) is one of the species that fruit in spring, mostly in the mountains east of the Cascade crest. The light yellowish fruitbodies are medium to large, with an often massive white stipe that develops brown stains in age. It has fairly long (9.5–14 × 3–5 µm) smooth or slightly ridged spores and clamped basidia. The flesh has a slow, weak amyloid reaction. Similar to other spring-fruiting corals, most of the fruitbody is buried in the soil, and the young branches resemble heads of cauliflower emerging from the soil and needle litter. *Ramaria magnipes* is an edible species, but Orson Miller reported that, in some people, it has laxative effects.

Ramaria rasilispora var. rasilispora Marr and D. E. Stuntz

Ramaria rasilispora var. *rasilispora* (subgenus *Laeticolora*) is a very common member of the PNW's spring mycota. It is a lovely pale yellow when fresh, although it often stays mostly buried and covered with soil, and can reach fairly large size. The stipe does not bruise brown and does not react with iron sulfate, but does exhibit a very slow, weak amyloid reaction. The spores are smooth or very finely warty and 8–11.5 × 3–4.5 µm, and the basidia have clamps at the base. *Ramaria rasilispora* var. *rasilispora* often is hard to

Ramaria gelatinosa var. *oregonensis*

Ramaria magnipes SAT-06-154-03

Ramaria rasilispora var. *rasilispora* SAT-07-124-07

Ramaria rubrievanescens

Ramaria rubripermanens SAT-07-123-08

distinguish from *R. magnipes*, which is brighter colored when fresh and has slightly longer spores. *Ramaria rasilispora* var. *scatesiana* differs in being somewhat paler colored, and occasionally occurring in fall, although it too is primarily a spring-fruiter. All these are eaten by many people.

Ramaria rubrievanescens Marr and D. E. Stuntz

Ramaria rubrievanescens and *R. rubripermanens* Marr and D. E. Stuntz both of the subgenus *Ramaria*, are two medium to large, often bulky, whitish corals with coral-pink to pinkish red branch tips. One way to sometimes tell them apart is to check the calendar: *R. rubrievanescens* fruits in fall only, *R. rubripermanens* in spring and fall. In addition, the tips of the latter retain their color, whereas those of *R. rubrievanscens* fade rapidly, and its stipe often is brown-bruised and dingy-looking, making iden-

Ramaria stricta

tification of older fruitbodies difficult. The spore sizes overlap (10.5–13.5 × 4–5.5 µm in *R. rubrievanescens*, 8–15.5 × 3.5–5 µm in *R. rubripermanens*), so often they are not particularly informative. However, spore size is useful in separating these two species from the very similar *R. botrytis*, which has larger spores (11–17 × 4–6 µm) and fruits in fall. The large size of all these species make them attractive as edibles but, as is common with ramarias, they have a laxative effect on some people, so proceed with caution and moderation if you choose to sample them.

Ramaria stricta (Persoon: Fries) Quélet
Ramaria stricta (subgenus *Lentoramaria*) is a widespread species that occurs on rotting wood, in the PNW, usually that of conifers. The fruitbodies are small to medium-sized, grade upward from a whitish base to reddish tan lower branches to pale yellowish upper branches, stain brownish overall, and have a distinctive upright habit. Microscopically, the spores are 7–10 × 3.5–5.5 µm and warty, and the cords that extend from the stipe base into the substrate are formed from two different types of hyphae. It is found throughout much of the U.S. and Canada and also in Europe. Several similar species grow on wood in the PNW, including *R. apiculata* with branch tips blue-green in one form and pale grayish orange in another, and relatively narrow ellipsoid spores, *R. concolor*, ocher-tan or tan without yellow or greenish yellow colors, *R. rubella* (= *R. acris*) with pinkish tan coloration and average spore length shorter than 7.5 µm, and *R. tsugina* with green stains. None of these has the yellow branch tips and brown bruising reaction of *R. stricta* or quite as well developed upright habit.

Ramaria testaceoflava SAT-00-285-02

Ramaria testaceoflava (Bresadola) Corner
Ramaria testaceoflava (subgenus *Laeticolora*) is characterized by its small to medium size, pale chocolate-brown branches, yellow branch tips, white fuzzy stipe base, rapid brown-bruising reaction, and flesh that turns green in iron sulfate. The brown coloration is unusual among the members of *Laeticolora*, as is the iron sulfate reaction in combination with clamped basidia. No other species combines all three of these characters.

OTHER CORAL-LIKE SPECIES
The other coral-fungi differ from the ramarias in having white, mostly smooth spores. In addition, most are paler in color than nearly all the ramarias.

Calocera viscosa (Persoon: Fries) Fries
Calocera viscosa looks very much like a clavaria or clavulinopsis, especially in its bright golden color. However, it actually is a jelly fungus, related to *C. cornea* and *Dacry-*

myces palmatus. Thus, microscopically, it is quite distinct from the other corals (having spores with single cross-walls produced on basidia that look like tuning forks or wishbones). Macroscopically, it is harder to separate, but its flesh is tougher and gelatinous, and the fruitbodies are viscid when moist. It is common, but rarely abundant, on rotting conifer wood in the forests of western North America, as well as in Europe and Asia.

Clavicorona pyxidata (Persoon: Fries) Doty

Clavicorona pyxidata (= *Artomyces pyxidatus*) is characterized by its wood-inhabiting, cream-colored to yellowish or brownish, erect, coralloid fruitbodies with branches that arise in a ring at the enlarged tip of a lower branch, resulting in the uppermost branch tips having a crown-like appear-

Calocera viscosa

Clavicorona pyxidata SAT-06-303-02

ance. The flesh is pliant, the spores white and amyloid (3.5–6×2–3 μm), and clamps and oil-containing cystidia are present. Despite its coralloid shape, its microscopic features and DNA evidence suggest that it is most closely related to the russulas, lentinelluses, and *Auriscalpium vulgare*. Other species of *Clavicorona* are distinguished by degree of branching, slight differences in spore shape and iodine reaction, and type of wood inhabited. These include *C. avellanea* (young branches grayish brown with pale tips, slightly broader spores, on conifer wood), *C. cristata* (only slightly branched, on conifer wood), *C. divaricata* (somewhat differently branched, on cottonwood logs), *C. piperata* (ornamented spores), and *C. taxophila* (only slightly branched, on conifer wood, spores nearly globose). Whether all these are deserving of recognition as separate species is not clear; more collection and critical study is needed to clarify the occurrence of clavicoronas in the PNW.

Clavulina cristata (Holmskjold: Fries) J. Schröter

Clavulina cristata (= *C. coralloides*) is a widespread and very common whitish to buff coral with pointed or toothed branch tips and white spores borne on two-spored basidia. Its shape is maddeningly variable, often making it difficult to recognize. It is ectomycorrhizal and usually occurs on soil, but at times can be found on well-rotted wood. Molecular analyses, as well as microscopic features, suggest that *C. cristata* is closely related to the chanterelles. Two similar species are *C. cinerea*, with lilac-grayish coloration, wrinkled branches, and less developed branching, and *C. rugosa*, with wrinkled (rugose) branches and only limited branching, especially at the tips. These

characters are not clear-cut and microscopic characters differ little among the three species, so one often encounters forms that are difficult to assign to one or another of them. The situation is further complicated by the tendency for *C. cristata* to be infected by the ascomycete *Helminthosphaeria clavariarum*.

Clavulina cristata

Clavulina cristata, infected by *Helminthosphaeria clavariarum* SAT-04-312-07

It produces gray to black colors in the clavulina (caused by formation of its minute fruitbodies) and seems to reduce branching of the tips, both of which can lead to confusion with *C. cinerea*.

Tremellodendropsis tuberosa
(Corner) D. A. Crawford

Like *Calocera viscosa*, *Tremellodendropsis tuberosa* is a coralloid relative of the jelly fungi. Its small, whitish to pale brownish fruitbodies usually arise from a single, long, whitish, stipe-like base and have a distinctive upright stature. The texture is quite tough. *Tremellodendropsis tuberosa* usually is

Tremellodendropsis tuberosa SAT-98-332-12

Stereopsis humphreyi

found on bare soil in forests; it is fairly common along the Pacific Coast, but is not well known, probably because it gets overlooked. The spores are generally ellipsoid to somewhat spindle- or almond-shaped, 12–20 × 5–9 µm, and are borne on basidia that are divided lengthwise, at least near their tips.

FAN-LIKE FUNGI
These fungi are superficially similar to the clubs and corals, but differ in having flat branches and generally tougher texture.

Stereopsis humphreyi (Burt) Redhead and D. A. Reid

Stereopsis humphreyi is a rare (or at least rarely reported) but distinctive fungus. The shape of the fruitbodies varies, sometimes looking like a kitchen spatula and at other times like a small fleshless chanterelle. Formerly, the species was considered a type of chanterelle (its original name was *Craterellus humphreyi*). It grows on cones and other litter of conifers, especially Sitka spruce, in rather wet areas. As far as we are aware, *S. humphreyi* has been reported only from coastal central Oregon, the west side of the Olympic Peninsula in Washington, and the Queen Charlotte Islands in B.C. It probably also occurs in southeast Alaska and northern California; whether it occurs farther inland is less certain.

Thelephora palmata Scopoli: Fries
Thelephora palmata is a candidate for stinkiest fungus in the forest. The fetid odor, combined with the somewhat coralloid appearance, flattened branches, and brownish gray coloration, usually with the tips being noticeably paler than the lower por-

Thelephora palmata

tions, makes it distinctive. It usually blends in with the conifer litter in which it grows and so may be smelled before it is seen. *Thelephora palmata* has a tough texture and, along with the other species in the genus, often is referred to as a leather fungus. It and other thelephoras also share irregularly shaped, brown, warty spores, an ectomycorrhizal lifestyle, and close relationship with spine-fungi such as hydnellums. *Thelephora palmata* is widespread and fairly common in North America, Europe, and Asia.

Thelephora terrestris Fries

Thelephora terrestris is another widespread inconspicuous leather fungus. Compared with *T. palmata*, the often abundant clusters are more frilly and flower-like and much less stinky, having very little odor. The fans are silky fibrillose on the upper surface and smooth or somewhat wrinkled underneath.

Thelephora terrestris SAT-98-195-06

Thelephora terrestris is ectomycorrhizal with conifers and is a very common "weed" in greenhouses and plantations where conifer seedlings are grown for reforestation purposes. It is even more widely distributed than *T. palmata*.

Polypores and Crust-Fungi

The fungi included here represent several growth habits, some with a stipe and cap, others that form rosettes, a number that form shelf- or hoof-like structures, and those that form flat sheets or patches attached to branches and logs. These fungi may be somewhat fleshy, as in *Albatrellus*, but most are tough-fibrous, leathery, rubbery, or woody in texture. Species with a stipe and pores underneath the cap may grow on wood or on the ground in soil and litter. The genera *Albatrellus*, *Boletopsis*, and *Coltricia* are typically terrestrial and ectomycorrhizal. *Bondarzewia*, *Onnia*, and *Phaeolus* cause root- and butt-rot of living trees.

Certain of these fungi fruit from logs, stumps, and snags and form single or multiple, small to large shelf-like caps that are tough, fibrous, rubbery, or leathery. The underside of the cap may have pores (*Bjerkandera*, *Ischnoderma*, *Laetiporus*, *Oligoporus*, *Trametes*), while others have a smooth, slightly bumpy or wrinkled underside (*Chondrostereum*, *Stereum*, *Hymenochaete*). Woody and tough, shelf- or hoof-like fruit-bodies of *Fomitopsis*, *Ganoderma*, *Phellinus*, and *Bridgeoporus* may grow for several years, and some can reach a rather substantial size.

Other wood-inhabiting fungi, such as *Coniophora*, *Meruliopsis*, *Phlebia*, and *Stereum*, grow as patches, crust-like coverings, or form shelf-like structures on the underside and sides of branches and logs. The spore-producing surface of these fungi is smooth to irregular or wrinkled or composed of tubes or spines. Generally one cannot easily remove these fungi from the substrate without destroying them, so it is best to cut off a portion of the wood with the fungus attached. Most of these fungi are wood decomposers, but a few, such as *Tomentella*, are ectomycorrhizal.

POLYPORES

Albatrellus avellaneus Pouzar

There are about ten species of *Albatrellus* in our region, including several rare or uncommon ones, and they occur on soil, litter, or wood. They are fleshy, but tough, and produce a single cap and stipe or multiple caps and stipes from a common base. *Albatrellus avellaneus* is a coastal to montane species associated with western hemlock and spruce, extending from California northward into Canada. It is medium-sized, and several fruitbodies often occur together. The cap is white to yellowish or orange-buff, sometimes with pinkish or purplish tones. In age, yellow and orange colors become more prominent, and the surface becomes fibrillose to scaly, with the scales sometimes slightly brownish. The tubes are decurrent and white, often staining yellow or orange in age. The stipe is whitish above with brownish tones toward the base, and stains yellow to rusty orange in age. Dried specimens often develop orange and red colors. *Albatrellus avellaneus* is very similar to *A. ovinus*, which apparently does not occur in our region, and *A. subrubescens*, a species of montane pine forests that stains yellow to orange when bruised or in age. All these fungi have white smooth spores; those of *A. avellaneus* and *A. ovinus* are non-amyloid while those of *A. subrubescens* are amyloid.

Albatrellus avellaneus SAT-04-296-01

Albatrellus dispansus (Lloyd) Canfield and Gilbertson

The fruitbodies of *Albatrellus dispansus* are complex, arising from a short thick base and branching out into numerous overlapping, sometimes fused, often irregularly shaped, caps. The caps are yellowish, dry, and tomentose to scaly; the tubes and pores are white when fresh, and the pores are angular; the stipe is whitish. *Albatrellus dispansus* occurs in montane mixed conifer forests, sometimes associated with woody debris or buried wood. The fruitbodies turn dark red when dried and stored.

Bjerkandera adusta (Willdenow: Fries) P. Karsten

Bjerkandera adusta forms flat or shelf-like, often overlapping, tough fruitbodies with smoke gray tubes and small, angular dark smoky gray or blackish pores. The surface of the caps is tomentose to somewhat hairy, cream to butterscotch in color, and not distinctly zoned. It is frequent on decaying hardwood logs and woody materials, rarely on conifers. *Bjerkandera fumosa* occurs on similar substrates in our area.

Albatrellus dispansus SAT-05-267-13

It differs from *B. adusta* by having thicker flesh and buff to pale smoky gray pores and a dark line above the base of the tubes (cut through fruitbody). Both these fungi could be mistaken for species of *Stereum* or *Trametes*. The former, however, have a smooth surface under the cap, while the latter have white to pale gray pores and their caps are more or less zonate.

Boletopsis grisea (Peck) Bondartsev and Singer

The genus *Boletopsis* is related to some of the spine-fungi such as sarcodons and hydnellums as well as thelephoras, and, like them, is ectomycorrhizal. While considered fleshy, the fruitbodies are rather tough and long-lived. The flesh is solid, white, and bitter-tasting. The spores are brownish and angular in outline, a feature that helps separate this genus from *Albatrellus* and *Polyporoletus*. Various names have been applied to our western boletopsises and, indeed, the number of species and their tree hosts remain unclear. Current thought suggests that at least three species could occur in the PNW. Our commonest one seems to be *B. grisea* (= *B. subsquamosa*), which apparently occurs mostly with pine; it has a dull gray to blackish, often radially streaked, cap that sometimes is slightly scaly near the center. The similar *B. leucomelaena* occurs mainly with spruce. *Boletopsis smithii* is known from a single collection in Washington and is distinctive by the orange coloration of the cap and stipe.

Bondarzewia mesenterica (Schaeffer) Kreisel

Bondarzewia mesenterica (= *B. montana*) typically produces large fruitbodies at the base of conifers. It develops from a sclerotium, and forms one or more fan-shaped caps, often irregular and overlapping from a common, rooting base. The surface of the cap is tomentose, often zoned in shades of brown and gray-brown. The pores are whitish, rather large and coarse, angular and lacerate in age. The flesh is whitish and, when fresh, has a pleasant odor. *Bondarzewia mesenterica* causes a white-rot of roots and butts, and can persist for long periods in stumps and dead trees.

Bridgeoporus nobilissimus (Cooke) Burdsall, Volk, and Ammirati

Bridgeoporus nobilissimus is the largest and most spectacular polypore in western North America. It occurs primarily on very old noble firs, at the base of living trees and snags or on top of stumps. Its fruitbodies are perennial and can form massive shelves up to 1.5 m (5 ft.) wide. The upper surface is covered by a mat of coarse fibrils that are white at first, become brownish, and then often greenish due to the presence of algae among the fibrils. As the fruitbody expands at the edge or from a short stout base, it can engulf plants or woody debris such as twigs.

Bjerkandera adusta SAT-05-282-02

Boletopsis grisea SAT-00-296-65

Bridgeoporus nobilissimus

Bondarzewia mesenterica

Plants may also grow on its surface. The flesh is ivory-colored and corky, and the layers of tubes are separated from one another by thin layers of flesh. Each new sterile layer makes the lower surface smooth initially, but soon small, ivory to buff, circular to angular pores develop, which may become pale brownish in age. *Bridgeoporus nobilissimus* is very rare, known only from forests of western Washington and Oregon, and is a protected species in both states.

Chondrostereum purpureum

Coltricia perennis SAT-01-276-01

Chondrostereum purpureum

(Persoon) Pouzar

Chondrostereum purpureum is commonly found on hardwood logs, snags, and stumps, and rarely on conifer wood. The cap surface is hairy to tomentose, grayish to yellowish buff or pale cinnamon to darker brown, often with a distinct pale edge. Unlike that of polypores, the spore-producing underside is smooth, and is violet to brown-violet and waxy-looking. *Amylostereum areolatum*, on conifer wood, is similar but has a zoned cap that often is moss-covered.

Coltricia perennis (Linnaeus) Murrill

Coltricia perennis has a rather slender, tough, brown, velvety stipe, and a funnel-shaped, velvety cap with concentric zones of grayish brown, golden to cinnamon-brown, or darker brown, and usually a pale irregular edge. The flesh is brown, thin, and leathery. The tubes are decurrent with pores that are yellowish white to brownish and bruise brown when handled. *Coltricia perennis* can be found during much of the mushroom season on the ground or on woody debris and is most characteristic of disturbed areas such as trail edges and roadsides in conifer forests. It is ectomycorrhizal, often grows in groups, and may have fused cap edges. The closely related *C. cinnamomea* has a silky, shiny, reddish brown cap with less well defined zonation.

Fomitopsis pinicola (Swartz: Fries) P. Karsten

RED-BELT CONK

Fomitopsis pinicola causes a brown-rot primarily in conifers, but occasionally in hardwoods, especially black cherry. It is our most common conk and a major player in the recycling of wood into soil. While normally forming a woody, rounded to shelf-like fruitbody, it also can grow as a simple layer of tubes on the underside of logs. The surface of the cap is usually banded with orange, reddish orange, or grayish to black, and has a whitish rounded edge. The interior is woody and fibrous, with multiple tube layers. The pores are very small and white, yellowish when bruised. When growing shelf-like, *Heterobasidion annosum* can appear rather similar, but lacks reddish colors.

roots of conifers and, occasionally, hardwoods. It can persist in dead woody materials for a long time. Its fruitbodies are sometimes difficult to find without some experience. They typically occur on the underside of logs, in cavities of trees, snags, and stumps, and often as a flat layer of tubes on the underside of woody substrates. The cap is often encrusted, rough and irregular, and brown to blackish in age. The pores are circular to angular and whitish to cream buff,

Ganoderma oregonense Murrill

The genus *Ganoderma* is best known for the medicinal fungus *G. lucidum*, commonly known as reishi or ling zhi, and *G. applanatum*, the artist's conk, a common perennial species on conifers and hardwoods in our region. *Ganoderma oregonense* and *G. tsugae* are two annual species that are somewhat similar to *G. lucidum*, but differ from it in coloration and substrate. *Ganoderma oregonense* and *G. tsugae* are almost impossible to separate from each other and might actually represent only one species. Both typically develop a medium-sized to large, shiny, ochraceous to reddish brown or mahogany cap with a lateral stipe; less often, they develop multiple caps or grow shelf-like. In older specimens, the varnished crust often cracks extensively. The pore surface is cream-colored and turns brownish when bruised or upon drying. The flesh of the cap can be rather thick, and is soft fibrous and whitish. Both *G. oregonense* and *G. tsugae* cause a white-rot in conifers.

Heterobasidion annosum (Fries) Brefeld

Heterobasidion annosum is one of the most destructive fungal parasites of forest trees, causing a white-rot of butts and

Fomitopsis pinicola

Ganoderma oregonense

Heterobasidion annosum, a bracket-like specimen

Heterobasidion annosum, a more typical crust-like specimen

Ischnoderma resinosum SAT-05-266-15

and change in color as the pore surface is rotated back and forth in incident light. The flesh is rather hard and corky. In recent years, some studies have suggested that *H. annosum* actually represents a complex of many species.

Ischnoderma resinosum (Schrader: Fries) P. Karsten

Ischnoderma resinosum is a widespread annual species that occurs as single or imbricate shelf-like caps with even or lobed edges on wood of conifers and hardwoods. When young and actively growing, the fruitbody is rather thick and fleshy, contains a sappy substance, and has a whitish, rounded edge, sometimes with liquid droplets, and a brownish tomentose cap. Later the fruitbodies become hard and corky, dark brown, and concentrically zoned, and the surface develops a dark resinous crust and becomes radially wrinkled. The pores are white to pale brownish and, when fresh, stain dark brown where bruised. Fresh specimens have an aromatic smell and the exposed wood sometimes has an anise-like odor when the fruitbodies are removed. *Ischnoderma benzoinum*, with darker flesh, occurs on hardwood.

Laetiporus conifericola Burdsall and Banik

SULFUR SHELF

This magnificent annual polypore (long known as *Laetiporus sulphureus*) often forms large clusters of overlapping bright yellow and orange shelves on living trees, logs, stumps, snags, and even utility poles. When fresh the fruitbodies are soft and somewhat fleshy to fibrous, and often watery, but later they become tougher and harder, and, eventually, fade and become soft and crumbly.

The pores are bright yellow when fresh, discolor somewhat when bruised, and become paler in age. Fresh specimens have a pleasant odor. In North America, several species of *Laetiporus* are now recognized. In the west, we have two species—*L. conifericola* on conifer wood, and *L. gilbertsonii* on hardwoods. The sulfur shelves also are called chicken-of-the-woods. When young, the growing edge is soft and edible, but once the caps mature, they become tough and chalky.

Laetiporus conifericola SAT-97-254-07

Oligoporus leucospongia (Cooke and Harkness) Gilbertson and Ryvarden

Oligoporus leucospongia is a spring fungus of the western mountains that grows on conifer and sometimes aspen wood that has been buried in snow. It can be found fruiting in association with snowbanks, but soon after snowmelt the fruitbodies rapidly deteriorate. They appear as single shelves, become elongated, or sometimes form simple pore-layers on the underside of logs. The cap is tomentose and white to buff, and the rounded margin often grows downward partially enclosing the pore surface. The pores are white when fresh, circular to angular, and become lacerated in age. The most amazing feature is the soft, cottony flesh and the corresponding light weight of the fruitbodies. They seem as though they could float right out of your hand. *Oligoporus fragilis* is somewhat similar but is denser and turns reddish brown when bruised or dried.

Oligoporus leucospongia SAT-07-147-01

Onnia tomentosa (Fries: Fries) P. Karsten

Onnia tomentosa (= *Inonotus tomentosus*) and its relatives cause a white pocket-rot in roots and butts of conifers and often form terrestrial fruitbodies under spruce and

Onnia tomentosa SAT-05-231-18

other trees of the pine family. The caps often develop on a rather thick, short, brownish, tomentose stipe, one or more arising from a common base, or they may grow directly from the base of a tree. The cap surface is tomentose, yellow-brown to darker brown, often with a pale edge when actively growing, and often zonate. The flesh is rather thick and has a soft, spongy upper layer and firm, fibrous lower layer. The pores are whitish to brownish, angular, and often become lacerated in age. *Onnia tomentosa* is most easily confused with terrestrial polypores in the genera *Coltricia* and *Phaeolus*.

Phaeolus schweinitzii (Fries)
Patouillard
DYER'S POLYPORE

Phaeolus schweinitzii is well known to foresters for its brown-rot of butts and roots of living conifers. The fruitbodies usually are terrestrial, forming one or more circular to irregularly shaped caps from a short, thick stipe, or with several caps forming a rosette; occasionally, it forms shelf-like fruitbodies on the sides of stumps and snags. The upper surface is tomentose to hairy, sometimes zonate, light yellowish brown to brownish orange near the margin and deep to dark brown toward the center, often with a pale edge when growing. The pores are circular to angular or labyrinthine, and become tooth-like in age. When fresh, they are greenish, yellowish, or orange-tinted and bruise brown, then become grayish to brownish in age. The yellowish brown to reddish brown flesh is soft and watery at first, then dry and brittle with age. As its common name indicates, *P. schweinitzii* is often used for dyeing wool. It yields an array of earth tones, the exact colors varying greatly with the age of the fruitbody.

Phaeolus schweinitzii SAT-97-254-06

Polyporus melanopus Persoon: Fries
From spring through fall, species of *Polyporus* can be found on hardwood and conifer logs, around stumps, and on the ground from a buried sclerotium or wood. They have in common stipes that are central to off-center, caps that are depressed in the center, small to larger pores that are often decurrent, and tough, corky to leathery flesh. In the PNW, there are four species that look very similar—*P. melanopus*,

Polyporus melanopus SAT-97-283-01

P. badius, *P. elegans*, and *P. varius*. All have brownish caps, very small white pores, and a black velvety covering on a portion of the stipe. In *P. melanopus* and *P. badius*, the black extends nearly to the apex of the stipe, while in *P. elegans* and *P. varius* only the base or lower half is black. *Polyporus badius* can be separated on the basis of its lack of clamp connections. *Polyporus elegans* usually is smaller than the other three species. In practice, applying these species concepts to collected specimens can be very difficult. *Polyporus tuberaster* also occurs in the PNW. It has larger pores and develops from an underground sclerotium. *Jahnoporus hirtus* is another stipitate polypore in our area. It has a gray-brown, finely pubescent cap and eccentric stipe that is usually deeply embedded in the substrate, tough flesh, iodine odor, and bitter taste.

Porodaedalea pini (Brotero) Murrill

Porodaedalea pini (more familiarly *Phellinus pini*) produces hoof-shaped to shelf-like, hard woody fruitbodies on logs or the trunks of living trees or occasionally forms only a flat tube-layer on the substrate. The upper surface is brownish orange to reddish brown then nearly blackish, rough, and often has concentric grooves and ridges. The brownish orange flesh is hard and wood-like. The brownish pores are circular to elongate and angular or labyrinthine. *Porodaedalea pini* is widespread in conifer forests, where it causes white-rot of heartwood.

Pycnoporellus alboluteus (Ellis and Everhart) Kotlaba and Pouzar

Pycnoporellus alboluteus is a common high-mountain fungus in spring and summer, fruiting on conifer logs, especially those of spruce, and occasionally on aspen. Its

flesh is very light and papery, and it usually forms a mass of pores on the wood surface rather than a bracket-like fruitbody. It occurs throughout the western mountains, and also has been reported occasionally from the northeastern U.S. and eastern Canada. *Pycnoporellus fulgens* is very similar in appearance, substrate, and distribution, but has smaller pores (0.3–0.5 vs. 1–3 mm), ellipsoid rather than cylindric spores, and less of a tendency for a portion of the fruitbody to lift away from the substrate.

Porodaedalea pini SAT-05-231-13

Pycnoporellus alboluteus SAT-98-174-03

Trametes hirsuta (Wulfen: Fries) Pilát

Trametes hirsuta forms flat patches or shelf-like, often overlapping, fruitbodies on hardwood logs or other woody substrates. The cap is white to gray, covered with short hairs, sometimes with a yellowish, tomentose margin, and usually is less obviously zoned than *T. versicolor*. The pores are circular to angular and white to tan then grayish when older. The flesh is relatively thick, tough and corky, and has a duplex structure—an upper, gray, soft fibrous layer separated from a lower whitish layer by a thin black line. *Trametes pubescens* has a tomentose, cream to buff, un-zoned cap, and the flesh is not duplex.

Trametes versicolor (Linnaeus: Fries) Pilát

TURKEY TAIL

Turkey tail is a very common polypore in our region, occurring extensively on hardwood substrates and rarely on conifer wood. It can be found almost any time of the year, but is most common in summer and fall. The thin, flexible fruitbodies are produced annually, but they are tough-fibrous and persist for a long time. The velvety to silky caps with concentric zones of different colors—white, buff, yellowish, brown, reddish brown, blue, and black—make this species easy to recognize in the field. The pores are white to yellowish white or grayish, thin-walled, small, and circular to angular, and the flesh is whitish with a black layer below the surface tomentum. *Trametes ochracea* is white to buff or reddish brown in color, less distinctly zoned, and usually has a more rigid structure. Several species of *Stereum* are similar to *Trametes* species, but have a smooth undersurface. Other thin, tough polypores include the genus *Trichaptum*, whose members have angular to tooth-like violet-tinged pores, and *Cerrena unicolor*, which has elongated pores and corky duplex flesh, with a pale brown lower layer separated from a darker upper layer by a narrow dark zone. *Trametes versicolor* has a history of medicinal use in Asian cultures and now is the subject of western medical research.

Trametes hirsuta SAT-06-276-06

Trametes versicolor SAT-07-261-05

Coniophora puteana SAT-99-330-04

CRUST-FUNGI

Coniophora puteana (Schumacher: Fries) P. Karsten

There are a large number of crust-fungi on logs and stumps in our area. For most, identification is almost impossible without access to a microscope and technical literature. Nonetheless the group is important ecologically since it includes a broad range of species that, for the most part, decompose wood and are important nutrient recyclers in forest ecosystems. *Coniophora puteana* causes a brown-rot in both hardwood and conifer wood, including building timbers, boats, and other substrates. The fruitbodies, which start as small patches, can develop into extensive membranous to somewhat fleshy flat continuous masses that are attached tightly to the substrate. The surface is smooth to irregularly warty, at first cream-colored then ochraceous, olivaceous, or dark brown, with a whitish edge and numerous small white strands. *Coniophora arida*, a similar species, usually occurs on conifer wood.

Meruliopsis corium (Persoon) Ginns

Meruliopsis corium is a striking fungus, especially when it fruits extensively on downed branches of hardwoods in brush piles. It can be found almost any time of the year but is most common in fall. The cap protrudes from the substrate and has a fibrillose to tomentose white to ochraceous surface. The underside is composed of shal-

Meruliopsis corium SAT-99-030-01

low pores, bumps, and wrinkles and is white to ochraceous with a distinct white cottony fibrillose edge. The consistency is leathery and tough but often pliable.

Phlebia merismoides (Fries) Fries

Phlebia merismoides (= *P. radiata*) is rather common in our area on hardwoods, especially alder snags and logs, and occurs much less often on conifer wood. The fruitbody typically is flat, circular to irregularly shaped, gelatinous to waxy, tough, and closely attached to the substrate. The surface has shallow ridges and irregular folds that sometimes form a radial pattern, and vary from orange to red or violet to brownish.

Phlebia tremellosa (Schrader: Fries) Nakasone and Burdsall

Phlebia tremellosa (= *Merulius tremellosus*) is mainly a fall fungus and occurs on stumps, logs, and woody debris of both hardwoods and conifers. The fruitbodies can consist of flat patches, but more often form overlapping, fused, undulating to irregular caps. The consistency is soft, elastic, and gelatinous when fresh. The cap is white to yellowish or pinkish, hairy to tomentose, and typically has a white to translucent edge. The undersurface is yellow, orange, or salmon-pink and composed of folds and ridges that form net-like shallow pores, often in radial rows.

Phlebia merismoides SAT-05-282-03

Phlebia tremellosa SAT-06-308-07

Puffballs, Earthballs, and Earthstars

Puffballs are basidiomycetes that produce large masses of spores that, by a variety of passive means, are introduced into the air for dispersal. Because they produce their spores internally, puffballs often are called gasteromycetes or stomach fungi. They come in a wide variety of forms and although generally similar in several features, they apparently are not closely related to one another; for instance, some are closely related to gilled mushrooms and others to boletes. Puffballs occur in a variety of habitats, from lawns and pastures to forests and even deserts. Many are widespread and common.

Close inspection will show that most puffballs are attached to the substrate at a central point and are usually rather easily removed. When young the interior of most species is white, with a texture like marshmallow; the portion where the spores are

formed is called the gleba. This fleshy interior is surrounded by a peridium, a thin to thick skin that may have more than one layer. As the spores develop and the puffball matures, the gleba begins to self-digest, becoming watery and gluey, and changing from pure white to yellowish or olivaceous. Once this process is completed, the moisture gradually escapes from the gleba, leaving behind a mass of dry spores. The peridium then develops a pore, splits open, or becomes torn in some manner, and the spores are released over time, sometimes with the aid of falling raindrops or the stomping of human feet. Some puffballs—such as those in the genera *Lycoperdon* and *Vascellum*—have a sterile base that functions like a stipe and elevates the spore sac into the air. Species of other genera, such as *Tulostoma* and *Battarrea*, develop relatively long, tough woody stipes. Earthstars are puffballs with thick, multi-layered peridiums in which the outer layer splits to form star-like rays that spread and bend backward, elevating the sac of spores.

Although constructed similarly, earthballs are not closely related to puffballs but rather to some boletes. The most common genus is *Scleroderma*, although *Pisolithus tinctorius* is probably the most widely known species due to its role in mycorrhiza research. The peridium of earthballs is thick and relatively hard. The gleba is solid, hard, and may be whitish at first but soon becomes purple-brown or darker, often with narrow white veins. The gleba remains hard for a long time, but eventually forms a mass of spores that are released passively following breaking or splitting of the peridium, sometimes in a star-like pattern.

Puffballs, especially the larger ones with a completely white, marshmallowy interior, often are collected for food. However, there is always the possibility of mistakenly gathering buttons of mushrooms such as the deadly poisonous *Amanita ocreata*. To prevent serious consequences, cut each alleged puffball in half, from top to bottom, and check the interior for the outline of a stipe, cap, and gills. Earthstars usually are not noticed until they are mature, by which time they are too tough to consider for the table. Many earthballs are quite poisonous, especially for pets, and so should be avoided altogether.

Calvatia fumosa

Calbovista subsculpta SAT-07-125-13

Calvatia fumosa Zeller

The genus *Calvatia* is well known, although perhaps not by name, because of the giant puffball *C. gigantea*, often pictured with a young child for scale. In our region, we have a different giant puffball, *C. booniana*, which occurs in sagebrush steppe habitats and other open grassy areas, along with several other calvatias. *Calvatia fumosa* is a more mundane small to medium-sized species that is common in montane conifer forests during spring and summer. It is attached to the soil by a persistent white cord that is connected to a pleated base. The white to grayish surface is smooth to roughened or shallowly cracked. The peridium is thick and persistent, eventually breaking open or chewed through by rodents to release the spores. The soft white gleba becomes yellowish then dark brown and powdery. During development it often has a very strong unpleasant odor, which seemingly would deter those seeking to eat them. *Calvatia sculpta* is a striking species, with large pyramidal warts, and *Calbovista subsculpta* Morse ex M. T. Seidl is a less striking species with low, somewhat flattened, pyramidal warts; both have a distinct sterile base below the gleba and occur in the mountains in late spring through summer. *Bovista* fruitbodies are similar to the smaller calvatias, but they become detached at maturity. They have a two-layered peridium—the outer one sloughs off while the inner one is persistent and develops a pore through which the spores are released as the windblown puffball tumbles across the ground.

GENUS *LYCOPERDON*

Lycoperdon or "wolf fart" is a widespread genus of puffballs, occurring in forests, grasslands, and other habitats from the lowlands to the alpine. Like the genus *Vascellum* it has a fat, stipe-like sterile base that elevates the spore sac a short distance into the air. All species develop an apical pore, which usually appears as a small bump at first. The color and structure of the surface of the peridium are particularly important features for identifying lycoperdons. Often there is an outer layer of granules, warts, or spines which usually is sloughed off as the puffball matures, leaving behind a smooth or patterned surface.

Lycoperdon nigrescens (Persoon:
Persoon) Persoon
Lycoperdon nigrescens (= *L. foetidum*) is widespread and occurs in summer and fall in conifer and hardwood forests as well as alpine habitats. The fruitbodies are some-what pear-shaped with a distinct stipe and fine strands attached to the base. It is one of the darker-colored species with light to dark brown pyramid-like spines that break away, leaving a reticulate pattern on the exposed surface of the peridium. Between the spines the surface is smooth and brownish to blackish brown.

Lycoperdon perlatum Persoon:
Persoon
Lycoperdon perlatum is the most common of our smaller puffballs. Its often densely clustered fruitbodies typically are white at first and become brownish in age. The species is distinctive by virtue of the outer layer of large conical warts, interspersed with smaller ones, that leave a reticulate pattern of shallow depressions over the tough, membranous inner layer as they are sloughed away. The inner peridium eventually develops an apical pore, through which the olive-brown spores are propelled by a bellows action when the spore sac is hit by raindrops or nudged by an inquisitive mushroom-hunter. *Lycoperdon perlatum* can be found in disturbed sites, such as forest

Lycoperdon nigrescens SAT-97-183-07

Lycoperdon perlatum

Morganella pyriformis

small granules, warts, scales, or blunt spines that eventually wear away. The color of the surface is white to ochraceous then brownish and often it develops shallow cracks as the puffball enlarges. The flesh of the sterile base presents a key feature for identifying *M. pyriformis*: it remains white at maturity unlike that of lycoperdons.

Vascellum pratense (Persoon) Kreisel

Vascellum pratense (= *V. depressum*) is a rather common species of grassy places that is easily confused with lycoperdons unless it is sectioned top-to-bottom for a look at the interior. Vascellums and lycoperdons all have rounded to pear-shaped fruitbodies with a distinct sterile base. However, when viewed in long-section, the sterile base in vascellums can be seen to be separated from the gleba by a thin papery membrane; lycoperdons do not have such a membrane. In *V. pratense* the outer surface of the fruitbody is granular or minutely spiny, and whitish to yellowish then brownish. This thin outer covering sloughs off, and the inner peridium becomes shiny and develops an irregular pore. Over time, the inner layer disintegrates down to the papery membrane at the base of the gleba as the spores are lost. The gleba is spongy white at first then becomes yellowish and eventually dark brown when the spores are mature. The sterile base is white to yellowish and composed of small chambers. *Vascellum pratense* can be found in late summer and fall in lawns, golf courses, and other grassy areas.

Scleroderma verrucosum (Bulliard: Persoon) Persoon

Earthballs of the genus *Scleroderma* are easy to recognize by their thick peridium and the development of the gleba, which is fleshy

roadsides, from late summer through fall whenever there is sufficient moisture.

Morganella pyriformis (Schaeffer) Kreisel and D. Krüger

Morganella pyriformis (= *Lycoperdon pyriforme*) is one of the more common puffballs in our area. It often produces clusters of many fruitbodies on rotting or buried wood to which it is connected by distinct white strands. The species name refers to the pear-shaped fruitbodies, the surface of which is covered by and white at first but soon becomes gray, violet, or brown, marbled with white lines forming lens-shaped islands. At maturity, the entire gleba develops into powdery dry spores, which escape through a splitting or tearing of the peridium. The fruitbodies are more or less spherical and attached by heavy white cords or, in some species, by a thick rooting stipe-like base composed of thick cords and soil. Sclerodermas are ectomycorrhizal and are found in most forested areas, often occurring on bare soil. They are also quite common in gardens and parks where oaks and other ectomycorrhizal trees occur. *Scleroderma verrucosum* typically has a short to well-developed rooting, stipe-like base with some sterile tissue at the base of the gleba. The surface of the fruitbody is buff to yellowish brown or pale brown and is covered with small patches of flattened scales.

Vascellum pratense SAT-05-263-01

Geastrum saccatum Fries

Earthstars are not particularly abundant in forested areas of the PNW. Many species are more characteristic of drier woodlands and even deserts, so the diversity of earthstars and many other gasteromycetes is much higher in the southwestern U.S. One small to medium-sized species that is found in PNW conifer forests is *Geastrum saccatum*. Its spore case sits directly on the usually five- to eight-rayed base formed by the thick outer peridium, unlike many species in which the spore case is elevated on a short stipe. The pore through which the spores are released has a radially fibrillose margin and is demarcated from the rest of the spore case by a ring that usually is lighter in color than the surrounding tissue. *Geastrum saccatum* is widely distributed in the Northern Hemisphere, and we have seen it, or a dead-ringer for it, in Tasmania, Australia.

Scleroderma verrucosum SAT-97-203-01

Geastrum saccatum

Jelly-like Fungi

A number of fungi produce gelatinous to rubbery fruitbodies, most commonly on wood but also on other fungus fruitbodies. Most of the more conspicuous species live as wood decomposers or parasites on other fungi. However, there are many more inconspicuous ones that live on the surfaces of living plants or as mycorrhizal associates with plant roots. The fruitbodies vary in habit—flattened waxy gelatinous layers, irregularly rounded or brain-like masses, leaf-, ear-, bracket-, or spoon-shaped, or simple slender clubs or corals. Usually the spores are produced over the entire surface of the fruitbody; however, in a few, spore production is localized, as on the spines of *Pseudohydnum gelatinosum*, the jelly-tooth. The fruitbodies come in many colors, including white, yellow, orange, reddish, purplish, brownish, blackish, and olive. Most jelly-fungi are apparent only when they are fully moist and expanded; when dehydrated they often fade to a hard knot or powdery crust. Many have the ability to survive several cycles of wetting and drying. Some ascomycetes are jelly-like, but the name jelly-fungi usually is used for a large number of basidiomycetes. In these, the structure of the mature basidium has been used to separate different groups—for instance, shaped like a tuning fork in *Dacrymyces*, transversely septate in *Auricularia*, and longitudinally septate in *Exidia*, *Pseudohydnum*, *Tremella*, and *Tremiscus*. While few species are used in cooking, *Tremella fuciformis* and species of *Auricularia* (wood ears) are well known for their culinary value.

BASIDIOMYCETE JELLIES

Dacrymyces palmatus (Schweinitz) Burt

Dacrymyces is a rather common genus of jelly-fungi, forming variously shaped, watery to firm gelatinous fruitbodies throughout the year. While most species are yellow or orange, some can be colorless and others are brown. In texture and appearance they are somewhat like *Tremella*, although many species of the latter have tougher fruitbodies. It often takes microscopic examination to confirm the genus—two-spored tuning fork basidia in *Dacrymyces* and four-spored, longitudinally septate basidia in *Tremella*. *Dacrymyces palmatus* (perhaps better called *D. chrysospermus*) often begins as a small disc or cushion, sessile or with a small stipe, and eventually expands and becomes irregular to lobed. The fruitbody is bright yellow to orange and has a rather tough consistency. The outer surface often has loosely arranged whitish hairs. *Dacrymyces palmatus* occurs on conifer wood. *Tremella mesenterica* is similar in appearance and texture, but grows on hardwoods and often is associated with the wood-rotting fungus *Stereum hirsutum*.

Dacrymyces stillatus Nees

Dacrymyces stillatus (= *D. deliquescens*) is rather common on conifer wood and occasionally on hardwood substrates. It often occurs on cedar-board fences becoming apparent every time it rains. It comes in two forms, one is dark orange or reddish orange

Dacrymyces stillatus SAT-98-332-08

Dacrymyces palmatus SAT-05-281-05

and rather soft and produces asexual spores. The sexual form is usually watery gelatinous to firm, yellow, orange, or reddish orange, sometimes with a short stipe and rather small and cushion-shaped, but sometimes forming larger confluent masses.

Heterotextus alpinus (Tracy and Earle) G. W. Martin

Heterotextus alpinus (= *Guepiniopsis alpina*) is known to most spring mushroom-hunters because it is commonly seen then in groups on wet conifer wood. However, it may also occur during other times of the year. The fruitbodies are bright yellow to orange, smooth on top but with a dense covering of hairs externally, small (3–8 mm), cone- to bell-shaped with a depression in the center, and a distinct point of attachment. They often hang like gumdrops from the woody substrate.

Heterotextus alpinus

Tremella foliacea Persoon: Fries

Tremella is a prevalent genus on the wood of hardwood trees, and occasionally that of conifers. The golden *T. mesenterica* (witch's butter) is the species most commonly seen in the woods, while the large white *T. fuciformis* more often is encountered in desserts at Asian restaurants. Tremellas are noted for their association with species of wood-rotting fungi, at times developing directly on the other fungus's fruitbody. Some also grow in association with lichens. *Tremella foliacea* usually occurs on wood with bark still attached, and develops as a cluster of leaf-like lobes from a common base. It is typically some shade of brown, sometimes blackish brown, often with a violet or reddish orange cast. Few things in our area could be confused with it.

JELLY-LIKE ASCOMYCETES

Ascocoryne sarcoides (Jacquin) Groves and Wilson

A number of discomycetes (cup-forming ascomycetes) produce gelatinous to rubbery fruitbodies. Some form distinct small to large cups with a gelatinous flesh while others, such as *Ascocoryne sarcoides*, produce small spherical to cup- or disc-shaped gelatinous fruitbodies on stumps, logs, and branches of conifers and hardwoods. Gener-

Tremella foliacea SAT-00-210-05

ally it appears in fall and continues to grow late into the season. It forms pink to violet-pink fruitbodies, often clustered together, and eventually the cup surface becomes irregular with a distinct dark edge. When *A. sarcoides* reproduces sexually, eight colorless, two-celled spores are formed in each ascus. However, when young, it may produce only asexual spores.

Cudoniella clavus (Albertini and Schweinitz: Fries) Dennis

Cudoniella clavus, like *Ascocoryne sarcoides*, is an inoperculate discomycete and not a true basidiomycete jelly-fungus. However, its appearance often is more similar to the jelly-fungi than to the cup-fungi and so we place it here. The fruitbodies range from shield-like, with well-formed stipes, to more or less like squatty gumdrops, but always are more or less cream-colored, sometimes with grayish, ocher, or violaceous tints. *Cudoniella clavus* occurs in spring and early summer on very wet plant debris, such as cones and twigs, often at least partly submerged in running water. It is widespread, but not particularly common.

Cudoniella clavus SAT-07-159-08

Ascocoryne sarcoides

Morels, False Morels, and Elfin Saddles

The morels, false morels, and elfin saddles are ascomycetes that, with few exceptions, have a fruitbody with cap and stipe, which allows them to more effectively release their spores into moving air. Unfortunately, like many common names, these are not used uniformly by mushroom-hunters. Here we use them in the following sense—morels are members of the genus *Morchella*, false morels are members of *Gyromitra* and *Verpa*, and elfin saddles are members of *Helvella*.

Morels have hollow stipes, the cap projects above the stipe apex for at least some distance, and the surface of the cap is composed of distinct ridges and pits. Verpas have hollow stipes when mature, but initially they are stuffed with white cottony material. The caps are smooth to wrinkled, conic to bell-shaped, and attached thimble-like to the apex of the stipe. Gyromitras have caps that are folded, wrinkled, brain-like, or lobed, or occasionally cup-like, with an ochraceous, orange-brown, red-brown, or darker brown surface. The stipes are slender or rather thick, simple or more complex and convoluted to marbled, with one or more chambers (make a cross-section to see this). Elfin saddles are quite varied, and some species are similar in shape and stature to gyromitras. The surface of helvella caps or cups usually is white, tan, dull brown, gray, or black, and lacks the warm orangish or reddish tones usually found in gyromitras. They can be cup- or saddle-shaped, rounded and wrinkled to irregular or lobed. The stipes can be slender to rather thick in relation to the cap diameter, and may be simple and cylindrical to distinctly ridged or ribbed, sometimes with furrows or pits.

Edibility runs the gamut from excellent and choice to deadly poisonous, so learning to identify these mushrooms is not merely an academic exercise. Even the best edibles in this group, the morels, should always be well cooked, as raw and undercooked specimens are responsible for a large number of poisonings every year.

MORELS

Morchella elata Fries
BLACK MOREL

Morels have a conic to rounded, sponge- to honeycomb-like cap with a network of ridges and pits and a whitish hollow stipe with a granular surface. We are using the name *Morchella elata* to refer to the group called the black morels. *Morchella conica* and *M. angusticeps* are other names for black morels. Like morels in general, black morels come in a variety of sizes and shapes. They are characterized by conic to bell-shaped, sometimes pointed, caps with ridges that are gray to grayish tan when young and then darken to black with maturity; in some forms, however, they are essentially black from the beginning. The pits are often narrow and the ridges elongated, but the pattern is variable. Black morels are very com- mon in western conifer forests, especially following fires, when they often fruit in huge numbers. They also can be found in smaller numbers in areas with hardwoods and in landscaping and other disturbed areas. They begin fruiting in April or May in some areas, but can be found well into summer at higher elevations. *Morchella deliciosa* sometimes is considered to be related to this group, but with a sterile zone between the edge of the cap and the stipe, more oval pits, and more yellow-brown to olivaceous colors. *Morchella semilibera*, usu- ally found with hardwoods, can be similar in color to *M. elata*, but its cap and stipe are fused only from about the middle of the cap upward (hence its epithet, "half-free"). All these morels are edible and considered good to wonderful by most people. However, a large proportion of the population is sus- ceptible to severe digestive upset when they

Morchella elata SAT-99-144-02

are eaten raw, and not everyone can tolerate them even when well cooked. So caution is advised until you determine into which group you fall. *Verpa bohemica* often is mistaken for a morel, but its caps are wrinkled and attached to the stipe only at the apex.

Morchella esculenta (Linnaeus)
Persoon
YELLOW MOREL

Morchella esculenta is a medium to large species with rounded to conic or elongated caps, with rather deep pits, elongated ridges, and irregular cross ridges. The caps are whitish to pale grayish tan when young and later become whitish, tan, or rusty ochraceous, sometimes with reddish spots. *Morchella esculenta* is widely distributed in the west and occurs in spring to early summer with conifers and hardwoods, in plantings, orchards, and burned areas. Like all

Morchella esculenta SAT-07-122-02

morels, it is edible and highly sought-after by mycophagists. *Morchella crassipes* has sometimes been used for a large form of *M. esculenta* with a very thick stipe base.

FALSE MORELS

Verpa bohemica (Krombholz)
J. Schröter

Verpas are similar in appearance to morels, but the cap is attached only at the apex of the stipe so that the sides of the cap hang freely, like a lampshade. *Verpa bohemica* is characterized by its brown, bell-shaped, strongly wrinkled cap and whitish stipe. It occurs early in spring, usually a week or two before morels begin to fruit. It can be found in a number of wooded habitats, but especially along rivers and streams under cottonwoods. If the attachment of the cap is noted, the only morel that it could be confused with is *Morchella semilibera*, in which the cap is free from the stipe for about half its height. However, the distinctly ridged and pitted morel cap is very different from the wrinkled cap of *V. bohemica*. This false morel is collected and eaten by many people, and some even prefer it to true morels. It seems to cause digestive upset in a greater proportion of people than morels do, so use caution and sample them in small amounts until you ascertain your tolerance.

Verpa conica (O. F. Müller: Fries)
Swartz

Verpa conica has a conic thimble-like cap that hangs free from the stipe apex. The surface of the cap is smooth or slightly wrinkled to irregular but not strongly so. The stipe is ivory to cream with brownish or

Verpa bohemica SAT-07-125-14

ochraceous blushes, and often has a banded pattern on its surface. It is a widespread but uncommon species that fruits early in the spring in a variety of habitats, including montane conifer forests. It is possible that we have more than one species in the PNW passing under the name *V. conica*, but the critical studies necessary to clarify this have not been carried out.

Gyromitra esculenta (Persoon: Fries) Fries

Gyromitra esculenta produces caps that are irregular to slightly lobed or saddle-shaped, with a brain-like wrinkled surface that varies from dull red to rusty red, reddish brown, or darker brown, sometimes with yellow or orange tints. In age, the caps often are black. The stipe is hollow at maturity

Verpa conica

and tinted with the cap color but often also with pinkish or grayish purple tones near the base. The edge of the cap often is curved toward the stipe or fused with it. *Gyromitra*

Gyromitra esculenta

Gyromitra infula SAT-06-320-01

esculenta is a spring or early summer species. It is associated with conifers and hardwoods and may be found on soil or rotten wood. It can be very common and is frequently encountered by morel-hunters. The species name (Latin for "edible") is misleading since it can be poisonous and has caused serious illness and deaths (see Appendix 1), although none of these incidents occurred in western North America. *Gyromitra infula* and *G. ambigua*, also poisonous, are similar species that occur in late summer and fall.

Gyromitra infula (Schaeffer: Fries)
Quélet

Gyromitra infula has a cinnamon-brown to amber-brown or reddish brown, somewhat saddle-shaped cap, with a smooth to somewhat irregular, but not strongly wrinkled, surface. The stipe is round in cross-section or somewhat compressed and furrowed, white or tinted pinkish red with white mycelium at the base. *Gyromitra infula* and *G. ambigua* typically occur in late summer and fall with conifers and hardwoods on soil and wood. Although *G. ambigua* normally has stronger purple tones on the stipe base and somewhat darker caps, determining which of these species you have usually requires checking spore size (mostly 20–23 µm long in *G. infula* and 22–30 µm long in *G. ambigua*) and, even then, the answer might not be clear. Both species are very poisonous (see Appendix 1).

Gyromitra melaleucoides (Seaver)
Pfister

Gyromitra melaleucoides has a broad shallow cup-shaped "cap" which may become irregular in age but is not strongly lobed. The color of the interior surface of the cup is light to dark brown, and the exterior is light brown to whitish, without prominent ribs, although it can be broadly folded. The brownish to whitish stipe has blunt ridges and is short to rudimentary. *Gyromitra melaleucoides* is known from northern California north to B.C. and east to Colorado on or near rotting conifer wood. Because of its overall shape, it could be confused with discinas, but the latter have, at most, a rudimentary stipe and much shorter spores (10–14 vs. 25–35 µm).

Gyromitra melaleucoides SAT-01-139-07

Gyromitra montana Harmaja

Gyromitra montana is closely related to the European species *G. gigas* and the eastern North American *G. korfii*, and can be common in our montane conifer forests. It occurs in spring and early summer, often near melting snowbanks. The cap is yellowish brown to brown or reddish brown and strongly convoluted to folded with an irregular edge that is pushed against or fused with the stipe. The white stipe is thick, short, and convoluted to folded, and its interior is composed of several anastomosing channels. Although considered edible and good by some, we recommend that it be cooked well and not eaten frequently or in large amounts.

Gyromitra montana SAT-97-166-10

ELFIN SADDLES

Helvella compressa (Snyder) N. S. Weber

Helvella compressa has a saddle-shaped, gray to brown cap, the margin of which is curved inward at first and then gradually unfolds and is flattened against the stipe when mature. The outer surface of the cup is pale

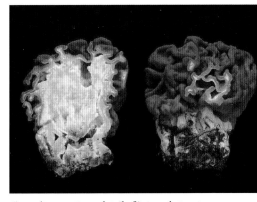

Gyromitra montana, detail of internal structure

Helvella compressa SAT-01-111-01

Helvella elastica

and more or less finely hairy. The stipe is round in cross-section, hollow, rather slender, equal or tapered upward, whitish, and finely hairy. The flesh is thin, brittle, and pale gray. It occurs with hardwoods and conifers along the coast in spring. *Helvella stevensii* is a very similar, mostly eastern, species that has a paler cap and smaller spores.

Helvella elastica Bulliard: Fries
Helvella elastica typically has a saddle- to broadly bell-shaped cap with the lower lobes frequently turned down toward the stipe and sometimes fused with it. The upper cap surface is buff to brown, sometimes with a violet tint, and the underside is whitish and hairless. The stipe is slender, hollow,

Helvella lacunosa

Helvella lacunosa, infected with Hypomyces cervinigenus

equal or tapered upward, cream to pale buff. *Helvella elastica* occurs in summer and fall in both conifer and hardwood forests.

Helvella lacunosa Afzelius: Fries

Helvella lacunosa is the most frequently encountered helvella in our region and often looks like it is made of wax. The caps are saddle-shaped or lobed, sometimes irregularly so, and the margin is sometimes fused with the stipe. The upper cap surface is even to wrinkled and gray to black, although pale forms can be found. The underside is somewhat paler and may be ribbed. The stipe is deeply furrowed, with single- or double-edged longitudinal ridges and pits (lacunae), chambered in cross-section, and usually white to gray or blackish. *Helvella lacu-nosa* occurs in conifer and hardwood forests and in lawns and plantings under ectomycorrhizal trees such as oak and hazel. It often is attacked by the mold *Hypomyces cervinigenus* or, less often, is host to the parasitic mushroom *Clitocybe sclerotoidea*. While most common in fall, it can occur at nearly any time. *Helvella crispa* is an all-white version, while *H. maculata* has a brownish cap and whitish stipe.

Helvella leucomelaena (Persoon) Nannfeldt

Helvella leucomelaena forms gray to dark brownish gray or blackish, urn- to cup- or star-shaped fruitbodies. The outer surface of the cup is finely pubescent and similar in color to the inner surface with a whitish

Helvella leucomelaena SAT-07-124-03

Pseudorhizina californica

lower portion. The short stipe, if present, has broad folds and ribs that extend a short way onto the cup. *Helvella leucomelaena* is found in spring and early summer in conifer forests, especially along paths and roadsides. *Helvella acetabulum* is similar, but with usually larger and paler tan cups with more pronounced ribs extending upward to near the cup margin.

Pseudorhizina californica (W. Phillips) Harmaja

Pseudorhizina californica has the appearance of a hybrid mushroom—a gyromitra-like cap mounted on a helvella-like fluted stipe—and, indeed, it has been classified in both of those genera. It is another member of our late spring and summer ascomycete community, and can be found in conifer forests on rotting logs, along trails, and near seeps. The thin- and brittle-fleshed cap reminds one of gyromitra—relatively broad, saddle-shaped to lobed, gray-brown, brown, or olive-brown on the upper surface and whitish and minutely tomentose beneath. The deeply fluted, wax-like stipe is cream-colored when young, yellowish in age, and has beautiful pink, red, or vinaceous blushes at the base. Some of the stipe ribs extend onto the undersurface of the cap.

Cup-Fungi

The cup-fungi (discomycetes, or cup and saucer fungi as mycologist Alan Bessette likes to call them) are ascomycetes whose fruitbodies are, as you would expect, more or less cup-shaped. The asci that produce their spores typically line the inner or upper surface of the cup, along with sterile cells called paraphyses, and often forcibly eject the spores upward into the wind for dispersal. Based on the structure of the ascus, two major groups of cups traditionally have been recognized, the so-called operculate and inoperculate discomycetes. Operculate asci have a hinged lid (operculum) at their tips which opens when the spores are discharged. The operculate cups tend to be larger and more readily observed in the field. Inoperculate asci typically have thick-walled tips that are penetrated by a tunnel or pore through which the spores are exuded. The inoperculate cups generally are quite small and usually overlooked by mushroom-hunters; however, they often are exquisitely

beautiful when viewed through a handlens or dissecting microscope. Cups are produced by fungi belonging to many different evolutionary lines, so they are not necessarily closely related to one another. The cup-fungi are a major element of the spring mycota in the PNW. Although many species fruit in fall, they are noticed less because of the much greater abundance of other fungi at that time. Some of the cups are edible, but none of them are particularly popular.

OPERCULATE CUPS

Aleuria aurantia (Persoon: Fries)
Fuckel
ORANGE-PEEL FUNGUS
Aleuria aurantia does indeed look like orange peels turned inside-out and scattered by a passing hiker or motorist. The inner fertile surface is a brilliant deep orange, the outer surface paler with a somewhat dandruffy

Aleuria aurantia

Aleuria rhenana

texture. The spores are ellipsoid, 13–24 × 7.5–10 µm, and covered by a network of ridges. *Aleuria aurantia* is very common in the fall, and is especially abundant along gravelly forest roads, in campgrounds, and at trailhead parking areas. It is one of several ascomycetes that will discharge many spores simultaneously when disturbed, producing a visible smoke-like cloud. Sometimes this can be induced by breathing on the cups; at other times it will occur on its own when the fruitbody is removed from its collecting container. *Aleuria aurantia* is widespread in the Northern Hemisphere; it is edible, but brittle and hard to collect intact, and has little taste. *Aleuria rhenana* Fuckel (= *Sowerbyella rhenana*) is similarly colored, with smaller cups borne on clustered stipes; it is much less frequently encountered, seemingly preferring old-growth forests.

Pseudaleuria quinaultiana Lusk

Pseudaleuria quinaultiana is a rare cup that looks somewhat like *Aleuria aurantia*. It differs in being more saucer-like than cup-shaped, having a more reddish fertile surface, occurring in ones or twos rather than large groups, having smooth ellipsoid spores (15.5–21.5 × 7.5–10.5 µm), and fruiting in spring rather than fall. The species was described from a collection made near Lake Quinault, in the southwestern portion of the Olympic Peninsula, and it has been found primarily in old-growth forest with Sitka spruce, western hemlock, and Douglas-fir. As far as we know, it occurs only in Washington and Oregon but, because seemingly suitable habitat is present from northern California to B.C. and southeast Alaska, it could well occur in those areas too.

Caloscypha fulgens (Persoon: Fries) Boudier

Caloscypha fulgens is another medium-sized orange cup that could be confused with *Aleuria aurantia*. Like *Pseudaleuria quinaultiana*, however, it is a spring-fruiter, and is one of the common members of the western montane snowbank mycota that fruit in areas recently uncovered by melting snow. In addition to its habitat and fruiting season, it can be distinguished from the other orange cups by the blue to green staining that occurs as the fruitbodies age. *Caloscypha fulgens* is a parasite of conifer seeds. Although most common in the western mountains, it occurs across North America, as well as in Europe and temperate Asia.

Cheilymenia fimicola (De Notaris and Baglietto) Dennis

The genus *Cheilymenia* is characterized by small, stipe-less, flattened saucers bearing conspicuous (under a handlens) eyelash hairs and growing on dung, rich soil, plant debris, or other materials. It appears to be closely related to *Aleuria*. *Cheilymenia fimicola* (= *C. coprinaria*) is one of the dung-dwellers, occurring on cow-pies as well as the droppings of wild animals. When fresh the fruitbodies are reddish orange, lightening to yellowish orange in age; the hairs are brownish, and all are unbranched. *Cheilymenia stercorea* (= *C. ciliata*) also occurs on mammal dung, but has branched brownish hairs near the base of the cup. *Cheily-*

Pseudaleuria quinaultiana SAT-99-209-03

Caloscypha fulgens

Cheilymenia fimicola SAT-99-128-05

Humaria hemisphaerica SAT-04-312-03

Sarcosphaera coronaria SAT-07-140-07

menia theleboloides occurs on rotting plant remains, or horse manure and straw; its cups have whitish hairs and are more yellow. *Cheilymenia crucipila* grows among mosses or on bare ground under grasses or other herbaceous plants; it has branched brownish hairs near the base of the cup like those of *C. stercorea*. *Cheilymenia fimicola* occurs virtually worldwide; it probably is edible if found in large enough numbers and cleaned well.

Humaria hemisphaerica (F. H. Wiggers: Fries) Fuckel

Humaria hemisphaerica is a smallish to almost medium-sized cup with whitish to grayish flesh and a contrasting exterior attractively decorated with brown hairs that, under the microscope, are pointed, thick-walled, and partitioned by cross-walls. The spores are large ($20–27 \times 10–15$ μm), ellipsoid, covered with small irregular warts, and contain two large oil drops. Several species of *Trichophaea* are similar in color, shape, hairiness, and habitat, but they are usually smaller and the spores are smooth; some mycologists feel these differences are too small to warrant placement in a separate genus. In the PNW, *H. hemisphaerica* is not uncommon, usually in moist, shady settings on damp mossy ground or well-rotted wood. It is widely distributed in the temperate Northern Hemisphere.

Sarcosphaera coronaria (Jacquin) Boudier

Sarcosphaera coronaria (= *S. crassa*, *S. eximia*) is one of the larger, fleshier cups. Young fruitbodies may be overlooked as they tend to be nearly buried in the soil or duff. When found at this stage, they are spherical and can be confused with truffles; later they crack open and expand into ragged-edged, star-shaped cups (hence its epithet, Latin for "crown"). The interior usually is some shade of violet and contrasts beautifully with the whitish to pale grayish exterior that often retains a coating of soil. The spores are broadly ellipsoid (13–22 × 7–10 µm) with blunt ends and usually two large oil drops. *Sarcosphaera coronaria* occurs in spring, mostly in the mountains, often near melting snow, and is a harbinger of morel season. It also occurs in Europe.

Discina perlata (Fries) Fries
PIG'S EAR

Discina perlata (= *D. ancilis*) can be described as a gyromitra without a prominent stipe. It sometimes appears as a shallow cup, but often is more cushion-like with a barely upturned or even turned-under edge. The upper surface is brown and usually wrinkled, the underside somewhat whitish, and a rudimentary stipe usually is present. The spores are 25–45 × 8–16 µm and have one large oil drop and prominently thickened tips with a single point. Similar species in the PNW include *D. leucoxantha*, rather large (up to about 10 cm, 4 in., across), with a yellowish upper surface and spores 30–40 × 12–18 µm with two-humped tips, and *D. olympiana*, fairly small (less than about 5 cm, 2 in., across), with a brown upper surface and spores 28–36 × 13–16 µm with inconspicuously ornamented tips. Like many of the ascomycetes, the spores of discinas are slow in maturing and so, frustratingly often, fruitbodies are found in which spores cannot be found and, thus, cannot be confidently identified to species. However, even when mature spores are present, the differences among species are small enough that identification still can be very

difficult. *Discina perlata* is common and widespread throughout temperate North America; in the PNW, it fruits on wet soil or rotting wood in the mountains in spring, often as part of the snowbank mycota.

Geopyxis carbonaria (Albertini and Schweinitz: Fries) Saccardo

Geopyxis carbonaria is one of a group of ascomycetes that fruit in eye-popping numbers after conifer forest fires. The fruitbodies look like small goblets with reddish tan interiors, yellowish tan exteriors, and

Discina perlata

Geopyxis carbonaria SAT-01-139-09

slightly ruffled, pale rims. A stipe usually is present but, at times, it can be rather short. The spores are smooth, ellipsoid, 11–18 × 6–9 µm, and do not contain prominent oil drops. *Geopyxis vulcanalis* is more yellowish tan in color, has larger spores (14–21 × 8–11 µm) without oil drops, and is found mostly in unburned areas. *Tarzetta cupularis* grows on soil or among mosses and has spores (19–23 × 10–15 µm) that contain two large oil drops. *Tarzetta catinus* (18–24 × 10–13.5 µm) is another soil-dweller, but with a lon-

ger stipe and larger cups (up to 2.5 cm, 1 in., across). Different mycologists interpret all these species differently, so it is often very difficult to identify collections unambiguously or to understand their distributions.

Otidea concinna (Persoon) Saccardo

The name *Otidea* (from the Greek for "ear") refers to the shape of the fruitbodies which, in some species, is much like that of a rabbit ear. Other otideas look as though the top part of the ear had been chopped off. *Otidea concinna* (= *O. cantharella*, *Flavoscypha cantharella*) belongs to the latter group. It has bright yellowish fruiting bodies that occur singly or close together in groups. The spores are smooth, ellipsoid, 10–12 × 5–6.5 µm, and contain two large oil drops. The paraphyses are slender, bent at the tips, and encrusted with yellow material. Similar dull yellow or yellowish brown species include *O. microspora* (= *O. alutacea* var. *microspora*), dull yellow, with spores 9–10 × 5–6.5 µm, and *O. alutacea*, pale yellowish brown, with spores 14–16 × 7–9 µm. Differentiating among these species is not a simple task, and reliable distribution information will not be obtainable until the species concepts are better defined, including consideration of molecular data.

Otidea concinna SAT-00-324-01

Peziza arvernensis Boudier

The genus *Peziza* includes many plain-Janes of the discomycete world, distinctive only because of their relatively large size. The fruitbodies are smallish to medium-large, but most come in generally boring shades of translucent medium brown. Microscopically, an important character is the blue-staining reaction of the ascus tips when treated with Melzer's reagent. *Peziza arvernensis* (= *P. sylvestris*) typifies the basic

Peziza arvernensis SAT-00-153-02

brown woodland peziza. The inner surface is medium brown, the exterior somewhat paler. The spores are smooth or very finely roughened, ellipsoid, 15–20 × 9–10 µm, and lack large oil drops.

Peziza vesiculosa Bulliard: Saint-Amans is paler brown than most pezizas, and can be found throughout much of the year growing on manure heaps, old straw, or composted soil. Its fruitbodies tend to be clustered together and remain strongly cup-shaped throughout their lives. The spores are smooth, ellipsoid, 18–24 × 9–14 µm, and lack oil drops.

Peziza violacea Persoon: Fries is probably the prettiest of the pezizas, at least when it is fresh and deep violet-colored. As it ages, it becomes increasingly brown. It occurs on burnt ground, and often can be found in and around campground fire-pits in the spring before the summer campers return and start lighting fires again. Its spores are smooth, ellipsoid, 16–17 × 8–10 µm, and lack large oil drops. *Peziza praetervisa* is a brownish purple species that also grows on burnt ground. Microscopically it differs from *P. violacea* by having spores 11–15 × 6–8 µm, ornamented with low warts, and containing two oil drops. Because, in Europe, both names have been applied to a fungus answering the description of *P. praetervisa* given here, a third name was coined, *P. subviolacea*, to remove the confusion. However, the solution seems not to have been wholeheartedly adopted. Nonetheless, eventually what is called *P. violacea* in the PNW could require a new name.

Neournula pouchetii (Berthet and Riousset) Paden

Neournula pouchetii is an uncommonly reported, spring- or summer-fruiting, woodland species. The inner surface of the cup

Peziza vesiculosa

Peziza violacea

Neournula pouchetii SAT-02-132-01

is pinkish brown, the exterior whitish to tan to violet-brown, and the edge is somewhat toothed or split; the stipe is covered with whitish tomentum and usually is buried in the substrate. The spores are ellipsoid, 23–32 × 8–10 µm, warty when mature (the roughened spores are the main character used to separate *Neournula* from the smooth-spored genus *Urnula*), and sometimes contain small oil drops. *Neournula pouchetii* is known from scattered locations throughout the PNW, North Africa, and France, although it is likely to occur elsewhere too.

Plicaria endocarpoides

Plectania nannfeldtii

Plicaria endocarpoides (Berkeley) Rifai

Plicaria is a small genus whose species fruit in burned areas, usually in spring. They are similar to pezizas (and are included in *Peziza* by some mycologists), but have a dark brown to black fertile surface and spherical rather than ellipsoid spores. *Plicaria endocarpoides* produces dark brownish cup-shaped fruitbodies with a tendency to flatten out in age; the spores are smooth, 8–10 µm diameter. *Plicaria trachycarpa* is generally smaller, darker with a black warty inner surface, flattens out sooner, and has finely warted spores 10–16 µm diameter. Most mushroom-hunters who forage in burned areas are focused on morels and pay little attention to dark brownish cups that can be hard to identify; thus, our knowledge of the distributions of the plicarias is limited.

Plectania nannfeldtii Korf

Plectania and *Pseudoplectania* are two, closely related, small genera of small to small-medium cups that are black at maturity and may or may not have stipes. The plectanias have ellipsoid spores, and the cups often are deeper, compared to the pseudoplectanias. *Plectania nannfeldtii*, one of our western snowbank fungi, seems to be restricted to western North America. The fruitbodies resemble champagne saucers and often can be found completely surrounded by snow, through which the mushroom has grown, its metabolic heat melting a path. The cups seldom exceed 2 cm (0.8 in.) across, and the stipes usually are relatively long in relation to the cups. The spores are smooth to finely roughened, ellipsoid, 21–35 × 10–15 µm, and lack large oil drops. *Plectania milleri* differs in having at most a short stipe, cups with a toothed edge and hairier exterior, and slightly smaller spores (21–26 × 9–11 μm). *Plectania melastoma* is very similar to the latter species in having at most a short stipe, hairy exterior, and spores 20–25 × 8–12 μm, but the cup exterior bears reddish orange granules, and the spores are warty.

Pseudoplectania vogesiaca (Persoon) Seaver (better known in North America as *P. melaena*) appears in late winter or early spring on twigs and other woody debris, usually of conifers. The cups usually are rather shallow and the interior is medium to deep olivaceous brown at first; in age, however, the entire cup becomes black. A stipe usually is present but never is as long as that of *Plectania nannfeldtii*. The spores are smooth and round, 10–17 μm, and contain one large oil drop. *Pseudoplectania nigrella* is similar but somewhat smaller, with at most a rudimentary stipe, a darker interior, and a hairier exterior. Both species are fairly common in the PNW, but their early appearance and dark colors help them escape notice.

Pseudoplectania vogesiaca

Sarcosoma mexicana (Ellis and Holway) Paden and Tylutki

Sarcosoma mexicana has somewhat the look of a bean-bag ashtray, with a shallow black cup perched above a bag filled with gelatin rather than beans. The combination of color, density, and jiggliness is distinctive. The spores are smooth, ellipsoid to slightly sausage-shaped, 23–24 × 10–14 μm, and contain one to three oil drops. It is found in spring on wet ground or wood, often in the mountains shortly after snowmelt. *Sarcosoma latahensis* is similar but smaller (to about 4 cm, 1.6 in., in diameter vs. about 10 cm, 4 in., for *S. mexicana*), less gelatinous, with the gelatin diminishing greatly as the fruitbodies age, and cups with a gray,

Sarcosoma mexicana

rather than black, exterior. The spores are smooth, ellipsoid, 24–37 × 9–12 μm, and lack oil drops at maturity. It occurs in the same sorts of habitat as *S. mexicana*.

INOPERCULATE CUPS

Bisporella citrina (Batsch: Fries) Korf and S. E. Carpenter

Bisporella citrina is perhaps the most noticeable of the inoperculate discomycetes, as it is very common, bright yellow, and fruits

Bisporella citrina SAT-05-275-01

in large numbers on hardwood branches that have lost their bark. Although there are other small, yellow, cushion-like discomycetes, none of them are as common or fruit in such abundance. The spores are ellipsoid, medium-sized (8–14 × 3–5 μm), and have one cross-wall and two oil drops at maturity. *Bisporella citrina* occurs throughout the temperate Northern Hemisphere.

Chlorociboria aeruginascens
(Nyland) Kanouse

The turquoise to greenish or olivaceous color of the small cups makes *Chlorociboria aeruginascens* and the very similar *C. aeruginosa* quite distinctive. Both grow on rotting barkless wood in a wide variety of forests. Even when not fruiting, the presence of the fungus is advertised by the turquoise color imparted to the wood by its mycelium. This wood has been prized by woodworkers for use as a decorative inlay material. *Chlorociboria aeruginascens* is characterized by larger fruitbodies (up to 7 mm, 0.25 in., across) that often arise several from a common base, flesh that is the same color as the exterior of the cup, and small spores (5–8 × 1–2 μm), whereas *C. aeruginosa* has smaller fruitbodies (less than 5 mm, 0.2 in., across) that usually arise singly, yellow-orange flesh, and larger spores (9–14 × 2–4 μm). The two species are frequently confused, so it is difficult to specify their ranges; however, one or the other or both occur across North America and in Europe and Asia.

Ciboria rufofusca (Weberbauer)
Saccardo

Ciboria rufofusca produces shallow translucent brown cups on slender stipes and, as such, they look like many other small discomycetes. However, their occurrence on cone scales of true firs sets them apart and makes identification easy. The spores are smooth and ovoid (5–7.5 × 3–3.5 µm), sometimes with two oil drops.

Dasyscyphus bicolor (Bulliard: Fries) Fuckel

Dasyscyphus bicolor (= *Lachnum bicolor*) is a beautiful example of an inoperculate discomycete. It is found most frequently on the old canes of salmonberry and other *Rubus* species but is also common on branches of hardwoods such as alder (some mycologists recognize two varieties or species based on substrate and small morphological differences). The cups have a bright yellow-orange fertile surface, and the outer surface is densely covered by white hairs; although a short stipe may be present, the cups usually appear to be seated directly on the substrate. When dry, the cups curl up and then look like small hairy snowballs. The spores are very slender (6–11 × 1–2 µm), paraphyses are lance-shaped and project beyond the asci, and the hairs are encrusted with granular material that sometimes forms discrete crystals. *Dasyscyphus virgineus* (= *L. virgineum*) is another very common species; it is entirely white, externally hairy, has an obvious stipe, and occurs primarily on hardwood debris. Both species, like many of the tiny inoperculates, are very widespread, though rarely noticed.

Lachnellula arida (W. Phillips) Dennis

Species of *Lachnellula* are very similar to those of *Dasyscyphus*, the main difference being microscopic—the paraphyses have narrow to slightly club-shaped tips in lachnellulas, whereas they are lance-shaped in

Chlorociboria aeruginascens SAT-99-128-05

Ciboria rufofusca

Dasyscyphus bicolor

Lachnellula arida SAT-05-227-02

Lachnellula agassizii SAT-07-140-04

Lachnellula suecica SAT-07-147-04

dasyscyphuses. They differ ecologically as well—lachnellulas are found only on conifers, whereas dasyscyphuses are found overwhelmingly on angiosperm wood or debris. All lachnellulas have a golden yellow to bright orange fertile surface, and the species are differentiated by the color of the cup exterior, size and shape of spores, color and nature of the hairs and paraphyses, structure of the flesh, and type of wood inhabited. *Lachnellula arida* is distinguished by its brown exterior and hairs, relatively broad (6–8 × 2.5–3.5 µm) spores, and growth on the wood of true firs (*Abies* spp.). *Lachnellula agassizii* (Berkeley and M. A. Curtis) Seaver has a creamy yellowish fertile surface, white or pale yellow exterior, relatively broad (6–8 × 2.5–3 µm) spores, and occurs on fir, hemlock, and pine branches; it is very similar to *L. calyciformis* and *L. subtilissima* and is our most common lachnellula. *Lachnellula suecica* (de Bary: Fuckel) Nannfeldt (= *L. chrysophthalma*) is relatively large (cups up to about 1 cm, 0.4 in., across), has a bright orange fertile surface, white exterior, small spherical spores (4.5–5 µm), and occurs mostly east of the Cascade crest on ponderosa pine branches. All these species fruit primarily in spring and early summer. Their distributions are not well known, because of confusion over names and species concepts; however, fungi answering more or less closely to these descriptions are found in many parts of the world.

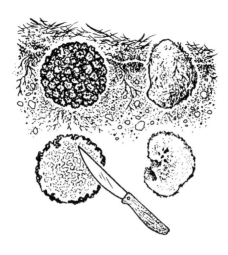

Truffles and False Truffles

Both the ascomycetes and basidiomycetes include species that produce hypogeous (below-ground fruiting) more or less spherical or otherwise potato-like fruitbodies. These are similar in appearance, with a relatively thin peridium (outer skin) and a spore-producing interior (gleba) that is firm and solid or chambered. Often a microscope is required to determine if one has a truffle (ascomycete) or false truffle (basidiomycete) and almost always to identify genera and species, which often are based on characteristics of the spores. Superficially, truffles and false truffles are not unlike some puffballs; however, most hypogeous fungi do not produce a powdery spore mass at maturity (the deer truffles, *Elaphomyces*, are an exception), a characteristic of almost all puffballs. In addition, puffballs occur on the surface of the ground (hence are epigeous) or sub-

strate, while most hypogeous fungi remain within the soil or, at most, become partially exposed. Mature truffles and false truffles typically produce strong and characteristic odors that attract various rodents and other mammals who dig them up, consume them, and eventually distribute the fungus spores in their feces. Truffles and false truffles are ectomycorrhizal partners with various trees, and the animals that disperse the spores help maintain the association.

Most of the strong odors produced by truffles and false truffles are unpleasant or, at best, "interesting" for most people. Some PNW species, such as the Oregon black truffle and the Oregon white truffle, are deemed, by North Americans at least, to be on a culinary par with the finest Euro-truffles, at a much lower price.

297

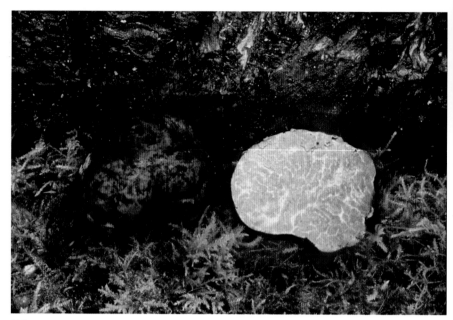

Tuber oregonense

TRUFFLES

Tuber oregonense Trappe and Bonito
nom. prov.

OREGON WHITE TRUFFLE

To some people, the only "true" truffles are those in the genus *Tuber*. The fruitbodies of tubers are spherical to irregular in shape, potato-like, and have gleba composed of islands of fertile tissue among meandering pale veins that sometimes extend to the peridium. The large, often thick-walled, and strongly ornamented spores are produced in large spherical asci but are not ejected at maturity. Some European tubers such as *T. melanosporum*, the Périgord truffle or black diamond, and *T. magnatum*, the Italian white truffle, are highly esteemed and quite

pricey edibles because of their complex aromas. Historically, European truffle-hunters used sow pigs to locate these truffles by smell but, nowadays, a trained dog is the helper of choice, because it is less likely to eat the finds. Extensive efforts have been made to cultivate truffles in North America, especially the black diamond, and some have been successful. However, commercial truffle-growing is not yet big-business here.

In our region we have three principal native truffles that are highly sought-after for food and collected for sale in markets. One is the Oregon black truffle, *Leucangium carthusianum*; the others—*Tuber oregonense* and *T. gibbosum*—are both known as Oregon white truffle. *Tuber oregonense* has an opaque whitish to yellowish or olivaceous peridium that develops prominent reddish orange to cinnamon colors. The gleba initially is whitish, then becomes brownish with white marbling. The odor is complex—a mix of garlic, spices, cheese, and other, indescribable components. It occurs from fall to late winter, principally with young, vigorously growing Douglas-firs. *Tuber gibbosum* is a very similar species that occurs in the same habitats as *T. oregonense*, but fruits during late winter and spring; it also differs in its almost translucent peridium, and less of a tendency to develop reddish colors in age. In Oregon, attempts to grow these truffles in Christmas tree farms apparently have been successful.

Leucangium carthusianum (L. R. Tulasne and C. Tulasne) Paoletti
OREGON BLACK TRUFFLE

The Oregon black truffle (formerly classified in the genus *Picoa*) is among our most beautiful fungi. The often large fruitbodies are brown to black with a smooth to rough exterior that encloses a solid, gray to olive or brownish gleba, which is separated into pockets by pallid sterile veins. The spores are smooth and very large (up to 100 µm long). *Leucangium carthusianum* often occurs in association with Douglas-fir along the coast but can also be found in urban areas. People who excavate them from their garden (which must have a suitable tree nearby) often think they have found a lump of coal. As with all truffles, this species has a strong pungent fruity (often like pineapple) odor when mature. It is a highly sought-after edible and is collected commercially.

Geopora cooperi Harkness

Geopora cooperi is a fuzzy truffle that can become the size of a baseball. It typically is nearly spherical but often has an irregular to convoluted surface due to infolding of the peridium. The outer surface is brownish and covered with a mass of coarse flattened hairs. The gleba is whitish and pale brown and composed of multiple chambers. Similar to many cup-fungi and unlike most truffles, *G. cooperi* produces long cylindrical asci, each with eight smooth, broad elliptical spores that are forcibly ejected at matu-

Leucangium carthusianum

Geopora cooperi

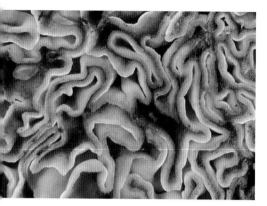

Geopora cooperi, detail of internal structure

Hydnotrya cerebriformis

short hairs. The interior is white to yellowish and composed of a series of narrow labyrinthine channels. The spherical and minutely roughened spores are produced in cylindrical asci on the surface of the walls. The odor is somewhat garlic-like, but is pungent and not at all enticing, even to garlic-lovers. It was powerful enough to escape several layers of containment in the refrigerator.

FALSE TRUFFLES

Alpova diplophloeus (Zeller and C. W. Dodge) Trappe and A. H. Smith

Alpova diplophloeus is essentially a small version of a rhizopogon, differing from them by its gelatinous gleba. Its well-developed peridium is light pinkish at first but soon darkens to brown or reddish brown (or stains those colors). The gleba is viscid-gelatinous and pale yellow to olive when young, and soon becomes orange-brown to reddish brown and marbled by white veins that divide it into chambers. At maturity the smooth, thin-walled, elongate, and colorless to pale brownish spores are borne in a jelly-like matrix. *Alpova diplophloeus* occurs only in association with alders, although other alpovas occur with other trees. The genus *Melanogaster* also has a gelatinous gleba, but it is brown to black and the spores are thick-walled and brown to purple. The generic name honors Alfred H. Povah, who collected the specimens on which the genus is based.

rity. It is ectomycorrhizal with conifers, widely distributed, and occurs almost year-round. The smell of *G. cooperi* is faintly aromatic, and it is considered a good edible species that can be used much like morels.

Hydnotrya cerebriformis (L. R. Tulasne and C. Tulasne) Harkness

Hydnotrya cerebriformis is a species of montane conifer forests. It has subspherical, lobed fruitbodies whose surface is pinkish to reddish brown and covered with fine

Rhizopogon occidentalis Zeller and C. W. Dodge

Rhizopogon is a large and difficult genus taxonomically, especially in western North

America. In the PNW, rhizopogons are probably the most common false truffles in pine and Douglas-fir forests. They can be found throughout the year, often partially emergent, especially in loose soils along road edges where they can push up as clusters of fruitbodies. Somewhat surprisingly to most people, the closest relatives of rhizopogons are not other false truffles, but boletes in the genus *Suillus*. Likewise, suilluses are more closely related to rhizopogons than they are to other boletes. *Rhizopogon occidentalis* is a common representative of the genus. It has a yellowish white to yellow peridium, often with orange to red areas and a network of fine yellow to orange fibrils over the surface. The gleba is white to gray or yellow at first, then becomes some shade of olive or brown. At maturity the gleba is dry or somewhat powdery. The spores are smooth, thin-walled, and often elongated to spindle-shaped. *Rhizopogon occidentalis* occurs with two- and three-needle pines in the mountains and, especially, the pine woodlands on coastal dunes. Truffle experts rate it as "palatable."

Alpova diplophloeus SAT-99-300-02

Truncocolumella citrina Zeller

Truncocolumella citrina has a yellow felty peridium, and the gleba is gray to olive or brown, chambered, with a distinctive pale yellow to yellow columella. The spores and most other features are very similar to those of rhizopogons; the major difference is the presence of a columella. *Truncocolumella citrina* is common under Douglas-fir on the west side of the Cascade crest and also extends into interior conifer forests as far as the Rocky Mountains. The potato-like fruitbodies are often found partially exposed at the surface of the soil or litter. They are edible, but are reported to have little flavor.

Rhizopogon occidentalis SAT-05-301-04

Truncocolumella citrina SAT-99-233-08

Odds and Ends

This section includes a variety of species that are difficult to fit into our other categories. Some of them are specialists that occupy narrow ecological niches. Some are ascomycetes and others are basidiomycetes. We have subdivided this bunch into secotioid species, parasites on other mushrooms, bird's nest fungi, and "all the rest."

SECOTIOID MUSHROOMS

Within the gilled mushrooms and boletes, a number of species have evolved in which the gills or pores have become modified, often folded and contorted, to the extent that the spores are no longer actively released (and so cannot give a spore-print). The cap shape, thickness, and outline may be altered, so that there is less tissue, and the stipe often is reduced, sometimes remaining only as a sterile columella inside the fruitbody. Often

the edge of the cap does not fully expand and instead remains pressed against the stipe or continuous with it. Together, such secotioid fungi, as they are often termed, do not form a natural evolutionary group, but rather belong to a number of different evolutionary lines.

Endoptychum depressum Singer and A. H. Smith

The genus *Endoptychum* includes two species that occur in the PNW—*E. depressum* (= *Agaricus inapertus*) and *E. agaricoides* Czernajew (= *Chlorophyllum agaricoides*). *Endoptychum depressum* typically occurs in mid- to higher elevation conifer forests in the late summer and fall. It is medium-sized and the cap is whitish, yellow-staining, and depressed in the center with the margin turned down and connected to the stipe. The spores are thick-walled and develop as a black powdery mass at maturity. The gleba is composed of closely packed, contorted gills. *Endoptychum agaricoides* is less mushroom-like, with a bulky, somewhat bullet-shaped cap and a stipe that is present mostly as a prominent columella.

Gastroboletus turbinatus (Snell)
A. H. Smith and Singer

The genus *Gastroboletus* comprises secotioid fungi that are similar to species of *Boletus*. Usually a cap is present and typically it is rounded or flattened with the margin turned down. However, in *G. ruber* (= *Truncocolumella rubra*), the cap is so reduced that it looks like a false truffle without a complete peridium. In most *Gastroboletus* species the tubes are elongated, curved or contorted, and often olive to brown. The stipe is usually short and stout or sometimes forms a columella. *Gastroboletus turbinatus* is our most common species, occurring

from spring through fall. At first glance, the fruitbody looks like *Boletus chrysenteron*—the cap is velvety and brown with yellowish and reddish areas, the stipe is rather short, pointed below, yellowish with small reddish scales and granules, and the pores are rather large, reddish, and stain blue. The tubes are

Endoptychum agaricoides SAT-99-233-07

Endoptychum depressum SAT-05-259-01

Gastroboletus turbinatus SAT-06-276-08

Nivatogastrium nubigenum SAT-03-153-03

Thaxterogaster pinguis SAT-97-176-02

long, curved, yellow to greenish yellow, and clearly indicate its secotioid nature. The flesh is yellowish, with some red just below the cap cuticle, and the whole interior stains blue after cutting.

Nivatogastrium nubigenum
(Harkness) Singer and A. H. Smith

Nivatogastrium nubigenum is a wood-inhabiting species, often on *Abies* logs, that often occurs near snowbanks in higher elevation conifer forests in California and Oregon. It can be found from spring into early summer. The fruitbodies are attached to the substrate by a short whitish stipe. The cap is ochraceous to brownish or, when faded, whitish, and rounded with the edge turned down to the stipe. When cut lengthwise, the stipe inside can be clearly seen. The spore-producing tissue is made up of short reddish brown gill-like sections and chambers, and a partial veil is present. The growth on wood and smooth brown spores with a small germ pore are two lines of evidence that *N. nubigenum* is most closely related to pholiotas.

Thaxterogaster pinguis (Zeller)
Singer and A. H. Smith

Thaxterogaster pinguis is somewhat similar in stature to *Nivatogastrium nubigenum* but usually has a somewhat longer stipe. It is closely related to gilled mushrooms in the genus *Cortinarius* and, like them, has brownish roughened spores and fruits on soil, often partially buried. It is usually found in the mountains under true firs, from summer into fall. The genus name honors mycologist Roland Thaxter; the specific epithet refers to the greasy nature of the cap surface.

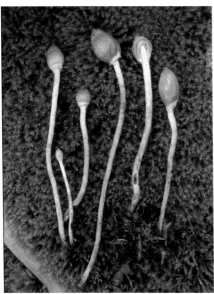

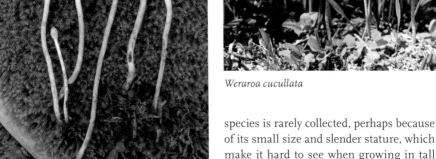

Weraroa cucullata

Weraroa cucullata

species is rarely collected, perhaps because of its small size and slender stature, which make it hard to see when growing in tall grass. It appears to be most closely related to stropharias and psilocybes.

Weraroa cucullata (Seaver and Shope) Thiers and Watling

Weraroa cucullata is a small slender mushroom found in moist meadows and other wet areas at higher elevations in conifer forests. It is relatively uncommon and sometimes is found with *Galeropsis polytrichoides*, another small secotioid mushroom. Both look like large moss capsules, as the cap does not expand but remains appressed to the stipe enclosing the reddish brown gills, which often are fused and irregularly shaped. The cap of *W. cucullata* is narrowly conic, shiny, cream buff to ochraceous buff or gray-buff, sometimes with small brownish scales near the margin. The stipe is slender and covered with small pallid scales over a brownish background. The pale partial veil soon disappears. The large, moderately thick-walled spores have a germ pore. This

PARASITES ON OTHER MUSHROOMS

Asterophora lycoperdoides (Bulliard: Fries) Ditmar

A number of basidiomycetes parasitize other mushrooms, including, in our area, *Collybia cirrhata* and its close relatives, and two species in the genus *Asterophora*, *A. lycoperdoides* and *A. parasitica*. Both the latter species infect russulas and lactariuses. The fruitbodies are relatively small, with a cap and stipe, either with distinct gills or thick, distant, and reduced ones. While both species are capable of producing basidiospores, they are noted for their production of asexual spores (chlamydospores). *Asterophora lycoperdoides*, the larger of the two, soon has the surface of its rounded cap covered by a brownish powder of star-

Asterophora lycoperdoides, growing on *Russula albonigra*

Asterophora lycoperdoides, powdery cap surface from production of chlamydospores

shaped chlamydospores. It has a short, stout, whitish stipe, and the gills are poorly developed. *Asterophora parasitica* has a more conic, whitish, brownish, grayish or faintly lilac cap that forms large, smooth, elliptical chlamydospores on the gills.

Hypomyces aurantius (Persoon) Fuckel

The species of *Hypomyces* are ascomycetes that form small flask-shaped fruitbodies, often on other mushroom-fungi, although some species grow on other substrates. The name *Hypomyces* is used in cases where sexual reproductive structures are produced by the fungus. However, many species reproduce asexually as well and then receive different names. *Hypomyces aurantius* is usually found on polypores but also can occur on decaying wood and litter. When growing on a polypore, it typically develops over the pore surface as large numbers of spherical orange-yellow flasks that develop from a yellow felt-like covering. It is most commonly found in spring, often on decaying conks of *Fomitopsis pinicola*.

Hypomyces aurantius

Hypomyces chrysospermus, showing both white and yellow stages

Hypomyces chrysospermus L. R. Tulasne and C. Tulasne

Hypomyces chrysospermus parasitizes boletes, decaying their fruitbodies in a relatively short time. Susceptible boletes are infected by the fungus early in their development. The ill-fated victims first become covered with a white coating of hyphae and asexual spores, and later turn bright yellow to rust yellow as a second generation of asexual spores mature. The sexual stage of *H. chrysospermus* is rarely seen; it involves formation of ascospores inside tiny flask-shaped fruitbodies. This fungus is widespread and commonly seen on *Boletus zelleri*, *B. chrysenteron*, *B. mirabilis*, and other boletes.

Hypomyces chrysospermus, early stage of infection

Hypomyces lactifluorum SAT-00-251-03

Stages in development of the lobster mushroom, *Hypomyces lactifluorum*, along with an uninfected *Russula brevipes*

Hypomyces luteovirens

Hypomyces lactifluorum (Schweinitz) L. R. Tulasne and C. Tulasne
LOBSTER MUSHROOM

Hypomyces lactifluorum grows in the tissue of certain russulas and lactariuses, especially *Russula brevipes* in the PNW, and turns the host mushroom into a dense mass of mummified tissue. The surface of the lobster mushroom becomes bright orange and the gills are reduced to low blunt ridges. At maturity, the minute, reddish-orange, flask-shaped fruiting structures of the hypomyces develop on the surface of the mushroom (use handlens). The flesh of the host usually remains white and brittle. *Hypomyces luteovirens* (Fries) L. R. Tulasne and C. Tulasne (= *H. tulasneanus*) is another parasite of russulas and lactariuses, typically developing over the gills as an olive-yellow to dark olive-green mold, eventually producing sexual reproductive structures. Lobster mushrooms are edible and can often be found at PNW produce stands and farmers' markets. The warnings against eating them usually are based on the assumed uncertainty of the host mushroom's identity; however, we are not aware of any serious poisonings caused by them.

BIRD'S NEST FUNGI

In the PNW several species of bird's nest fungi are widely distributed in a number of habitats and on various substrates including woody debris, herbivore dung, and soil. Almost all produce small cup-like "nests" inside of which are produced a number of tiny lens-shaped "eggs" (peridioles). The spores are produced inside the peridiole, more or less like a puffball. Inside each cup, which is enclosed by a cover until maturity, the peridioles develop in a glutinous

Cyathus striatus

matrix. At maturity, the cover falls away and allows falling raindrops to splash the peridioles out of the cup and onto the surrounding substrate. Eventually the peridioles break down, and the spores are released. These fungi are basidiomycetes, although the cups superficially look like those produced by ascomycetes. The common genera in our region are *Cyathus*, in which a long, thin, thread-like cord remains attached to each peridiole when it is ejected from the cup; *Nidula*, in which the peridioles are free in the cup with no cord; and *Crucibulum*, in which each peridiole is attached by a very short, simple cord that leaves a tiny stub on the base of the peridiole when it leaves the cup. *Nidularia* also occurs in our area. It is similar to the other bird's nest fungi but the cup never develops; instead, the fruitbody dissolves into a glutinous mass which dries on the surface of the peridioles.

Cyathus striatus (Hudson) Willdenow

Cyathus striatus occurs in a number of different habitats on decaying plant materials such as wood chips, small branches, and needles. It can be common in gardens where woody materials have been added to the planting beds. The species name refers to the vertical grooves on the inside of the mature gray-brown cups. The exterior of the cups is densely covered by rust-brown to dark brown hairs and tomentum. The lens-shaped peridioles are whitish gray in color. *Cyathus stercoreus* is very similar but has non-grooved cups and usually grows in dung.

Nidula candida (Peck) V. S. White

We have two common, widespread species of *Nidula* in our region, *N. niveotomentosa* and *N. candida*. Both have a wooly covering on the exterior of the cup, which is grayish

Nidula candida

mosses when dried. Recently, a number of more typical gilled mushrooms, such as *Clitocybe epichysium*, were transferred to *Arrhenia*. *Arrhenia retiruga* is grayish white to grayish brown, fades quickly on drying, is very thin, and the fertile surface is nearly smooth or with very shallow, slightly reticulate veins. It is widely distributed and can be found in both urban and forested areas. *Arrhenia lobata* is a moss-associated species often found in fens, along streams, or in association with melting snow. Old faded specimens can be confused with *Cyphellostereum laeve*.

to brownish in *N. candida* and white in *N. niveotomentosa*. *Nidula candida* is considerably larger than *N. niveotomentosa*, and its cup has a wide-flaring mouth. *Nidula candida* occurs on woody debris and soil, and the empty cups are persistent and can be found throughout the year. *Nidula niveotomentosa* is often found among mosses but also can be associated with the debris of bracken ferns and other substrates. Nidulas are most likely to be confused with crucibulums, the peridioles of which are attached by short cords before they are dispersed.

ALL THE REST

Arrhenia retiruga (Bulliard: Fries)
Redhead

Arrhenia in the traditional sense includes small, thin, pliable-fleshed mushrooms that are spoon-, petal-, or cup shaped, often lobed, and without a stipe or with a lateral one. The fertile surface is smooth, or bears anastomosing veins or blunt gills. They occur on soil or in association with mosses and often can hardly be seen among the

Cyphellostereum laeve (Fries) D. A.
Reid

The tiny basidiomycete *Cyphellostereum laeve* forms whitish spoon- to irregular-shaped, thin, soft fruitbodies with spores produced on the undersurface. It occurs on mosses, usually hair caps (*Polytrichum* spp.), and is common in late summer and fall in our moist conifer forests, especially along trails and other areas where mossbeds are found. The spores are white, non-amyloid, smooth, rounded, and $4–5 \times 2.5–3$ µm.

Onygena corvina Albertini and
Schweinitz

Small mushroom structures with a cap and stipe are found in several groups of ascomycetes, for example, the fruitbodies of *Cordyceps*, *Vibrissea*, and *Mitrula*, and the club-shaped earth-tongues. Though similar in appearance to these fungi, the very small fruitbodies of *Onygena* species differ in that the cap surface breaks into a powdery spore mass at maturity. The two most common species are *O. corvina*, which occurs on owl pellets, bird carcasses, hair, and wool, and *O. equina*, found on the decaying horns and hooves of cattle and sheep. *Onygena corvina* reaches at most 2.5 cm (1 in.) in height, and has a whitish stalk and an ocher to light brown cap. These fungi are widely distributed but infrequently collected because of their small size and occurrence on animal remains, which are avoided by most mushroomers.

Rhytisma punctatum (Persoon) Fries
TAR SPOT FUNGUS

In our region, *Rhytisma punctatum* is extremely common on maples, especially bigleaf maple, in both forest and urban areas. Around mid-August, islands of small black spots (structures that will produce sexual spores in the following spring) surrounded by yellowish tissue develop on the living leaves. Later

Arrhenia retiruga SAT-98-302-02

Cyphellostereum laeve SAT-98-290-02

Rhytisma punctatum

Onygena corvina

in fall when the leaves have turned mostly golden and fallen, the "tar spots" can be seen surrounded by a circle of green tissue that remains photosynthetic long after the leaves have fallen to the ground. The fungus overwinters in the dead leaf and, in spring, releases spores that are transported by winds to infect new young leaves. Two other species, *R. americanum* and *R. acerinum*, also occur in our region. All three occur widely in North America, and the latter is thought to have been introduced from Europe.

Sparassis crispa SAT-06-293-02

Sparassis crispa, detail of flattened branches

Sparassis crispa (Wulfen: Fries) Fries
CAULIFLOWER FUNGUS

Although *Sparassis crispa* is commonly known as the cauliflower fungus, it actually looks less like that vegetable than do many ramarias, such as *Ramaria magnipes*. To us, the broad, flat, cream-colored, fan-like branches are much more similar to short egg noodles. Regardless of its vegetable likeness, this fungus can hardly be confused with any other in the PNW (there are other species of *Sparassis* elsewhere that can cause confusion). The spores are white and may be produced on both surfaces of the leaf-like branches. *Sparassis crispa* can grow quite large from its root-like base (fruitbodies weighing over 50 pounds, 22 kg, occur), although the older giants usually are of lower quality for the table than younger, smaller individuals. Such young specimens are among the most highly sought-after edible mushrooms in the PNW. *Sparassis crispa* is a parasite of tree roots, especially those of Douglas-fir, and fruitbodies often will recur in the same spot, although not necessarily every year. It occurs in northern North America, Europe, and Asia.

TO LEARN MORE

Mushroom Clubs

The best way to learn about mushrooms and mushroom-hunting is to join one of the many mushroom clubs (often called mycological societies or associations) in the Pacific Northwest. Most hold regular meetings with featured speakers and, in-season, collected mushrooms can be brought there to be identified. Some of the larger clubs host informative Web sites or e-mail discussion groups, offer classes in identification, and hold an annual exhibit or large overnight foray (both a trip in search of mushrooms and a multi-day mushroom get-together are called "forays"). Nearly all hold forays, usually on Saturdays, during the peak season. Here you will be exposed to a wide range of people from whom you can begin to learn. Despite the bad pun, mushroomers really are a down-to-earth, if sometimes a tad eccentric, bunch and generally enjoyable to be around. Mingling at meetings and on forays is also a good way to learn about other resources and events that might interest you. Northwest clubs of which we are aware follow.

Alaska (southern)

Alaska Mycological Society, Homer
Glacier Bay Mycological Society, Gustavus
Greater Anchorage Mycological Association, Eagle River
Southeast Alaska Mycological Association, Sitka

British Columbia (southern)

Fraser Valley Mushroom Club, Mission
South Vancouver Island Mycological Society, Victoria
Southern Interior Mycological Society, Lake Country
Vancouver Mycological Society, Vancouver

California (northern)

Humboldt Bay Mycological Society, Arcata
Mount Shasta Mycological Society, Mount Shasta

Idaho

North Idaho Mycological Association, Hayden
Palouse Mycological Association, Moscow
Southern Idaho Mycological Association, Boise

Montana (western)

Kootenai Valley Mycological Society, Libby
Southwest Montana Mycological Association, Bozeman
Western Montana Mycological Association, Missoula

Oregon

Cascade Mycological Society, Eugene
Lincoln County Mycological Society, Otter Rock
Mount Mazama Mushroom Association, Medford

North American Truffling Society,
  Corvallis
Oregon Mycological Society, Portland
Wild Rivers Mushroom Club, Brookings
Willamette Valley Mushroom Society,
  Salem

Washington
Kitsap Peninsula Mycological Society,
  Bremerton

Northwest Mushroomers Association,
  Bellingham
Olympic Peninsula Mycological Society,
  Chimacum
Puget Sound Mycological Society, Seattle
Snohomish County Mycological Society,
  Everett
South Sound Mushroom Club, Olympia
Spokane Mushroom Club, Spokane

Mushroom Web Sites

Because of the dynamic nature of the World Wide Web, we were hesitant to include addresses for many Web sites, as they change so often; however, the following two sites have been amazingly stable (both of them for well over a decade), so we feel reasonably safe in giving them. In addition to being very informative in themselves, they provide many links to other sites of interest.

Tom Volk's Fungi: http://botit.botany.wisc. edu/toms_fungi/
Tom Volk is a professor at the University of Wisconsin and his Web site has won numerous awards for presenting information in an extremely entertaining fashion. His "Mushroom of the Month" is a long-running favorite.

MykoWeb: http://www.mykoweb.com/
MykoWeb is the pet project of San Francisco Bay area mushroomer Mike Wood. Although a large portion of its content is focused on California, there is much of general interest and many links to mushroom sites of all types.

GLOSSARY

aborted, abortive: arrested in development and only partly formed

acrid: with a sharp biting taste, hot and peppery

acute: pointed or sharp-edged

adnate: describes gills that are attached to the stipe along all or most of their height

adnexed: narrowly attached; describes gills that are attached to the stipe along only a part of their height, or appear as though a small part of the gill had been cut away next to the stipe

alliaceous: with an odor or taste similar to onion or garlic (plants in the genus *Allium*)

amyloid: staining blue, blue-gray, to blackish in Melzer's reagent; compare dextrinoid

anastomosing: describes gills that split and re-join in network fashion, like a braided stream

annulus: a skirt-like ring

apex (-ices): the uppermost part of some-thing, usually in reference to a stipe or spore

apical: occurring at the apex of a structure

apiculus: short projection at the base of a spore by which it was attached to the sterigma

apothecium: open cup-shaped fruitbody characteristic of some ascomycetes

appendiculate: hung with bits of veil tissue; in reference to a cap margin

appressed: flattened onto a surface

arachnoid: silky fibrillose, cobwebby

areolate: cracked like dry mud

ascomycetes: the largest group of fungi, characterized by production of spores in an ascus

ascospore: spore produced in an ascus

ascus (-i): a sac-like cell in which sexual spores are formed

atomate: covered with minute shining particles

basidiomycetes: a large group of fungi, characterized by production of spores on a basidium

basidiospore: spore produced by a basidium

basidium (-ia): an often club-shaped cell on which sexual spores are formed

binding hypha (-ae): branching, thick-walled, usually non-septate hypha that tends to bind other hyphae together, which lends strength to the tissue

bloom: a thin surface covering, often found on blueberries and grapes

bolete: a fleshy mushroom with a tube layer on the underside of the cap

boletinoid: similar to a boletinus, usually in reference to the radially arranged elon-gated pores of many *Suillus* species

boletoid: similar to a boletus, usually in ref-erence to the shape of spores

brown rot: type of wood decomposition in which the cellulose is broken down, but not the lignin, leaving a reddish brown residue in small brick-like chunks

buff: a pale yellow color with slight gray-ish tones

bulb: swollen base of a stipe

button: young, unopened mushroom

caespitose: see cespitose

campanulate: bell-shaped

cap: the broad expanded umbrella-like portion of a typical mushroom, which bears gills, tubes, spines, or a smooth surface on its underside

capillitium: sterile hyphae of puffballs and similar fungi, often thread-like, thick-walled, and branched, part of the gleba

capitate: having a head, or small knob at the tip

carminophilous granules: see siderophilous granules

cartilaginous: rigid and brittle, breaking with a snap; usually in reference to a stipe

caulocystidium (-ia): sterile cell located on the surface of a stipe

cellulose: a major component of wood, fibrous and pale-colored; it is the main constituent of paper; see also lignin

cespitose (caespitose): growth form (habit) in which stipes of several fruitbodies arise very close together

cheilocystidium (-ia): sterile cell located on the edge of a gill or pore

chlamydospore: a thick-walled spore produced asexually

chrysocystidium (-ia): sterile cell, the contents of which turn yellow when mounted in potassium hydroxide or ammonia and viewed under a microscope

clamp connection: half bagel- or doughnut-like protrusions present at the cross-walls of the hyphae of many basidiomycetes; often shortened to "clamp"

clavate: club-shaped

close: in reference to spacing of gills, farther apart than crowded, but closer together than subdistant

columella: sterile stipe-like tissue within some false truffles or puffballs

conifer: a cone-bearing tree, usually evergreen, such as pine, spruce, or Douglas-fir

conk: a hard, bracket- or hoof-shaped fruitbody of certain polypores; term often used by foresters

connate: fused at the base and for some distance upward; in reference to mushrooms growing in a cluster

context: the flesh of a mushroom, particularly that of the cap

convex: rounded, like an upside-down bowl

coprophilous: dung-inhabiting

coriaceous: leathery

cortina: a silky fibrillose, cobwebby partial veil, found in cortinariuses and some other mushrooms

crenate, crenulate: scalloped, finely scalloped, usually in reference to the edge of a gill or cap

crowded: in reference to spacing of gills, packed closely together

cuticle: the outermost layer ("skin") of a cap or stipe

cystidium (-ia): a sterile cell (actually a hyphal end), usually larger than, and projecting beyond, nearby cells; often with distinctive appearance and much used for classification purposes

decurrent: describes gills that are attached to, and extend down, the stipe

deliquescence: liquefaction of the gills of ink-caps and certain other mushrooms to facilitate release of spores

dentate, denticulate: toothed, finely toothed

depressed: in reference to the cap, having the central portion sunken relative to the margin

dextrinoid: staining dark red or red-brown in Melzer's reagent; compare amyloid

dichotomous: split in two, forking, like a wishbone or tuning fork

disc: the central portion of the cap surface

distant: in reference to spacing of gills, rather far apart

duff: plant litter making up the surface layer of forest soil; usually applied in conifer forests

eccentric (or excentric): off-center, often in reference to the attachment of stipe to cap

ectomycorrhiza: a mutualistic symbiosis between the hyphae of certain basidiomycetes and ascomycetes and the fine roots of certain plants (see "Ecology of the Mushroom-Fungi" in Preliminaries)

ellipsoid: in reference to spores, elongated with rounded ends and curved sides

entire: even, smooth, not toothed or broken up; usually in reference to the cap or gill margin

epigeous: above-ground; compare hypogeous

epithet: the second half of a species' scientific name (the first half is the genus to which the species belongs)

equal: of the same diameter throughout; usually in reference to a stipe

eroded: irregularly toothed; usually in reference to the gill edge

excentric: see eccentric

farinaceous: odor or taste like that of freshly ground meal; when strong, somewhat like that of cucumber or watermelon rind

fascicles: bundles, like pine needles or sheaves of grain

fibril: small slender fiber

fibrillose: composed of fibrils

fibrous: tough and stringy

floccose: with tufts of loose cottony material

free: describes gills that are not at all attached to the stipe along their height

friable: easily breaking into pieces, crumbly

fruitbody: large sexual reproductive structure produced by certain fungi

fusiform, fusoid: tapering from the middle toward both ends, spindle-shaped

gasteromycetes: fungi, such as puffballs, in which the spores are formed within cavities inside the fruitbody and not discharged forcibly

gastroid: like a gasteromycete; similar to a puffball or earthball

genera: plural of genus

generative hyphae: typical thin- to thick-walled hyphae that are the fundamental components of the fruitbody

genus: a group of similar, presumably closely related, species

germ pore: an apparent opening (actually a thin area) in the wall at the apex of a spore

gill: blade-like, or sometimes fold-like, structure, borne radially on the underside of a cap, and the faces of which are covered by fertile tissue

gill trama: the sterile tissue in the center of a gill, "sandwiched" between the two fertile layers

glabrous: smooth, naked

glandular dots: tufts of caulocystidia that exude a sticky fluid; usually in reference to the stipe of certain suilluses

gleba: in gasteromycetes, the tissue in which the spores are formed; may include capillitium

globose: approximately spherical

glutinous: glue-like, gooey

granulose: covered with small sugar-like particles

gregarious (habit): occurring in groups

habit: morphological form, such as pleurotoid, or manner of growth, such as solitary, scattered, gregarious, and clustered

hardwood: flowering trees with broad leaves such as alder, maple, madrone, and oak; may be deciduous or evergreen

herbaceous: describing plants that have no (or very little) woody tissue; most live for only one growing season

herbarium: a permanent organized repository for dried, or otherwise preserved, fungus or plant specimens

hygrophanous: changing from translucent to opaque, and often markedly fading in color (expallent), upon drying; usually in reference to the cap surface

hymenium: the spore-producing, or fertile, tissue of a mushroom, such as the layer of basidia and other cells on the face of a gill, or the layer of asci lining the inside of a cup-fungus

hypha (-ae): long tube-like elements that make up the body (mycelium) of a fungus; may or may not be septate

hypogeous: below-ground; compare epigeous

imbricate: overlapping like roof shingles

inferior ring: ring borne on the lower portion of a stipe

infundibuliform: deeply depressed, funnel-like

inoperculate: a type of ascus in which the pore through which the spores are released has no lid; compare operculate

lacunose: covered with pits or indentations

lamella (-ae): gill

lamellula (-ae): a gill that does not extend the entire distance from cap margin to stipe

lateral: attached at one side, as in the short stipe of many shelf-fungi

latex: watery or milky fluid; produced by lactariuses and certain other fungi

lignicolous: growing on wood

lignin: a major component of wood, extremely resistant to decay; see also cellulose

longitudinal: along the long axis of a structure; especially in reference to a stipe or spore

lubricous: slightly greasy or slippery to the touch

macroscopic: visible with the naked eye, or at low magnification such as obtained with a 10-power handlens

marcescent: withering or drying up; see also reviving

margin: edge; especially in reference to a cap or gill

marginate: having a distinctly marked border, such as a gill with differently colored edge or bulb on stipe bearing a sharply flaring rim

Melzer's reagent: an iodine-containing solution used, both microscopically and macroscopically, to test for color changes; see amyloid and dextrinoid

membranous: thin and pliable, like a membrane

merulioid: indicates a spore-producing surface that is composed of shallow pits or tubes separated by irregular ridges, often correlated with a membranous to gelatinous fruitbody texture; the fruitbodies may be flat against the substrate, with or without extended edges, or form narrow shelves or a series of fused to overlapping caps

micrometer (μm): unit of measurement in the metric system, equal to one-millionth of a meter; informally referred to as a micron

microscopic: visible only with a microscope

morphologic(al): pertaining to the form and structure of an organism or other object

mycelial cord: root-like structure formed by the aggregation of hyphae; superficially similar to but anatomically different from rhizomorphs

mycelium: the body of a filamentous fungus, composed of a network of complexly branched hyphae

mycoflora: all the species of fungi that inhabit a given area (= mycota)

mycologist: one who studies fungi

mycology: the study of fungi

mycophagy, mycophagist: the eating of fungi, one who eats fungi

mycorrhiza: a nearly universal mutualistic symbiosis between the hyphae of fungi and the roots of plants (see "Ecology of the Mushroom-Fungi" in Preliminaries)

mycota: see mycoflora

obtuse: blunt, not pointed

ocher: a dingy orangish yellow color, also spelled ochre

ochraceous: having an ocher color

operculate: a type of ascus in which the pore through which the spores are released has a lid like the hatch of a ship; compare inoperculate

ornamentation: the surface features (spines, warts, ridges, wrinkles) of a non-smooth spore

ovoid: egg-shaped

pallid: a very pale shade of any color, almost white

papilla: a small, nipple-shaped projection

paraphysis (-es): sterile hyphal ends that, along with the asci, comprise the hymenium of cup-fungi

parasitism: a form of symbiosis, in which an organism (the parasite) obtains its nutrition from a live, usually much larger organism (the host)

partial veil: a thin membranous or fibrillose tissue that extends from the cap margin to the stipe of an unopened mushroom and covers its gills or pores

pendant: hanging downward like an icicle or stalactite

peridiole: small chambers in the gleba of some gasteromycetes, or the "eggs" of bird's nest fungi; spores are produced within them

peridium: the outermost layer of a fruitbody such as a puffball or truffle

perithecium (-a): a flask-like fruiting structure characteristic of some ascomycetes; usually many are embedded in a mass of fungus or host tissue

persistent: retaining its shape or position for a long time

pileipellis: the outermost layer of the cap (pileus), the cap cuticle

pileocystidium (-ia): cystidium located on the cap surface

pileus: cap

plage: a smooth area near the point of attachment of a spore

plane: flat

pleurocystidium (-ia): cystidium located on the face of a gill or tube

pleurotoid (habit): shelf-like, lacking a stipe or with a short lateral one

pliant: flexible, can be bent without breaking

plicate: folded like a fan or pleated skirt

pore: small opening, or the mouth of the tubes of boletes and polypores

primordium: very young undeveloped mushroom

pruinose: finely powdery

pubescent: finely hairy

punctate: covered with tiny scales or spots

radicating: with a root-like projection

resupinate: flat-lying fruitbody, with the upper "cap" surface attached to the substrate (usually a log) and fertile surface facing outward

reticulum: net-like system of ridges; often in reference to a stipe or spore

reviving: a marcescent fruitbody that

assumes its fresh condition and resumes releasing spores when re-moistened

rhizomorph: root-like structure formed by the aggregation of hyphae and often found at the base of a stipe; superficially similar to but anatomically different from mycelial cords

rimose: with small cracks or crevices

ring: membranous skirt-like remnant of a partial veil borne on a stipe

ring-zone: band of fibrillose remnants of a partial veil borne on a stipe; often colored by the accumulation of falling spores

rugose: coarsely wrinkled

rugulose: finely wrinkled

saccate: shaped like a sack

saprotroph: an organism that obtains its nutrition by decomposing dead organic material

scaber: tufts of short stiff hairs, usually in reference to those on the stipes of leccinums

scabrous: covered with scabers

scale: torn portion of a cuticle that projects from the surface of a cap or stipe; these can take a wide variety of forms—membranous, fibrillose, flat, soft, erect, and so on

scattered (habit): fruitbodies occurring singly here and there over a relatively wide area

sclerotium: a hard round knot of fungus tissue and sometimes soil, often functioning in vegetative reproduction

scrobiculate: with shallow pits or depressions

seceding: refers to gills that are initially attached, then tear away from the stipe as the fruitbody develops, usually leaving lines on the stipe surface

secotioid: a fruitbody similar to a gilled mushroom or bolete, but with a cap that does not expand, gills or tubes that are close-packed and crumpled, and often a reduced stipe; conceptually midway between a normal mushroom and a false truffle

septate: having septa

septum (-a): cross-wall of a hypha

sericeous: silky

serrate, serrulate: saw-toothed, finely saw-toothed

sessile: attached at the base, without any sort of stipe or stalk

siderophilous granule: small dark purple to nearly black particle observed in the basidia of some mushrooms when stained with acetocarmine

skeletal hypha: type of thick-walled, non-septate, often unbranched hypha found in polypores and certain other mushrooms

solitary (habit): fruitbodies occurring singly without others nearby

sordid: dirty or dingy

species: the lowest category in the classification of organisms (although some species are further divided into subspecies, varieties, or forms); variously defined, but can be considered to represent a single kind or type of organism

sphaerocyst: a more or less globose cell, commonly found in clusters in russulas and lactariuses

sphagnum: general term for members of one of the two main groups of mosses; it often forms extensive dense growths in (peat) bogs and cold, wet forests

spore: single-, or sometimes multi-celled, reproductive propagule formed by fungi and many of the "lower" plants such as ferns and mosses; functionally similar to the seeds of gymnosperms and flowering plants

squamulose: covered with tiny scales (squamules)

squarrose: covered with stiff upright scales

stature: overall form, such as tall and slender or short and stocky

sterigma (-ata): branch-like extension of a basidium, on which a spore is formed

sterile: non-spore-forming parts of a mushroom

stipe: stem

stipitate: having a stipe

striate: having small parallel or radiating lines or grooves ("striped"); often in reference to a cap margin or spore

subdistant: in reference to spacing of gills, farther apart than close, but closer together than distant

substrate: medium in which the vegetative body (mycelium) of the fungus is growing and from which the mushroom projects; usually soil, woody material, or leaf litter, but can be such things as insects or other mushrooms

sulcate: with deep parallel or radial grooves; between striate and plicate

superior ring: ring borne on the upper portion of a stipe

synonym: an alternate, usually less preferred, name for the same organism

tacky: slightly sticky

taxonomy: the naming and classifying of organisms

terrestrial: growing on the ground, in soil

toadstool: informal term sometimes used to refer to a poisonous mushroom

tomentum: covering of long, soft, matted hairs

translucent-striate: appearing striate as a result of the gills being visible through the very thin flesh of the caps of some small mushrooms, especially mycenas, galerinas, and small ink-caps

truncate: appearing as though an end was cut off; usually in reference to spores or the fruitbodies of some otideas

tube: in boletes and polypores, a hollow cylinder the inner surface of which is lined with fertile tissue; the exposed ends of the close-packed tubes are referred to as pores

umbilicate: shaped like a navel; usually in reference to the center of a cap

umbo: hump or raised area in the center of a cap

umbonate: bearing an umbo

universal veil: a membranous, fibrillose, or friable tissue that entirely covers an unopened mushroom; often leaves remnants in the form of a volva, bands on the stipe, or a patch or warts on the cap

ventricose: fattest in the middle and tapering toward both ends; usually in reference to a stipe

verrucose, verruculose: warty, slightly warty

vinaceous: said to be the color of red wine; in practice, not so deeply colored and with duller gray to brown tones, yielding more of a dark salmon-pink

virgate: streaked

viscid: sticky

volva: remnants of a universal veil found at the base of the stipe

warts: isolated remnants of the universal veil left on the cap; can be peeled off without disrupting the cap surface

white rot: type of wood decomposition in which both the cellulose and lignin are broken down, leaving a soft, wet, stringy, pale-colored residue

zonate: with concentric bands of different color or different shades of one basic color; usually in reference to the cap surface

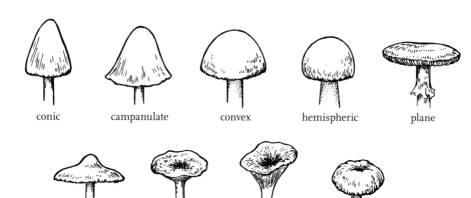

conic   campanulate   convex   hemispheric   plane

umbonate   depressed   infundibuliform   umbilicate

Cap shapes. Illustration by Marsha Mello.

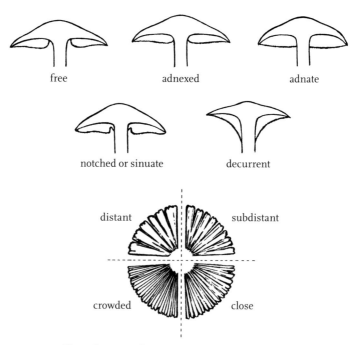

free   adnexed   adnate

notched or sinuate   decurrent

distant   subdistant

crowded   close

Gill attachment and spacing. Illustration by Marsha Mello.

Partial veil and remnants   skirt-like ring   cortina   appendiculate margin

Universal veil and remnants   volva with collar-like rim and warts or patches on cap   volva remains as rings of tissue and warts on cap   saccate volva

Veils. Illustration by Marsha Mello.

equal   tapered   clavate   bulbous

Stipe shapes. Illustration by Marsha Mello.

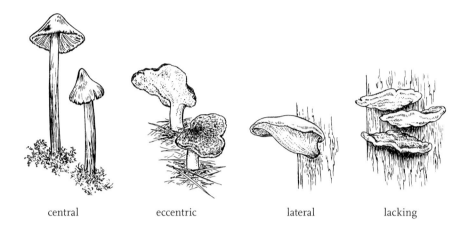

central   eccentric   lateral   lacking

Types of stipe attachment to cap. Illustration by Marsha Mello.

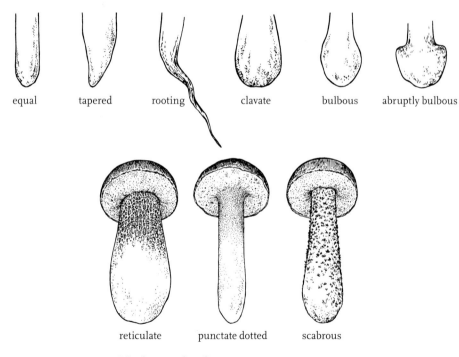

equal   tapered   rooting   clavate   bulbous   abruptly bulbous

reticulate   punctate dotted   scabrous

Stipe bases and surfaces. Illustration by Marsha Mello.

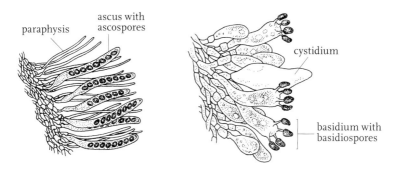

Hymenium of an ascomycete (a typical cup-fungus) and a **basidiomycete** (a typical gilled mushroom). Illustration by Marsha Mello.

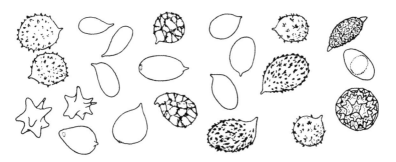

Examples of mushroom spores. Illustration by Marsha Mello.

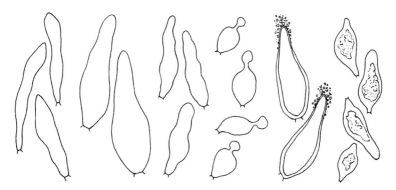

Examples of cystidia. Illustration by Marsha Mello.

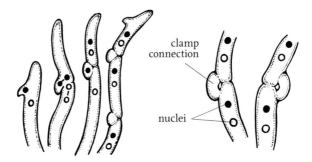

Formation of clamp connections allows many basidiomycetes to maintain two different types of nucleus in their hyphae. Illustration by Marsha Mello.

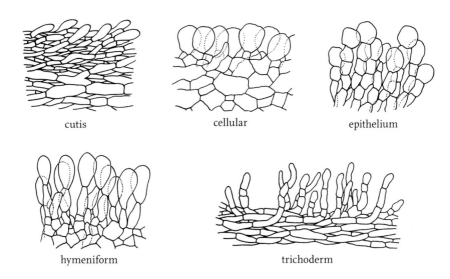

cutis

cellular

epithelium

hymeniform

trichoderm

Types of cap cuticle structure. Illustration by Marsha Mello.

APPENDIX 1. Types of Mushroom Poisoning

Mushroom poisoning is not a simple matter. The mushrooms vary in the types and amounts of potential toxins they contain, and people vary in how they react to these, as well as to other, nontoxic components of fungi. So learn to unfailingly recognize the potentially deadly species and avoid them. For the others, use caution and eat mushrooms in moderation even after you know a particular mushroom is safe for you.

Some types of mushroom poisoning can be traced to particular chemical compounds whose modes of action and effects are well known. These are fairly easy to categorize. However, other types of poisoning and the toxins that cause them are less well understood, and they are not always so easy to categorize. Traditionally, myco-toxicologists have recognized eight types, based primarily on the symptoms produced. A brief summary of these and a ninth type caused by *Amanita smithiana*, follows, including type of toxin, its mode of action and effects, and examples of the species that contain the toxin. For those who are interested in going into greater depth, an excellent source of information about mushroom toxins and poisonings is the book *Mushrooms: Poisons and Panaceas* by Dr. Denis Benjamin.

Amatoxins

Poisoning by amatoxins should be permanently on the radar of anyone who contemplates eating wild mushrooms. Although fatal incidents are rare, they do occur despite being largely avoidable. One of the first things a mushroom-hunter should do is learn to recognize on sight the mushrooms that contain these toxins and how to distinguish them from similar species.

Toxic agent and mode of action

Two groups of potent cyclopeptides (compounds that essentially are small proteins with ring structures) are produced in these fungi. Because they were isolated first from *Amanita phalloides*, the death cap, they were named phallotoxins and amanitins. Although the phallotoxins can be highly toxic when injected into an animal or applied to cell cultures, they are not absorbed from the gastrointestinal tract in an active form, and so are believed to play no role in poisonings. It is the amanitins that are responsible, and the cellular mechanism by which they work is well understood. Amanitins inhibit the action of the enzyme RNA polymerase II, and this blocks the synthesis of cellular proteins. Without their normal complement of proteins, cells cease to function, with the effects becoming critical first in cells that rapidly turn over proteins. Liver and kidney damage is common, primarily because they are exposed to higher concentrations of the toxins than are most other organs.

Onset and symptoms

Amatoxin poisoning often occurs in four phases. For a period of time—typically on the order of 8 to 12 hours—there is no indication of a problem. In severe cases, the onset time can be 6 hours or less; in mild cases it can take 2 to 3 days. Then, with little warning, the victim experiences severe abdominal pain and cramping, vomiting, and watery diarrhea, which may last for as much as 48 hours. At that point, the symptoms usually subside and often the victim feels the ordeal is over. For perhaps 24 hours, no further symptoms are felt. However, in the fourth, sometimes fatal phase, the abdominal pain returns, progressively accompanied with bloody diarrhea, onset of jaundice, possible kidney failure, convulsions, coma, and death in approximately 10–15% of victims.

Species involved

By far, the most common cause of fatal mushroom poisoning is consumption of amanitas in the destroying angel group. In North America, the most common of these are *Amanita phalloides*, *A. ocreata*, and *A. bisporigera* (= *A. virosa*). However, many other species can cause the same type of poisoning. Mushrooms in at least three other genera have sufficiently high concentrations of amanitins to present a serious risk—*Conocybe*, *Galerina*, and *Lepiota* in the narrow sense. Species include *C. filaris*, *G. marginata* (= *G. autumnalis*, *G. venenata*), *L. subincarnata* (= *L. josserandii*), and likely *L. felina*, *L. castanea*, and other closely related lepiotas.

Orellanine

This group of toxins was discovered in the 1950s with considerable surprise because most mycologists had assumed that all the types of mushroom poisoning would have been recognized long ago. Only after 102 people in Poland became ill, and 11 of them died, was the link between eating certain species of *Cortinarius* and poisoning established.

Toxic agent and mode of action

The chemical nature of the toxin(s) responsible for the poisoning still has not been well characterized. One school of thought believes they are cyclopeptides called cortinarins, similar to the amatoxins; the other school feels they are bipyridyls. Likewise, the mode of action has not been firmly established, but the critical target is the kidneys.

Onset and symptoms

Orellanine poisoning has a delayed onset, even more so than amatoxin poisoning, ranging from about 2 days to 3 weeks. The first symptoms are vomiting and diarrhea, followed by frequent urination, intense burning thirst, headache, chills and shivering, lethargy, generalized muscle and joint pain, and, finally, progressive kidney failure. The death rate is estimated to be about 15%.

Species involved

Three species of *Cortinarius* are known to cause orellanine poisoning—*C. orellanus*, *C. orellanoides*, and *C. rubellus* (likely the same as *C. speciosissimus*). *Cortinarius rainierensis*, described from Washington state, is likely the same as *C. rubellus*, but this remains uncertain. Nonetheless, species related to *C. rubellus* occur in Washington, British Columbia, and in the boreal forest of North America. Until recently, whether any cases of orellanine poisoning had occurred in North America was an open question. However, in 2008, a well documented poisoning occurred in Michigan, involving mushrooms closely related to *C. orellanus*.

Amanita smithiana Nephrotoxicity

Amanita smithiana has caused at least one fatality, due to kidney failure, and more than 14 poisonings dating back to the mid-1970s, many also involving kidney failure. In one case, liver function also was lost. In the PNW, almost all cases of poisoning appear to have resulted from *A. smithiana* being mistaken for *Tricholoma magnivelare*, American matsutake.

Toxic agent and mode of action

The toxins are thought to be 2-amino-3-cyclopropylbutanoic acid and/or 2-amino-4,5-hexadienoic acid. The mode of action is not well understood.

Onset and symptoms

Amanita smithiana produces symptoms similar to orellanine poisoning except for the much more rapid onset. Abdominal pain, nausea, vomiting, and diarrhea typically develop 4 to 11 hours after ingestion and can continue for several days, followed much later by difficulty urinating. Kidney failure has occurred in some victims 5 to 6 days after ingestion. Death due to kidney failure has been known to occur.

Species involved

Amanita smithiana is the species in our region known to be toxic. It and other potentially dangerous species are in the subgenus *Lepidella*, which is much more common in the southeastern U.S. than it is in our region. Similar poisonings have been reported in France, Spain, and Italy (caused by *A. proxima*) and in Japan (caused by *A. pseudoporphyria*).

Gyromitrin

Probably the most confusing issue surrounding mushroom poisoning involves gyromitrin. Although it has been shown conclusively to cause fatal poisonings, mostly in Europe, but also in a small number of incidents in eastern North America, many mushroomers in western North America eat gyromitras, apparently without ill effects. Even in instances of fatal poisoning, it is not unusual for other persons who have eaten as much of the mushrooms as the victim to suffer only mild or no effects from the meal. These seeming contradictions have at least four contributing factors. First, people vary widely in their susceptibility to the toxins. Second, there is a rather small difference between a non-symptomatic dose and a toxic one. Third, proper preparation destroys most, if not all, of the toxin. Fourth, there is some evidence that the toxin accumulates in the body and can trigger symptoms when a sufficient concentration is reached. Another possible factor, but one that has not been addressed in any depth, is variation in the concentration of the toxins in mushrooms from different geographic areas. Perhaps our western fungi just do not have sufficient levels of toxins to make them acutely poisonous. The jury remains out on these questions, however, and until there is a better understanding of them, we urge following the advice of Charles McIlvaine, who was no shrinking violet when it came to testing and eating wild mushrooms: "It is not probable that in our great food-giving country anyone will be narrowed to *Gyromitra esculenta* for a meal. Until such an emergency arrives, the species would be better let alone."

Toxic agent and mode of action

Gyromitrin is one of a number of closely related hydrazines that are responsible for this type of poisoning. These are broken down to a simpler compound, monomethylhydrazine (MMH), which is the active agent. All these are rather volatile and can be removed by thorough cooking. MMH has been used as rocket fuel, and a lot of what is known about its effects came from studies carried out by the aerospace industry. The main effect of MMH is disruption of the action of vitamin B6, which is an important factor in many cellular processes. Thus, a wide variety of symptoms can result from gyromitrin poisoning. Liver and kidney damage often result, and breakdown of red blood cells occurs in a smaller percentage of cases.

Onset and symptoms

In its early stages, the symptoms of gyromitrin poisoning are similar to those of amatoxin poisoning. Onset of symptoms usually occurs about 6 to 12 hours after consumption, earlier in severe cases, and longer in milder ones. Initial symptoms come on suddenly and include the usual gastrointestinal ones—feeling of fullness and bloating, abdominal pain, vomiting, and severe headache. Diarrhea and fever may or may not occur. At this point, most victims recover in 2 to 7 days, without further ill effects. In severe cases, there is a progression to liver and sometimes kidney damage. There is no "false recovery" period as there is in amatoxin poisoning. Jaundice develops, red blood cells may be destroyed, and convulsions and coma may be experienced. Death occurs in about 15% of cases. The database of poisoning reports maintained by the North American Mycological Association contains about one report of gyromitrin poisoning per year, with liver damage occurring in one-third of the cases.

Species involved

The principal species involved in gyromitrin poisoning is *Gyromitra esculenta*, whose species epithet ironically means "edible." *Gyromitra infula* and *G. ambigua* also have been implicated, but the presence of toxins is less certain in them. Suspicion has fallen on several other species, but even less is known about their toxicity; among these are the PNW species *G. montana* and *Pseudorhizina californica*. The former is generally regarded as edible among PNW mushroomers and is eaten by an unknown number. The latter is not as common and probably is not eaten frequently.

Coprine

Coprine poisoning is unusual in that a mushroom that is ordinarily a good edible causes symptoms in conjunction with the consumption of alcohol. Because the effects can be triggered by a drink for perhaps 2 to 3 days after the mushroom meal, one must choose which is more important—the fungus or the wine!

Toxic agent and mode of action

Coprine is the agent responsible for this type of poisoning. It acts by interfering with the metabolism of alcohol. In the body, alcohol is first converted to acetaldehyde and then to acetate and carbon dioxide. A breakdown product of coprine blocks the action of the enzyme that catalyzes the aldehyde-to-acetate reaction, and the consequent buildup of aldehyde causes the symptoms.

Onset and symptoms

Symptoms typically appear within 5 to 10 minutes of consuming alcohol anywhere from 30 minutes to 3 days after eating the mushroom. They may include a sensation of warmth, elevated blood pressure, flushing, tingling in the arms and legs, nausea and vomiting, a metallic taste, rapid heartbeat, pounding headache, sweating, anxiety, weakness, dizziness, confusion, and, occasionally, fainting. These symptoms have come to be known as the Antabuse syndrome, after the name of a drug used in the treatment of alcoholism that produces the same effects in the same general way. In most cases the effects of coprine are mild and, even when more severe, they have not been found to have a lasting effect.

Species involved

Coprine poisoning is pretty much restricted to one species—*Coprinopsis atramentaria*. A few other *Coprinopsis* and *Coprinus* species have been reported to contain coprine, but they are much less commonly eaten. In addition, other mushrooms, such as *Clitocybe clavipes*, have been reported to produce the same effects with alcohol, but appear to not contain coprine. Still other fungi, including morels, pholiotas, and boletes, have been implicated in alcohol-related poisonings, but the symptoms vary from those of the coprine syndrome and often can be attributed to the mushroom being toxic on its own, usually with gastrointestinal irritants.

Ibotenic Acid

Although the toxicity of *Amanita muscaria* often is said to be caused by muscarine, that is not the case. *Amanita muscaria* actu-ally contains only tiny concentrations of that compound which, however, is present in many other mushrooms and is responsible for many poisonings. The compound that is responsible for poisonings by *A. muscaria*, ibotenic acid, also occurs in related amanitas, sometimes at higher concentrations. Not all poisonings by ibotenic acid are accidental; in many cases, the mushrooms are consumed specifically with the intent of experiencing their psychoactive effects. Much has been written, for instance, concerning the ceremonial or ritualistic use of *A. muscaria* in parts of Siberia and elsewhere, and it even has been proposed that this mushroom was involved with the origins of Christianity. However, enjoyment of the psychoactive effects often is outweighed by the unpleasantness of the physical effects. Ibotenic acid is also responsible for a high percentage of poisonings of dogs, sometimes with fatal results.

Toxic agent and mode of action

The compound responsible for most of the physiologic effects in humans is muscimol, a breakdown product of ibotenic acid, the primary substance found in the mushrooms. Chemically, muscimol is very similar to GABA (γ-aminobutyric acid), an inhibitory neurotransmitter, and by binding to GABA receptors, muscimol alters the functioning of the nervous system. Both ibotenic acid and muscimol belong to a family of compounds known as isoxazole derivatives, and that term is sometimes used to describe this type of poisoning. As is the case with many mushroom toxins, the concentration of ibotenic acid in mushrooms is highly variable, both within and among species. Thus, it is difficult for those who would intentionally ingest these mushrooms to determine how much is necessary for an appropriate dose.

Onset and symptoms
The effects of ibotenic acid often are described as inebriation, although quite different from those produced by alcohol consumption. Effects usually begin between 30 minutes and 2 hours after the meal, but can take up to 6 hours in some cases. They peak about 2 to 5 hours later, and may last 8 to 24 hours. Nausea is usually the first symptom, sometimes accompanied by vomiting, especially in children. Other effects are incoordination, confusion, dizziness, difficulty in walking, and abrupt waxing and waning of activity, sometimes involving rather vigorous and excited outbursts. Muscle twitching, tremors, cramps, and spasms are common, and generalized seizures occasionally occur. Although true hallucinations seem not to occur, perception is altered such that objects often seem larger than they are or take on different colors. The final stage usually involves a deep coma-like sleep from which it is difficult to arouse the victim. Usually there are no aftereffects, although sometimes a hangover headache occurs. In many cases, especially those involving children found grazing on a mushroom, the effects of treatment probably are more harmful than those of the mushroom.

Species involved
All the species confirmed to be involved in ibotenic acid toxicity are closely related amanitas—*Amanita pantherina*, *A. muscaria* in its many forms, *A. gemmata*, *A. aprica* (probably), and others that are not known to occur in the western U.S. Toxin levels are highly variable for reasons that are unclear. In general, *A. pantherina* contains higher concentrations than *A. muscaria* (such that pantherine is another name applied to this type of poisoning). One study of a color-series of dark brown through paler brown *A. pantherina* to brownish yellow and finally yellow *A. gemmata*, showed that toxin levels were positively correlated with darkness of color. In another study, specimens of amanitas collected in summer had ten times the toxin levels as specimens collected in fall.

Muscarine
Although muscarine was first discovered in *Amanita muscaria*, it usually is present in very small concentrations and seems not to be important in poisonings by that species. Other mushrooms, however, do contain concentrations high enough to cause problems, even death in extreme cases. The incidence of poisonings is relatively low, perhaps because few of the species are large, inviting-looking, and abundant, and few closely resemble popular edible species.

Toxic agent and mode of action
Muscarine acts by binding to acetylcholine receptors associated with the autonomic nervous system, which controls involuntary muscle actions and glandular secretions such as tears. When acetylcholine binds at a receptor site, it triggers an action and then is rapidly degraded, which removes the stimulatory effect. When muscarine binds to a site, it too acts as a trigger but is not degraded quickly, so its effects continue much longer than those of acetylcholine. Atropine, which is an effective antidote, acts by displacing the muscarine without triggering the receptors.

Onset and symptoms

The symptoms of muscarine poisoning begin about 5 to 30 minutes after the mushrooms are eaten. Profuse sweating is the most frequent symptom, often accompanied by salivation and lacrimation (production of tears); an alternate name for this type of poisoning is PSL syndrome (for perspiration-salivation-lacrimation). The victim may experience blurred vision and feel nauseated, and abdominal pain, vomiting, and diarrhea often occur. Less often, victims show constriction of the muscular region at the back of the mouth, a painful urge to urinate, difficulty in breathing due to constriction of the bronchial region or blockage of airways by mucus, and decreased heart rate and blood pressure. The alkaloid atropine quickly blocks the effects of muscarine and recovery often occurs within 30 minutes. Without treatment, the symptoms can persist for many hours before disappearing.

Species involved

The principal species of concern are most, if not all, inocybes and several clitocybes, including *Clitocybe dealbata*, *C. connata*, *C. gibba*, and, possibly, *C. nebularis*. Other species, such as *Amanita muscaria* and *A. pantherina*, contain muscarine but at levels too low to be physiologically active. Still others, from several different genera, either contain, or are suspected of containing, sufficient muscarine to cause poisoning, including *Mycena pura* and certain species of *Boletus* and *Omphalotus*.

Hallucinogens

Referring to the effects of these "magic" mushrooms as "poisoning," while sometimes an accurate representation, often is misleading. Most ingestions occur with the intent of experiencing the psychoactive effects of the fungi. Although many people enjoy these effects, they can vary considerably according to the dose received and can be quite frightening when the mushrooms are mistakenly or unknowingly consumed.

Toxic agent and mode of action

The compound of interest found in greatest concentration in magic mushrooms is psilocybin, although the effects probably are triggered by psilocin, which is formed from psilocybin upon ingestion. Other closely related compounds are found in certain species. All these compounds are indole alkaloids derived from hydroxytryptamine. Psilocin produces effects, mostly through stimulation of the autonomic nervous system, because of its similarity to neurotransmitters in the brain; the details of just how it does this, however, are not yet well understood.

Onset and symptoms

The effects are noticed soon after ingestion, usually within 10 to 30 minutes. Initially, these include nausea, abdominal discomfort, dizziness, shivering, weakness, anxiety, restlessness, and numbness of the lips. Within an hour, symptoms include a feeling of euphoria, visual effects (such as blurring, brilliant undulating or vibrating colors, and floating visual patterns with the eyes closed), increased hearing sensitivity, facial flushing, decreased concentration, feelings of unreality, incoordination, and impaired speech. After an hour or two, the visual effects become stronger, objects may take on wave-like motions, and the passage of time may seem slow. After about 2 hours, the effects gradually wane and have usually disappeared by 4 to 12 hours after ingestion of the mushrooms. Later effects can include headache, fatigue, a sense of calm, decreased appetite, uncontrollable laughter, or none at all.

Species involved

Most of the magic mushrooms are species of *Psilocybe* or *Panaeolus*, although both of those genera include a number of non-psychoactive species. Common active species in the PNW include *Psilocybe baeocystis, P. cyanescens, P. semilanceata,* and *P. stuntzii* as well as *Panaeolus subbalteatus*. Several other genera contain active species, including *Conocybe* (e.g., *C. smithii*), *Gymnopilus* (e.g., *G. junonius*), *Inocybe* (e.g., *I. aeruginascens* and *I. corydalina*), and *Pluteus* (e.g., *P. salicinus*). Not all of these are known to occur in the PNW.

Gastrointestinal Irritants

This is by far the most common type of mushroom poisoning although, perhaps surprisingly, relatively little is known about its details. This is due to the symptoms being the same as those of many other types of poisoning, the variety of mushrooms and the compounds they contain being very large, and the fact that the effects of a particular species can be felt to very different degrees by different people. The poisonings are rarely serious, but the symptoms can be highly unpleasant while they last—in other words, while you may not die, you might wish you had.

Toxic agent and mode of action

For some species, the toxins have been isolated and characterized chemically but, for many others, the toxins remain unknown. Where known, the toxins belong to a wide array of chemical groups, and so the mechanisms behind poisoning are probably quite varied.

Onset and symptoms

Symptoms usually appear between 15 minutes and 2 hours after the meal and normally include abdominal pain and nausea with vomiting and/or diarrhea. They usually pass fairly quickly, especially if vomiting occurs soon after ingestion and removes most of the toxic material from the victim's system. In severe cases, such as those caused on occasion by species such as *Tricholoma pardinum*, complete recovery may take several days.

Species involved

Many different fungi cause gastrointestinal irritation. Some are consistent in affecting nearly everyone, while others bother relatively few individuals. Some are toxic only when raw, insufficiently cooked, or eaten in too great a quantity. Nationwide, the number-one culprit is *Chlorophyllum molybdites*, which, if present at all in the PNW, is neither common nor widespread. However, we do get our share of problem fungi, including *Agaricus moelleri, A. hondensis, A. silvicola,* some armillarias (honey mushrooms), red-pored boletuses such as *Boletus pulcherrimus,* collybias such as *Gymnopus dryophilus* and *G. acervatus,* certain hard-to-identify fleshy entolomas, *Gomphus floccosus* and *G. kauffmanii,* hebelomas such as *Hebeloma incarnatulum* and *H. mesophaeum,* acridtasting lactariuses and russulas such as *Russula emetica, Laetiporus conifericola,* undercooked morels, *Phaeolepiota aurea, Pholiota squarrosa,* some ramarias, especially the gelatinous-fleshed ones, *Sarcosphaera coro-*

naria, sclerodermas, some slimy suilluses, and a large number of tricholomas including many brown- and gray-capped species and, especially, *Tricholoma pardinum*. Many more species can cause problems, and thus we emphasize again the importance of accurately identifying all fungi you propose to eat and determining their edibility before you sample them.

There are a number of other species that have produced serious poisonings, including deaths, and whose basis is only very sketchily understood. These include *Paxillus involutus*, *Tricholoma equestre* (= *T. flavovirens*?), and *Pleurocybella porrigens*. All these species are included in this guide, and every PNW mushroom-hunter should learn to recognize them.

APPENDIX 2.
Information Often Included
in Descriptions of Gilled Mushrooms

General Information

- Date, collection number, location (including GPS coordinates), and filename(s) for digital image(s).
- Growth habit. For example: solitary, scattered, gregarious, cespitose, clustered, connate, pleurotoid.
- Substrate. For example: soil, wood, woody debris, leaf litter/duff, other mushrooms, burned soil.
- Habitat and names of nearby plants and fungi. For example: mixed conifer forest, riparian forest, coastal pine woodland, sagebrush steppe, grassy meadow, urban lawn, park, landscaping.

Macroscopic Features of the Fungus

- Spore-print color (or a spore print is attached).
- Cap: diameter; shape in side and top views; color of surface and color changes as mushroom ages, dries, or is bruised; other surface characteristics such as shininess, wetness, texture, and presence of universal veil remnants; surface features of margin and its shape in cross-sectional, side, and top views; thickness, color, color changes, consistency, taste, and odor of flesh.
- Gills: attachment; spacing; relative thickness; waxy-appearing or not; forked or

not; presence of partial gills; width and shape in edge-on view; color and color changes as mushroom ages (and spores mature), dries, is bruised, or latex dries; shape and color of margin; appearance of gill face; presence/absence, color, and color changes of latex.

- Stipe: attachment to cap; length and diameter; shape in long- and cross-sections; solid, hollow, or stuffed; color of surface and color changes as mushroom ages, dries, or is bruised; other surface characteristics such as shininess, wetness, and texture; presence, position, and nature of partial and/or universal veil remnants; color, color changes, consistency, taste, and odor of flesh.

Microscopic Features

- Spores: color (specify mounting liquid); attachment; shape and degree of symmetry; length, width, and ratio (Q-value); type and height of ornamentation; chemical reactions.
- Basidia: shape, dimensions, number of spores per, and chemical reactions.
- Cystidia: position, type, shape, dimensions, pigmentation, ornamentation, contents, and chemical reactions.
- Gill trama: type(s) of hyphae and their dimensions, presence/absence of clamp

connections, pigmentation, contents, and arrangement in different parts of the hymenium (fertile tissue).

- Cuticle: number of layers; morphology; chemical reactions; presence of cystidia or other distinctive elements and their position, type, shape, dimensions, pigmentation, ornamentation, and chemical reactions.

- Flesh of cap and stipe: hyphal types; presence/absence of clamp connections; pigmentation; chemical reactions; presence of cystidia or other distinctive elements and their position, type, shape, dimensions, pigmentation, ornamentation, and chemical reactions.

- Veils: hyphal/cell types; pigmentation; chemical reactions.

INDEX

STEVE TRUDELL is affiliate professor in the College of Forest Resources and lecturer in the Biology Department at the University of Washington. He has been identifying and photographing mushrooms and studying their ecology for over 30 years. Steve writes for several mycological publications, and frequently serves as foray mycologist or invited lecturer for mycological societies and other nature groups. His research interests include the roles of fungi in forest nutrient cycling.

JOE AMMIRATI is professor of biology and teaches mycology and botany at the University of Washington. His research focuses mainly on the classification and evolutionary relationships of the gilled fungi, particularly in the genus *Cortinarius*, but also includes mushroom biogeography, co-evolution, and diversity. Joe is the scientific advisor to the Puget Sound Mycological Society.

MARIA ALICE NEVES

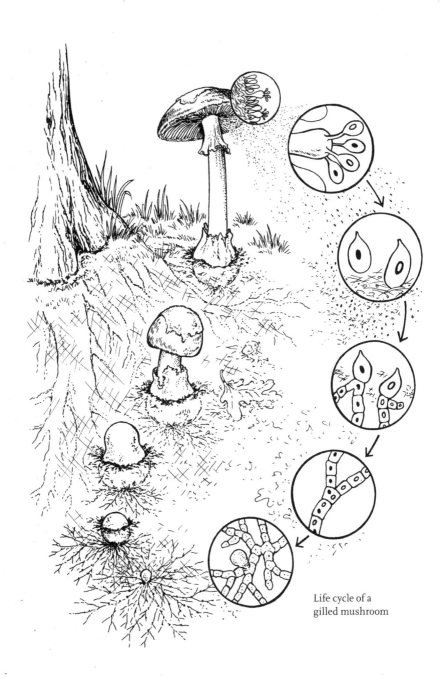

Life cycle of a
gilled mushroom